Entangled by
White Supremacy

NEW DIRECTIONS IN SOUTHERN HISTORY

SERIES EDITORS
Peter S. Carmichael, *West Virginia University*
Michele Gillespie, *Wake Forest University*
William A. Link, *University of Florida*

Entangled by White Supremacy

Reform in World War I–era South Carolina

Janet G. Hudson

THE UNIVERSITY PRESS OF KENTUCKY

Editorial and Sales Offices: The University Press of Kentucky
663 South Limestone Street, Lexington, Kentucky 40508-4008
www.kentuckypress.com

13 12 11 10 09   1 2 3 4 5

Library of Congress Cataloging-in-Publication Data

Hudson, Janet G., 1959–
Entangled by white supremacy : reform in World War I–era South
Carolina / Janet G. Hudson.
p. cm. — (New directions in southern history)
Includes bibliographical references and index.
ISBN 978-0-8131-2502-2 (hardcover : alk. paper)
1. White supremacy movements—South Carolina—History—20th century.
2. South Carolina—Race relations—History—20th century. 3. South
Carolina—Politics and government—1865–1950. 4. African
Americans—South Carolina—Politics and government—20th century.
5. Whites—South Carolina—Politics and government—20th century.
6. Social reformers—South Carolina—History—20th century. 7. World War,
1914–1918—Social aspects—South Carolina. I. Title.
F280.A1H83 2009
305.800975709'04—dc22
                                        2008039303
This book is printed on acid-free recycled paper meeting
the requirements of the American National Standard
for Permanence in Paper for Printed Library Materials.

Manufactured in the United States of America.

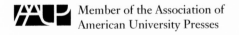

Member of the Association of
American University Presses

For Lacy, Travis, and Sonya

Contents

Illustrations

Tables

Maps

Acknowledgments

A journey as long and arduous as writing this book can only be completed with the assistance of countless individuals. I would like to acknowledge and thank a very few of those people. Many of the limitations of this book spring from my determined yet futile search for self-sufficiency, but without the assistance of William A. Link, one of the New Directions in Southern History series editors, its weaknesses would be even greater. Bill offered the needed balance of encouragement, criticism, and push. He read the entire first draft, willingly and quickly, simply because I asked. He generously read and commented on several subsequent drafts, offering timely and cogent advice. I am also indebted to the 2003 National Endowment for the Humanities Seminar on the Modern Civil Rights Movement at Harvard University, directed by Patricia Sullivan and Waldo Martin. This valuable seminar and those who participated in it convinced me that I had something to say and motivated me to resurrect this long-dormant project, which began as my dissertation. I am especially grateful to Susan Youngblood Ashmore for her encouragement. She helped me believe it was possible when I had become convinced it was impossible.

I appreciate the staff at the University Press of Kentucky, especially Ann Malcolm, acquisitions editor, and Cheryl Hoffman, freelance copy editor, as well as the anonymous reader who raised important questions and offered needed criticism. I am appreciative of David Carlton and Elizabeth Robeson, who read portions of the manuscript and steered me clear of a few disasters. Thanks to Marjorie Spruill, Jim Farmer, and Carl Abrams, who offered comments on the portions they read in the form of conference papers; and to

Bobby Donaldson and Tim Tyson, who answered questions and offered advice. Thanks to Joyce Hughston, who patiently read every word and provided valuable editing suggestions. A special thanks to Eugene Hill, my sixth-grade teacher, whose exceptional human relations skills opened my eyes, as a young girl, to the racial injustices that permeated my community, region, and culture. The insights I gained from Mr. Hill have continually shaped my perceptions of the world. Thanks to my parents, who instilled in me a work ethic that was essential for this project, whose rewards are primarily intrinsic. While I have never worked as hard as they do and perhaps have not applied my diligence to the ends that they would most appreciate, I am grateful for the dedication and steadfastness they have always modeled for me.

My greatest debt is to Lacy Ford, my husband and mentor, for his remarkable patience and historical judgment. He never grew tired of reading drafts, offering suggestions and encouragement, and repeating advice that I ignored until I grew to appreciate it. No one could be happier that the project eventually advanced beyond our countless private conversations. Thanks also to my children, Travis and Sonya, who grew up with this project as background noise. Although they could never fully appreciate why it seemed so important to me, they offered encouraging nods. They have always provided me motivation and perspective. Although I tend to forget it, their lives serve as consistent reminders of my great good fortune.

Introduction

When we are reading a novel or watching a film, nothing shapes our perceptions or inhibits our imagination as much as knowing the conclusion in advance. A critic poised to divulge a surprise ending or an unforeseen plot twist issues a spoiler alert. Beware, the critic warns; what is about to be revealed may jeopardize one's ability to experience the unfolding narrative with fresh eyes or may subvert the ability to consider many possibilities. With advance knowledge of the conclusion we may be dismissive of particular characters or underestimate the significance of actions that lead away from the revealed ending. We may also ignore evidence that appears irrelevant to an ending that no longer holds any mystery. Familiarity with the ending may encourage the perception of its inevitability. Interpreting events through the lens of a known conclusion could lead to a misunderstanding of the context or to a diminished appreciation of the narrative's complexity and rich insights.

The challenge of this book is to reconsider a historical narrative with a well-known outcome and to seriously consider possibilities that contemporaries imagined but which never reached fruition. When long shots fail, it is difficult to recapture the sense of possibility that motivated those involved to take the required risks. But if we can put aside the skepticism derived from knowing the ending and reflect upon once-imagined possibilities, we can recognize how white supremacy prevented the full realization of contemporaries' imagined possibilities. Moreover, we can achieve a better understanding of the expectations of World War I–era South Carolina reformers, black and white, who were entangled by white supremacy.

The narrative to reconsider carefully is the relationship between

1

white supremacy and reform during the World War I era, 1914–1924.[1] For a brief period, war-related demands offered unusual and unexpected opportunities. South Carolina benefited economically from the war as commodity prices increased for agriculture and the textile industry enjoyed record profits. Additionally, the introduction of new military bases stimulated economic growth in selected areas of the state. The prosperity that accompanied the war helped South Carolina's white reformers believe their state had the financial means to accomplish their ultimate goal of a better-educated and economically prosperous state, with a higher standard of living, adequate health care, less crime and violence, better roads, and a more diverse economy.[2]

But if the war generated economic opportunities that white reformers welcomed, it simultaneously introduced challenges that whites feared, challenges to the recently constructed institutionalized forms of white supremacy: segregation and disfranchisement.[3] The federal government's war mobilization efforts that precipitated the military draft, construction of new military training bases, labor shortages, new employment opportunities, black migration, and woman suffrage threatened the stability of the existing racial hierarchy. Market forces, which drove up the price of labor during the war, also challenged the artificially constructed racial order. Yet most disturbing to whites, the war to make the world "safe for democracy" had kindled hope among South Carolina's African American reformers, who channeled their hope during and immediately after the war into challenging the structures of white supremacy. Challenges to white supremacy from black reformers ignited whites' anxiety as well as intensified their resolve to resist any erosion of their control. While black reformers welcomed and exploited the war-related challenge to white supremacy, white reformers confronted the potential paradox that these desired opportunities also threatened white control. They responded to this paradox by both seizing the unique wartime reform opportunities with enthusiasm and resolutely seeking the best method for maintaining white supremacy. Balancing both the opportunity and the threat proved complicated.[4]

Despite its importance in world and American history, World War I has seldom been identified as an important turning point in southern history because it did not trigger substantial economic, political, or social change in the South. In 1917, however, South Carolina reformers—black and white—saw their world poised on the brink of momentous change, especially since the war had brought South Carolina new economic opportunities and a glimpse of prosperity that they imagined would foster long-term improvement. From their vantage point in 1917, they could not foresee that the opportunities presented by the war would be short-lived, that an agricultural depression would further erode the fleeting opportunities as it followed on the heels of the armistice and continued for two decades, or that the Jim Crow racial order would survive the challenge and remain firmly in place well beyond midcentury. This well-known ending may entice you to dismiss as inconsequential both the challenge to white supremacy and the serious attempt at reform, but resist that temptation.

While institutional white supremacy endured the war-related challenge, the assault had consequences that would complicate white reformers' postwar legislative agenda and ultimately lead to the attenuation of reform. The wartime challenge to white supremacy, especially African Americans' activism, created a tangible and exploitable fear of white supremacy's vulnerability. White South Carolinians were particularly cognizant of and sensitive to any threats to white supremacy because they held power as a minority in a black-majority state. If white control was tentative or potentially jeopardized, as whites supposed, then great care was necessary to protect it from all perceived threats. In the aftermath of heightened anxiety about challenges to white supremacy associated with World War I, an anxiety intensified by African Americans' activism, South Carolina white reformers pursued their fundamental progressive reform agenda: tax and education reform. If white reformers anticipated achieving their reform goals, they had to assuage white anxiety with a dogged defense of white supremacy and all its practical manifestations, especially since wartime black activism had eroded whites' confidence in its stability. Hence, white reformers had to become masters of white supremacy politics and contend against other skilled practitioners of the art.[5]

As white reformers aggressively pursued the reform agenda they deemed essential for South Carolina's economic and social progress, they encountered opposition from other white South Carolinians.[6]

White reformers' opponents often included traditional conservatives, large landowning elites and industrialists, who guarded their
economic interests first, as well as the white working class, white
tenants, and small farmers, who frequently saw reform as a threat to
their autonomy. Yet the political contests over reform depended on
far more than the merits of or substantive objections to proposed
reform. Instead, the class tensions, factional rivalries, and economic
conflicts among whites about reform were contested as disputes about
whose class interests, political faction, or legislative proposal most
threatened white supremacy. As a corollary, they also debated who
best defended the shared ideal. This rhetorical jousting often mas-
queraded as an authentic competition. The conflict and competition
among whites was real, as real as whites' commitment to white supremacy. Yet the politics of white supremacy, the political context in
which competing white interests contended, was crafted to disguise
the substance of these differences by appealing to everyone's whiteness as a distraction.[7]

Using white supremacy as a distraction was a strategy that
tempted all factions because whites' commitment to white supremacy
was so constant, intense, and broadly shared—a nonnegotiable value
among whites. The cultural consensus around white supremacy,
however, did not ensure harmony or always facilitate agreement
among whites, as the collective commitment might suggest. Instead,
the shared allegiance of white South Carolinians to white supremacy
created an illusion of unity among whites who otherwise were divided by class tensions, economic competition, regional rivalries,
and factional loyalties. The effectiveness of the rhetorical appeal to
white supremacy was its breadth of connotation. Politicians and
policymakers, who regularly asserted their allegiance to white supremacy, preferred to keep the concept ill defined and to draw upon
its power to allude. Whites' consensus around maintaining white
dominance splintered if and when other, more controversial aspects
of white supremacy were too precisely delineated. The broadly shared
and entrenched belief in white supremacy among white voters of
competing class, economic, and political interests ensured a political
culture of constant manipulation—manipulation that involved the
disfranchised and franchised alike.

The existence of this nonnegotiable cultural value, white supremacy, invited all white social classes to champion their own interests by linking them to this fixed axiom. Thus, all factions boasted of their stubborn defense of white control. This pandering technique strategically served interests other than white supremacy's preservation.[8] Yet reformers' proposed changes arguably introduced more uncertainty than their opponents' recommendations to simply maintain the status quo. Whether that meant existing laws, voting schemes, informal traditions, or public policies, the status quo, advantageously, had already proven capable of sustaining white control. Therefore the white supremacy consensus, which shaped relationships of power, political alliances, and public policy debates, bolstered conservatism and hindered reform. Moreover, the wartime challenge to white supremacy in a black-majority state had heightened whites' fear and made them more resistant to change, especially when other whites argued that the changes reformers advocated jeopardized white control. Thus the wartime challenge further constrained white reformers, and their eventual results, because the strategies essential for preserving white domination favored the status quo and eschewed the risks that fundamental reforms required.

The development of this interpretation occurs in two parts. Part 1 examines the challenge that World War I posed to white supremacy. Chapter 1 captures black reformers' hope in the immediate postwar era. As leaders of the state's African American majority, this small but determined cohort of educated black leaders seized the initiative for change during and immediately after World War I. The first chapter not only introduces the background and agenda of this understudied group of black reformers but also details the state's demography and economic structure, its pervasive poverty, and the oppressive environment that whites had created to control African Americans. Chapter 2 introduces the white reformers, their perspective on South Carolina's problems, their motivation, recent efforts to implement their truncated progressive agenda, and their vision for future improvement. The second chapter also examines white supremacy, providing a brief history of its institutional construction and an explanation of its core premises.

The next four chapters explore African Americans' activism stimulated by the country's direct involvement in the war. Chapter 3 examines the challenge that war mobilization posed to white supremacy. Chapter 4 details black and white reformers' tentative and tepid cooperation in meeting the civilian war-mobilization demands. More specifically, it explores black reformers' efforts to use white reformers' desire for blacks' cooperation as a form of authority to push their own agenda. However, when peace commenced, black and white reformers' expectations clashed. Chapter 5 explores the clash. White reformers no longer needed African Americans' cooperation, so they vehemently resisted African Americans' postwar reform initiatives that they perceived directly challenged the practice and principle of white dominance. Thus, constantly rumored, anticipated, and executed racial violence characterized 1919. Chapter 6 surveys the black migration and the ensuing labor shortages as African Americans threatened white economic control by leaving South Carolina. This more indirect form of black agency exposed economic differences among whites that fueled bitter debates about the best method for maintaining white supremacy.

Part 2 shifts the analysis of white supremacy away from the interplay of white and black reformers in the World War I era, when both groups of reformers attempted to capitalize on unique opportunities presented by the war. The second half of the book provides an analysis of the internal dynamics among various white interests in the context of white supremacy politics. Analyzing these dynamics involves discussing elections, factional politics, coalition building, and legislative maneuvering. The war-generated activism of black reformers, especially their push for political rights, had sensitized all political debates and directly influenced political discourse among whites. Since black reformers were not involved in these internal dynamics among whites, they become more peripheral in this half of the book.

With analyses of three war-era elections, chapter 7 demonstrates why harsh racial rhetoric saturated political discourse and why white reformers operated within a loosely constructed political coalition within the Democratic Party that left them with few reform allies. Chapter 8 provides an analysis of the woman-suffrage debate in South Carolina that reveals that both proponents and opponents of the Susan B. Anthony amendment evoked white supremacy in defense of their positions. Chapters 9 and 10 analyze the political complexities involved in undertaking tax reform, which white reformers viewed as the most fundamental reform necessary for securing a more activist state and generating revenue, equitably, to fund all other reforms. Finally, chapters 11 and 12 examine the dismal problem of an illiterate and undereducated population. White reformers' broad reform agenda, which included attracting capital investment, implementing scientific agriculture, diversifying economic opportunities, raising the standard of living, and expanding humanitarian institutions, depended on dramatically reducing illiteracy and educating the general population. Although white reformers designed educational improvements primarily to benefit white South Carolinians, they encountered numerous obstacles from opponents who charged that their reforms threatened white control.

Finally, exploring white supremacy during a time of challenge reveals its complexity, vitality, and multifaceted nature. It demonstrates that white supremacy impinged on almost every issue, especially when whites sensed the vulnerability of their control. The purpose of examining the challenge World War I posed to white supremacy and examining the determined reform effort it inspired is not to argue that these succeeded at either overthrowing white dominance in South Carolina or transforming the state into a progressive society. Rather, an examination of both the challenge and the vigorous defense of white supremacy, in the context of a determined reform effort, recaptures a sense of historical contingency and enables a glimpse at the dynamics of a culture entangled by white supremacy. While white reformers saw no contradiction between advocating reform for South Carolina and holding steadfastly to white supremacy, the incongruity of their "whites only" progressivism helps explain its limited success.

Part 1

Wartime Challenges

Chapter 1

Black Hope

On February 21, 1919, thousands lined the downtown streets of Columbia waiting for the excitement to begin. The capital city had hosted numerous parades since the United States entered the Great War, but on this Friday onlookers knew they were about to see battle-hardened heroes. The men who would soon parade had fought in the climactic Champagne offensive in France and demonstrated their valor on the front lines at Verdun, one of Europe's most infamous dying fields. These returning soldiers wore medals—American and French military decorations that testified to their battlefield courage. South Carolinians who assembled along Main and Hampton streets came to honor the bravery and sacrifices of the 371st, a regiment composed primarily of South Carolinians. Family, friends, neighbors, church members, and curious strangers gathered to welcome home the men who, they had learned from the national press, had helped the Allies secure victory while sustaining casualties at a rate of almost 45 percent. Understandably proud, parade watchers relished the opportunity to see fellow South Carolinians hailed as international war heroes. What made this military homecoming unusual in a culture suffused with white supremacy was that the audience gathered in admiration of African American soldiers. Approximately 1,400 returning African American soldiers marched with their two or three dozen white officers. Bursting with pride to glimpse men fresh from the battlefields, African Americans left homes, jobs, and popular rendezvous to attend the parade. One reporter, observing the large African American turnout, remarked condescendingly that "more dinners were left uncooked and more babies left unnursed" during the hours of the parade "than at any time since Sherman invaded the city." Whites attended primarily as curiosity seekers, some peering out of downtown windows and doorways while others observed from nearby street corners.[1]

The uncommon circumstances of the parade matched the distinctiveness of the 371st and its service. Nationwide approximately four hundred thousand African Americans had served in World War I, and almost half of these men served in France. Eighty percent of the two hundred thousand African Americans who served overseas received noncombat service unit assignments and were responsible for loading and unloading supplies, clearing roads, digging trenches, removing disabled equipment and barbed wire, and burying dead soldiers. Only one in five black soldiers serving in the war zone participated in combat, a much lower ratio than the two in three white soldiers who served in combat units. While discriminatory military practices relegated most black soldiers to labor battalions, the 371st by contrast was a combat infantry regiment, one of only four combat regiments attached to the Ninety-third Division, which was one of only two all-black divisions—the other being the Ninety-second—organized in World War I.[2] The 371st was also the only infantry regiment in the Ninety-third Division created with only conscripted soldiers. The core members of the division's other three regiments came from prewar National Guard units. Composed of draftees primarily from South Carolina and neighboring North Carolina, the 371st regiment, which would disband within days of this parade, had originated at Camp Jackson in Columbia in August 1917.[3]

Not only was the 371st Infantry Regiment included among the 10 percent of African American combat soldiers, the men in this combat unit also represented an even smaller fraction of African American combat soldiers who served directly with the French. Desperate because of the war-induced manpower shortage, the French begged Gen. John J. Pershing for fresh troops to assist its battle-weary forces in concluding the four-year struggle against Germany. General Pershing, commander of the American Expeditionary Force, furnished the French with four American units, the four infantry regiments from the all-black Ninety-third Division. The commander's perceived generosity satisfied the desperate French, who welcomed more soldiers, regardless of race, and enabled Pershing to avoid integrating the black units directly into his force. Consequently the 371st became one of only four African American combat regiments to fight within a French brigade. Recruited and trained at Camp Jackson, the 371st left South

Carolina for the French battlefield in April 1918 as the first draft regiment to see combat. Assigned to the French 157th division—the famous "Red Hand," commanded by Gen. Mariano Goybet—these men trained with the French using interpreters and were issued French equipment to complete the full immersion.[4]

After a few weeks of preparation with the French and their weapons, these newly trained recruits, without combat experience, were sent in June to Verdun, where they served three months on the front lines. White officers in the regiment initially doubted the ability and resolve of these enlisted black men to fight. Yet under intense German machine-gun fire Lt. John B. Smith's doubts vanished. Smith, a white officer from Greenville, commended the unit. The men quickly cohered and proved themselves "splendid fighters," he observed. After the unit proved their skill and tenacity during the summer at Verdun, the French transferred the 371st in September to the Champagne campaign, where they stayed weeks past the armistice signing. This epic final battle against the Germans was hard-fought. The 371st lost 1,065 of its 2,384 men in nine days of intense fighting. While sustaining a high rate of battlefield casualties these men advanced and secured territory. They captured prisoners, confiscated ammunition, and shot down three German planes with rifle and machine-gun ground fire, exceeding all previous regiments' record of shooting down only one enemy plane. Capt. A. V. R. Richey, a white officer, declared proudly that the "whole regiment fought like veterans, and with a fierceness equal to any white regiment." Richey, a Laurens native, further remarked that when repeatedly shelled, they stood like "moss-covered old-timers," and even when surrounded by heavy casualties the men "never flinched or showed the least sign of fear."[5]

Not only did the unit's white officers acknowledge these men's contributions but so did the French military. For its extraordinary bravery the French awarded the entire regiment the Croix de Guerre with palm and awarded select members the highest French military honor, the Croix de Guerre.[6] As the men left Europe, French general Goybet offered his personal commendation, affection, and gratitude in a farewell replete with unmistakable suggestions of equality.

> For seven months we have lived as brothers at arms, partaking in the same activities, sharing the same hardships and the same dangers. Side by side we took part in the great Champagne battle,

which was to be crowned by a tremendous victory. . . . Officers,
noncommissioned officers, and men, I respectfully salute our glo-
rious comrades who have fallen. . . . Our brotherhood has been
cemented in the blood of the brave and such bonds will never be
destroyed. Remember your general, who is so proud of having
commanded you, and be sure of his grateful affection to you all
forever.[7]

Enthusiastic onlookers in Columbia that Friday afternoon in February 1919 followed the parading soldiers to Allen University, an African Methodist Episcopal (AME) educational institution, where
community leaders expressed appreciation for the soldiers and voiced
expectations for the future. Following comments from prominent
white guests—Robert A. Cooper, South Carolina's newly inaugurated governor; Gen. W. A. Cole, commander of Camp Jackson; and
C. S. Monteith, city attorney, who represented Columbia's mayor—
several prominent African American ministers, including Nathaniel
F. Haygood, pastor of Sydney Park Church; Jacob J. Durham, pastor
of Second Calvary Baptist Church; and AME bishop William D.
Chappelle, addressed the expectant crowd. The Reverend Haygood
assured the men that they had proven themselves the equal of any
soldier. Consequently, he encouraged them to demand and insist.
Haygood suggested that the returning soldiers' mantra become,
"Give me what belongs to me." Then he asserted that these young
men deserved a "man's place," which he defined as service on grand
juries and in local police departments. Bishop Chappelle offered the
frankest conclusions when he declared emphatically: "The war was
fought for democracy. We want democracy in our own country."
Furthermore, he noted, "We want freedom." To ensure that his audience understood that he invoked these twin principles as more than
rhetorical ideals, the bishop specifically explained that democracy
and freedom required access to the ballot box and the jury pool.[8]
While the pomp and circumstance of this unique occasion enjoyed
the official sanction of city, state, and military white leaders, African
American leaders' use of this occasion to present a provocative wish
list linking military service with political rights challenged the pa-
rameters of acceptable public discourse in this time and place.

One white resident quickly penned his response to the postparade oratory, which had called for political rights as African Ameri-

cans' reward for military sacrifice. Their list of expectations, which included serving on school boards, juries, and police forces, was consistent, he reasoned, with the "socialistic propaganda that is floating about the world." Furthermore the writer declared that blacks would not be satisfied until they had achieved "universal suffrage and race amalgamation."[9] This slippery-slope argument that reasoned if whites were ever to concede that African Americans had any appropriate, integrated role in public life then the entire society would collapse was a familiar and often repeated one. Frustrated with this obvious distortion of the reasoned demands made for returning war heroes, M. W. Garrick, an African American woman from Sumter, offered her retort by asserting that black men deserved the ballot even before the war. Furthermore, she warned, African Americans would not be satisfied "so long as we are deprived of the rights belonging to us." Garrick also refuted the perpetually provocative suggestion that black men's political demands merely cloaked their desire for sexual access to white women. "The self respecting negro loves the black woman who gave birth to the race of which he belongs," she emphasized.[10] Garrick's direct and public rebuke of white hyperbole signaled a renewed determination among African Americans to claim their freedom. Whites resented such direct demands, which implicitly challenged their authority. Some expressed their opposition publicly, while others shared their anxiety privately, but all concerned white South Carolinians contemplated how to handle the black soldiers' demands and expectations. The military prowess of these young black men clearly haunted whites, who sensed that such a harrowing and socially leveling experience on a foreign battlefield would perpetually jeopardize white control.

The courageous assertions of the ministers who addressed the postparade crowd and Garrick's bold defense of black men's political rights exemplified African Americans' burgeoning optimism inspired by World War I–era opportunities. Evidence mounted in 1919 that African Americans' confrontational spirit would neither quietly nor quickly dissipate. Expressing this daring hope most articulately were African American reformers, a small but diverse group of leaders. During the war they sensed that the unique wartime circumstances, which required a rapid, national mobilization for a total war, offered them a distinctive chance to expand African Americans' freedom—a chance they seized during and immediately after the war. These black reformers, who came mainly from the professions, were business owners, lawyers, health-care professionals, journalists, educators, and ministers. Primarily urban dwellers from Charleston and Columbia, South Carolina's two largest cities, reformers also resided in smaller county-seat towns across the state. As members of the state's small black elite, these reformers were an even smaller group since not all members of the black elite shared the reformers' agenda. This small collection of reformers also stood in contrast to the vastly larger African American population who labored in South Carolina as agricultural tenants, sharecroppers, laborers, and domestics. Seventy-five percent of black South Carolina lived on farms. Eight of every ten African Americans who engaged in agriculture were landless, making black tenants and sharecroppers the largest class of African Americans.[11]

Yet this small group of black reformers advocated for the majority of South Carolinians. In World War I–era South Carolina, 55 percent of the state's population was black, making South Carolina one of only two states with a black majority (Mississippi was the other). African Americans' majority status in South Carolina enhanced both their leverage and their vulnerability. White landowners depended on African Americans' labor, especially since landowners' strategy for economic prosperity rested on maintaining an abundant supply of surplus, cheap labor. War-era labor shortages distressed large landowners and exposed whites' economic dependence on black labor, a dependence that provided some leverage for blacks. Yet African Americans' long-term interest was not well served by meeting whites' needs for cheap labor. With numerical dominance African Americans potentially held the balance of political power in the state, if their constitutional rights had been fully protected, which they were not. Yet this political possibility inspired whites' constant vigilance to prevent that from ever happening.[12]

Despite theoretical possibilities for black political power, in reality whites systematically excluded African Americans from politics. This exclusion and uneven distribution of power greatly disadvantaged black reformers, who had to cooperate with whites as they led reform initiatives during and immediately after the war. Black reformers' cooperation with whites—either directly or indirectly—required craft and nuance as reformers navigated within a complex environment

dominated by whites, who were committed to maintaining white supremacy. Thus the asymmetrical collaboration of black reformers with
white power brokers could be, and often has been, misconstrued as
black reformers' deference, naiveté, or selfish ambition.[13]

This cohort of African American reformers, especially its older
members, had come of age in the nineteenth century. They understood personally, through their parents' generation, the promises of
Reconstruction, expressed through the Thirteenth, Fourteenth, and
Fifteenth Amendments to the Constitution, which had abolished slavery, guaranteed citizenship rights of due process and equal protection,
and established universal manhood suffrage. Reconstruction's brief
but radical experiment in interracial democracy included widespread
African American political participation, federal government protection, expanded black landownership, creation of a public school system,
and personal freedom. Blacks held a two-to-one majority in the South
Carolina General Assembly's lower house, a feat accomplished in no
other state. Black South Carolinians held office between 1867 and
1876 as the lieutenant governor, secretary of state, adjutant general,
secretary of the treasury, speaker of the house, and president pro tem
of the senate. Moreover, nine black men had been elected congressional representatives for the Palmetto State. This black political power,
exercised through leadership of the Republican Party, had undermined
white control. Consequently, threatened white South Carolinians
generated unyielding opposition to undermine the goals of Reconstruction and terminate the experiment in interracial democracy.[14]

As federal resolve waned in the 1870s, the generation of newly
freed people, filled with hope and expectation, watched white South
Carolinians forcefully regain political control of the state by employing a combination of fraud, intimidation, and violence. White
Democrats launched an aggressive, violent campaign to reestablish
white hegemony the summer before the pivotal 1876 election. In the
small, westernmost South Carolina town of Hamburg, whites employed terror tactics in the infamous Hamburg Massacre to intimidate blacks, eradicate interracial cooperation, undermine an
already-weakened Republican Party coalition, and set the stage for
the Red Shirts' campaign season of violence and intimidation. The
bitter, divisive, and wholly corrupt 1876 election and the resulting
national Compromise of 1877 satisfied former Confederate general
Wade Hampton and his Red Shirt followers' intentions to restore

white rule in South Carolina and to curtail abruptly African Americans' progress toward equality. After the so-called Redemption, the Democratic Party, the party of white supremacy, dominated South Carolina. Moreover, for generations to come, whites incessantly referenced Reconstruction as an era of humiliation in which whites had suffered under a corrupt, tyrannical, and oppressive government controlled by inferior blacks and manipulative outsiders. Consequently they concluded that perpetual vigilance was necessary to ensure that such degradation would never return.[15]

As the Democratic Party grew in power, the briefly influential Republican Party suffered diminished authority in South Carolina and functioned increasingly as simply a vehicle for distributing patronage among the handful of party faithful during subsequent Republican presidential administrations. As the black reformers' generation moved into adulthood, it faced an even more vitriolic racism and aggressive political exclusion than the previous generation had encountered with the paternalist racism of Wade Hampton and the Conservatives. Championing the cause of the white yeomen and tenants, Benjamin "Pitchfork Ben" Tillman challenged Conservative rule in South Carolina during the late 1880s and early 1890s. After successfully maneuvering for his own election as governor and winning control of the legislature for his insurgent faction, Tillman orchestrated a call for a constitutional convention for the express purpose of disfranchising African American voters.[16] Because the Fifteenth Amendment to the U.S. Constitution prohibited the restriction of voting on the basis of race, the Tillmanite architects of South Carolina's 1895 constitution developed voting restrictions that relied on attributes that closely correlated with race: illiteracy and poverty. To vote in South Carolina, the 1895 constitution required that adult men pay a poll tax and demonstrate the ability to read and understand the state constitution. Since, in 1890, 65 percent of South Carolina's black men of voting age were illiterate, such restrictions effectively disfranchised the majority of potential African American voters. While technically African American men who could read and understand the constitution and retain proof of paying the poll tax could vote, and some did, the practical method for disfranchising the remaining black men was the all-white Democratic primary.[17]

By the World War I era, South Carolina's African American reformers had seen the wrath of two decades of the state's oppressive political structure at work, with its statewide white primary and constitutional restrictions on voting. During these twenty years the political system worked essentially as its creators had hoped. African Americans were almost completely disfranchised, with only three thousand to five thousand blacks still voting in general elections. Without political power, African Americans lacked leverage to secure resources for education, health care, and justice in the courts, and they suffered at the hands of indifferent and malicious white leaders. While governor on the eve of World War I, Coleman "Coley" Blease expressed this callous attitude by quipping that resources devoted to educating the state's black population were merely "ruining a good plow hand and making a half-trained fool." Most white educators recoiled from such frank rhetoric, but the reality of educational funding and bureaucratic policies closely mirrored Blease's bluntness. South Carolina's segregated school system offered trifling educational opportunities to African Americans, spending annually a meager $1.90 per black student while allocating $17.02 per white student. More than 90 percent of African American schools were the one-room, one-teacher style, long after educators had recognized the inefficiency of one-room schools. School sessions for African American students averaged just over three months per year statewide with very few opportunities beyond fifth grade.[18]

When possible, African Americans substituted the defective public education the state offered with a private alternative. Funded by philanthropic and religious organizations, private education provided, among other things, three-fourths of the high schools for African Americans in South Carolina before World War I. The Julius Rosenwald Fund, Anna T. Jeanes Fund, General Education Board, John F. Slater Fund, and others provided private funding for African Americans to address educational needs that public education wholly neglected. This money built schools, paid teachers' salaries, funded administrative-oversight positions, underwrote vocational training, and supplemented public school funding. Most black public school teachers received their training from private "normal schools." Yet the philosophy of these schools, expressed through the northern philanthropists who supported them and the southern educators who implemented the philosophy, remained entangled with white supremacy values. As Carter G. Woodson pointed out, the priority of these self-proclaimed sympathizers, which focused heavily on vocational training for agricultural and domestic jobs, was serving the interests of the white-dominated agricultural economy rather than educating African Americans to pursue their interests and human potential.[19]

Minimal education reinforced minimal employment opportunities. South Carolina's economy further illustrates the dismal opportunities for African Americans, who comprised 56 percent of South Carolina's labor force. Nearly 80 percent of South Carolina's workforce found employment in either agriculture or manufacturing. Of the remaining 20 percent of working South Carolinians, 7 percent worked as domestics and 3 percent worked for either railroads or public utilities. Only one in ten South Carolinians held white-collar jobs. The comparative paucity of professional and commercial occupations resulted in the slow growth of a middle-class in the state, and African Americans held a fraction of these professional positions.[20] Agriculture absorbed two-thirds of the state's total labor force. Yet agriculture captured the labor of a higher proportion of African Americans than whites. Nearly three out of every four black South Carolinians in the labor force worked in agriculture, whereas less than half of whites did.

Manufacturing, the second-largest sector of the South Carolina economy, employed 16 percent of all workers in the state, but African Americans held few of these positions because the textile industry, the state's major manufacturer, deliberately excluded them from all but the most menial jobs. This informal practice of excluding African Americans from textile employment arose with the industry as a means for mill owners to pacify landless whites who found themselves becoming permanent wage earners, a status that had always been despised. Investors and mill owners willingly made this concession to working-class whites since it assured them of a loyal workforce. In 1915 the legislature explicitly provided statutory protection for the informal practice of racial segregation that already existed in the textile industry. The law prohibited cotton-textile manufacturers from hiring "different races to labor and work together within the same room, or to use the same doors of entrance and exit at the same time . . . use the same stairways and windows . . . toilets, drinking water buckets." Mills that violated these restrictions were fined.[21]

African American women had the least economic opportunity of all South Carolinians. Ninety-five percent of black women working in South Carolina performed either agricultural or domestic labor and barely 3 percent worked in manufacturing. Only 2 percent of black women in the labor force held clerical or professional jobs, and most of the professionals were teachers. African American women did more than 90 percent of the domestic work. Most domestics were servants, housekeepers, laundresses, and untrained nursemaids. By her late teens, Lilla Woodruff, a young black woman from Spartanburg, had already plotted a career path that resembled the one taken, out of necessity, by many other African American women. Lilla had a fifth-grade education, the maximum available to African Americans in her community. Before acquiring her job at Piedmont Laundry, which paid $2.50 per week, Lilla had worked for less money as a housekeeper. When work was scarce in town, she picked cotton. Lilla's coworker, Lucile Smith, also worked at Piedmont Laundry because she made more money as a laundress than as a nursemaid, her previous job. Yet Lucile conceded that after buying groceries for her siblings, with whom she lived, her week's pay had vanished.[22]

The brutality of whites' dominance and their minimal interest in African Americans' education and employment opportunity was also reflected in the state's criminal justice system. Whites occupied every office of authority in the discriminatory system: police officer, sheriff, county magistrate, juror, judge, and lawmaker—and most attorneys were white. African Americans participated in the system almost exclusively as accused and convicted criminals. South Carolina's prison system had not adopted twentieth-century ideas of rehabilitation. Instead, the state prison, located in Columbia, operated as a self-supporting, profit-oriented institution of punishment. The state provided no appropriations for the penitentiary. Prisoners sentenced to hard labor generated income for the institution by working on the prison farm and in the chair factory. The state penitentiary housed anyone—men and women, black and white—but African Americans comprised more than 80 percent of the prison population. The network of county chain gangs served as an informal labor force for road construction and an informal labor pool leased to local landowners through the convict-lease system. More than 90 percent of those convicted to hard labor on the chain gangs were black.[23]

The criminal justice system was particularly cruel to black children. Juvenile justice for white South Carolinians was managed through state industrial schools for training and rehabilitation, one in Florence for boys and another in Columbia for girls. But comparable institutions did not exist for African American youth. The state provided nothing for black girls. Consequently, black reformers, primarily women working through the State Federation of Colored Women's Clubs, privately operated the Fairwold Home for Neglected Colored Girls during the war. The reformatory designated for African American boys, located inside the state penitentiary, operated simply as a prison. While the institution incarcerated youth under sixteen, about half of the boys were under twelve years old. Boys as young as eight, nine, and ten received harsh sentences for minor crimes. For example, Lee Wilkins received a ten-year sentence for stealing a sack of flour. The reformatory offered no merit system for parole and provided no education or training for these children who came of age behind bars. Observers described the facilities as "bare, desolate, and dirty," without cooking equipment, a laundry, or even towels and toothbrushes. Serious conditions of "gross injustice" in these institutions were difficult to overstate, as an advocate for abolishing the existing prison, chain gang, and reformatory system grimly reported.[24]

The pervasive and entrenched quality of the problems African Americans faced discouraged hopefulness. Yet the admirable service and sacrifice from the young men in uniform who marched through South Carolina's capital city in February 1919 inspired seasoned African American leaders at home to hope and develop a strategy for parlaying their military successes into civilian opportunities. The parade and postparade speeches—intentional, bold, and organized—were hardly the first, and far from the last, such efforts in World War I–era South Carolina that signaled an emerging hope among African Americans, an optimism that energized and motivated a long-oppressed people to challenge their oppressors. Their vigilance reflected African American leaders' deliberate effort to seize every opportunity created by wartime service and sacrifice, which they had done since the nation's initial involvement in the war. Moreover, these local and state leaders in South Carolina built on the inspiration and national leadership of W. E. B. DuBois, editor of the National Association for the Advancement of Colored People (NAACP) monthly, the *Crisis*, who tirelessly campaigned to link African Americans' war support with peacetime opportunities.[25]

Under the auspices of the Lincoln Memorial Association, a black civic organization, black leaders met several times at local churches, raised money, and rallied the community for a "monster celebration" honoring the returning soldiers' service. Those who organized the parade and reception that followed comprised a veritable who's who of Columbia's African American reform-minded leaders. These men and women, whether religious leaders, educators, business entrepreneurs, doctors, or lawyers, served the community in many capacities other than their professions. They led numerous civic organizations dedicated to improving education, health care, juvenile justice, and economic opportunity for African Americans. Several of these forward-looking leaders organized a Columbia branch of the NAACP during the war and served as its executive officers, dedicating themselves to expanding political opportunity. Their names had graced numerous petitions seeking fair access to state resources for African Americans. Many of the parade organizers had already been privately fingered to the governor as dangerous leaders too interested in politics. These black leaders strategically used an accustomed and respected ritual, like the military welcome-home parade, as an occasion for suggesting tangible rewards for military service.[26]

Henry E. Lindsey, president of the Lincoln Memorial Association, appointed Isaac Samuel "I. S." Leevy, one of South Carolina's determined reformers, to chair the steering committee for the parade and festivities that followed. Leevy and the host of other committee members responsible for the "monster celebration" that welcomed home battle-weary soldiers embodied the characteristics of African American reformers who highlighted inequalities and fought to extend justice for African Americans. A unifying characteristic of reformers was their commitment to education. They had earned education credentials, advocated expanding and improving education for others, and believed in education's transforming power. Leevy, business owner and tireless civic leader, graduated from Hampton Normal and Agricultural Institute in Virginia in 1906. He once told his father that his four years at Hampton, an educational institution committed to training black educators and promoting Booker T. Washington's self-improvement philosophy, had revolutionized his life and convinced him of life's possibilities and his ability to improve his life. Leevy was a native South Carolinian, like most of the state's reformers. An infant when Reconstruction collapsed and whites re-captured political control of the state, Leevy grew up in Camden, just east of Columbia. He only left South Carolina for his four years of education at Hampton, which he attended with the encouragement and assistance of Richard Carroll, a Booker T. Washington protégé who operated as a minister/missionary in South Carolina and knew Leevy's family. After graduation Carroll facilitated Leevy's move to the capital city where he lived out his ninety-two years creating a lengthy record of struggle and achievement.[27]

Leevy possessed other common characteristics of reformers: middle-class optimism and a strong work ethic. With this determined optimism that he brought to Columbia, Leevy directed his ambition toward business. His first business venture, as a tailor and merchant, led to his second, owner-operator of I. S. Leevy Department Store at 1131 Washington Street, located in the heart of the black business district in downtown Columbia. Other businesses owned, operated, and patronized by blacks found on Washington Street included an undertaker, drugstore, insurance office, real estate agency, shoe repair shop, dentist, physicians, attorneys, barbershops, a shaving parlor, lunch cafés, tailors, cleaners, a billiard parlor, and a hotel. Leevy Department Store, which housed a barbershop, beauty salon, tailoring shop, and dressmaking department, became the largest black-owned business in the state. While Leevy was an identifiable member of the black elite, he came from modest circumstances in Kershaw County, where he lived until his late twenties when he left to attend Hampton. Applying the philosophy he absorbed from Hampton, Leevy worked hard at improving himself and used his position of growing prominence to improve the lives of other African Americans. Booker T. Washington's influence was evident in Leevy's life, but he was not constrained by those ideas.[28]

Leevy shared with other black reformers a desire to combine his personal ambition and individual work ethic with cooperative group efforts. Leevy was an officer in the Capital City Civic League, a local organization whose stated purpose was "contesting and contending for our every Constitutional right, privileges and immunity, in a quiet, legal and peaceful manner." Under the auspices of the Capital City Civic League, Leevy served on the executive committee that organized, in 1917, Columbia's first NAACP branch. One of the early branches organized as the NAACP expanded into the South,

Columbia's NAACP included men and women as charter members, and two of the nine executive committee members were women. When the Civic League members expressed an interest in organizing a branch of the NAACP, Mary Childs Nerney, secretary of the association, commended them on their "radical spirit" especially for a group operating "so far south." Leevy's leadership in the Capital City Civic League and the NAACP testified to his commitment to political rights. Further evidence of this commitment, Leevy, a registered voter, sought the Republican nomination for a congressional seat in 1916 and 1918. In towns throughout South Carolina, black reformers organized to secure their political rights.[29]

Ahead of Columbia by a few weeks, Charleston's black reformers organized a local NAACP branch in Charleston, the state's invaluable coastal port, which had a large and diverse black population. Edwin "Teddy" Harleston, who had been a student of W. E. B. DuBois at Atlanta University, initiated the formation of South Carolina's first NAACP branch. Teddy was the middle child of the Harlestons, an elite black Charleston family. Teddy's father, Capt. Edwin Gaillard Harleston, was the son of an enslaved woman and her white plantation owner, a mixed heritage not uncommon in Charleston. The elder Harleston owned the preeminent African American funeral home on Calhoun Street in Charleston, Harleston Funeral Home. The Harlestons' wealth enabled Teddy to become a professional artist while assisting his father in the family mortuary business. Harleston enlisted his extended family in the effort to organize an NAACP branch. To expand interest beyond his family, Harleston invited his mentor, W. E. B. DuBois, to visit Charleston. On his brief Charleston trip, DuBois visited every black church in town, owing to their importance. A week following DuBois's March 2, 1917, visit, twenty-nine pledged members started South Carolina's first NAACP branch. Eighteen of the charter members were men and eleven women. Most of the members were middle-class professionals. The membership elected Teddy Harleston president and his cousin, Richard "Dick" H. Mickey, a fellow Atlanta University alumnus, secretary. Harleston's activism in Charleston, expressed through his leadership of the NAACP, was so dominant that the organization earned the nickname "Harleston chapter." By 1919 the Charleston NAACP had exponentially increased to 646 members. Harleston carried his enthusiasm and heightened expectations to the first postwar national NAACP conference. At the Cleveland conference in 1919, Harleston reported to the national delegates that even as far south as South Carolina it was now "possible to make a manly fight for our rights, without giving up our self respect."[30]

Both Teddy Harleston and I. S. Leevy, one a mortician and artist, the other a business entrepreneur, embodied many characteristics of black reformers anxious for change. Joining these community leaders were other business professionals. For example, Lazarus A. Hawkins, a realtor in Columbia, advocated reform and served on Columbia's NAACP executive committee. Yet many black business professionals preferred to steer away from controversy and avoid these activities, which invited white retribution against their businesses.

Reformers were also found in the ranks of the state's black attorneys, an elite but meager collection of professionals. Long after the window of opportunity presented during Reconstruction and long before Charles Hamilton Houston aggressively recruited and trained black lawyers at Howard University in Washington, D.C., African American attorneys were scarce in the era of the Great War. South Carolina had fewer than a dozen black lawyers in 1919. Nearly half of these men practiced in the low country, mostly in Charleston, and half in the central portion of the state, mostly in Columbia. No African Americans practiced law in the Piedmont and only one in the Pee Dee. One of the state's most promising attorneys, William T. Andrews, educated at Fisk University and Howard Law School, left South Carolina during the war for better opportunities elsewhere. While the South Carolina bar admitted at least eighty African American men as lawyers in the nineteenth century, only four had been admitted since the turn of the century. With a few exceptions, most of the eighty lawyers who had been educated and had begun practicing law in the nineteenth century had either retired or died by World War I. One of the exceptions was Edward J. "E. J." Sawyer of Bennettsville. The only black Pee Dee attorney, Sawyer was exceptional in many respects. Also a large landowner, realtor, postmaster, principal, newspaper editor, banker, secret-society leader, Sawyer's legal skills facilitated his other pursuits. The number of active black attorneys had dwindled with the erosion of educational opportunities. The law school at South Carolina College, which had been fully integrated during Reconstruction, became an all-white institution again after Reconstruction. Claflin College and Allen University, the two private, black institutions that attempted to fill the void in legal education after Reconstruction, collapsed by 1900, leaving no opportunity for African Americans to pursue a formal legal education in the state.[31]

Of course not all lawyers were reformers, but all three of Columbia's black lawyers—Butler W. Nance, Green Jackson, and Nathaniel J. Frederick—were activists, NAACP members, and advocates for African Americans' political rights. Butler Nance, a native of Newberry, had worked as a railway clerk and teacher before establishing his law office in Columbia. Like I. S. Leevy, Butler had been a member of the Capital City Civic League. He wrote W. E. B. DuBois in 1915 inquiring about the NAACP's interest in expanding its New York–based civil rights organization to South Carolina. When Columbia founded its NAACP branch, the charter members elected Nance president. Green Jackson, an Allen University graduate, was admitted to the South Carolina bar in 1898. He was active in the NAACP and particularly respected for his work with voter registration. Jackson, a man of enthusiasm, had been recommended to James Weldon Johnson as an excellent spokesman for the NAACP.[32] N. J. Frederick, the youngest of the three, became the most prominent.

The progressive leadership of Frederick, who was admitted to the South Carolina bar in 1913, enhanced his statewide reputation. A graduate of Claflin and the University of Wisconsin, he was an educator before beginning his legal career. For at least thirteen years Frederick was principal of Howard School, South Carolina's first public black high school. Along with Leevy and Nance, Frederick belonged to the Capital City Civic League, a forerunner to the NAACP, and he was a charter member of the Columbia NAACP, organized in 1917. At the war's conclusion Frederick edited one of South Carolina's black newspapers, the *Southern Indicator*, a Baptist paper. In addition to belonging to many fraternal organizations, Frederick was secretary of the Colored State Fair Association. Frederick and the other officers of this fair for black South Carolinians promoted it as more than entertainment. The Colored State Fair provided annual opportunities to promote black progress, provide vendors business, and furnish artisans and craftsmen a market for their crafts. As an educator, editor, and lawyer, Frederick participated in a wide array of civic, educational, and political activities; such diversification typified black reformers of this era. By 1925 he owned and edited his own newspaper, the *Palmetto Leader*. By the end of the decade Frederick developed a national reputation representing several high-profile South Carolina clients that the NAACP supported: the Lowman family of Aiken in 1926 and Ben Bess in 1928. Frederick persuaded the South Carolina Supreme Court to grant a new trial for three Lowman family members who had been convicted of killing a sheriff's deputy. In retaliation, whites lynched the Lowmans to prevent the new trial. Two years later, Frederick convinced the state supreme court that Governor John G. Richards should not rescind the unconditional pardon he had granted to Ben Bess after the white woman Bess had been convicted of raping publicly confessed that she had lied about the rape. Late in Frederick's career Charles Hamilton Houston identified him as one of the "notable exceptions" of his generation of black lawyers, noting that he did not shy away from conflict and remained unafraid of controversy.[33]

South Carolina's most esteemed leader and seasoned reformer by the World War I era was Thomas E. Miller, a low-country lawyer who had fought to extend African Americans equality in the South Carolina House and Senate, and the U.S. Congress. Originally from Beaufort, Miller had become a Charlestonian by 1919. Born a free black in Beaufort in 1849, Miller was very light skinned, and many contemporaries could not distinguish him from his white colleagues. Yet Miller identified himself as black and consistently championed African Americans' rights. As a lawyer, Republican Party activist, and politician, Miller used legal and political advocacy as his tool for resisting oppression. The state's oldest black attorney, Miller had been a member of the South Carolina bar since 1875. He represented Beaufort, a black-majority low-country county, for five terms in the state house (1874–1880, 1886–1887, 1894–1896) and a partial term in the state senate (1880–1882). He served one term as a congressional representative from the seventh district, 1889–1891. While in the general assembly and Congress, Miller fought against, among other things, unjust labor laws, which he insisted offered no protection for black laborers against white landowners. He also opposed the convict-lease system that primarily ensnared African Americans in a de facto forced-labor system.[34]

Beaufort also selected Miller as a delegate to the state constitutional convention of 1895. Miller fought for woman suffrage and against disfranchisement measures targeted at African Americans, losing both struggles. Yet at the constitutional convention Miller did not lose every fight. He, along with the five other black delegates, lobbied for a publicly supported college for African Americans. At the time, the state provided modest appropriations to Claflin College, a private black school with Methodist Episcopal oversight and northern influence. Miller won this fight by exploiting whites' concerns about their lack of control over this religious institution with nonsouthern ownership. With the constitutional provision approved, Miller sponsored a bill, which the legislature approved in the 1896 session, creating the Colored Normal, Industrial, Agricultural, and Mechanical College of South Carolina (known as South Carolina State) in Orangeburg adjacent to Claflin. Miller became the new college's president. He served as president until 1911, when Governor Coleman "Coley" Blease pressured him to resign. Miller had aggressively campaigned against Blease's election in 1910, so the newly elected governor, who publicly supported lynching, retaliated. During World War I Miller served on the all-black subcommittee of the Civic Preparedness Commission that mobilized and encouraged African American support for the war. Immediately after the war Miller rallied African Americans to oppose a long-standing practice in the Charleston public schools of only hiring white teachers to teach in segregated black schools. The desire to open more teaching positions for African American teachers would soon galvanize black Charlestonians.[35]

Some reformers were in business, some were lawyers, and some health-care professionals. Dr. Charles C. Johnson, born in Virginia and educated at Howard University, moved to South Carolina in 1888, becoming the first African American physician to practice medicine in Columbia. Johnson organized the Palmetto Medical Association for African American doctors. After serving twenty years as a physician in Columbia, Johnson moved his practice to Aiken. When war mobilization began, Johnson chaired Aiken's civic preparedness committee. Another physician, South Carolina native James R. Levy, practiced in Florence. Levy and Johnson, just months apart in age, were both born as the Civil War began. A longtime active Republican, Levy had served as a delegate to every national Republican convention since William McKinley. Like Johnson, Levy chaired his county's civic preparedness committee when mobilization began.[36]

In Columbia several physicians actively participated in reform efforts. John H. Goodwin, a native of Richland County and educated at Shaw University in North Carolina, served on the executive committee of the Columbia NAACP. He was president of the Colored State Fair Association, the organization in which N. J. Frederick was secretary. Goodwin, along with Drs. Henry H. Cooper, Lewis M. Daniels, and Matilda Evans, served on the steering committee for the Columbia welcome-home parade chaired by I. S. Leevy. Cooper, a dentist in Columbia, left South Carolina for dental school at the University of Pennsylvania but returned and established a practice in 1910 on Washington Street in Columbia.[37] Cooper, along with Leevy, Frederick, Goodwin, and others, served on the executive committee of the Columbia NAACP. A Charleston physician, William H. Johnson, helped organize the Charleston NAACP. A native Charlestonian, Johnson obtained his medical education at Howard University and returned to practice in his hometown. By 1919 Johnson was chief surgeon at Cannon Street Hospital, the city's hospital for African Americans. As a leader in the local NAACP, Johnson advocated compulsory education, property ownership, and voting as essential strategies for racial advancement.[38] These doctors' leadership in their local NAACP and community activities demonstrated the activism of physicians in reform efforts outside their profession.

These were not the only black doctors in South Carolina, but they were the ones active in community reform efforts. One of the most active was Matilda Evans. As South Carolina's first licensed female physician, Evans was a pioneer who continually developed strategies to meet the overwhelming health-care needs of black South Carolinians. Born in Aiken, a small town west of Augusta and the Savannah River, which provides the boundary between Georgia and South Carolina, Evans attended Aiken's Schofield Normal and Industrial School, one of South Carolina's better-known Reconstruction-era northern philanthropic private schools. The school's Quaker founder, Martha Schofield, encouraged Evans to continue her education outside South Carolina. Evans eventually received her medical training and credentials from the Woman's Medical College of Pennsylvania. Aware of the overwhelming need for health care for African Americans in her home state, Evans returned, in 1897, to serve South Carolina in Columbia. She developed a public-school health-testing program to identify systematic health problems among the school-age population. She opened a public health clinic in Columbia to educate families in proper health maintenance. When Evans first arrived, Columbia had no hospitals available for the majority of the city's population, who were African Americans, so she cared for patients in her home. Within a few years she founded the Taylor Lane Hospital and Training School for Nurses. The teaching and supervising demands of the only hospital that served the black community led her to give up private practice and serve as superintendent of the hospital. She also founded the Negro Health Care Association of South Carolina to facilitate statewide health and hygiene instruction.[39]

Another woman active in Columbia's health-care community was Lillian Rhodes. Although not a physician, she shared Evans's determination to expand and improve hospital care for African Americans. Rhodes and her physician husband, Swan Rhodes, founded the Good Samaritan Hospital and Nurse Training School for Columbia in 1910. Noted as a woman with exceptional business skills, Rhodes became solely responsible for the business side of the hospital when her husband died two years after opening the hospital. Rhodes's activism transcended easy categorization. She was an active member of the South Carolina Federation of Colored Women's Clubs (SCFCWC), an umbrella organization that both networked many smaller, local clubs and linked South Carolina's efforts with the National Association of Colored Women. Rhodes pursued business opportunities, managed the hospital, and advocated for improved health care. Rhodes was one of two women who served on the executive committee of the Columbia NAACP. The other woman, Dixie B. Brooks, was also secretary of Columbia's NAACP and executive secretary of Associated Charities.[40]

As Matilda Evans's, Lillian Rhodes's, and Dixie Brooks's activism demonstrates, black women exercised leadership in reforming South Carolina. Black women participated jointly with men in the same organizations, working together more often than white men and women did. Women served on the executive committees of Columbia and Charleston's NAACP. Every committee of black reformers that petitioned the legislature for community needs included men and women. At least four women served on the committee that organized the coming-home parade for the returning 371st soldiers: the extraordinary physician Matilda Evans, Lillian Rhodes, Estelle Perrin, and Sara B. Henderson, one of the original founders of the

SCFCWC. Women also engaged in reform independent of men. They most often channeled that independent leadership through the network of women's clubs. The philosophy of black club women, "Lifting as We Climb," acknowledged their social status and asserted their aspirations. Although limited themselves by racial discrimination, educated black women dedicated their volunteerism and fundraising to improving conditions in African American communities by promoting education, better health care, disease prevention, and care for young women whom society had neglected and forgotten.[41]

Club women's activism transcended narrow boundaries. Women held multiple leadership roles and engaged in a variety of reforms. Susie Dart Butler, an original founder of the SCFCWC, exemplified the overlapping community involvement of women reformers. In addition to the state organization, Butler's leadership in South Carolina's club women included belonging to and holding offices in the Phyllis Wheatley Club and Modern Priscillas of Charleston. Professionally, Butler was a teacher, milliner, and founder of Dart Hall, the first public library for African Americans in Charleston. Moreover, she was a charter member of Charleston's NAACP and its treasurer. Jeannette Cox, founder and president of Charleston's Phyllis Wheatley Club and wife of Avery Institute's president, was also a charter member of the NAACP. As the NAACP leadership of Cox, Butler, Evans, Rhodes, and Brooks indicated, club women worked for racial justice. They also worked for social change. In 1919, at the state organization's annual meeting, a member spoke in favor of woman suffrage, declaring, "Many crooked paths will be made straight when women cast her vote."[42]

South Carolina's most influential African American club woman was Marion Birnie Wilkinson, who served as state president for decades. In 1909, a group of women that included Wilkinson met at Sydney Park Church in Columbia and founded the SCFCWC. An Avery graduate and a Charlestonian by birth, Wilkinson lived her adult life in Orangeburg. This midstate county was home to South Carolina State College, the state's only public college for African Americans. Her husband, Robert Shaw Wilkinson, became the college president in 1911 after Thomas Miller resigned. During the war, Wilkinson led the organization to take responsibility for providing a home for young women sexually exploited by the influx of soldiers into the state. Originally named Fairwold, the home later changed its name to Wilkinson Home in honor of her long-term leadership supporting this institution, which relied on African Americans' private funding. With the formation of the Commission on Interracial Cooperation soon after the war, Wilkinson took an active leadership role in this new effort.[43]

In addition to business leaders, a few attorneys, health-care providers, and community leaders, some of the most prominent reformers were educators: university presidents, principals, and teachers at private and public schools. Many club women active in community reform were professional educators. Celia D. Saxon, charter member of the SCFCWC, and Rachel Monteith, a charter member of Columbia's NAACP, stand as just two examples of Columbia women who were lifelong career teachers and active participants in many facets of reform. Community leaders who eventually pursued business, law, medicine, and the ministry often began their careers as educators. For example, I. S. Leevy taught a year before launching his tailor business, and N. J. Frederick had been principal of Howard School. Anderson native M. H. Gassaway devoted thirty years as a teacher and principal of the local grade school. Gassaway organized a branch of the NAACP in his up-country county and soon experienced serious consequences for this boldness. Columbia had only two black public high schools, Howard and Booker T. Washington. The latter was a relatively new high school completed in 1916. Several years earlier I. S. Leevy had petitioned the local school board to build a new school for the city's black children. Howard, the only black high school in Columbia at the time, was overcrowded. Leevy picked the school name to honor his fellow Hampton alumnus.[44] In 1919 Cornell A. Johnson, principal of Booker T. Washington, and Isaiah M. A. Myers, principal of Howard School, the first public high school created for black South Carolinians, actively participated in reform initiatives.

While the state provided few public high schools for black South Carolinians, private high schools helped fill the education void. One of the most prominent private high schools was Avery Institute in Charleston. Numerous charter members of Charleston's NAACP were Avery alumni. Benjamin F. Cox, Avery's first black principal since Francis L. Cardozo's Reconstruction leadership, had become the principal at Avery Institute in 1914. Born in Mississippi, educated at Fisk, Cox became a professional educator with the American

Missionary Association (AMA), the northern missionary association that founded and supported Avery. He had served AMA schools in Albany, Georgia, and Florence, Alabama, as preparation for his move to Charleston. Cox's wife, Jeannette, was a Fisk graduate. Benjamin and Jeannette, acting as a team, brought Avery their expertise and appreciation for black history and culture, which they integrated into the curriculum. Before their arrival, Avery had gradually been incorporating more black and fewer white teachers into its faculty. The Coxes accelerated this trend, creating an all-black faculty at Avery by 1916. Both joined with forward-looking Charlestonians in forming the Charleston branch of the NAACP. As charter members (Benjamin also served on the executive committee), they facilitated a close relationship between Avery and the NAACP. Avery's financial independence of local whites made it an obvious haven for NAACP activities, protecting participants from economic retaliation and intimidation.[45]

Black business leaders, lawyers, physicians, hospital administrators, and educators all, directly or indirectly, relied on whites even as they pursued reform. In an era when white supremacy subordinated black professionals and created dependency, black churches, by contrast, stood as autonomous sanctuaries. Thus ministers, the leaders of these community beacons, held a unique status of influence among African Americans. While many ministers were not reformers and avoided these activities, every reform endeavor included ministers in its ranks. Those most interested in reform and expanding opportunities for African Americans found that the ministry facilitated their goals more than other professions. Allen University, an AME school in Columbia, enjoyed greater independence from whites than other African American colleges, which relied on white philanthropy. By contrast, African Americans founded, funded, and staffed Allen, which among other missions educated teachers and ministers. Allen's chancellor and the denomination's presiding bishop of South Carolina, W. D. Chappelle, was a bold reformer.[46]

Chappelle delivered the keynote address at the February welcome-home parade. A Winnsboro native, Chappelle, like many African Americans of his generation, was born into slavery. He attended school during Reconstruction at Fairfield Normal Institute, the new school in his county operated with northern Presbyterian philanthropy and northern white educators. Chappelle spent his life as an AME minister, climbing the ranks within the hierarchically structured church, becoming a prominent leader in and beyond the state. As a young minister he attended Allen University. Later he would serve two terms as its president and become a life trustee and chancellor of the university. As an AME bishop, Chappelle served briefly outside the state in Oklahoma and Arkansas from 1912 to 1916 and returned as the presiding bishop of South Carolina just before the nation's entry into World War I. Chappelle's contemporaries described him as "practical, forceful and progressive" and applauded his willingness to push others and work for tangible results. Without hesitation Chappelle spoke truth to power, publicly criticizing white leaders for their discriminatory treatment of African Americans. A recognized leader within the church, Chappelle extended his leadership far beyond it too.[47]

Other reform-minded black ministers in Columbia included the two men who shared the podium with Chappelle after the welcome-home parade: Jacob J. Durham, Second Calvary Baptist pastor, and Nathaniel F. Haygood, Sydney Park Methodist pastor. Collectively these three ministers' addresses embodied the black reformers' war-era message. Their public activities reinforced their insistence on change. Durham also served on the executive committee of Columbia's NAACP. Moreover, Chappelle and Haygood, along with two other ministers, Joseph C. White, pastor of Zion Baptist Church in Columbia, and E. H. Coit, a Charleston pastor, had been identified to Governor Cooper in 1919 as some of the "most officious Negro political leaders."[48] Such criticism authenticated their reform credentials.

Another minister, Erasmus Lafayette Baskervill, demonstrated leadership within his denomination, the Episcopal Church. A native Virginian, Baskervill came to Charleston in 1913 to serve as rector of Calvary Episcopal Church. Within a year he became archdeacon of the Diocese of South Carolina. Like Chappelle, Baskervill employed his activism beyond the church as well. Active in all facets of the community, Baskervill belonged to the NAACP and the YMCA and served as a trustee of Voorhees Normal and Industrial School, to name just two of his community leadership roles. Like many reformers he actively encouraged African Americans' participation in the war effort. He served as an officer in the state's United War Work Campaign. He organized rallies and protests. He linked his responsibilities as a minister with the fight for equality. G. Croft Williams, a white reformer who promoted interracial cooperation, expressed concern about Baskervill's activism. "The old Abolitionist is working mightily," Williams lamented, "stirring them [African Americans] up to all kinds of hazardous daring."[49] Although not a Charlestonian or a South Carolinian, Baskervill exhibited a reform style that fit better with NAACP president Teddy Harleston's assertive style than with that of the rival low-country reformer, Daniel Jenkins.

As in all human relationships, diversity and conflict existed within the African American community. In Charleston, Daniel Jenkins was a polarizing leader. Many respected and admired him, while others resented his growing influence. Known as "the Orphanage Man," Jenkins had a commanding physical presence and a personal confidence that was constantly on display. A Baptist minister, Jenkins operated Jenkins' Orphanage, which he founded in Charleston in the 1890s. He worked his way out of the hardscrabble poverty of his sharecropping roots and consequently believed that self-help could work for everyone. This fierce, independent attitude and belief that individual initiative could solve all problems put him at odds with many others. Jenkins, not formally educated like most black reformers, trusted whites, curried their favor, and depended on them for funding his orphanage. City officials provided a modest annual appropriation for the orphanage and then felt justified in sending black youth offenders there. Jenkins supplemented the city funds with private fund-raisers. His most dependable source of revenue was the orphanage brass bands that Jenkins created to tour the nation as well as play for local tourists. An admirer and imitator of Booker T. Washington, Jenkins prized manual labor and promoted obedience. He also published and edited the *Charleston Messenger*, in which he touted his self-help ethic. Whites encouraged Jenkins, believing his philosophy of hard work and strict discipline for black orphans benefited society. Charleston's existing black elite conflicted with Jenkins's style and philosophy. Everything about Jenkins, a self-educated, dark-skinned man with roots in Barnwell County, clashed with the light-skinned, privately educated Charlestonian elite, who had been rooted in Charleston for generations. Moreover Jenkins's Booker T. Washington accommodationist philosophy conflicted with their support of and friendship with W. E. B. DuBois. Yet Jenkins's influence was undeniable.[50]

Another minister who created divisiveness among blacks was Richard Carroll, who operated from Columbia. Carroll shared with Daniel Jenkins a cozy relationship with whites. All African American reformers worked with whites, solicited their understanding, and sought their assistance. W. D. Chappelle once remarked that working with white leadership was nonnegotiable. If blacks stood alone against whites, Chappelle explained, "on one side [would be] education and wealth and on the other ignorance and poverty."[51] Yet Jenkins and Carroll claimed whites' attention by criticizing other black leaders and promoting their own efforts as uniquely harmonious with white expectations. While most black reformers viewed whites' economic and political power as an impediment that required careful negotiation, Jenkins and Carroll interpreted powerful whites as allies who desired their collaboration. Of course the interracial partnership that both men prided themselves in fostering was asymmetrical. They, more than their colleagues, served as pawns of white leaders, but they relished the proximity to power.

Carroll greatly admired Booker T. Washington and wholly embraced his self-help philosophy. Referenced on public occasions as the "Booker T. Washington of South Carolina," Carroll corresponded with Washington and invited him to speak in South Carolina several times. He once told Washington that "if Jesus Christ came down from Heaven and was permitted to speak, I believe that he would have said just what you said in Zion church to the colored men."[52] Such sycophantic declarations characterized Carroll's style. Carroll's contemporaries remarked on his smooth style and eloquent expressions of admiration, especially of his esteem for whites. Carroll's close relationship with whites began early. Carroll's mother, his only acknowledged parent, died when Carroll was a child, leaving him in the care of the Rices, the Barnwell County white family who had owned her during slavery. Carroll, born in 1860, had also experienced slavery as a young child. W. D. Rice, an avid Southern Baptist, introduced Carroll to Christianity through this evangelical, white protestant denomination. Carroll attended Benedict College in Columbia and Shaw University in North Carolina and then entered the ministry as a Baptist missionary to African Americans, funded by a white missionary society, the American Baptist Publication Society. He was a chaplain in the army during the Spanish-American War in 1898. He promoted his self-help philosophy by helping found the state Reformatory for Negro Boys in 1900 and briefly operated an industrial school.[53]

Carroll recognized the same problems other black leaders identified, but his solution was always to advocate exemplary individual behavior by blacks as the impetus for change rather than suggest a change in the racist structure that ensnared African Americans. White leaders applauded Carroll and supported his efforts because he articulated their perspective and their solutions. Ironically, Carroll's mentor acknowledged but disapproved of his consistent kowtowing to whites that earned him their favor. Booker T. Washington privately confided to Oswald Garrison Villard of the NAACP that Carroll had "many qualities that neither you nor I would admire, but at the same time there is no discounting the fact that he has tremendous influence with the white people of South Carolina."[54] While Carroll openly criticized violent and extreme expressions of racism, he ignored whites' responsibility for creating the unjust educational, economic, political, and social disparities that oppressed African Americans. Moreover, he overlooked that whites exercised the power they held to serve their ends and to benefit from the resulting inequities. Instead Carroll insisted, "Righteous living on the part of the negro will cause righteous living on the part of white people." Further, Carroll explained in a pamphlet he distributed at his first race conference: "If we commit crime, [whites] commit crime. If we be law-abiding, they will be law-abiding."[55] Carroll seemingly imagined justice emanating from the continual sacrifices of the "least of these," who were expected to uphold exemplary standards never expected of those who held the power and resources.

Carroll promoted his views through the South Carolina Race Conference, which he organized in 1907 and continued to arrange through the World War I era. Carroll intended the race conference, which he held as a series of annual meetings in various cities across the state with interracial audiences, as a setting for promoting harmony and understanding between blacks and whites. Carroll enlisted white leaders to speak, and most years the governor of South Carolina spoke at his race conferences. Whites readily supported his conferences because he planned benign topics, such as "fidelity and loyalty" and "how to raise turnips," that fit their view of race relations. Carroll also published his own newspaper, the *Southern Plough-*

man, in which he promoted his views that conflicted with those of other African American leaders, particularly other ministers.

In addition to his accommodating activism and harmony-inducing rhetoric, Carroll ingratiated himself with whites by explicitly steering clear of politics. He frequently touted his own successful intentions to shun politics. While encouraging other blacks to follow his example, Carroll criticized publicly any African American reformers who advocated voting rights for blacks. This behavior was another quality that distinguished him from most black reformers. Moreover, while other black reformers were prominent ministers, Carroll held one of the most unusual positions a black minister could hold: whites employed him to evangelize African Americans. As a missionary of the Home Mission Board of the white-controlled Southern Baptist Convention, Carroll worked among blacks at the pleasure of whites. This position as a Baptist missionary facilitated his frequent travels, extensive audience, and financial dependence on whites. His broad acceptance among whites led Governor Richard Manning to appoint Carroll to chair the segregated, black counterpart of the South Carolina Council of Defense, the organization that facilitated African American war mobilization.[56]

Together Carroll's uplift rhetoric that supported white political control, his position as a Baptist minister in a white denomination, and the formal endorsement by the white power structure enhanced his popularity among whites. His close relationship with prominent white leaders, ironically, made him influential with other black reformers, who despised his methods but could not risk alienating him. Carroll's cultivated relationship with the white elite made him a formidable rival for other black leaders. Other black reformers who needed white support had to navigate through the accommodating, deferential maze that Carroll created. Consequently, Carroll's prominence and presence fostered, among black leaders, a broad pressure to conform.

As African Americans gathered in February 1919 to honor returning soldiers and to remember those who had sacrificed their lives, black reformers in South Carolina were filled with hope and expectation that the time had arrived to press against their dismal status, oppressed conditions, and limited opportunities. While African Americans' struggle for freedom and equality did not begin in 1919, it gained energy and a sharpened focus that year. The United States' involvement in World War I, which had ended just a few months earlier, had been the immediate catalyst for African Americans' rising hope. Anticipating that their support of the nation's war effort would leverage future economic and political opportunities, many African Americans readily looked for chances to serve the nation and then parlay that wartime cooperative service into meaningful and tangible opportunities. John McClellan, a Columbia minister, articulated the sentiment clearly: "We pray God, in the midst of shot, blood shed and shells, that out of this great struggle for democracy, a new democracy may be born which shall measure a man by his mind and not by his face."[57]

Black reformers appealed to the legacy of Reconstruction for inspiration. For this generation of black leaders, Reconstruction connoted a spirit of hope and promise, reminding African Americans of the time when blacks voted in large numbers and held public office at the local, state, and national levels. As an "unfinished revolution" Reconstruction heartened African Americans and evoked a historical memory of a "golden era" they longed to resurrect and fulfill completely. Their reform ideals imagined for the state's black majority improved educational opportunities, higher-paid and more-qualified teachers, longer school terms and more public high schools, less employment discrimination yielding a broader range of job opportunities, widespread landownership opportunities, higher-quality and more-accessible health care, and fair treatment in the criminal justice system. African American reformers' list also included the demand for political rights, a prerequisite for pursuing all other goals but a demand that directly threatened white political control, whites' perceived cultural imperative.

Chapter 2

White Resolve

"It is possible, indeed likely," declared *The State*'s editor, William Watts Ball, "that the South Carolina and the South that we have known will be, on account of this war, unrecognizable in the course of a few years." Ball's optimistic forecast demonstrates aptly that World War I inspired hope. Not only were South Carolina's African American reformers hopeful, but the war also fostered high expectations among whites who styled themselves progressive reformers. They dreamed of a progressive South Carolina with a diverse and prosperous economy, an effective state highway system, expanded educational opportunity, compassionate treatment of the mentally ill, rehabilitation for wayward juveniles and adult prisoners, and an improved standard of living. Moreover, Ball continued, "To the old timers, accustomed to the jog trot of Southern manners and living, the changes will bring disturbance, annoyance and perhaps inconvenience under which they will chafe and fret: some of these one may decry in the close future, but by and large, the changes will be salutary."[1] Here Ball alludes to white reformers' perception of themselves as leaders who embraced change eagerly, anticipating positive outcomes.

South Carolina white reformers, drawn from the state's relatively small middle class, included lawyers, journalists, university professors, public school educators and administrators, ministers, businessmen, doctors, civic leaders, agricultural scientists, agricultural extension agents, and others. These middle-class professionals pursued widely varying goals, emphasized different priorities, and often pushed conflicting agendas. Yet this small, active cohort of reformers shared a broadly articulated vision in the World War I era of a better-educated and economically prosperous state, with a higher standard of living, adequate health care, less crime and violence, better roads, and a more diverse economy. Fundamentally, they desired to move South Carolina from the bottom tier of so many lists that served as indicators of economic well-being and a satisfactory standard of living. Like their national counterparts, South Carolina reformers were imbued with notions linking efficiency and progress, believing that the appropriate expertise could remedy any of society's economic, political, and social ills. They wanted to bring order and effectiveness to state government and business.[2]

Progressives deemed an educated population essential to all other reform endeavors. They especially recognized the importance of extending educational opportunities to broader segments of the population. As educated leaders they enjoyed a privilege not available to the overwhelming majority of South Carolinians. During their adolescence the state provided only seven years of public education. South Carolina created its first public high schools after 1907, and those were not widely available across the state. Consequently all formal education beyond the seventh grade required private funds. Thus the mark of every reformer was a credentialed education, acquired from both private and public colleges and universities, in and outside the state. From grade school to college, educational improvement received attention from reformers because of South Carolina's manifest deficiencies at all levels.[3]

White reformers advocated improving the economy through commercial and industrial development. Moreover, they focused on strengthening the economy by helping South Carolina diversify its agriculture, become much less dependent on cotton, and implement more-scientific agricultural methods. Most reformers advocated construction of a state network of highways, believing that improved transportation facilitated all other economic development strategies. Some white reformers directed their energy and attention to reforming the institutions of state government, which seemed wholly inadequate for administering the programs that reformers thought the state needed.[4]

Since additional state revenue was so fundamental to any reform, revising South Carolina's tax structure loomed large on many reformers' agendas in the postwar era. They wanted a new tax system that would generate adequate revenue to fund their long list of public needs. In addition to filling the state treasury with ample funds, they expected a reformed tax system to distribute the public financial burden fairly among landowners and to tax all income-generating sources, not simply property owners. In the pursuit of improved humanitarian institutions, some reformers highlighted as serious social ills South Carolina's horrendous prison conditions, its inadequate reformatories for errant youth, its labor-exploitative chain gangs, and the employment of children in the textile industry. Others crusaded for improvement in public health, better mental health facilities, county almshouses for the elderly indigent, and restrictions on child labor in industry. Like their counterparts in other southern states, some South Carolina reformers crusaded for an improved system of criminal justice and against extralegal violence, including lynching, which many hoped to eliminate.[5]

Yet white reformers wanted changes that they prescribed and could control. As southern progressives, they remained resolved to guarantee whites' economic, political, and social dominance. They carefully devised reform initiatives that ensured their efforts would benefit whites first and foremost.[6] They did not want "disturbance, annoyance and perhaps inconvenience" coming from black reformers whose dreams imagined a different end. Black reformers directed their hopeful anticipation toward improving African Americans' lives, which was not a priority for white reformers. Consequently, South Carolina's white and black reformers welcomed the Great War as a catalyst for change that would facilitate fulfillment of their respective reform agendas. Each group envisioned that America's participation in the war would channel resources from war profits and federal spending toward addressing entrenched educational, economic, health, and infrastructural problems. But their visions clashed, making these two sets of reformers asymmetrical competitors rather than collaborators.

The progressive agenda that whites articulated embraced wide-ranging and diverse goals, but it included a nonnegotiable provision—white supremacy—which brought their aspirations into conflict with black reformers' goals. Whites found common ground with white supremacy, even whites whose social worlds rarely met, whose political allegiances clashed, and whose economic interests competed. White South Carolinians, whether landless sharecroppers, low-wage mill workers, school principals, or bank presidents, agreed on at least two core premises of white supremacy. First, they relied on the assumption of whites' inherent supremacy, conceiving of themselves as intellectually and culturally superior to blacks. Most whites accepted the corollary supposition of African Americans' genetic, thus permanent, inferiority. Second, white supremacy also meant that in a biracial society, like the American South, whites believed they should necessarily secure and maintain control over all aspects of the culture: political institutions, law, the economy, education, social values, and religion. While whites readily embraced white supremacy as a set of ideas that rationalized and enhanced their world, African Americans experienced the detrimental realism of the society that whites had constructed to embody these beliefs. Framed from the perspective of African Americans, white supremacy stifled their efforts and limited their human potential as they struggled under its oppression. Black South Carolinians had few prospects for education, economic opportunity, and self-fulfillment because the dominant white culture subscribed to a set of beliefs that insisted that the tools necessary for success be permanently locked away from them. W. E. Smith, an African American from South Carolina, concisely defined white supremacy as "the idea that one race must be discouraged, limited and throttled in every avenue of human endeavor in order that the other might rise to heights unknown."[7]

The white reformers who advocated a progressive vision for reform in the World War I era proudly assembled under the banner of white supremacy, as did all other whites. By the second decade of the twentieth century a culturally constructed white supremacy united whites, even political adversaries, in a shared determination to preserve white control. Without apology, U. B. Phillips, a contemporary southern historian, asserted that white southerners held a "common resolve indomitably maintained—that [the South] shall be and remain a white man's country." This sentiment, Phillips insisted, "whether expressed with the frenzy of a demagogue or maintained with a patrician's quietude," united white southerners. White society drew confidence and self-assurance from the belief in its inherent superiority, using the term "white supremacy" openly, frequently, and proudly. Billy Sunday, the prominent white evangelist, told a South Carolina audience that he believed in "Protestantism, Americanism, and the supremacy of the white race." A Columbia resident explained his belief about African Americans in stating that "God in His wisdom created him the inferior of the white man." The editor of Anderson's *Farmer's Tribune* warned that any "white man who believes in social equality is worse than the most damnable rape fiend on earth." Benjamin "Pitchfork Ben" Tillman, infamous U.S. senator from South Carolina, proudly proclaimed from the floor of Congress that for thirty years he had upheld his duty to "stand forever opposed to any idea of political or social equality on the part of the negro with the whites of South Carolina."[8] This public rhetoric exemplifies the openness and pride that whites attached to expressions and justifications of white dominance.

This shared, unapologetic commitment to white supremacy emerged long before the twentieth century. White supremacy was both more than and different from racism and prejudice. While racism and prejudice have permeated human relationships through time and across cultures, a systematic white supremacy had emerged in the United States in response to specific historical circumstances that included slavery.[9] Slavery, a racially justified institution, was not the only foundation for white supremacy, but in the Old South, most whites deemed slavery the surest or best foundation for maintaining white supremacy in their biracial society given their economic need for agricultural labor and the high proportion of enslaved black people in the population.[10] The Union's victory over the Confederacy in the American Civil War permanently destroyed slavery and the institutional sanction that had nurtured and protected white supremacy. Military defeat and emancipation, however, did not weaken whites' commitment to regain power and reassert white authority.

As a legally and politically sanctioned ideal, white supremacy suffered briefly during Reconstruction under federal action that facilitated emerging African American citizenship. With the introduction of the Fourteenth and Fifteenth Amendments to the Constitution, the Republican architects of Radical Reconstruction departed ideologically from the national, antebellum white consensus, which held that blacks were inferior and not entitled to the same rights as whites. These amendments, which guaranteed blacks citizenship, equal protection under the law, and voting rights for men, was a direct affront to white supremacy and an assault on white southerners' relegation of African Americans to an inferior status. Moreover, white domination of the political system ended abruptly in South Carolina with black enfranchisement and officeholding. Yet support and enforcement of these constitutional guarantees proved short-lived. Following the fraudulent and corrupt 1876 election, white Democrats regained political control of the state, federal troops withdrew, and the brief experience in interracial democracy was finished. With "Redemption" white South Carolinians had not yet resurrected institutional protection for white supremacy, but the momentum had shifted in favor of it.[11]

By the twentieth century white supremacy was again institutionalized, this time through disfranchisement and segregation, both institutions that whites constructed to satisfy their perceived need to subordinate African Americans and maintain political dominance, economic advantage, and social control. White South Carolinians had succeeded at undermining the intent of the Reconstruction amendments with ratification of the 1895 constitution, designed by Ben Tillman as the instrument for disfranchising African Americans. Whites also gradually codified segregation. In 1896, the U.S. Supreme Court endorsed the legal subterfuge with *Plessy v. Ferguson*. Segregation and disfranchisement, which whites complexly constructed over many years in the late nineteenth and early twentieth centuries, granted white supremacy new institutional strength, which had been lost when emancipation destroyed slavery—the initial institution that sanctioned white supremacy.[12]

With white supremacy securely constructed and enjoying institutional status, white reformers felt free to pursue progressive changes that would improve the quality of life for the state's white citizens. In this pursuit, white reformers confronted innumerable challenges, whose magnitude is partially revealed by the state's demography. South Carolina's white reformers, like other progressives throughout the nation, emerged primarily from the town-based middle class. Yet World War I–era South Carolina was overwhelmingly rural, poor, and black and generated a relatively small white middle class that severely limited the ranks of white reformers. With 85 percent of its population living in rural districts, South Carolina was one of the least-urban states in the nation and more rural than most neighboring southern states. In 1920, when the census offi-

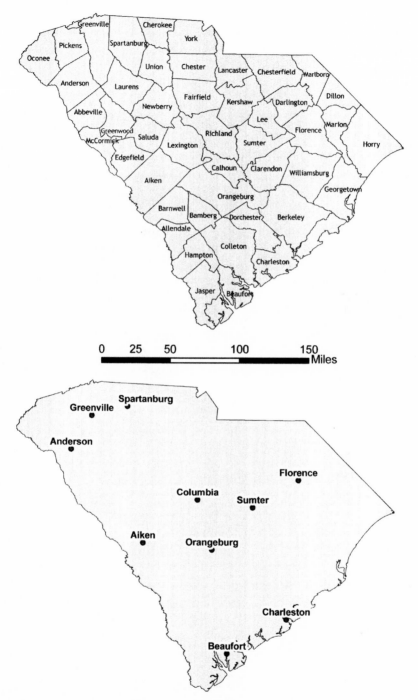

South Carolina counties (above) and selected cities (below). (Map by W. Lynn Shirley)

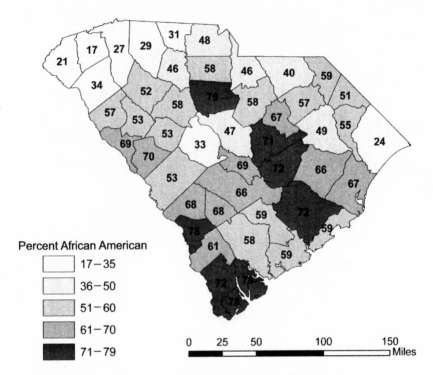

South Carolina racial demography. (Map by W. Lynn Shirley)

cially recognized that the majority of Americans resided in urban areas, only four states were less urban than South Carolina, and two of these were the sparsely settled Dakotas. In addition to being a disproportionately rural state, South Carolina was also poorer than most. Shortly before the war broke out in Europe, the Palmetto State's per capita wealth was $869, 44 percent of the national average, $1,965. Only three states ranked lower in per capita wealth. Moreover, 55 percent of South Carolinians were black, the second highest percentage of African Americans in any state, just behind Mississippi, whose population was 56 percent black. South Carolina and Mississippi were the only states to have African American majorities.[13] As a black-majority state, South Carolina not only differed sharply from the rest of the nation in terms of racial demography, but the presence of a black majority also influenced white South Carolinians' attitude on every issue of public policy.

Not all white South Carolinians perceived the state's black majority in the same way. African Americans' presence affected whites differently depending on a range of factors including whites' geographical location, economic status, and social class. Whites' desire to dominate African Americans was generally most pronounced in areas where blacks were a larger portion of the population. Since maintaining white supremacy depended on white economic, political, and social control, whites who lived as a minority in their district, county, city, or state insisted on developing more-elaborate strategies of control over the African American majority in their midst. South Carolina's black majority was neither spread evenly through all counties nor proportionately represented in all economic pursuits. African Americans represented 60 to 78 percent of the population in the coastal low-country counties, and their proportion of the population diminished gradually as you moved north and westward toward the up-country Piedmont counties, where a few counties had white majorities.[14] (See racial demography map, page 48.) White power brokers who lived as a minority among African Americans, whom they deemed inferior, encouraged stubborn resistance to all changes that they thought might threaten white control.

South Carolina's black majority provided a particularly daunting challenge for white reformers who desperately wanted to create a white majority. Reformers callously blamed the African American victims of poverty for causing the state's intractable problems associated with poverty. They simplistically imagined that a proportionately smaller black population would mean fewer problems. Moreover, the black majority proved a political liability for reformers because in the Jim Crow age racial demography influenced the structure of political and economic power. The shape it took in South Carolina tilted the balance of power in favor of reform opponents. Generally, white South Carolinians who lived in counties or regions with proportionately high black majorities favored local control and resisted accepting state government as a partner in solving economic, educational, and social problems affecting the entire state.[15] This embrace of localism and resistance to statewide solutions directly conflicted with white reformers' goals and strategies. Consequently, the dictates of white supremacy made South Carolina's racial demography an important factor in public policy that constrained reform initiatives.

To combat the notion that change threatened white supremacy, South Carolina's white reformers promoted the compatibility of change and white dominance. White reformers envisioned progress within the context of a securely constructed system of white supremacy. The twin commitment to progress and white control received perhaps its best expression from an influential reformer, Irvine F. Belser, Columbia native, Yale graduate, lawyer, and adjutant of the state American Legion. Belser voiced his support for development and progress in South Carolina at an organizational meeting of the South Carolina Development Board, a progressive, post–World War I venture committed to economic development. At the meeting Belser noted that the American Legion stood for "progress at all times," and "white supremacy at all times."[16] White reformers imagined no contradiction in advocating reform, which demanded change, and embracing white supremacy, which thrived on continuity and stability. Yet as white reformers pursued their reform agenda with its nonnegotiable provision, maintaining white supremacy, they confronted two distinct obstacles: African American reformers, and whites who opposed their vision for reform.

All reformers, black and white, seized on World War I mobilization as a potential agent for change. Yet the vision of South Carolina's white reformers conflicted with African Americans' aspirations because it included a significant caveat: whites first and foremost. African American reformers, for the most part, wanted precisely the same things for the state's black majority that white reformers wanted for the state's white population: improved schools, higher-paid and more-qualified teachers, a broader range of job and landownership opportunities, improved health care, and fair treatment in the criminal justice system. Additionally, however, African Americans' list included the demand for political rights, a prerequisite essential for pursuing all other goals but a direct threat to white political control. Ironically, had the dictates of white supremacy not loomed so large, black and white reform leaders might have found common cause, but in World War I–era South Carolina, such coalition building across racial lines terrified whites, who believed that such alliances signaled civilization's inevitable demise. Compounding whites' ideological resistance to biracial cooperation was the existing disfranchisement machinery that had reduced the number of African

American voters to a few thousand. Such small numbers proved an immediate and practical obstacle to pursuing such forbidden coalitions. Absent a partnership, white reformers viewed black reformers simply as troublesome agitators who aroused the whites' political opponents. African Americans' struggles for freedom and equality provoked anxiety among all whites. Reform opponents exploited this fear to defeat reform initiatives that advocated change, a strategy that particularly alarmed white reformers, who resented war-related black activism, perceiving that such activism jeopardized their chance to seize the unique opportunities created by war-stimulated economic growth.

While African American reformers complicated white reformers' plans, white reformers simultaneously had to prevent political control of state government from falling into the hands of their white political adversaries, who, to one degree or another, opposed the reform agenda. White reformers distinguished themselves from traditionalists, with whom they disagreed vociferously about a wide array of political, economic, and public policy issues. Reformers advocated change when most other whites defended the status quo. From the reformers' perspective, all white South Carolina traditionalists were their foes, and reformers contended broadly with two distinct groups of white traditionalists. On one end of the economic spectrum stood conservative elites, including agrarian conservatives, particularly the state's large landowning elite; affluent businessmen; and many industrialists. All these groups fought reform initiatives because they anticipated that the cost would fall heavily on their particular economic interests. Several of these opponents also embraced economic strategies that relied heavily on an abundant supply of cheap labor. So they resisted all reforms that threatened their labor-intensive business model. On the other end of the economic spectrum came opposition from South Carolina's sizable white working class, led by Cole Blease, the state's most notorious racial demagogue. Textile-mill operatives expressed deep suspicions of state action, which they feared would impose middle-class values on them and their families; thus they relished Blease's obstructionism.

Ironically, the weapon traditionalists used to thwart white reformers was white supremacy, the same blunt instrument white reformers used to extinguish the dreams of black reformers. Compounding the

irony, white reformers faced intense criticism from reform opponents, who claimed to be preserving white hegemony with their opposition. In spite of reformers' firmly pledged support to the
well-entrenched axiom of white supremacy, they continually faced
the charge that proposed reforms threatened that supremacy. Such
accusations supplied part of the theater and rhetorical style of white
supremacy politics that saturated political discourse of this era. The
allegations did not serve as evidence that white reformers intended to
undermine white supremacy. To the contrary, white reformers steadfastly refused to challenge institutional racism and the legitimacy of
white privilege. Rather, reform opponents' baseless allegations that
reformers intended to undermine white supremacy reveals the political machinations at work in a culture suffused with a nonnegotiable provision to which all other considerations were forced to
yield.

White reformers' fundamental challenge was implementing their
vision, which necessitated maintaining white supremacy while navigating the obstacles that black reformers, other whites, and white
supremacy itself imposed. Reformers' significant opposition, their
diverse goals, small numbers, and loose-knit coalition shaped their
strategy and encouraged newspaper editors to become the movement's leaders. Because they publicly articulated the movement's visions and policy expectations, editors were some of the most
well-known reformers. Newspapers were an easily accessible medium
for communicating with a scattered but comparatively well-educated
constituency residing primarily in cities and towns. Other political
movements in the state, such as those led by Ben Tillman and Cole
Blease, relied more heavily on building political support through
physical proximity, rallies, and local organizations. The agrarian
revolt led by Tillman, who organized farmers into local Farmers'
Associations, had created grassroots networks across the state. The
frustrated white working class, which rallied behind Blease, was concentrated in the Piedmont, where workers lived in textile-mill villages and worked in the textile industry. Whereas the earlier farmers'
movement and the contemporary textile-workers' movement relied
on local organizations, oral tradition, and personal contact, the
widely scattered progressive coalition proved less amenable to face-
to-face organization. Thus white reformers understood that owning

and editing local newspapers extended their voice and influence beyond their personal contacts and into their communities. The larger city newspapers like *The State* in Columbia, the *News and Courier* in Charleston, and the *Greenville News* spread the message through entire regions of the state. These progressive editors used their platform to garner political support, promote progressive public policies, critique opponents, and generally rally public support to the reform cause. Moreover, several editors held other positions of responsibility and influence, including elected office.

For example, J. Rion McKissick, son of textile magnate and business executive A. Foster McKissick, came to enjoy influence in Greenville, a Piedmont town heavily dependent on the textile industry. McKissick graduated from South Carolina College and Harvard Law School. A Union County native, Rion McKissick expected to practice law, but the journalistic tug was stronger. Fellow South Carolinian James Hemphill offered McKissick a job as a reporter for the prestigious *Richmond Times-Dispatch* in 1909. Several years' experience as a reporter and assistant editor at the Virginia paper positioned him to return to South Carolina and become editor of the *Greenville News* from 1916 to 1919. In 1919, McKissick bought the controlling interest in the *Greenville Piedmont* and became its editor and president. Before returning to South Carolina, McKissick turned down an editorial position with the *New York Press*, a position that would have advanced his journalistic career. A colleague identified this decision to choose service to South Carolina as his primary profession as McKissick's turning point. McKissick considered journalism a calling analogous to the ministry or medicine. Like many reformers, he believed in using his talents for purposes greater than his own career. One of his first challenges upon returning home from Richmond was helping elect Richard I. Manning, the reformers' candidate, governor in 1914. Celebrating this victory, McKissick asserted that Manning's administration would put South Carolina in the "company of enlightened and progressive commonwealths." McKissick was one of the few South Carolina editors to endorse woman suffrage.[17]

Another progressive editor, Harry Watson, enjoyed broad influence in his hometown, Greenwood. Watson, editor and owner of the *Greenwood Index-Journal*, supported progressive causes through his editorials. Watson's authority in Greenwood was evident from the number of influential executive posts he held in his small town. He served as director of Greenwood's Chamber of Commerce, hospital, fair association, public library, Southeastern Life Insurance, and Oregon Hotel Company. He was president of the local bank and a trustee of Furman University and chaired the board of trustees of Greenwood city schools. Watson's pervasive and overlapping leadership in the community typifies the broad activism of some small-town reformers.

Another small-town reformer who paralleled Watson's town leadership was W. W. (William Wightman) Smoak, editor, publisher, and owner of the *Walterboro Press and Standard*, the only newspaper in Colleton County. Smoak developed a reputation in this small low-country town as a progressive advocate of "public improvement." After establishing his journalistic credentials at the *Press and Standard*, he briefly left South Carolina for journalistic experience in Madisonville, Kentucky. Like McKissick, he returned, first to Anderson and then to Walterboro, where again he became owner and editor of the *Press and Standard*. Smoak, a native of Colleton County, garnered support for local initiatives and promoted various state reforms through his editorial column. He represented his community in the state legislature for one term during World War I. Rather than seek reelection to the state legislature, he became mayor of Walterboro in 1920. He was president of the South Carolina Association, a development organization that served four low-country counties at the southeastern tip of the state.[18]

The most influential editor among the reformers was William Watts Ball, who edited numerous major newspapers in South Carolina and later served as the first dean of the School of Journalism at the University of South Carolina, which opened in 1923. The Laurens native, who referred to himself simply as an up-countryman, had a passion for politics that shaped his editorials. A graduate of South Carolina College, Ball studied law at the University of Virginia and was admitted to the South Carolina bar in 1890 but pursued journalism as his profession. For the first two decades of his career Ball moved from paper to paper in a frustrated search for a platform that matched his aspirations.[19] In 1913, President Woodrow Wilson unknowingly created Ball's much-anticipated opportunity. From

1909 to 1913 Ball had been managing editor of *The State*, the capital city's newspaper. Wilson appointed its editor, William Gonzales, ambassador to Cuba. With Gonzales's departure Ball was promoted from managing editor to editor in chief of *The State*, South Carolina's most important newspaper. This promotion put Ball exactly where he longed to be, at the center of South Carolina politics when factional politics reached its zenith.[20]

While John Stark and others identify Ball as a conservative, that label is broadly defined and a misleading description of Ball's entire life. Ball identified with South Carolina's elites who staunchly opposed Ben Tillman in the late nineteenth century, and this position is labeled conservative. Yet South Carolina's politics experienced realignment in the early twentieth century. In this repositioning, Ball clearly identified himself with progressives, just as many other former conservatives had. By the 1930s, however, Ball's bitterness against the New Deal made him a colorful and outspoken reactionary against Franklin D. Roosevelt's policies, which greatly expanded the federal government's involvement in ordinary Americans' lives.[21]

Within a year of Ball's becoming editor of *The State*, Richard Manning was elected governor. Ball became a regular consultant to Manning, who committed his governorship to a progressive reform agenda. Many credited Ball with Manning's hard-fought 1916 reelection win against Cole Blease, the ardent antireformer. By 1919, Ball, as editor of *The State*, had led three campaigns against Cole Blease (1914, U.S. Senate; 1916, governor; 1918, U.S. Senate). His relentless public fight against Blease, begun immediately after taking the helm, made him a potent political force for the reform agenda. Reflecting after these elections, Ball shared his perception of his role in South Carolina politics: "Circumstances put on me a considerable part of the task the last ten years of trying to unite the most intelligent and patriotic people of this state against raids by the unscrupulous politicians," of whom, according to Ball, Blease was the most unscrupulous. "My work," Ball explained, "is to prevent division among those men," the reformers and their allies. In addition to using *The State*'s editorial page to shape policy and build a reform political coalition, Ball maintained an extensive private communication network with state political leaders. He remained editor of *The State* until 1923, when he resigned to become the first dean of the School of Journalism at the University of

South Carolina, hoping to influence the next generation of South Carolina journalists.[22]

Another state leader with newspaper interests and a commitment to progressive reform was Niels Christensen Jr., of Beaufort. Christensen purchased Beaufort's local paper, the *Beaufort Gazette*, in 1903, owned it until 1922, and edited the paper off and on during these two decades. Christensen's ownership of the *Beaufort Gazette* roughly paralleled his political career. Christensen represented Beaufort in the South Carolina Senate for almost twenty years, from 1905 to 1924. He used the *Beaufort Gazette* to promote his progressive agenda. When Christensen chaired the Senate finance committee, the *Beaufort Gazette* developed the largest mail circulation of any weekly in South Carolina, evidence of his assertive leadership. In his twenty-year state senate career Christensen advocated for tax reform, woman suffrage, prison reform, and greater state responsibility for health care, the mentally ill, and public education. His long public service record as a state senator created his statewide reputation. Christensen not only supported progressive reform but also sponsored significant reform legislation. While serving in the legislature and editing the *Beaufort Gazette*, Christensen also worked in the family hardware, lumber, and building supply business, N. Christensen and Sons, and managed Christensen Realty. He was also a commissioned naval officer during World War I.[23]

Unlike most other white reformers, Christensen did not have deep southern roots. His father, Niels Sr., immigrated to the United States from Denmark in 1862. Sensing his best opportunity as a new immigrant was serving in the Union army, a motive distinct from patriotic attachment to his adopted country or antislavery idealism, Niels Sr. volunteered with the 145th New York Infantry and reenlisted three times. His first visit to South Carolina was marching in Sherman's army as a captain in the Forty-fourth U.S. Colored Infantry. He settled in Beaufort during Reconstruction as a federal government representative who cared for the graves of Union soldiers. Abbie Holmes Christensen, Niels's mother and a Massachusetts native, moved to Beaufort in 1864 at age twelve with her family, who participated in the missionary experience at Port Royal, an educational and religious outreach to the newly freed slaves in the South Carolina low country. She married Niels Sr. in 1875. Abbie exhibited a lifelong passion for reform as an activist on such issues as temperance, woman suffrage, and African American education. Through her initiatives, the Christensens founded Port Royal Agricultural School for African Americans in Beaufort. They secured private funding and recruited a Tuskegee graduate as principal to lead the school on the Booker T. Washington model. Abbie Christensen and her son Niels served as trustees for many years. Compared to many white South Carolinians, Niels Jr. advocated moderate reforms, such as increased agricultural education and anti-lynching legislation, yet he never shared his mother's inclination toward social equality for African Americans. Her abolitionist, missionary background and social activism for gender and racial equality set her at odds with the culture and her son, who embraced the southern tenets of white supremacy.[24]

By World War I, Christensen was a seasoned progressive leader in state politics. A much younger politician, Claud N. Sapp, also promoted a reform agenda. Always proud of his roots in Sapp's Crossings in rural Lancaster County, Sapp championed progressive causes that he envisioned would improve the lives of ordinary white South Carolinians. Gifted with a strong, analytical mind, Sapp earned his A.B. degree from Wofford College in 1907 and graduated from the University of South Carolina Law School in 1911 and was admitted to the South Carolina bar the same year. He began his law career in Lancaster, where he served as city attorney and later as county attorney. He represented Lancaster County in the state house of representatives in the 1913–1914 term. In 1916, Sapp moved to Columbia, where he became South Carolina's first assistant attorney general, an office he held until 1919. After World War I, he returned to the state house, this time representing Richland County, from 1921 to 1924. As a reformer, Sapp envisioned a prosperous South Carolina that would educate its citizens, modernize its infrastructure, and integrate itself more fully into the economic mainstream of the nation. He tirelessly advocated for improved public education and generous public spending to broaden educational opportunities for South Carolina's rural white population. Although Sapp embraced middle-class, town values in adulthood, he pushed for expanded opportunities to rural areas because of his rural experiences. When he became chair of the powerful house ways and means committee, he used his influence to advocate increased state responsibility and funding for education.[25]

If Niels Christensen Jr. and Claud Sapp exemplified progressive leadership in the general assembly, South Carolina's quintessential reformer occupied the governor's mansion for two terms, 1915–1918. A patrician by any standard, Richard Irving Manning of Sumter was the third Manning to be governor of South Carolina. As a Sumter native, he proudly considered himself a practical farmer, but business owner and banker more aptly described his profession. His business interests began and remained primarily banking and included manufacturing, cotton warehouses, utilities, automobiles, and insurance. Manning's four years as governor coincided with World War I and followed the governorship of Cole Blease, the state's most reactionary opponent of progressive reform. Manning made numerous trips to Washington on official war business during his second term and enjoyed the confidence of President Woodrow Wilson, who frequently consulted him on domestic war issues.

Manning's political career began in the 1890s, when he represented Sumter in the South Carolina House for three terms and in the state senate for two terms. He served as a Conservative in the General Assembly from 1893 until 1906, at a time when South Carolina's political factions were divided between Tillmanites (followers of Benjamin R. Tillman) and Conservatives, the traditional patrician leadership who opposed the agrarian reformers. Tillman, who forged a coalition of agricultural landowners, tenants, and sharecroppers, had wrested control of state government from the Conservatives, who had been in power since Redemption, the era when Democrats regained power from Reconstruction-era Republicans. Tillman's lasting legacy was the restoration of white supremacy embodied in the disfranchising clauses of the 1895 constitution. Once elected to the U.S. Senate in 1894, Tillman was less involved in state politics. By the second decade of the twentieth century new political divisions and rivalries had emerged to replace the Tillmanites-versus-Conservatives split that had dominated turn-of-the-century politics. Manning was a seasoned progressive who had once been a Conservative in the older Democratic Party factional rivalry. His patrician roots and earlier conservative allegiances illustrate the conservative inclination of South Carolina reformers. The distinctions between the reformers and the conservatives were often subtle, since reformers were also drawn from the elite and closely allied with business interests.[26]

Asbury Francis "Frank" Lever pursued reform causes at the national level, representing South Carolina's progressive interests in Washington. Lever, a Lexington County native, received his formal education at Newberry College, pursued a law degree at Georgetown University in Washington, D.C., and was admitted to the South Carolina bar in 1899 but never practiced law. Instead, he pursued a political career, first in the state house and then in the U.S. House of Representatives, where he served for two decades, 1901–1919. He chaired the House Agriculture Committee for almost ten years, years that coincided with Woodrow Wilson's presidency. Deeply committed to agricultural reform issues, Lever wanted to address the systemic problems of rural poverty, cotton dependency, and high tenancy rates. A high tenancy rate in cotton agriculture contributed significantly to South Carolina's poverty. While agriculture dominated the state's economy and cotton dominated agriculture, tenant farmers and sharecroppers dominated cotton growing.[27]

Only 35 percent of South Carolina farms were operated by their owners, leaving the state with a 65 percent tenancy rate, much higher than the national rate of 38 percent. Not surprisingly, tenancy throughout the South was high, but only in Georgia and Mississippi, both with 66 percent tenancy rates, was tenancy as pervasive as in South Carolina. The incidence of tenant farming in South Carolina closely paralleled cotton production patterns. Counties with higher tenancy rates were generally those where cotton production dominated the economy. While tenancy rates were high among both white and black South Carolinians, nearly seven of every ten tenants were African American. As non-landowners, tenant farmers naturally made up the lower economic strata of the state's rural population, and most of these South Carolinians were black. African Americans made up the majority of tenants in all but seven predominantly white counties. High farm tenancy encouraged the development of smaller farms, undercapitalization, the use of fewer modern farming techniques, less use of machinery, and an abundance of poor and often quite mobile farm families.[28]

At a conference held in 1919 devoted to understanding the problems of agriculture in the nation's most rural areas, Lever joined fellow conferees in declaring farm tenancy a "constantly increasing menace to a permanently prosperous agriculture and a contented country life." The conference declaration further stated that tenancy had contributed to "the loss of the priceless fertility of the soil—the creation of an unsettled farm population—illiteracy—an inefficient country school system—a drift from farm to city—and unprofitable methods of agriculture."[29] Arguably farm tenancy should not have shouldered the entire responsibility for all these problems. Nevertheless both tenant farmers' families and the larger society suffered the consequences of high tenancy rates. As a reformer, Lever believed experts armed with appropriate knowledge could solve these agricultural problems through cooperative local, state, and national efforts.

Lever's most memorable contribution to progressive agricultural reform was cosponsoring the Smith-Lever Act of 1914, which created the Cooperative Extension Service. Exemplifying the progressive ideal of applying expertise and education as problem-solving tools, the Smith-Lever Act mandated that the federal government, through the U.S. Department of Agriculture, fund research at state agricultural colleges, which would then "extend" their expertise to ordinary rural farmers. Lever partnered with U.S. senator Hoke Smith of Georgia in sponsoring this legislation, which promised to provide "useful and practical information on subjects related to agriculture and home economics" and to encourage practical application of research-based knowledge. Beginning in 1915 South Carolina's legislature appropriated funds to receive the Smith-Lever matching federal dollars. Clemson College, South Carolina's land-grant institution, provided the expertise and mandatory public service through two agricultural extension agents for each county. In 1919, Lever was serving his tenth consecutive term in the House when he resigned to accept an appointment to the Federal Farm Loan Board.[30]

David R. Coker, agribusiness leader from Hartsville, in the Pee Dee region, championed progress for southern farmers and shared Lever's commitment to scientific agriculture. Coker admired ordinary white farmers, although he came from a merchant/planter family of considerable means. His father, James Lide Coker, brought modernity to Darlington County as an entrepreneur and lead investor in the county's first railroad, its only bank, and its infant industry, which included a cotton mill, fertilizer mill, cotton-oil mill, paper mill, paper products mill, and J. L. Coker and Company, the core family business and largest mercantile firm between Richmond and

Atlanta. The Cokers also founded a private women's college in Hartsville, Coker College. The second son, David R., known affectionately as "Mr. D. R.," benefited from his family's business network, resources, and influence, which facilitated his passion, improving agriculture. Cotton agriculture dominated the Pee Dee, a region in northeastern South Carolina that benefited and suffered as cotton profitability rose and fell. The relationship between science and farming intrigued Coker, a graduate of South Carolina College. He experimented with cottonseed breeding and in 1914 created Coker's Pedigreed Seed Company. With the fervor of an evangelical missionary, Coker preached the gospel of scientific agriculture and promoted his seeds nationally.[31]

While advocating for improved agricultural techniques and crop diversification, Coker supported a wide array of reforms he hoped would save "rural civilization." He advocated creating and improving roads to accommodate the rapidly growing popularity of the automobile. A decade before the war South Carolina had no paved roads and only about three hundred miles of crushed-rock road. By the time the United States entered World War I, more than forty thousand motor vehicles were registered in the state. Yet South Carolina lacked a highway system. Counties built or neglected their own roads with chain-gang labor. The army trucks moving across the state during mobilization for World War I constantly complained about inadequate roads.[32] Coker supported the creation of a state highway system rather than the existing, inefficient county system. In addition to improving rural life with better roads, Coker supported land reform that would reduce white tenancy, and he promoted educational improvement at all levels, from the rural elementary schools to college. Coker's progressive credentials and combined expertise in business and agriculture made him Governor Manning's obvious choice to lead in the statewide war mobilization effort. Thus in May 1917 Manning appointed Coker chair of the South Carolina Council of Defense.[33]

While white reformers were not a homogeneous group, they shared a faith in education's transforming power and understood that comprehensive progress rested on public education reform. In this era, 70 percent of South Carolinians never reached the fifth grade. Many interrelated economic and social factors explained the state's inadequately educated citizenry. As a poor state with a low tax base, South Carolina lacked the financial resources needed to fund quality education. Compounding this problem, champions of education programs found voting majorities elusive as they sought compulsory school attendance and substantial public spending increases for improving education. Much of the relatively uneducated electorate held jobs that required little education, and large numbers of South Carolinians either openly resisted formal education or treated it with indifference because they perceived little economic advantage to it. Most families earned their household income from either agriculture or textiles. These South Carolinians perceived that the skills needed for life were best learned "on the job," and they often embraced cultural values that disparaged "book learning." Additionally, these same families depended on their children's labor for a significant portion of their family income. In 1915, almost 18 percent of textile workers were sixteen years old and younger. Therefore, many parents opposed lengthy school days and terms that competed for time when young adolescents could be earning money.[34] Moreover, a majority of South Carolina's school-age children were black. The white electorate, committed to white supremacy ideals, exhibited little interest in promoting or improving education among people they deemed inferior.

Without a consensus for state support of educational spending, local communities funded their own schools. Such localism heightened the discrepancies in educational opportunities among different portions of South Carolina due to existing economic disparities among regions. The difference between town and rural schools in all measures of school quality, such as length of school term, availability of high schools, attendance ratios, and teachers' salaries, illustrates precisely how localism created divergent educational opportunities along class lines. On the eve of the United States' involvement in World War I, town school terms for white students averaged thirty-four weeks, significantly longer than the school term for rural white schools, which averaged just twenty-seven weeks.[35] While by every measure of quality, educational opportunity was found wanting in South Carolina schools, the discrepancy in spending and attention between white and black schools in the dual educational system reveals both an intentional discrimination against African Americans designed to ensure their permanent subordination to whites and an egregious indifference to their plight. School sessions for African American students, both rural and town, averaged just over three months per year statewide, considerably shorter than sessions for white students. More than half of South Carolina's school population was black, but these students were taught by barely a third of the teachers. While spending for white students totaled only $17.02 per child, state spending for black students was a meager $1.90 per child per year.[36] South Carolina's public schools—discriminatory and wholly inadequate to address the state's needs—tallied endless victims.

All white reformers supported expanding educational opportunity, but John E. Swearingen, a Trenton, Edgefield County, native, was the institutional face of early education reform. Swearingen served seven consecutive two-year terms as state superintendent of education, from 1908 to 1922. During his tenure as superintendent of education South Carolina's commitment to funding education grew, largely owing to Swearingen's leadership. Swearingen fought for increases in education funding, longer school terms, better-trained teachers, and expansion of high schools. While he favored a state organizational structure and generous state financial support, he prized local initiative and local control and worked with county superintendents to heighten enthusiasm for education among local communities. Swearingen's dogged determination and professional commitment to education grew from his personal experience with adversity. A South Carolina College graduate, Swearingen was blinded at thirteen by an accidental shooting while hunting. Family, peers, and professors marveled that Swearingen not only adjusted to total blindness but also excelled at every endeavor. Graduating from college with all-sighted faculty and students in the late nineteenth century was remarkable for any blind student. Yet Swearingen managed to graduate with honors at the top of his class. At Swearingen's 1899 commencement from South Carolina College, Professor Edward Joynes remarked that the young man's "intellectual achievements under the most arduous difficulties in every department of study are monumental in the history of this historic college."[37]

Whereas John Swearingen, the state superintendent of education, represented the broad crusade for improving public education, Wil Lou Gray became the state's voice for remedying adult illiteracy.

An avid crusader, Gray completed her early education at two of South Carolina's women's colleges, Columbia and Winthrop. After beginning her lifelong career as an educator, she pursued graduate education at Vanderbilt and Columbia University. Only after leaving her home state for Vanderbilt did Gray recognize the systemic problem of adult illiteracy. While almost 40 percent of black South Carolinians were unable to read and write, what bothered Gray and other white reformers more was the high white illiteracy rate, the second-highest in the nation. Most white illiteracy existed in rural communities and textile-mill villages.[38] After completing a master's degree at Columbia University in 1911, Gray rejected a professorship at Louisiana College to accept the school supervisor position in Laurens County, her home. During her four years in Laurens she developed a professional teaching staff and opened seven night schools for adults staffed with volunteer teachers. This experimentation in adult night schools became her passion and received some modest state funding beginning in 1916, the same year Governor Richard Manning created the South Carolina Illiteracy Commission after heavy lobbying from the state Federation of Women's Clubs. In 1918, after the first two years of the commission's merely pro forma existence, Gray became its executive secretary. The next year the Illiteracy Commission pushed the legislature to establish the first statewide, state-supported adult education program, with Wil Lou Gray at the helm.[39]

Women who actively advocated reform most often engaged in collective, organized efforts, predominantly within the state's numerous women's clubs, which organized under the umbrella South Carolina Federation of Women's Clubs. These women promoted education, libraries, health initiatives, and children's interests. As historian Joan Marie Johnson describes them, these elite South Carolina women worked for reform, cautiously advocating progress but always in the context of southern tradition, particularly white dominance. For example, they promoted kindergartens and libraries for whites in mill villages and rural communities but not for rural black children. Moreover, they never advocated improving black education or narrowing the public-spending gap between white and black schools. As wives and daughters of the state's elite, they avoided direct criticism of industry, as evidenced by their promotion of compulsory school attendance as an indirect means of addressing the industrial child labor problems that concerned them. Johnson explains that club women lobbied the legislature to support their club projects but rarely with any success. Despite shared race and class identity, middle-class white women reformers encountered persistent resistance to their political activism, which most legislators, reformers included, interpreted as an unwelcome intrusion.[40]

Two University of South Carolina professors, G. Croft Williams, professor of sociology, and Josiah Morse, professor of philosophy and psychology, were actively engaged in reform. Both were civic leaders. Williams, a clergyman from Aiken, served as secretary of the state Board of Charities and Corrections and the state Board of Public Welfare. Morse, a Virginia native, served as state director of the American Red Cross and during the war was field director for the Red Cross at Camp Jackson. In addition to their commitment to health and social-service reform, both men served as the face of interracial cooperation among South Carolina's white reformers. Williams was a South Carolina representative to the Commission on Interracial Cooperation that met in Atlanta in 1920. Morse was also a member of the University Commission on the Race Question. Their concern for race relations was paternalistic and primarily focused on how race relations affected whites. These men, like all white reformers, supported white supremacy and condemned social equality.

White reformers, like these two university professors, had dreamed of a progressive state with a diverse and prosperous economy long before 1917. World War I did not introduce ideas of progress and reform. South Carolina white reformers had pushed for economic and social progress in their state since roughly 1900. By the time the United States officially entered the war, South Carolina's white reformers proudly included among their accomplishments state prohibition, child labor restrictions, compulsory school attendance, some fiscal restructuring of state government, a reorganized state mental hospital, and, most important, state aid for public schools. Most of the white reformers' legislative successes had come since they had seized control of state government with Richard I. Manning's 1914 gubernatorial victory. Manning followed South Carolina's most notorious demagogue, Cole Blease, who during his two terms (1911–1914) enjoyed the solid political support of the mill workers. Blease had used his veto power to thwart middle-class reforms deemed intrusive and unwanted by the state's white working class.[41]

Even the reforms undertaken in Manning's administration initiated modest changes that relied primarily on local initiative and control and only partially remedied the state's problems. For example, a loophole remained in prohibition that allowed South Carolinians to obtain a gallon a month of alcohol for medicinal purposes. Even though Commissioner of Agriculture, Commerce, and Industry E. J. Watson proudly announced in 1915, "It is now a recognized principle of government that the State shall throw every protection around the child worker and around the female worker, the mother of the oncoming generation," child labor laws only restricted employment of children under twelve years old, still younger than reformers wanted.[42] Compulsory school attendance was not statewide and remained optional for each school district, and few districts opted for it.

While the war did not launch the progressive movement in South Carolina, it gave white reformers a new sense of optimism. For several reasons, the war energized them and helped them believe success was imminent. First, the war stimulated the state's economy. It increased long-standing low and depressed agriculture prices, produced record profits for the cotton-textile manufacturing industry, and brought federal dollars into the state with the creation of several new military training camps. August Kohn declared in the war's aftermath that South Carolina was experiencing "abundant prosperity." This was a welcome declaration for one of the nation's poorest states with a per capita annual wealth less than half the national average. South Carolina was also an overwhelmingly agricultural state, devoting 70 percent of its land area and two-thirds of its labor force to farming.[43] Two aspects of South Carolina's agricultural economy contributed substantially to the state's poverty: an overdependence on cotton and the pervasiveness of tenant farming and sharecropping. South Carolinians not directly involved in producing cotton often worked in ancillary industries such as production of cottonseed oil and fertilizer or cotton ginning. Cotton dictated the terms of the credit system, ensuring bankers' and merchants' dependence on the cotton economy. Every spring, credit flowed freely to encourage the planting of a large crop of cotton. When harvest time arrived, creditors, who had extended the generous credit in spring, demanded that agricultural debtors pay their obligations quickly, regardless of the price of cotton. The state's heavy reliance on one cash crop, exemplified by cyclical debt and dependency, meant that South Carolina's entire economy rose and fell with cotton prices.[44]

Thus, thirty-cent cotton, the wartime price, immediately and pervasively increased income for the state's farmers. The annual value of agricultural goods in the state increased 90 percent in 1917, and the comparable value of industrial goods increased 40 percent for the same year. The commissioner of agriculture, commerce, and industries reported in 1918 that an "incidental blessing" of the war to make the world "free for democracy" was to make thousands of South Carolina farmers "free of debt." Commissioner Summers proclaimed that "30-cent cotton has set the 'one-horse farmer' free," enabling tenants to pay off lifetime debts.[45] In 1919 the new commissioner, B. F. Harris, reported that South Carolina farmers, merchants, bankers, and cotton manufacturers made record profits during the war. "The South has been kept down for 50 years—by cotton!" wrote Harris. "But our younger farmers are gaining confidence as they are acquiring cash balances—and their future is in their own hands." The textile industry, the state's largest industry, also had its most successful years of the new century during the war. In addition to windfall profits for owners and investors, textile mill operatives enjoyed wage increases.[46] This wartime prosperity signaled new possibilities.

South Carolina's economy also experienced a substantial boost from new military training facilities established in the state. The U.S. War Department's need to recruit, train, and deploy expeditiously at least five hundred thousand troops in Europe created a demand for several new military cantonments. The South's mild climate and southern Democrats' influence in the Woodrow Wilson administration made the region a likely host for many of the proposed training camps. South Carolina aggressively sought federal consideration as a site for some of the cantonments. The War Department approved three sites in the state, which became home to Camp Jackson, a permanent army base in Columbia; Camp Sevier in Greenville; and Camp Wadsworth in Spartanburg. Although located in Georgia, the training camp at Augusta, Camp Gordon, also helped South Carolina's economy because of its proximity to the state border. Moreover, as a result of wartime needs, the Marine base at Port Royal, near Beaufort, expanded greatly. With official entry into the war, the Charleston Navy Yard became the headquarters of the Sixth Naval District. Civilian employment went from 1,240 to 5,000, and the payroll jumped from $884,000 prewar to $9 million annually by war's end. Construction of the cantonments brought new jobs and new capital to the state. Once completed, the camps brought soldiers to the state.[47]

In addition to the economic boost the military training camps provided, white reformers saw the camps as an opportunity to alter the racial demography of South Carolina. White South Carolinians had developed various schemes in the early twentieth century to recruit whites from other states, hoping to erode the state's black majority, but these had never succeeded. As white military recruits from other states came to train in South Carolina, white reformers projected that many of them would make South Carolina their permanent home. Consequently they believed that South Carolina would benefit from a net growth in its white population. White reformers' expectation of creating a "whiter" South Carolina was raised not only by recruiting white soldiers but also by the migration of African Americans from the state stimulated by the war. With the out-migration of black South Carolinians and the influx of more whites, white reformers believed the war had renewed the opportunity for South Carolina to obtain a white majority in the near future.[48]

In addition to stimulating the economy, war mobilization highlighted systemic problems that progressives longed to remedy. The new military training camps created a welcome economic boom for the state and especially the local areas. Yet an insufficient supply of skilled labor for constructing the military training camps plagued the projects. South Carolina's antiquated road system, composed mainly of dirt roads and maintained by each county, could not readily handle troop mobilization.[49] Moreover, the draft revealed South Carolina's systemic problems associated with poverty: high illiteracy rates, a minimally educated citizenry, and poor public health. Shocking numbers of South Carolinians, white and black, failed the literacy tests and could not satisfy the physical and mental standards for the draft. South Carolina had difficulty meeting its national recruiting quotas because of its high rejection rate. In the early stages of the draft the rejection rate was reported to be 68 to 80 percent. Following the initial registration, the state averaged about a 25 percent rejection rate, also very high. Frank Evans, superintendent of education in Spartanburg, noted this as a "disgrace" and "humiliation." Others argued that the war had demonstrated that the high prevalence of illiteracy threatened the nation's ability to defend itself. Alarmed and embarrassed by the negative attention the draft brought to South Carolina, white reformers immediately called for the formation of a special commission to address the state's illiteracy and health problems. In 1916 the state Federation of Women's Clubs, frustrated by the prevalence of adult illiteracy, pressured Governor Manning to create an Illiteracy Commission. The commission was formed in 1916 but received funding only in 1918, when Wil Lou Gray, the new executive secretary, directly linked the high rejection rates with the larger problem of adult illiteracy in South Carolina.[50]

Despite the adverse spotlight, reformers welcomed the attention because it glaringly revealed what they already understood. One-quarter of South Carolina's population over ten years old was illiterate. Only Louisiana had a higher illiteracy rate. More than a quarter of a million African Americans, almost 40 percent of the state's black population, were unable to read and write because they had been afforded little or no educational opportunity for generations. While illiteracy among white South Carolinians, at 10.5 percent, was considerably lower than among African Americans, it was significantly higher than the 3.7 percent national average and even the regional average of 8 percent. Although having the second highest illiteracy rate in the nation was a burden, South Carolina's education problems extended far beyond its high illiteracy rate. In 1916, 75 percent of the state's population had less than an elementary education, and only 2.4 percent of students attended college. Obtaining a high-school degree in South Carolina had been possible for only a few years. The state organized its first public high school in 1907, and by 1916, only 164 high schools operated in South Carolina, and more than half of these high schools failed to meet the state's criteria for certification. Only 661 students in the entire state reached the final year in high school (11th grade) and were eligible for graduation in 1916, the last graduating class before the military draft began.[51] The national focus on South Carolina's problems during a crisis validated reformers' criticisms, leading reformers to hope for weaker opposition to proposed reforms in the future.

High rates of illiteracy and an undereducated population compounded every other problem. Inadequate education and income contributed to public health problems. Many South Carolinians lacked adequate sanitation; diets with eggs, fresh vegetables, and lean meats; access to physicians; health screening; and adequate housing. They died from influenza, malaria, diarrhea, measles, sexually transmitted diseases, pellagra, chicken pox, typhoid, tuberculosis, and other diseases. Even among "healthy" recruits, a U.S. Health Service study revealed that 23.5 percent of South Carolina recruits were infected with hookworm, a rate higher than the 17 percent infection rate among all southern recruits.[52]

Reformers welcomed the war mobilization because it stimulated South Carolina's economy, revealed systemic problems long ignored, and provided an experiment in state-level problem solving and organization. Wartime governor Richard I. Manning organized the South Carolina Council of Defense at the request of the secretary of war that states supplement the work of the Council of National Defense. The South Carolina Council of Defense organized and managed all state war mobilization efforts, marshaled the state's financial resources for the war, and promoted civilian support for the war. Governor Manning had close ties with the Woodrow Wilson administration, the first Democratic administration in the twentieth century. Manning actively supported the administration's war efforts. Secretary of War Newton Baker praised South Carolina's Council of Defense, ranking it "among the first in the entire nation because of the variety and value of its activities, the closeness of its cooperation with the National Council and the thoroughness of its local organization." David R. Coker, a leading reformer, chaired the Council of Defense. Manning appointed the original twenty-four members of the council. Intentionally stacking the council with members who shared his vision for reform, Manning distributed his appointments among professionals in agriculture, business, industry, and education.[53]

Thus the war facilitated a unique opportunity for reformers, who rapidly developed an organization with a statewide agenda. This state-level approach contrasted with the existing organizational system of entrenched localism and decentralized, personal authority. White reformers understood that implementing their goals necessitated using state government as an instrument for reform. Also, a more effective state government was needed to replace what currently existed. White reformers both identified and distinguished themselves with the term *progressive*, which connoted those who advocated state action as an essential and legitimate strategy for solving state economic and social problems. South Carolina's organizing successes associated with war mobilization convinced white reformers that the state's systematic problems should be tackled with a cooperative statewide effort.

On the heels of victory in World War I, prominent reformers in South Carolina launched an organization that became the South Carolina Development Board (SCDB). Although organized in early 1919 the board's founders dated its official beginning November 11, 1918, Armistice Day. Progressive state leaders self-consciously linked the Great War's conclusion with the inauguration of this private, statewide development board, which embodied their vision for postwar-era reform and progress. As president of the newly formed SCDB, Niels Christensen promoted the board's vision and explained repeatedly that desired reforms depended on state activism rather than local initiative. Reformers' postwar commitment to state-level reform, evident in the SCDB goals and activities, stemmed directly from wartime mobilization experiences.[54]

But implementation of white reformers' agenda for South Carolina required a more activist state government than many South Carolinians believed acceptable. Thus white reformers always had to contend with political opposition from those who preferred local control. Reformers also faced resistance from those who feared public policies that shifted power from informal, personal control to a bureaucracy. Wartime experiences convinced white reformers that effective organization could confront the persistent opposition. One reformer boasted of this postwar organization, stating, "We learned the trick during the war and are keeping it up."[55]

Yet the war era introduced unexpected challenges to white supremacy. Firmly established by the eve of World War I, disfranchisement and segregation together represented the strongest institutional expression of the strength of white supremacy in South

Carolina. With white supremacy deeply embedded in the state's laws and social structure, it had become the status quo. Constant justification or defense of white supremacy had become unnecessary since no serious challenge had yet been undertaken to dismantle it. Unexpectedly, the demands of war wrested control from white reformers, who watched the federal government, African Americans in the state, and those outside the region, black and white, exercise undesirable agency. African American hope, kindled by World War I opportunities, inspired black reformers' activism that challenged the status quo, creating resolve among white South Carolinians, who then vigorously resisted the challenge.

Chapter 3

Mobilization for War

The hope that South Carolina's African American reformers expressed in 1919 arose in part out of their recent experience with war mobilization. When the United States officially entered the Great War in the spring of 1917, the Woodrow Wilson administration rapidly mobilized the nation for total war, hoping to make an immediate and lasting difference for the Allies. Among other things, war mobilization precipitated a military draft, massive training of newly recruited soldiers, labor shortages, and new employment opportunities for all South Carolinians. These sweeping changes threatened the stability of South Carolina's existing racial hierarchy. Sensing that this potential instability nudged their segregated world closer to meaningful change, black reformers welcomed the war as an opportunity, as a catalyst for change from the past decades of oppression and bleak prospects for an improved standard of living. Yet black reformers were not the only South Carolinians who believed the Great War offered new opportunities for rapid change. White reformers also welcomed the war. Resolved to profit from the war-stimulated economy, an influx of new capital, and the war effort's pinpointing the state's shortcomings, white reformers embraced these positive changes. Yet they also demonstrated equal resolve in resisting the potential instability that had inspired black hope.

White South Carolinians' commitment to the subordination and control of African Americans was unyielding. All changes introduced into South Carolina society—those insiders deliberately sought, along with those outsiders imposed—had to uphold scrupulously the existing white-supremacy structures. Changes also had to fit consistently with formal as well as informal expressions of white social control. White reformers soon discovered, however, that war mobilization could not always be controlled. War mobilization empowered others, and change loosened the moorings that sustained white supremacy. Controlling change during World War I proved difficult because three catalysts propelling change were not under the direct influence of white southerners. One, African Americans, who lived in the South and outside the region, initiated change. Two, the federal government made war-related demands that conflicted with whites' racial-control priorities. Three, the invisible hand of the marketplace created economic stimuli that resisted control. As white reformers pushed for economic change, they also struggled to refasten the moorings that secured white domination. This anchoring maneuver hindered change to some extent, although it never stymied it completely. As white reformers considered the threat America's war mobilization posed to the state's elaborate system of white supremacy, their ambivalence revealed the complexity of maintaining an oppressive and hierarchical society while rhetorically calling for equal sacrifices and biracial cooperation for a common good.

African American reformers initiated change quickly. While Congress debated President Woodrow Wilson's plea for a declaration of war against Germany, prominent African Americans in South Carolina took preemptive action by calling a meeting of black South Carolinians in Columbia. On April 4, 1917, participants, who met at First Calvary Baptist Church, discussed the feasibility and desirability of African American men's serving as soldiers. The Columbia forum of African Americans drafted a resolution for Governor Richard I. Manning and President Wilson that expressed the following sentiment: "It is the sense of this meeting that the government, State or national, should provide at once for military training and instruction of those members of our race who are ready to enlist, that they may be able to render good and efficient service."[1] Anticipating the immediacy of war, these leaders used the patriotic circumstance to expand opportunity for black South Carolinians. These black reformers sided with the Wilson administration and believed that their support of war mobilization best served African Americans' interests in their struggle for equality. While national black leaders advocated a range of strategies regarding the war, most black leaders in South

Carolina worked to advance their rights in the context of endorsing the nation's war effort completely.[2]

At this meeting, Rev. Richard Carroll, the prominent black Baptist minister who advocated reform in the tradition of Booker T. Washington, urged that African Americans be allowed to serve in all ranks of the military from major on down. "We've had jim crow cars; jim crow street cars; jim crow cemeteries, churches and schools. Now let us have a jim crow regiment, surgeons and hospital corps," Carroll implored. Carroll called for African Americans' full inclusion with a request that was at once assertive and compliant. He challenged white authority by insisting on African Americans' complete participation, which whites had not yet accepted, but he insisted within the context of segregation, a condition whites would demand. More than most black reformers, Carroll cultivated close relationships with white leaders. Here he took advantage of his reputation of trustworthiness to pressure them. Without denying the legitimacy of segregation, Carroll's request compelled whites' consideration. Twelve men from this meeting, including key reformers from Columbia—Jacob J. Durham, pastor of Second Calvary Baptist Church; Nathaniel J. Frederick, attorney and principal of Howard School; Robert W. Mance, president of Allen University; and I. S. Leevy, business leader—personally delivered this resolution to Governor Manning. Manning summarily dismissed their plea for inclusion in military service, telling them their services were needed in capacities other than as soldiers. "Stay on the farm and work," Manning retorted brusquely.[3] Hoping to shape and limit African Americans' role in the war effort, the governor expressed white reformers' resolve with his dismissive response.

Despite Manning's rejection, African American leaders persisted in their petition for an opportunity for military service. Within days of the Columbia meeting, Beaufort's African American community followed with a public resolution pledging their commitment to military service. The resolution boldly declared the loyalty of Beaufort's African American population: "In spite of the discriminations, injustice and lack of protection under the laws, both local and national, [we] feel that we are still citizens of this great country." Furthermore, the resolution reminded its audience, African Americans had fought and died in every war since the American Revolution, and they offered the same commitment to the current conflict even while "we feel keenly the ill-treatment of the Negro by our State and national governments."[4] This resolution demonstrated black reformers' rhetorical skill when addressing disparate audiences, a skill honed from years of working in stifling oppression. With humility they pledged their loyalty, to assuage whites' doubts, while boldly asserting their cognizance of the injustice. Black reformers frequently negotiated this balance between seeking the respect of whites, to whom they had to accommodate to achieve their goals in the context of disfranchisement, and retaining their dignity and influence among African Americans of all classes.

Two prominent Charleston reformers asserted identical sentiments expressed by black reformers in Columbia and Beaufort. Archdeacon Erasmus L. Baskervill of Charleston penned a letter to the *News and Courier* reiterating the Columbia committee's request. "In this crisis I hope that the federal and state governments will authorize the organization of a negro regiment in this state and give the young men of my race in South Carolina an opportunity for military service against the enemy," Baskervill implored.[5] Another prominent African American leader followed with a similar demand. Thomas E. Miller, former Republican congressman from South Carolina and former president of South Carolina State College in Orangeburg, made a specific offer to both President Wilson and Governor Manning. In a letter addressed to both executives, Miller stated:

> I come to you in this hour of our nation's calamity, offering you the patriotic service of 30,000 American negroes of my native state to serve in the regular army and navy of our nation. . . .
>
> I come to you to bring no treasures from my people, for they are poor, but . . . in their name to offer to their country their fidelity, patriotism, devoted service and courage.
>
> I bring their manhood for service or for sacrifice upon the altar of a nation "conceived in liberty and dedicated to the principle that all men are created equal."[6]

As clergy, educators, lawyers, and entrepreneurs, these African American reformers had long worked to create opportunities, im-

prove the standard of living, and ameliorate some of the harsher re-
alities of poverty for South Carolina's black majority. Yet, as evidenced
by Manning's reaction, African Americans faced formidable difficulties when they called for just and equal treatment because they lacked
political and economic power, essential tools for producing significant change. As these resolutions reveal, African American reformers
fully understood white southerners' incontrovertible commitment to
white supremacy and the oppressive consequences that tenacious
axiom had on black South Carolinians. Yet within these constraints,
black reformers sought to capitalize on the contradictions that
emerged from the peculiar political, economic, and social structure
that white supremacy helped create in their state. While whites
feared the consequences of permitting African Americans to serve in
the military, black reformers recognized the potential opportunities
for economic and social improvement that military service might
provide them. Thus, many black reformers were anxious to afford
African Americans the opportunity to join the U.S. military. Moreover, they were anxious to exploit the contradiction of privilege and
responsibility associated with military service.[7]

South Carolina's black reformers not only contended with politically and economically powerful whites who sought to control them
and stifle their effort, but they also had to navigate among African
Americans with diverse views, experiences, and interests. Like whites,
blacks in the Palmetto State had varying opinions of the war. Black
South Carolinians who did not share the black reformers' enthusiasm
for war expressed indifference, resisted coercion, dodged the draft,
or moved, and some deserted. Black reformers marshaled their resolve in support of the war in the face of resistance among African
Americans. Moreover, black reformers reasoned, war opposition
among South Carolina's black population made their own leadership
essential to African American mobilization.[8] Some African Americans, who resented whites' manipulative schemes to control them,
showed less enthusiasm for wartime exploitation. At the April 4
meeting in Columbia, the prevailing sentiment held that black men
should have the opportunity to serve as soldiers, but a minority
strongly disagreed. One dissenter boldly declared, "The white folks
have the Winchesters, and you haven't even a little popgun. They'll
not ask you whether you want to enlist. They'll just take you out and

shoot you, if you don't." Shocked and dismayed, dozens of participants protested the comment. Pandemonium briefly prevailed, and the crowd's adamant disapproval prevented the speaker from continuing. Matilda Evans, prominent physician and community leader, brought order to the chaos when she began singing "My Country, 'Tis of Thee, Sweet Land of Liberty."[9]

South Carolina's white leadership did not readily embrace African Americans' call to arms, and they resented black reformers who pressed the issue. Until the federal government ordered the state to accept black recruits, military induction centers in South Carolina routinely rejected African American volunteers. Many whites discouraged blacks from seeking military service, hoping to avoid the complications that wartime experiences might present to white domination. Yet white South Carolinians quickly discovered, as they would again and again during mobilization, that the war diminished their prerogatives. Whites could not control all war-related decisions, or shape the national debate over such decisions, even though the consequences could disrupt their carefully crafted system of racial control. Congress's declaration of war against Germany on April 6, 1917, necessitated rapid deployment of troops to assist the Allies in Europe. The military's need for large numbers of soldiers, initially estimated at five hundred thousand, and the urgency of that need sparked a national debate about the possibility of enacting a draft rather than simply relying on volunteers for the necessary manpower.[10] Immediately, white citizens of South Carolina anguished over the possibility of implementing a national draft without racial distinctions.

Since military service connoted both privilege and obligation, the relative weight whites placed on these two competing conceptions of military service profoundly influenced their attitudes toward including African Americans in the proposed draft. Rhetorically, South Carolinians revered military service as honorable, sacrificial, and the highest form of patriotism. Practically, however, they, like other Americans, had recognized that military service was a risky endeavor and a burden most often imposed on the poor. White South Carolinians felt conflicted about the prospect that blacks would be drafted just like whites, train alongside whites, and eventually serve on the battlefield with whites. This implication of equality was repugnant to white South Carolinians who recognized that it directly conflicted with an imperative of white supremacy: that African Americans were inferior and should be segregated from whites. Opposition to including African Americans in the military prevailed when whites contemplated the rhetorical glories of war. One South Carolinian, who privately expressed reservations about African Americans' serving in Europe as soldiers, indicated that southerners should not consent to using black soldiers: "We should cling to the notion that arms is a gentleman's profession, therefore, a white man's profession!"[11] Governor Manning exhibited this attitude through his initial efforts both to limit military service to white South Carolinians and to quell the enthusiasm African Americans expressed for becoming soldiers. Whites' resistance to blacks' military participation exposed the inherent contradiction between the rhetoric of American patriotism and the reality of military service.

Manning persisted in suggesting that African Americans could best serve their country as civilians, and more specifically as laborers. The Commission for Civic Preparedness, chaired by prominent white reformer David R. Coker, organized much of the early war preparation by encouraging South Carolinians to plant gardens, assist the Red Cross, buy bonds, and "be loyal." After rejecting African Americans' offer to serve as soldiers, Manning quickly appointed a committee of eight black men to assist Coker with the African American counterpart to the preparedness commission. Consistent with other southern institutions, all aspects of civic war preparation were segregated, even patriotic rallies and parades.[12] By channeling African Americans into the domestic side of the war effort, white Carolinians hoped to prevent African Americans from experiencing social relations elsewhere that might conflict with the South's peculiar racial mores. Moreover, whites feared that African Americans would later return to South Carolina with attitudes and expectations incompatible with the South's racial order.

Constituents' communications to Congressman A. Frank Lever often relayed practical arguments against drafting African Americans as soldiers, rather than concerns about rhetorical allusions to the grandeur of military service or potential challenges to the culture's racial hierarchy. J. Harry Foster, distressed about labor shortages resulting from a military draft, told Lever he supported conscripting

African Americans, but as agricultural laborers and not as soldiers. Foster argued that farmers would find it increasingly difficult to secure an adequate supply of labor unless labor could be compelled. The crisis of war, Foster argued, should justify labor conscription.[13] Charles L. Rhame of Sumter also commented on the relationship between the emerging agricultural labor shortage and the desire of African Americans to serve in the military. Rhame acknowledged familiarity with whites' opposition to using black troops. But, he suggested, an investigation into this hostility would reveal that "large land owners who are not planting grains . . . but mostly cotton and merchants who expect to do a big business in cotton traffic after the war" were provoking this opposition.[14]

Fundamentally, the large landowners and merchants were protecting their cotton investment and feared all labor shortages that threatened their financial interests. Rhame's charge was consistent with widespread concerns about labor shortages during the war. Moreover, his suspicion that large landowners and merchants fomented the opposition to African Americans' serving as soldiers reveals how readily whites manipulated the shared commitment among whites to white supremacy. In Rhame's view, large landowners and merchants with a strong economic self-interest in maintaining an abundant supply of cheap labor could protect that supply more readily if black laborers could not be drafted. Thus they could exploit white supremacy, opposing the drafting of African Americans on ideological grounds, thus masking their economic self-interest.

Despite implications of social equality and fears of labor shortages, white South Carolinians' resistance to drafting African American men as soldiers was tempered by the harsh reality of military service, which, at a minimum, meant unwelcome disruption in one's life and potentially meant the abrupt ending of one's life. Those who supported conscription as the best method for raising an army emphasized the need for all Americans to share the military burden. Moreover, whites quickly realized that if African Americans did not serve in the military, a larger proportion of whites would be compelled to go to Europe, thus increasing the probability that more whites would be killed. The loss of one's life or that of a loved one proved a hard consequence for whites to accept, even in the defense of white supremacy. Because a majority of South Carolina men were black, meeting the state recruitment quota would impose a particularly heavy burden on whites if black men were prohibited from serving.

When some white South Carolinians considered the real hardships of war, their posture toward blacks' serving in the military reflected their belief that African Americans should not be allowed to escape the ordeal young white men faced. S. L. Kransnoff expressed this sentiment in his letter to the editor of *The State*. Kransnoff wrote that he would not want to see the "white flower of manhood sacrificed upon the battlefields for democracy without the negroes contributing their share."[15] Several business leaders from Columbia told Congressman Lever that they favored conscription so the honorable men, who would readily join the army, would instead stay home and provide an equally valuable service of operating the farms. In their stead, "the young men who patronize pool rooms and are parasites on their families" should serve in the army. Moreover, they believed African American men should be drafted if the state hoped to benefit from their labor since, these whites argued, the great "quantity of negroes leaving this section daily for the north, unless they are conscripted also for the army, will do us no good."[16]

Other whites supported conscripting African American men on the grounds of defending public safety. Consistent with whites' fears that African Americans posed an inherent danger to whites if inadequately supervised, Marvin M. Mann, clerk of the South Carolina Senate, suggested that if only white men went to war and left black men at home, those whites left behind, especially women, could be in great danger. Mann favored a system that would force the "idle" and "latent criminals" to perform either military or economic service. He argued that the federal government had a responsibility to protect those who remained at home if a community "gives up its best blood for the field of battle." A Rock Hill attorney reiterated this same concern: "The negro situation, at home would have to be made secure before you and other good men left our homes. We could not leave our wives and babies here even with the negro women. These things cannot well be talked, but we people of the South realize the situation."[17]

Ultimately, however, whites reconciled the dialectic between forbidding African Americans from becoming soldiers, with the accompanying implications of equality, and demanding that they share the burdens of war. In the struggle to synthesize these contradictory ideas, whites wrestled with the meaning of military service and social equality. Since equality of the races contradicted one of the core premises of white supremacy, white South Carolinians ultimately accepted the idea of black men serving as soldiers by emphasizing another tenet of white supremacy: paternalism. James L. Hunter Jr. of Graniteville argued in a letter to the editor of *The State* that whites had a responsibility for influencing African Americans in their communities. "The negroes of a community as a rule make a very good barometer or index to the characters of the white people who live there," Hunter maintained, "as they are in a great measure an imitative race and almost invariably try to do as near as they can the way the white people do. . . . [I]f the whites are sober, industrious, law abiding," he continued, "the negroes as a whole will be likewise; if you find them idle, vicious, ignorant look at the morals of the community and see if that is not the example set them by the white people."[18]

Hunter's letter was a defense of black southerners against the accusation that African Americans had been influenced by German agents, who allegedly incited them to rise up against whites and abandon their country by refusing to fight. After conferring with numerous black ministers, teachers, and laborers, Hunter was convinced that the leaders of the black community were not influenced by this antiwar propaganda.[19] He reasoned that few blacks opposed the war because few whites opposed it. Although willing to concede that some "very ignorant negroes might be led astray," Hunter insisted that it would be wrong of whites to "judge the negroes by their worst element" since he believed most whites were hardly willing to be judged by the same standard. He continued to note parallels in the behavior of whites and blacks by pointing out the exceptional few who did not support the war.

> If we find the negroes talking against the government you will find some white men, not necessarily German agents either, who are talking it first. In fact my attention was called to one white man who was advising the negroes not to fight and if they came after them to take their guns and go to the swamps. With such advice from a man whom they knew and who said he would not fight and that the country did not have any right to fight as our government was all wrong, can you blame them for saying that they would not go?[20]

Hunter urged all white men to influence their black neighbors to support the war effort. Perceiving that whites naturally held authority over blacks, Hunter reassured whites that blacks would not misinterpret their Christian charity as a gesture of equality. "The negro is not asking for social equality, he does not expect it," Hunter believed. He concluded his letter with further admonitions that detailed how whites perceived that they exercised controlling influence over African Americans in this situation: "It makes me satisfied that the negro will do his duty when shown wherein his duty lies. If the country wants them for soldiers she can get them, if she wants them in industrial occupations she can get them. However, if she decides for them to stay at home and work on as they are now doing she can do so with absolute safety and a mind at rest."[21]

Hunter expressed in his letter a paternalistic understanding of race relations that many white South Carolinians of this era shared. White reformers believed that modeling good behavior and guiding African Americans in approved directions ensured whites' social control over blacks. Paternalism, as Hunter and other whites reasoned, fostered the submissive behavior from blacks that whites desired. Moreover, they believed that paternalism thwarted challenges to white supremacy that discontented black reformers would otherwise instigate. Yet whites' paternalistic reasoning rested on the premise that African Americans adhered to whites' own self-delusional logic that if whites guided African Americans compassionately, then blacks would remain satisfied with a minimal status in society. Paternalism was a manifestation of white supremacy. Yet unlike the two core premises that all whites shared—the inherent superiority of whites and the necessity that whites dominate society's institutions—paternalism was a class expression of white supremacy, articulated most often by whites of economic means and education.

White South Carolinians' reservations about conscripting African Americans for military service became moot once Congress enacted the Selective Service Act in May 1917, which established a draft without racial distinction. The new law not only allowed but required, on June 5, 1917, that all African American men aged twenty-one to thirty should register for the draft on the same terms as white men. The draft-registration notices published in South Carolina echoed the theme of white paternalism. In addition to enumerating the basic legal stipulation, the draft registration notices encouraged whites to notify blacks personally. "The negroes should be informed. Their employers, their landlords, the merchants who supply them, their own preachers and doctors and teachers can do a good work for the State between now and registration day by seeing that every negro between the ages of 21 and 30, inclusive, is informed that it is essential for him to present himself at the registration booth on Tuesday, June 5." Despite whites' apprehension over the insult associated with African Americans serving in the military, black South Carolinians responded as required and often with eagerness. Robert Moorman, chairman of Columbia's draft board, reported that African Americans requested exemptions less often than white registrants and "negroes were keenly disappointed when they were rejected." Moorman attributed African Americans' enthusiasm for military service to the racial differential in job opportunities and pay scales, noting that "$30 a month, clothing and sustenance is far beyond what many of them can expect in civil employment."[22]

The majority of registrants in South Carolina were black, and African American draftees exceeded whites by 7,500, the highest differential of any state. At times white South Carolinians had trouble meeting their quotas. One reason was the competition between agricultural interests and the military's needs. Bright Williamson, a bank president from Darlington, complained to David Coker that the draft was taking too many white farmers away from their farms. Williamson told Coker fifty-four whites were needed to meet the draft quota in his county, but only eight white nonfarmers were available. "This means we need 46 white farmers to go. Help!!" Williamson exclaimed. Another reason whites had difficulty meeting their quotas was the uneven racial distribution of the population across the state. Low-country counties, whose black populations exceeded 70 percent, could not meet the white quotas set by the state. Therefore, more whites had to be drafted from counties with a higher density of whites to satisfy the overall state quota. Thus an ironic consequence of whites' demand for segregated mobilization was the drafting of more Piedmont whites.[23]

Debate over the national draft created introspection among South Carolinians, forcing them to confront the competing meanings of military service. Whites wanted compulsory military service for blacks, but they wanted it devoid of any connotation, even rhetorical, of equality. White supremacy demanded that whites control blacks and channel them into accepted pursuits, but the federal government's wartime call for mandatory service divided whites over what the appropriate expression of white supremacy would be in the new circumstances that they did not fully control. Simultaneously African American reformers seized the patriotic rhetoric, desperately seeking to link their actions with broad heroic meanings. Black reformers welcomed the opportunity to demonstrate their patriotism through military service in the hope of alleviating whites' doubts about blacks' willingness or ability to serve. Yet they confronted some opposition and indifference from African Americans, especially those in rural areas, who doubted that military service would do anything but serve whites' interests.[24]

On the heels of the debate about drafting African American men, white South Carolinians soon faced another challenge to white supremacy. The War Department, as it prepared to mobilize young draftees, announced in August its intention to conduct biracial military training in southern camps. The Wilson administration's failure to organize military training on a racially segregated basis offended white South Carolinians. Realizing that African American recruits would need to be trained, South Carolina officials had anticipated the possibility of biracial training and rejected it, proposing instead that black soldiers be trained elsewhere. But they thought the Wilson administration would honor their preemptive pleas for separate training camps for black soldiers outside the South, thus averting yet another public debate that placed them in the awkward position of having to defend the South's racial hierarchy during a national crisis that stressed common efforts to defend democratic principles. Yet, in August, when white South Carolinians learned that Washington planned to send all recruits from South Carolina, North Carolina, Florida, and Puerto Rico, regardless of race, to Columbia's Camp Jackson, they responded with outrage. They also quickly realized that their defense of segregation would have to be both public and determined.[25]

The War Department's intention to train black soldiers in newly created southern cantonments presented three distinct challenges to the existing white-supremacy system. First, it directly threatened the established principle of segregation. Second, this aspect of war mobilization would, southern whites thought, bring northern blacks, unaccustomed to segregation, into South Carolina with defiant attitudes. Third, whites feared that training all American soldiers together—regardless of race, class, or region—would expose black South Carolinians to ideas and influences that would jeopardize future white control. Ironically, the training camps, which South Carolina's white reformers fought hard to secure with political influence, became the source of a critical challenge to white supremacy. The irony of the training camp controversy again revealed the persistent difficulty of seeking economic development while struggling to maintain white supremacy. Economic progress involved change and often introduced unwelcome threats to the racial order, which required obstinacy for survival.

Months before the United States entered the war, Edwin W. Robertson, a banker, utility pioneer, entrepreneur, and civic leader, began pursuing for Columbia his vision of economic development that would also meet the military's need for a large training camp. Robertson traveled to Washington to propose that General Leonard Wood consider the value of the vast Wade Hampton estate, east of Columbia, for a training camp. In January 1917, army officials came to inspect the property. Convinced of the economic boon this proposed military training camp would create for one of South Carolina's largest cities, Robertson marshaled the Columbia Chamber of Commerce's support to aid in lobbying for the camp. The Chamber created a Cantonment Committee, with Robertson as chair, to raise the funds to purchase the site from the Hampton heirs, who were asking $59,000 for the property. At a legendary meeting of the Cantonment Committee, enthusiastic Columbians raised the desired funds in only forty-five minutes. Although a determined private initiative, pursuit of a training camp for South Carolina also enjoyed public support. Not only did the Chamber of Commerce members purchase the land and donate it to the federal government, but the city of Columbia also guaranteed light, power, gas, and an extension of the trolley line. Columbia was the first South Carolina city to seek this federal wartime opportunity. In early March Governor Manning assisted Columbia's efforts by promoting the two-thousand-acre site to Secretary of War Newton Baker. Rumors and private assurances circulated weeks before May 19, 1917, when Major Douglas MacArthur announced that Columbia had been accepted as the site of one of the sixteen national cantonments, which became Camp Jackson, a permanent army training base and South Carolina's largest military camp.[26]

Before Camp Jackson received the order to accept black recruits from North Carolina, Florida, and Puerto Rico, rumors abounded that black troops from New York would be sent to Camp Wadsworth in Spartanburg, another South Carolina cantonment camp pursued by white reformers seeking economic development. When Manning learned about the War Department's decision not only to train black soldiers in South Carolina but also to train them alongside white soldiers and send northern blacks to the state, he lodged a vigorous protest with Secretary Baker. Expressing sentiments common among white southerners, the governor voiced several concerns. He opposed training African American troops in South Carolina or anywhere in the South. He argued that allowing large numbers of armed blacks to train as soldiers in areas with large black civilian populations presented "dangers" to the white community. South Carolina whites also feared that allowing northern blacks, unfamiliar with the South's Jim Crow mores and possibly not easily controlled, to train with southern blacks would undermine the entire white-supremacy system.[27]

South Carolina congressman Sam Nicholls, representing the Fourth Congressional District in the Piedmont, also adamantly protested the rumored proposal to send black New Yorkers to Spartanburg's Camp Wadsworth. Quickly Nicholls received private assurances that the War Department had changed its plans and would not be sending the black unit from New York to the camp for military training. Thinking his protest had altered the War Department's initial plans, Nicholls proudly touted his achievement to the local newspapers.[28] Doubtless Manning hoped Washington would respond to his protest concerning Camp Jackson with a similar change of plans. But Baker had grown frustrated with southerners' constant complaining, so the War Department sent strong signals that it was uninterested in capitulating to southern racial protocol. Just a few weeks after Nicholls had offered assurances that black New Yorkers would not be coming to the state, the South Carolina press reported that the War Department planned to stick by its decision to train in southern camps African Americans who lived in the South. An army being raised to spread democracy to the rest of the world, the War Department reasoned, could not sanction racial distinctions in its own ranks.[29]

White South Carolinians responded with dismay and frustration when the Democratic Wilson administration suggested an arrangement that was clearly inconsistent with prevailing white supremacy ideals. Moreover, news that African American soldiers would train with white recruits galvanized white South Carolinians to defend their racial ideals and resist the War Department's order. Prominent citizens confronted Manning and expressed their emphatic disapproval of Washington's order.[30] Consequently, the governor went to Washington on August 20 to meet the South Carolina congressional delegation and lodge a personal protest against Secretary Baker's order. Accompanying Manning were agribusiness leader and chairman of the state's Council of Defense, David R. Coker; business leader and Charleston banker R. Goodwin Rhett, a future president of the national Chamber of Commerce; and George Baker, John W. Lillard, and William Elliot of the Columbia Chamber of Commerce. This prestigious delegation of South Carolina reformers represented key business and agricultural interests in the state.[31] Noticeably absent from Manning's delegation was Fred Dominick, a vocal critic of the Wilson administration and the lone South Carolina congressman to vote against the declaration of war. As Cole Blease's law partner, Dominick identified with the Blease faction and found himself at odds with the reformers. Dominick and Blease, adamant opponents of reform, relished the opportunity to highlight that reformers' aggressive pursuit of Wilson administration favors had threatened white supremacy. In making their case to Baker, Manning and his entourage focused on what they perceived as the most outrageous portion of the plan, training Puerto Rican recruits in South Carolina. The Puerto Rican contingent would probably include "many mulattoes and whites mixed together and their being accustomed to social equality, makes their proposed mobilization here still more undesirable," Manning contended.[32]

The State suggested that training large numbers of black troops in the South would offend white southerners and be "dangerous," yet the newspaper expressed confidence that the War Department would handle this "delicate subject in a manner that will avoid inconvenience to the people of the South." No doubt *The State* was most concerned about the "inconvenience" to white southerners. The *Charleston News and Courier* suggested that Washington's decision for biracial military training in Columbia had caused "utter astonishment" in the state. The "people of South Carolina know to pursue such a policy is to court disaster," the newspaper insisted. The *News and Courier* defended reformers who resisted the War Department's decision by outlining the centrality of white supremacy to white southerners: "The authorities in Washington cannot afford to forget that in the South the problem of the relations between the white people and the negroes underlies and overshadows nearly every other problem." The Charleston editorial argued that biracial military training directly conflicted with the policy of the state, "a policy which has become fixed through the process of years and which is accepted today by the people of both races."[33]

Judge Thomas E. Richardson of Sumter supported Manning in his "herculean task" of keeping black soldiers out of South Carolina and offered the governor some suggestions about how to persuade Washington that African American recruits could be better trained elsewhere. "The negro's *natural ability* to endure the hot and sultry climate of the sugar and indigo plantation in the West Indies," Richardson suggested, could be used as evidence to support training African Americans "under a tropic sun and in a climate best suited to their nature." Furthermore, Richardson said, "negroes thrive in malaria climates." He encouraged Manning to make this argument for training soldiers outside of South Carolina as though he were trumpeting the interests of black southerners first and foremost. Such "*a humanitarian view*," of the problem, Richardson believed, would "bring down blessing upon yourself and your country to say nothing of the negro."[34] Such self-interested strategies thinly laced with paternalistic concern for African Americans widened the gulf between black and white reformers. Black reformers both understood and experienced the humiliation of this paternalism, but they could not easily combat the exploitive power of white supremacy.

Not all South Carolinians supported this position against training black soldiers in South Carolina. Isaac Edwards made a paternalistic plea in favor of training African Americans in the state. "God has placed these creatures in our care," Edwards contended, "and it becomes our duty to give him that training for this duty that the South alone can give him." As long as the troops were segregated during their training, Edwards believed, white southerners should provide a place for black soldiers at Camp Jackson.[35] Secretary Baker's response to white South Carolinians' stubborn resolve resembled Edwards's suggestion. Baker insisted on his original plan that African American troops would be trained in South Carolina, but he accepted the condition of segregating the troops. He also relented on the plan to send Puerto Rican soldiers to South Carolina, although perhaps this portion of the plan had always been negotiable. South Carolinians who stormed to Washington in protest saved face by accomplishing something, and Baker attained his central purpose, keeping black southerners at southern training camps.

Baker's concessions were only partially satisfactory to South Carolina's political leadership. Thus they continued their resolute protests against having black soldiers in South Carolina. Just two days after Baker met with South Carolinians, African American soldiers became the subject of national hysteria because of an eruption of racial violence in Houston. On the night of August 23, 1917, more than one hundred African American soldiers from the Twenty-fourth Infantry, in defiance of their white officers, marched from Camp Logan to nearby Houston, armed and angry. In a frenzied state fueled by mounting frustrations and fear, these men believed Corporal Charles Baltimore, a military police officer and model soldier, had been killed that afternoon by local police, and they wanted answers. At the conclusion of their two-hour march on Houston, sixteen whites, including five police officers, and four black soldiers had been killed. Serious consequences awaited those perceived to be responsible for what became known as the Houston riot.[36]

Just weeks earlier, in late July, 654 nonsouthern, career black soldiers who made up the Third Battalion of the Twenty-fourth Infantry traveled from New Mexico to their new assignment at Camp Logan, a new military training camp three and one-half miles from downtown Houston. Washington assigned these soldiers the responsibility of guarding construction of the military camp. Immediately these African American soldiers experienced racial hostility and discrimination. White construction workers resented the authority of the black soldiers. They regularly harassed the soldiers, hurling racial slurs. White Houstonians, well practiced in white supremacy, refused to give newly arrived black soldiers the same respect they accorded white soldiers. Local whites reasoned that respecting these soldiers would imply equality and would raise the expectations of local blacks for similar consideration. Additionally, Houston's police force had a notorious reputation for brutality to its black population, the largest of any city in Texas. During the soldiers' off duty visits to town in the weeks that preceded the riot, Houston police regularly insulted, beat, and arrested black soldiers for minor infractions of local customs. Members of the Twenty-fourth Infantry resented this treatment. As proud and self-confident men who had spent the last few years in western states, the soldiers were not accustomed to the South's Jim Crow mores and regularly defied the injustice.[37]

The precise cause of the Houston violence is disputed. Some charged that the soldiers secretly plotted revenge. Others reasoned, more probably, that the soldiers reacted spontaneously to mounting frustrations brought on by repeated police abuse and white mob violence. Regardless of the cause, on the evening of August 23 emotions exploded. That day, two police officers beat and arrested an enlisted man, Alonzo Edwards, who tried to protect a local black woman from police harassment. Unlike local whites, Houston's black residents welcomed and revered the soldiers. Black Texans expected the soldiers, whom they viewed as heroes and leaders, to protect them. These expectations intensified the soldiers' humiliation since they had been unable to protect even themselves from police brutality. To quell escalating tensions between soldiers and the police, a negotiated agreement assigned twelve black noncommissioned officers as military police to monitor soldiers' behavior in town. Consistent with the agreement, Corporal Baltimore asked a police officer about Edwards's arrest, and the officer asserted that he did not answer to "niggers." The police officer struck Baltimore in the face with his pistol and shot at the corporal three times, chasing him into a vacant building. Although Baltimore escaped with his life, word reached camp that this highly respected MP had been killed.[38]

Cooler heads did not prevail in this difficult situation. Experienced leaders from the Third Battalion, black and white, had recently been transferred, and their replacements, especially the white commissioned officers, had not earned the men's trust. The new leaders proved inadequate for this challenge. That evening anger, confusion, and fear prevailed in the camp. Rumors of impending trouble led white officers to plead for calm, but shouts that the white mob was coming transformed the chaos into action. More than a hundred soldiers, following Sergeant Vida Henry's lead, scrambled for weapons and ammunition. They marched to Houston, targeting the police station in the Fourth Ward as their destination. The next two hours altered many lives, and Sergeant Henry killed himself before dawn, troubled that he had accidentally killed a fellow serviceman in the mayhem.

Following this riot, the army launched an extensive and hasty investigation that led to the largest court-martial in American military history, the prosecution of 118 African American soldiers. Of these, 106 men were found guilty of mutiny and murder; 19 of the convicted were executed, 63 were sentenced to life in prison, and the remainder received lesser sentences. White officers were not prosecuted nor were any white civilians tried.

News of the Houston riot traveled rapidly across the South, fueling existing racial animosity.[39] Richard Manning pointed to the riot to bolster his argument that integrated military training would never work, especially in the South. In a public statement issued the day after the riot, Manning said, "Knowing these things and knowing the social structure of the South, stabilized and bolstered by years of vigilance and trial and the southern white man's pride of position and the negro racial instincts, I hope the War Department will not offend in these things by placing negroes at South Carolina camps." Senator Ben Tillman assured his constituents that Secretary Baker understood the necessity of preventing racial violence. Yet Tillman also seized the opportunity to note that "since the people of Columbia have commercialized the camp they have to take the disagreeable things along with the good." The "good" to which Tillman referred was the economic stimulus that accompanied the cantonments. His critical tone suggested that he did not share the reformers' enthusiasm for commercial development. The targets of Tillman's sniping were the Columbia reformers who had long constituted the core of his political opposition.[40]

White South Carolinians demonstrated continual alarm that Washington ignored their demands for racial control of federal cantonments. They received another jolt when word leaked in late August that Baker intended to reinstate the original plan for training black New York soldiers at Camp Wadsworth. Despite Congressman Nicholls's confidence, expressed three weeks earlier, that this would not happen, the War Department's needs required a change. Saturated with the news from Houston, shocked Piedmont residents immediately launched a firestorm of protest. Spartanburg mayor J. F. Floyd reasoned that black soldiers from New York would "probably expect to be treated like white men." But, Floyd protested, in Spartanburg they would "not be treated as anything except negroes. We shall treat them exactly as we treat our resident negroes."[41]

The Spartanburg Chamber of Commerce, which had actively sought the creation of Camp Wadsworth, erupted over news of the unexpected complication. The Chamber's specific grievance focused on northern blacks' perceived attitude of defiance and equality. White South Carolinians feared that these strangers to Jim Crow would openly challenge the well-established racial boundaries, as black soldiers had in Houston. "If any of those colored soldiers go in any of our soda stores and the like and ask to be served they'll be knocked down," a chamber official warned, because "we don't allow negroes to use the same glass that a white man may later have to drink out of." The Spartanburg Chamber of Commerce drafted a resolution protesting the training of northern black troops at Camp Wadsworth. "The most tragic consequences would follow the introduction of the New York Negro with his Northern ideas into the community life of Spartanburg," the resolution declared.[42]

Despite white South Carolinians' protests, by early October the issue was settled and black soldiers were indeed coming to South Carolina. No amount of public blustering or behind-the-scenes maneuvering trumped war needs; war mobilization had snatched the reins of racial control away from white South Carolinians, who were unaccustomed to others steering on this terrain. When the provost marshal issued the final order, Manning released a public statement. He emphasized that the federal government had made the decision to draft and train African American soldiers. He said he was confident most soldiers would not cause trouble, although the possibility of racial conflict still existed. "We cannot ignore the existence of race prejudice," Manning noted in an intentional understatement. To avoid the kind of violence experienced in Houston, Manning said, "whites must not overstep their rights and the negroes must do nothing to cause irritation on the part of the whites and act in accordance with the adopted policy of the southern state, which provides for the separation of the races."[43]

Manning's warning notwithstanding, whites overstepped their bounds in South Carolina just as they had in Houston. In early October, the New York National Guard, organized as the Fifteenth New York Regiment and soon to be known as the 369th Infantry Regiment, received its official assignment to train at Camp Wadsworth and arrived soon afterward. Reeling from the humiliation of failing to prevent the federal government from sending black troops to their county, white citizens of Spartanburg regularly taunted the black troops who came to town on leave. Whites created opportunities to assert their dominance. Within a few weeks of arriving in South Carolina, Colonel William Hayward, regiment commander, was in Washington pleading for help to quell tensions that he thought were ready to explode. The previous Sunday evening, Noble Sissle, a black soldier from Camp Wadsworth on weekend leave, purchased a newspaper at a white hotel lobby in Spartanburg. When Sissle failed to deferentially remove his hat, the white proprietor called attention to the social faux pas. When Sissle refused to immediately correct this perceived blunder, the owner attacked the soldier, knocking him to the ground and kicking him. Lt. James R. Europe, a black officer, restrained his fellow soldiers in order to prevent retaliation. Angered beyond rational control, a group of soldiers marched to town the following evening, vowing to "shoot it up" as the Houston soldiers had done just two months earlier. With extraordinary coercion, Colonel Hayward managed to intervene and bring the soldiers back to camp, forestalling violence. Yet with the Houston memory raw in his mind, Hayward despaired that violence could be averted. Tensions between his soldiers and local white residents mounted. Hayward asked Emmett Scott, special assistant to the secretary of war in charge of African American troops, to visit his unit. Convinced of the volatility of the situation, Scott left Washington for South Carolina and met privately with the noncommissioned officers. Without any white officers present, Scott appealed to these black officers' patriotism and racial pride. Although the men bombarded Scott with reports of being continually subjected to bitter racial insults, he appealed to the men to show the greatest self-restraint and ignore the provocation from local whites.[44]

The soldiers followed Scott's admonishments, although tensions remained elevated. The War Department feared both keeping the soldiers at Camp Wadsworth and reassigning them. If the soldiers stayed and local community resistance persisted, War Department officials risked provoking another Houston-style riot. If the military reassigned the New York regiment, Washington empowered white southerners and invited endless protests and resistance from them. Faced with these two undesirable choices, the War Department created a third alternative. Although it was not yet prepared, the War Department ordered the regiment to France, making it the first black unit to go overseas. In France, the 369th became one of the most decorated and acclaimed infantry regiments of the war.[45]

As an undercurrent in this swirling debate about where and with whom black soldiers should be trained ran an internal political struggle between white reformers and their political nemesis, the Bleaseite faction. Fred Dominick, representative of the Third Congressional District, offered his complaint about the War Department's decision to train black soldiers in the South to Manning in the following telegram:

> It is an outrage on decency that negro troops should be placed in same camp with our white troops and it is hardly conceivable that such action should be even considered by a Democratic administration. Such action on the part of the government and the placing of negro troops by the side of white troops in our armies will undo the half century efforts of our people to prevent social equality of the races. South Carolina can well afford to lose all cantonments, camps and favors rather than suffer such disgraceful conditions within her borders.[46]

Dominick, law partner and avid supporter of Cole Blease in state politics, had joined Blease as a vocal critic of Wilson's administration and U.S. involvement in the war. While Dominick's opposition to the war initially diminished his popularity, he hoped to vindicate his criticism of Wilson by capitalizing on the administration's even more unpopular decision to train black troops in the South. By linking both the Wilson administration and South Carolina reformers, including Manning, to an attack on white supremacy, Dominick hoped to discredit the anti-Bleaseite faction in state politics. Cognizant of this strategy, Manning minimized his association with the Wilson administration's unpopular decision to train African Americans at South Carolina camps. He simply and forcefully opposed the decision by defending white supremacy. Manning dreaded the consequences this issue might have on state politics. In a note to himself, he wrote, "I am not overstating it when I say there are persons in South Carolina who [would] not be above exciting race troubles if they occur to throw the responsibility on the Administration."[47]

T. C. Duncan of Union, an observer of the heated rhetoric provoked by the War Department's decision, sensed that state leaders had overreacted. Duncan suspected that political maneuvering explained the excess. "I have known what to expect from the negro under any condition," Duncan commented, "for I have known from early childhood the negro from every viewpoint, and not for cheap politics do I intend to see him slandered and maligned." Employing paternalistic reasoning, he believed the concerns about social equality were overstated. "Now that war is upon us we need the negro and for social equality to loom up as an objection will not hold," he observed. "The negro knows his place and he has never moved out of it except when led by designing white men."[48] Dominick's political posturing and Manning's defensive response illustrate how readily and effectively a political faction could exploit white anxiety about the potential erosion of white control. Thus white supremacy operated as an effective rhetorical shield to disguise class motivations and factional interests and as a sword for attacking political opponents. Even Duncan's critique of both factions' political manipulation of white supremacy required him to confirm his understanding of the prescribed subordination of African Americans. In public disputes among whites about racial control, white participants had to brandish their white supremacy credentials to maintain credibility.

The idea of a universal draft troubled many white South Carolinians because it implied a racial equality that was inconsistent with white supremacy. The reality of the draft, however, was equally distressing because the practical task of preparing soldiers for war violated established white-supremacy practices. Woven throughout the debates about African Americans' serving as soldiers and training at southern bases were references to yet another challenge the war effort posed to white supremacy: the threat to its abundant supply of cheap labor. South Carolina's labor-intensive economy, both agricultural and manufacturing, depended heavily on surplus labor to keep wages low. The military's need for soldiers, the demand for labor generated by new industrial jobs in northern cities, and increased demand for agricultural products created labor shortages that either made laborers scarce or raised their wages. Because African Americans made up the majority of the state's agricultural labor and occupied the lowest rungs on the economic ladder, black agricultural laborers often found themselves snared in the middle of conflicts between agricultural interests and war demands.

Whites regularly complained to Congressman Frank Lever about South Carolina's labor shortages. Lever's response to such a query from an attorney in his district revealed whites' willingness to manipulate the law to coerce African American laborers. Lever suggested that local communities in South Carolina demand that sheriffs, magistrates, and other local law enforcement officers "enforce rigidly the vagrancy law and let the construction of that law be rather unlimited. There are a lot of darkies hanging around towns and cities, and on farms even, that should be put to work either on the farms and in places where they are needed or on the public works of the State." Apparently the congressman's suggestion was heeded. Numerous newspaper accounts throughout the war printed public warnings about strict enforcement of the vagrancy law and reported numerous arrests. The agricultural extension service's white leadership also entertained ideas about legal ways to coerce black laborers. J. F. Duggan, director of the agricultural extension service in Alabama, suggested to W. W. Long of Clemson, his counterpart in South Carolina, that South Carolina consider creating a Saturday Service League, which would require African Americans to work all day on Saturday during the busy farm season. Such a program was justified, Duggan suggested, because of the "common habit for negro farm laborers to take holiday for the whole of Saturday, or else for

Saturday afternoon." While Long favored the idea, he expressed doubt that it could be implemented. "If the colored people feel that this is an organized undertaking to force them to work on Saturday and does not include the white people, I am sure it will have little effect," he observed.[49]

The ethos of white supremacy insisted that whites were superior to blacks, and adherents of this belief system always endeavored to interpret human behavior in a manner consistent with its fundamental premises. At times, however, reality confounded the basic precepts. World War I had created situations that forced white southerners to reflect on precisely what the most appropriate subservient role for African Americans should be. War mobilization induced labor shortages that increased the price of labor—a windfall for laborers and a concern to employers. The shortages made all labor, including black labor, more valuable, and gave African American laborers new leverage that white South Carolinians resented. James Henry Rice Jr. blamed the Wilson administration for the problem. "It was not necessary to send the negro to France," Rice complained, nor was it necessary to raise wages to the currently "absurd figure." In Charleston, Rice complained, black plasterers made more money "than the ranking scientists of this land—more than you receive after a life time devoted to science." To illustrate his frustration Rice explained to Robert Ridgeway, leading American ornithologist of Olney, Illinois, that "barbers wear twelve-dollar shirts and house girls buy silk stockings that cost six dollars a pair."[50]

Julia Seldon of Spartanburg communicated to David Coker her frustrations with the unusual prerogative that she perceived black South Carolinians had gained because of the war effort. She complained that African Americans had "plenty of money now" and that they "take a pride in seeing how wastefully they can spend it." She asked Coker if "anything can be done about the negroes with their unskilled labor carrying from $60 to $100 a month. When the white man are giving up professions and offering their lives for $30? Is it possible to fight the high prices paid the laborers? It is a sinful waste of the money people have sacrificed." Seldon and Rice were offended by the irony that unskilled African American laborers profited from wartime labor shortages, which were partially created by the absence of whites, who made less money as soldiers.[51] Their attitudes further illustrate the irony that white southerners favored market forces when they kept labor cheap but abhorred the capricious power of market forces when they drove up the costs of labor, especially black labor.

While Seldon complained that white soldiers, risking their lives for their country, were underpaid at $30 per month, another South Carolinian argued that when the pay went to black soldiers it was exorbitant. R. Charlton Thomas, president of Thomas Company in Ridgeway, wanted to notify Washington that the federal government was paying dependents of enlisted black soldiers in the South too much. Thomas groused that African Americans were eligible to receive payments he perceived as excessive even if they did not work. Thomas complained that "negroes here receiv[e] from $25-$50 month, more money than they have ever had." Thomas argued that not only was the government spending "vast sums of money unwisely" but these payments were also "demoralizing what little labor is left in the country." He blamed interference from outsiders, in this case money from the federal government, for hindering white southerners' ability to control and compel black laborers as they believed they were entitled to do. No doubt Thomas perceived that these federal payments also drove up the price of labor he hoped to hire. Asserting that many African Americans who received payments were not actually dependent on the absent soldiers, Thomas advised authorities to review all applications and cull the list of dependents to only the "truly dependent." Thomas wanted to severely limit the influx of money into his community because, he maintained, "a negro will not work when he has money."[52] An editorial in early 1918 arguing for enforcement of vagrancy laws echoed Thomas's perception that black southerners would not work if they had money: "A nigger fellow with $3 in his pocket feels rich . . . and any negro in these days is able to get $3 to $30 in his pocket in a few days or weeks."[53] The war had clearly disrupted whites' controlling strategy of paying negligible wages that demanded that dependent laborers work constantly simply to survive.

For white South Carolinians the most troubling aspect of the war was their inability to control the changes that impinged on white supremacy. War and war mobilization empowered African Americans, the federal government, and market forces to disrupt and challenge, in several ways, the heretofore well-constructed structure of white supremacy. First, African American reformers mobilized public forums, calling for new opportunities and asserting black South Carolinians' willingness to serve. Second, the draft revived the issue of racial equality, or at least of how to defend inequality to the rest of the nation. Third, the War Department's need to train African American soldiers on southern bases threatened the newly fixed principle of formal, public segregation that had earned consensus as a day-to-day institutional expression of white supremacy. Military training of all soldiers at newly constructed cantonments threatened both to integrate military bases and to send to South Carolina African Americans from outside the region who were unfamiliar with formal segregation and its peculiar "etiquette." Fourth, and perhaps most fundamental, African Americans' response to wartime opportunities threatened South Carolina's abundant supply of cheap labor, a necessary component of South Carolina's economy in the minds of many whites. Finally, the economic changes that war mobilization induced—benefits as well as threats—were all viewed through the prism of white supremacy, even though all whites did not perceive them in precisely the same way. Refracting these questions at peculiarly southern angles distorted white South Carolinians' perception of war-related challenges, exaggerating problems that in the absence of white supremacy might have been understood merely as opportunities.

Chapter 4

Interracial Cooperation, 1917–1919

From the nation's initial engagement in World War I to the immediate postwar era, black and white reformers forged two distinct and seemingly parallel trajectories as they navigated war-imposed responsibilities. The dictates of white supremacy, of course, insisted that white reformers lead the state's war mobilization effort while engaging black reformers in a subordinate role of helping whites meet the national wartime objectives. White reformers needed African American reformers' cooperation and wanted their leadership among the state's black majority. Yet white reformers drew upon black reformers' leadership for whites' very limited war-related purposes while attempting to suppress black reformers' broader, independent wartime aspirations. With the principle of white supremacy well understood, both groups of reformers cooperated with each other during the war and accommodated each others' interests to some degree. Once the war ended, however, these white and black reformers drew distinctly different lessons from their brief period of war-driven cooperation.

World War I briefly gave African American reformers more leverage in their struggle for equality because whites needed their cooperation. Recruiting, drafting, and training soldiers were visible and important facets of war mobilization, but these were not the only challenges. Soldiers had to be clothed, fed, equipped, entertained, and paid. In the soldiers' absence, others had to perform their civilian labor. The war required soliciting seemingly endless financial resources. Consequently, successful execution of the war necessitated civilian cooperation, participation, and sacrifice. As the majority of South Carolina's residents, African Americans engaged in a collaborative endeavor with the state's white leadership that was crucial for meeting these civilian challenges. White reformers' desire for home-front success pressured them to cultivate black reformers' coopera-tion. South Carolina's need for African Americans' participation in the civilian war mobilization gave black reformers an authorized public forum for rallying the state's black majority. White reformers' need for this cooperation ironically and temporarily empowered African American reformers.

Not only did white reformers want blacks' cooperation to meet the great civilian war demands, they also needed black reformers to rally support and quell dissent among the state's African American population. Even before the United States entered the war against the Central Powers, fears of subversive German agents organizing blacks' opposition to the war gripped Americans. White southerners particularly scrutinized African Americans, anticipating their dis-sent and doubting their loyalty. Rumors quickly circulated that Afri-can Americans had succumbed to German spies who fomented blacks' dissatisfaction and exploited their resentment of white con-trol. This near hysteria facilitated development of a wartime bureau-cracy that investigated allegations of German subversion and provided close scrutiny of possible draft evasion.[1] By the end of the war the federal government had prosecuted a few domestic zealots who pledged loyalty to their European homeland in the company of African Americans, but no blacks were convicted of espionage. Rather than a gauge of African American's vulnerability to enemy manipulation, the wartime frenzy was testimony to the heavy hand of the federal government at war, whites' anxiety about losing con-trol, and whites' gross ignorance of African Americans' reasoned assessment of their own oppression. Dissent as well as indifference characterized many African Americans' response to the war effort, but they did not need encouragement from German spies to resent white supremacy's grip on their lives.[2]

The national frenzy concerning a potentially subversive black population reached South Carolina early. Within three days of the declaration of war B. F. McLeod of Charleston informed the Justice Department that a German agent in Lynchburg was organizing blacks in that small Lee County community to revolt. McLeod, no doubt, had heard the rumor from concerned family members who lived in the area. No revolt materialized. The next month Sheriff Lightsey of Hampton County notified federal authorities of a threatened uprising of blacks that he reasoned was likely provoked by German agents. Fueling these insurrection rumors were allegations that local blacks had received suspicious shipments and had stockpiled ammunition. When federal agent Branch Bocock found no relevant evidence to warrant an investigation in Hampton, Lightsey admitted that he had appealed to federal authorities because he feared a lynching unless he "appeased the crowd" with such an appeal.[3] Like many South Carolina counties, Lee and Hampton were black-majority counties. These rumors of German subversive agents resonated with whites, who sensed the potential havoc war disruptions might wreak on existing racial control strategies. Even if German agents had not fomented it, dissent among blacks alarmed whites and they needed black reformers to curtail it.

Whites wanted black reformers' cooperation to cultivate, coerce, and restrain the black population as needed, but they did not welcome the vulnerability that might come by seeking their cooperation too aggressively. So whites cloaked their desire for help, and most importantly their desire to control this help, with calls for patriotism. African American reformers, cognizant of their white counterparts' strategy, consistently heeded the calls for patriotism, demonstrating enthusiasm for civilian service, just as they had military service, by participating in every aspect of civilian auxiliary assistance. Hastings Hart of the Russell Sage Foundation reported to Governor Richard I. Manning that African Americans' organization and "active co-operation" in the home-front war effort in South Carolina "is surprising and is highly creditable to the Negro race." Black reformers accommodated whites' requests for wartime sacrifice as an investment in fighting for their own equality. Their first home-front challenge required a firm rebuttal to the rumors of German subversion. African Americans reaffirmed their loyalty while pointing to their historical record of allegiance. "We love our country today as in 1775, in 1812, in 1861–1865, in 1898, and in all the years of its existence," Beaufort's black residents noted at a public rally designed to assuage white doubt.[4] Soon after Congress officially declared war in the spring of 1917, African American reformers staged mass meetings, similar to the one held in Beaufort, in every South Carolina county.

These county events, often called Preparedness Day, were organized by black reformers who served on local black civic preparedness committees.[5] Hundreds of African Americans attended these public forums held at churches, schools, and courthouses. The rallies included patriotic singing and rousing oratory by local ministers, lawyers, educators, farmers, and county extension agents. In Darlington more than a thousand participants gathered to watch a parade and sing before the speeches began. Edward "E. J." Sawyer of Bennettsville, one of the wealthiest and most influential of the state's black leaders, addressed the large gathering with a speech "full of the best advice." Kershaw, Chesterfield, York, and Lexington, along with many other counties, pledged to increase food production to meet the nation's demand. Most counties' Preparedness Day included a community pledge of loyalty. Many counties adopted formal resolutions affirming their allegiance to the country, president, governor, and state war-preparation plans. Sumter residents pledged their loyalty even though it had been "slanderously asserted that German agents have 'conspired' and 'plotted' with the negroes of the South." African Americans from Aiken promised "thrift and economy" while agreeing that the "negro has no other flag but the Stars and Stripes." Intending to distinguish loyalty to the nation at war from satisfaction with injustice, the black citizens of Clarendon County pointed out that "we are not unmindful of past events bearing on the treatment of 10,000,000 Afro-American people in these United States, [yet] we stand now with no feeling of hatred or disloyalty to our government."[6]

As black reformers exercised county-level leadership across South Carolina, organizing demonstrations of African American loyalty, they simultaneously supported war mobilization as state leaders. The South Carolina State Council of Defense, initially organized as the Commission for Civic Preparedness, managed all civilian activities for the war's prosecution. Manning created a segregated counterpart to the State Council of Defense and appointed eight prominent African Americans from across the state to serve on it. The committee included Butler General, a prosperous cotton and tobacco farmer from Marion County; Jonas W. Thomas, a general store merchant from Bennettsville who built the only hotel in Bennettsville for African Americans and participated in the Negro Business League; Jacob J. Durham, pastor of the Second Calvary Baptist Church in Columbia; Thomas Miller, Charleston lawyer, retired politician and college president; and Ransom W. Westberry, a Sumter realtor with extensive experience in business and agriculture leadership. He had served as a county extension agent for five years and had been president of both the Negro Business League and the South Carolina Farmers Conference. Westberry chaired South Carolina's Food Conservation Colored Committee, the first black man in the nation appointed to that work.[7]

Hoping to control and orchestrate African Americans' participation in the civilian war effort, Manning appointed Richard Carroll, a black reformer he trusted, to chair this subcommittee. Whites historically had expressed confidence in Carroll, a conservative black minister who proudly renounced any participation in politics. Not all members of the committee took that position, however. For example, J. J. Durham was an executive committee member of Columbia's NAACP; while General and Miller were active leaders in South Carolina's Republican Party. In addition to these leaders who formed the state subcommittee, each county organized a local council of defense with a black auxiliary. Under the aggressive leadership of Hartsville agribusiness leader David R. Coker, who desperately wanted to unite South Carolina in service of the Wilson administration's war effort, the State Council of Defense authorized the African American state subcommittee and the auxiliary county councils to actively engage their communities for the war effort.

Across the state African American reformers met whites' expectations for loyalty and full civilian participation. In every county African Americans served on county councils of defense, organized mass meetings to communicate war needs and rally support for them, planted additional food crops, and supported the Red Cross. Benjamin Hubert, special agent, U.S. Food Commission, praised black South Carolina farmers for the "spirit of loyalty" they demonstrated in accelerating food production. "The negro farmer is no slacker," Hubert stressed. When tuberculosis was identified as a war problem, a prominent black leader from Marlboro County donated land for the site of the first TB sanitarium for South Carolina's black population. African Americans also responded to state leaders' requests for financial contributions. They participated in all four Liberty Fund drives with generous contributions, purchased War Savings Stamps, and cooperated fully in the final financial push, the United War Work Drive. Rev. Erasmus L. Baskervill of Charleston, black state director of the United War Work Drive, traveled across South Carolina delivering motivational speeches and encouraging broad participation among African Americans. "Give until it hurts and then double the amount," Baskervill implored.[8]

White Greenville reformers publicly praised African Americans for their thorough and sacrificial giving to the United War Work Drive. Their white counterparts praised them also for their creative approach to encouraging 100 percent participation in the campaign. J. A. Talbert and Charles Brier of the black executive committee proposed enlisting every man, woman, and child in the final war fundraising campaign by developing three levels of participation: the Honor Roll, the Givers, and the Slackers. Talbert and Brier anticipated that this three-tier approach for assessing participation would effectively compel broad community involvement. Moreover, they anticipated that publicly labeling nonparticipants as slackers would heap contempt on the nongivers. Praising black reformers for their organization and determination, white reformers concluded that African Americans had "heroically done what their white friends have hesitated to do": insist that community members give proportionate to their ability. Columbia's United War Work campaign received praise for its fundraising thoroughness. African Americans divided the community into blocks and assigned captains to contact every household and report to a ward chairman, who reported daily to the War Camp Community Service (WCCS) club.[9]

In every community located near a military camp African Americans served on a black auxiliary committee of the WCCS. Among other responsibilities, this committee had the task of entertaining black soldiers. The Columbia committee's first priority in 1917 was to keep harmonious race relations between the newly arriving black soldiers at Camp Jackson and the Columbia community. Whites' heightened anxiety about training African American soldiers in newly constructed cantonments made this a significant responsibility.

African American men and women served on the executive commit-tee of the WCCS. By the war's end the WCCS had opened a Red Circle Club, a community club for entertaining black soldiers, com-parable to the white soldiers' club. The Red Circle Club in downtown Columbia, located on Washington Street, served black soldiers sta-tioned at Camp Jackson. The club entertained approximately 17,000 soldiers during its brief existence. It gave parties for the soldiers at the Phyllis Wheatley Girls' Center, provided them car rides, spon-sored dances, and placed 650 soldiers into local homes for Christmas dinner. In November 1918 Columbia's Red Circle Club hosted the Nineteenth Regiment band, one of the "best colored bands ever heard." African Americans also prepared welcome-home parades for returning soldiers.[10]

National and state leaders stressed providing public entertain-ment for soldiers as an antidote to the private comfort many soldiers sought in local brothels or from young women who congregated near military bases. Military and federal government officials, wanting to minimize soldiers' exposure to sexually transmitted diseases, devel-oped strategies for protecting soldiers by keeping them away from infected women. Working with the newly created Commission on Training Camp Activities (CTCA), communities near military bases, in addition to providing the requested "wholesome" entertainment, aggressively patrolled and shut down red-light districts to comply with the Selective Service provision that prohibited prostitution within a five-mile radius of military training camps. But this provi-sion did not address what became the more serious problem: young women, not prostitutes, seeking the excitement they associated with the unprecedented gathering of tens of thousands of young men pre-paring for war.[11]

Alan Johnstone Jr., the federal official with the CTCA in charge of repressing vice near military training camps in the Southeast, identified South Carolina as a state in crucial need of help in address-ing the problem. On any given day, more than one hundred thousand soldiers were training in South Carolina, Johnstone explained in a Senate hearing, and 90 percent of women who had been arrested near military camps in Charleston, Columbia, Greenville, and Spar-tanburg had tested positive for syphilis or gonorrhea. South Caroli-na's legislature responded to the problem by establishing a reformatory for young women that would give the state a way to confine any young woman perceived as a health threat to the military population. The federal government offered money to help establish the reformatory if the state provided matching funds. So both contributed $40,000, and South Carolina started construction of its first home for wayward white girls. The state made no provision for black girls, although Johnstone had emphasized the need. Governor Manning suggested to Johnstone that this was simply an oversight, an improbable explanation, since the state legislature denied numerous subsequent funding requests for a similar facility for African American girls. Given the severity of the need and the unwillingness of whites to use state or federal resources for black girls, the black community would have to provide one themselves through private funds.[12]

Black women reformers active in the South Carolina Federation of Colored Women's Clubs undertook this major challenge. They raised $30,000 in private funds to purchase thirty acres of land ten miles north of Columbia and created Fairwold, a reformatory for black girls. Yet the women reformers who started Fairwold reframed the problem and emphasized a different need. While creating Fairwold during the war addressed the military's stated desire to remove problematic women from the vicinity of training camps, the club women stressed the young women's needs. Many were homeless or without family support and had fallen victim to the military presence. Rather than seeing the young women as preying on soldiers, the club women emphasized their vulnerability and argued that the military presence had exploited the most vulnerable. Fairwold became an alternative to jail for young women convicted of minor crimes. The next year, black leaders petitioned the governor for $10,000 to defray operational costs, pointing out that the white girls' home received $40,000 in state appropriations. The General Assembly refused in 1919, and for decades to come, all petitions for funding assistance.[13]

African American reformers who served on state and county councils of defense demonstrated loyalty by organizing community support, selling and purchasing war bonds, entertaining soldiers, and caring for forgotten and exploited young women were referred to by whites as "leading negroes." David Coker and white members of the State Council of Defense expected the black reformers who served on black subcommittees of white organizations to function as community monitors, ensuring that everyone met whites' expectations for loyal and appropriate participation. These prominent African American reformers met these expectations, but they often used their service on local councils for a twofold purpose. While promoting specific civilian war mobilization efforts that whites desired, many African American reformers simultaneously used their white-sanctioned positions of authority to help meet their community's needs. For example, Joseph C. White, pastor of Zion Baptist, the largest Baptist church in Columbia, characterized his war-related activities as serving this twofold purpose. As White became involved in every aspect of the war mobilization work, he said he was leading the black community to participate in a "way which was at once gratifying to his own race and a revelation to the white people of Columbia and the State," a close observer noted.[14]

Attending to multiple audiences and pursuing goals with conflicting purposes was nothing new for African American reformers who always had to navigate within oppression, viewing whites as both an obstacle and at times a means to a better end. Whites wanted to control South Carolina's black population. To retain that control, they organized the war effort around county-level committees led by black reformers. The leadership responsibility that whites assigned them also created a measure of influence and leverage for black reformers. By accommodating whites' expectations for civilian preparedness, black reformers could also use their new authority to resist systematic white oppression and push an African American agenda for progress.

African American reformers used their appointed positions on black auxiliaries of county councils of defense to help expand job opportunities for black laborers. War-induced labor shortages potentially expanded blacks' employment options. Richland County's black auxiliary council ran an employment service to develop that potential, a service not directly related to its preparedness responsibilities. Home of the state capital and located in the center of South Carolina, Richland County housed one of the state's largest black business districts in the heart of downtown Columbia. The county council established its headquarters on Washington Street at the North Carolina

Mutual Insurance building. (North Carolina Mutual was a black-owned insurance company headquartered in Durham, North Carolina.) At the council headquarters, newly created to coordinate civic preparedness, the council members also acted as job brokers by registering African Americans who needed jobs and identifying employers who had vacancies. Vowing to eliminate the alleged vagrancy problem that concerned whites, the black council leaders also planned to secure for African American laborers the "very best market" in the local area. This rapidly developed employment service established in the black auxiliary council's office exemplifies African American reformers' creative approach to expanding opportunities in directions whites had not anticipated or directed.[15]

Charleston's African American reformers also quickly demonstrated their determination to expand wartime employment options for black workers. As the nation geared up for war production, the Charleston Navy Yard clothing factory, the sole clothing manufacturer for the navy, announced in May 1917 its immediate need for six hundred new workers. The increased demand for sailors' uniforms required doubling the existing work force to operate the factory day and night. Marvin Taylor, representative of the Navy Yard Labor Board, noted, however, that only white women need apply. Other women who applied, he proclaimed, were "wasting time and carfare." Despite Taylor's warning, black women applied for the positions. Frustrated and puzzled by black women's desire for these well-paid jobs, local navy yard authorities speculated that Germans had encouraged them. They reasoned that German spies could create havoc by disrupting the only facility that made navy uniforms and consequently jeopardize the mandate to clothe enlisted men properly.[16] Yet the Charleston NAACP understood the enticement of higher pay. Members immediately fought for an opportunity for black women to obtain these jobs.

The Charleston NAACP had only been in existence for a few months when its members seized this opportunity.[17] Richard Mickey, representing the new Charleston NAACP branch, petitioned the Charleston Chamber of Commerce for assistance in overturning the navy yard's policy excluding black women from employment. Rather than inflame the situation and jeopardize the petition's success, Mickey addressed the local chamber under the auspices of the "Committee of Colored Citizens" rather than the NAACP. In their request for assistance, black Charlestonian reformers strategically appealed to white business leaders on a sensitive issue that gravely concerned white employers: out-migration of black labor. Black reformers told chamber members that qualified African American women wanted these job opportunities, but if these new jobs remained unavailable, the best black laborers would leave Charleston. "If these openings are made [available to black women], it will stem the migration tide; if not, the alternative only remains," Mickey stressed. Since the navy yard was an extension of the federal government rather than a local business, African Americans also looked to allies outside the state to fight this blatant discrimination against black women.[18]

The Charleston NAACP partnered with members of the Minneapolis branch of the NAACP, who enlisted the assistance of their congressional delegation. Several Minnesota representatives, after being contacted by the Minneapolis NAACP, contacted Secretary of the Navy Josephus Daniels, a native of North Carolina. This elaborate and well connected network yielded a direct response from Daniels, who diplomatically and carefully explained that federal civil service regulations for artisan positions with the navy rated applicants on experience and physical ability. Thus, Daniels reasoned, rejected applicants probably failed to meet the civil service regulations. Yet the loophole that Daniels only alluded to, but the Minnesota representatives highlighted, was that a local representative, serving on the Civil Service Commission of the Labor Board, had authority to enforce the regulations. Consequently, this authority provided the local representative with the opportunity to exercise broad discretion and conveniently to find all African American women incompetent. This information helped the Charleston NAACP leverage a practical change in the navy yard's hiring practices. These persistent yet stealthy maneuvers by dedicated black Charlestonians led to the employment of at least 250 black women, who earned collectively an estimated $150,000 a year at the Charleston Navy Yard's clothing factory.[19]

Black reformers not only fought against the economic manifestation of white domination, they also understood the need to resist the cultural reassurances of white supremacy. In Columbia, African American reformers used their civilian wartime authority and their proven record of success at rousing the black community in support of innumerable war activities to bolster their protest against showing the racially offensive movie *Birth of a Nation*. In May 1918, the Broadway Theater in Columbia planned to show D. W. Griffith's film that cast the Ku Klux Klan as courageous heroes who rescued white southerners from the dreaded grip of black rule during Reconstruction. Nationally African Americans, especially the NAACP, had protested the offensive film since before its 1915 release. Such a sympathetic white supremacist interpretation of Reconstruction greatly offended African Americans, even a conservative appeaser like Richard Carroll. Publicly, Carroll referred to *Birth of a Nation* as a "stirrer up of strife, an incubator of crime, of race hatred and race prejudice."[20] The film crassly portrayed nineteenth-century black southerners as stereotypically lazy, corrupt, and ignorant.

Black reformers, including Carroll, argued that showing *Birth of a Nation* would ignite racial antagonisms, as it had in other cities. Strategically, black reformers linked their protest of the film's showing with their proven record of war support. Carroll reasoned that blacks had contributed to the war "willingly and cheerfully" in every task the war demanded. Thus, as the nation faced the enemy in Europe, he insisted it was a time for unity, not division. Knowing that white reformers in South Carolina were anxious to maintain African Americans' cooperation in the war effort, black reformers petitioned white city leaders to use their influence with David Coker and the State Council of Defense to cancel *Birth of a Nation*.[21]

On Friday morning, May 24, the Columbia City Council held a special meeting to hear from black petitioners. A delegation of thirteen black reformers from Columbia presented their argument against the film's showing. Included in this delegation were black auxiliary members of the Richland County Council of Defense, Nathaniel F. Haygood, chair; Butler W. Nance, president of the Columbia NAACP; Richard Carroll, chair of the black State Council of Defense; and key Columbia ministers such as Joseph C. White of Zion Baptist, Mark G. Johnson of Ladson Presbyterian, D. F. Thompson, C. A. Harrison, and Charles Jaggers.[22] The city council invited S. E. Possey, manager of the Broadway Theater, to hear the blacks' request. Speaking for the petitioners, Joseph J. Atwell emphasized that African Americans had been loyal and patriotic and had fostered unity among all South Carolinians. Moreover, he argued that their sacrifices should not be denigrated or the existing racial harmony jeopardized by showing a film that emphasized racial conflict. Likely Atwell did not believe war mobilization had abruptly transformed long-standing racially hierarchical relationships into harmonious, cooperative ones, but he employed the rhetoric and appealed to white reformers' desire for order and calm.[23]

Cognizant of the petitioners' and Columbia City Council members' concerns, Coker consulted with Washington mobilization officers about the State Council of Defense's authority to cancel the film's scheduled showing. Arthur Fleming of the National Defense Council stated that while no such formal authority existed, he believed they should turn back any threat to peaceful race relations. Fleming told Coker that the state council should use its influence to minimize potential racial antagonisms. Coker concurred and reasoned that it would be unnecessarily provocative to show the film during the war in light of black reformers' protest and their wartime cooperation. Anxious to satisfy black reformers and avoid further escalating tensions, the State Council of Defense encouraged local white leaders to honor the black reformers' protest.[24]

Hoping to avoid a mandatory cancellation, the city council encouraged Possey, the theater manager, to negotiate with the African American delegation and reach an informal agreement. Yielding to this pressure, Possey agreed to cancel the scheduled showing of *Birth of a Nation*, and the city council applauded his cooperation as a gesture of wartime patriotism. Appreciative of Possey's "patriotic stand," the Columbia City Council passed a resolution declaring that "pursuant to the recommendation of the State Council of Defense, [city council recommends] that the film, 'The Birth of a Nation,' be not shown in the city of Columbia."[25] Again white reformers extended African American reformers unique wartime authority because they needed their cooperation and black reformers used that leverage in ways whites had not anticipated.

African American reformers were active not only in areas of the state like Charleston and Columbia, where blacks represented a majority of the population, but also in the Piedmont, where African Americans were a minority. African Americans in Greenville rallied their community when the Greenville City Council discussed passing a coercive employment ordinance that targeted African American women. Numerous white Greenville residents had complained to the city council that black women had recently quit their domestic jobs. They had been unable to hire replacements because many black women refused the job offers. Many of these African American women quit low-paying domestic jobs and refused other low-wage work because they received a monthly federal allowance from husbands serving as soldiers in the war.[26]

Whites could not tolerate this exercise of personal autonomy in defiance of white authority. These black women freely chose to care for their own homes and families when the salaries of their soldier husbands made it possible. In the accustomed racial order, whites exercised economic control over blacks, preventing such independent choices. Thinking only of their inconvenience, white women complained about the excessive hardship in their families, who needed cooks and laundresses but could not find them. Frustrated by the loss of the leverage that whites traditionally held over blacks, whites lashed out by labeling the black women "unpatriotic loafers." This wartime slander masked their fundamental concern: the breach of white supremacy. Further defaming the women by exaggerating the perniciousness of not working, whites claimed that many of these women became prostitutes after quitting their domestic jobs. Higher wages quite possibly could have persuaded black women to work, especially at a time when other jobs commanded higher pay. Yet whites did not turn to increased wages as a solution. To solve their perceived problem, white Greenville reformers proposed compelling these women to work with a "work or fight" ordinance requiring all able-bodied black women in Greenville to carry a labor card verifying that they were employed at least five days a week. Otherwise they would be jailed or heavily fined. Other southern states and towns had enacted similar ordinances, including nearby Georgia.[27]

Outraged by the discriminatory proposal, African American reformers organized a public forum for black Greenville residents to vent their frustrations and adopt a protest resolution. Rev. Green and Professor Charles Briar, who had organized the community, passionately offered their objections before the assembled Greenville City Council. They argued that black women were already engaged in useful occupations and should not be compelled to work for lower wages. They warned that such a discriminatory ordinance would impede war-related volunteer efforts and likely cause an exodus of African Americans from Greenville, a constant concern of whites who depended on cheap black labor. Mayor H. C. Harvley attempted to defuse the situation by assuring black reformers the council would gladly accept an informal solution. He claimed that the council had no serious plans for adopting a city ordinance. While agreeing with the petitioners' assertion that Greenville's African American population had consistently supported the war, he insisted that whites' complaints were legitimate. After all, the mayor had personal experience with the problem, he claimed, since his own cook had suddenly left him with three sick children. Governor Manning had privately voiced the same complaint about his servants leaving. When council members shared alleged evidence of callous black women, Green countered with contrasting instances of thrift and responsibility. For example, he told of a young soldier's wife who had recently deposited $50 of her $72 allowance in the bank, planning for an uncertain future. Green agreed that idleness was a vice he could not condone. He promised to encourage local ministers to emphasize the need for thrift and industry. Yet Green rejected the council's earlier suggestion that black women with inclinations toward unwarranted leisure and extravagances were widespread problems in Greenville.[28]

Recognizing that the public discussion about passing a coercive labor ordinance for black women had angered African Americans in Greenville, one council member reassured them that African Americans' contributions were noticed and appreciated. Henry T. Mills, a white business leader, reminded the audience that Greenville's black community had contributed $7,000 to the latest Liberty Bond drive, and he wanted "no humiliation for such patriotic people." Blair returned the gesture of harmony by assuring Mayor Harvley he would find him a good cook immediately. This incident in Greenville demonstrated again that outside influences, in this case the federal government's guidelines for paying soldiers' spouses, upset the balance of power within long-standing relationships where the dictates of white supremacy had traditionally been the controlling element. Whites resented not only African American women exercising economic independence, but also the federal government diminishing whites' prerogative while facilitating blacks' freedom. The exchange at the city council meeting illustrated that African Americans' resistance as well as their cooperation influenced whites' behavior.

Emboldened by their participation in the war effort and sensing they were living in a time of rapid change, African Americans pushed harder and persistently made demands even as the armistice approached. During the final months of the war African American reformers from Charleston organized an intensive campaign in their city to reverse a long-standing humiliation. Unlike all other segregated black public schools in South Carolina, where black teachers taught black children, Charleston's public schools for African Americans students hired only white teachers. While white teachers often taught in black private schools, these teachers, who generally came from outside the South, were possessed of a strong sense of either missionary zeal or philanthropic dedication and were well received by African Americans. Black Charlestonians resented the white teachers in the public schools; however, because they were white southerners who treated the children as inferior. Black parents believed that effective teachers needed a parental bond of affection and sympathy with children. Thus they reasoned that the white teachers who clung to white supremacist ideas implicitly taught the children self-hatred and could not inspire black students to reach their maximum potential. Although the anomalous circumstance of whites teaching black children had remained formally unchallenged for half a century, African American reformers exuded a sense of optimism, buoyed by the war to "make the world safe for democracy," that spurred them to experiment with democracy at home.[29]

After months of preparation through the local NAACP, a representative committee petitioned the Charleston city school board at its January meeting for a permanent reversal of the policy. The committee proposed that the board allow well-qualified African American teachers to teach in the black schools of Charleston. The petitioners insisted that black students should not continually be taught by those who deemed them inferior. The all-white Charleston city school board rejected the request. Undaunted, the Charleston NAACP, with assistance from the Columbia branch, raised the stakes and petitioned the state legislature directly for a law that would prohibit white teachers from teaching in black public schools. Of course, these African American petitioners appealed to an all-white legislature that did not represent their interests. Such a disadvantage required a sensitive strategy, which began with assembling distinguished petitioners. The chair of the petitioning committee was Thomas E. Miller, who most recently had served on the governor's Committee for Civic Preparedness and had formerly served in Congress and as president of South Carolina State College. The members of the committee were two doctors, William H. Johnson and John M. Thompson; Rev. Charles C. Jacobs; and Edwin A. Harleston, president of the Charleston NAACP. Since Senator Arthur R. Young of Charleston sympathized with the white teachers and refused to sponsor the bill, this committee of low country African American reformers looked elsewhere for assistance. They planned to divide whites by exploiting sectional tensions among them. Hoping to profit from Piedmont resentment of Charleston's elitist attitudes, black reformers turned to a Piedmont senator, John H. Wharton of Laurens County, who submitted the bill for consideration.[30] Ironically, the black Charlestonians' request played to the basic segregationist logic that resonated well in white majority counties: If schools were segregated, why allow white teachers in Charleston's black schools? Consistency, if nothing else, supported the NAACP position. Charleston whites were asking to remain an exception, and Piedmont legislators never liked considering Charleston exceptional.

The black petitioners from Charleston appeared personally before the house committee on education, chaired by Fairfield representative Richard A. Meares, to make their case. Among other things, the petitioners argued that black Charlestonians paid more in taxes than they received in public school support. Armed with data that supported this assertion, Charleston's black reformers found this information, compiled during their extensive preparation, helped quell opposition from committee members outside of Charleston. Dealing with white Charlestonian opposition required another tactic.[31]

A committee of three white commissioners from the Charleston school board appeared to oppose the black reformers' request. These commissioners insisted that white women should not be displaced from their positions because of blacks' complaints. The white Charlestonians argued that the black petitioners represented an elite perspective and not the viewpoint of the majority of African Americans in the school district. In refuting this charge, black Charlestonians again demonstrated their cleverness and extensive preparation. To counter the accusation that black reformers were elites and unrepresentative of Charleston's larger African American community, they presented the education committee with the signatures of five thousand heads of household. These signatures represented approximately twenty-five thousand black Charlestonians, nearly three-fourths of the city's black population. The pages of signatures represented skillful and stealthy grassroots organization. Local NAACP members had held more than a dozen meetings in churches throughout the city where they emphasized the importance of opposing white teachers in black schools. They encouraged the community to sign the petition conveying their desire to have black teachers for their children.[32]

The determination, careful strategy, and sheer boldness of Charleston's black reformers paid off. The white Charleston commissioners knew the volume of signatures their opponents presented undermined their best argument, so they proposed a face-saving compromise that involved allowing the local school board rather than the state legislature to change the policy. The house education committee agreed to table the proposed bill that would have criminalized hiring white teachers for black schools. In return, the Charleston superintendent agreed to adopt the stated policy for its schools. Senator Young made the quiet arrangements. Charleston school superintendent A. B. Rhett independently announced the desired policy change, stating, "On or before the scholastic year commencing September 1, 1920 no white teachers shall be employed in the public school of the city of Charleston to teach negro pupils." As promised, Meares withdrew the proposed bill from the legislature's agenda.[33]

The successful struggle of Charleston's NAACP to secure better teaching positions for black teachers signaled that the war's conclusion had not ended African Americans' push for greater opportunity. Rather, black South Carolinians began expecting other postwar dividends on their wartime investments. Black activism that began during the war had met with success. African American reformers had used white appeals for wartime cooperation and sacrifice as a fulcrum for moving their agenda, an agenda that sought to ameliorate harsh inequalities and to narrow the economic disparity between whites and blacks. In modest ways white reformers accommodated these demands, primarily because meeting them facilitated African Americans' cooperation, which white reformers perceived they needed to execute the civilian war demands successfully. Since war mobilization and voluntary preparedness had created new opportunities, African Americans hoped the war's aftermath held additional promise for South Carolina's oppressed majority. As the United States transitioned from the war to the postwar era, black reformers became more emboldened and anticipated tangible rewards for African Americans' collective military service and wartime cooperation. Jesse O. Thomas, president of Voorhees Normal and Industrial School in Denmark, South Carolina, directly linked service and reward. "When the Negro is called upon to help America and her allies—the white man—make the world safe for Democracy by offering upon the altar of sacrificial service his own life," Thomas explained, "there is a growing feeling in the bosom of every black man that the white man of his country ought now to be willing to assure him that America will be made safe for the Negro."[34] As World War I concluded successfully, black reformers' agenda increasingly became a push for African Americans' full rights of citizenship. Yet African Americans' spotlight on injustice and attempts at securing their citizenship rights sounded an unwelcome alarm for white South Carolinians who dreaded more war-related turmoil.

Chapter 5

Interracial Tension, 1919

Celebrations commenced November 11, 1918, hailing the armistice that signaled an end to the Great War. With the ending and winning of the war, black reformers anticipated an accelerated loosening of oppressive constraints that had eased somewhat during the war. They expected rewards for their loyalty and commitment, tangible results for their dutiful wartime cooperation. With heightened expectations, black reformers grew more impatient with their inequality and bolder in their insistence on change. Yet the war's conclusion quickly diminished the war-generated leverage African Americans had briefly enjoyed. White reformers, by contrast, waited eagerly for an end to the fluidity of race relations that they had grudgingly but necessarily tolerated because of war needs. Whites desired an immediate halt to the accommodations they perceived had been made for black reformers. They wanted a rapid return to the seemingly stable, prewar racial structure that whites had more readily controlled. As the wartime need for blacks' cooperation dissipated, whites increasingly resisted African Americans' raised expectations and their intensified postwar activism. Consequently, the parallel paths that black and white reformers traveled in wartime began to converge in the immediate postwar era, putting them on a collision course in 1919.

African American reformers in Columbia summoned the imagery of freedom and new beginnings on January 1, 1919, as they gathered to celebrate Emancipation Day and to draft a series of resolutions that reflected their determination. As the postwar year dawned, African Americans celebrated by publicly protesting discrimination and resolving to change the future. After a parade at Benedict College, Rev. James Kirkland of Darlington addressed the gathering by first praising the soldiers' valor and the civilians' cooperation. While Kirkland cautioned African Americans against discouragement, he readily acknowledged the obstacles in their path. At the annual community commemoration of freedom, a freedom first promised fifty-six years previously with the Emancipation Proclamation, African Americans of Richland County highlighted present injustices. They decried the inadequate and inferior railroad accommodations. They admonished the legislature for its meager education appropriations for black schools, as they deplored mob violence and lynch law. They also identified the solution for these inequalities: the ballot. Calling on whites to live up to the American ideals of freedom and equality, black reformers quoted the Declaration of Independence, asserting their belief that "governments derive their just powers from the consent of the governed." As their rhetoric revealed, black reformers understood that whites had corrupted American political ideals with disfranchisement, which denied consent to a majority of South Carolina's citizens. Drawing on the spirit of the war era, the committee of black reformers who drafted the Emancipation Day resolutions challenged whites to attend a "cooperative conference" where whites and blacks could hold a "frank but dispassionate" discussion of these problems.[1] The bold and optimistic assertions black reformers made on January 1 signaled the tone they sustained that momentous postwar year.

Perhaps African Americans' boldest challenge to institutional white supremacy was the call for increased political participation, a direct threat to whites' calculated disfranchisement of African Americans. On February 4, 1919, African American reformers from across the state met in Columbia for a conference where they discussed the challenges black South Carolinians faced. They debated potential solutions to the problems and articulated their vision of harnessing renewed energy and enthusiasm into a plan of action reminiscent of the Reconstruction era. African American reformers who met in the capital city decried the current political system in South Carolina as "unjust, unfair and unlawful." In addition to condemning the injustices, they affirmed that voting was the fitting strategy for addressing these systematic problems. Participants at the Columbia conference resolved to encourage and register eligible

African American voters. The conference called upon all ministers to urge qualified congregation members to register to vote. Additionally, they requested that each black precinct and ward chairman in South Carolina organize and reach the masses, drafting a plan to register eligible voters within a year.[2] Most of the state's black leaders in attendance pledged their allegiance to the Republican Party, which had garnered their support since Emancipation, but not without reservation and frustration. The state party's white chairman, Joe Tolbert, ran the party primarily to direct federal patronage toward a small band of maverick whites and a smaller handful of black allies. Tolbert showed little interest in African American issues.

Knowing the indifference of the state Republican Party's white leadership, Bishop William D. Chappelle, prominent AME leader and tireless champion for change, articulated a political desire that struck at the heart of whites' informal disfranchising strategy and aroused their greatest fear. "What I want to see," Chappelle stated, "is the Democratic party divided."[3] Chappelle understood that real political power for relatively small numbers of eligible African American voters was possible only if blacks served as power brokers in a divided Democratic Party. White South Carolinians knew that political division among the state's white minority was only possible if all whites honored the Democratic Party's loyalty oath to support the primary winner in the general election no matter how bitter the primary contest. Consequently, African American reformers desperately wanted to exploit the class and regional differences among whites.

So enticing was the prospect of a divided Democratic Party that Chappelle, a minister of the gospel, confessed, "I would be willing to follow any one, even the old devil himself part of the way, who could split the Democratic party." Here Chappelle publicly proclaimed a strategy he had quietly pursued in 1916 when he mysteriously invited Cole Blease to speak to an all-black audience at Allen University soon after Blease's close and bitter loss in the Democratic primary. No doubt many African Americans equated Blease with the "old devil himself." Chappelle's critique of the state's impotent Republican Party and his proposed alternative led the conference to adopt a compromise resolution. They agreed that each member of the conference would "pledge anew his loyalty to the Union Republican party, or *any other political organization* that will give us the right(s) to which we are entitled." Within three days *The State* editor reminded white readers that bold statements like Chappelle's served as a warning of the continual need for white political unity.[4]

In addition to debating political strategy, the Columbia conference of African American reformers issued reports that expressed the goals of their uplift campaign. They wanted to improve the dismal status of education for African Americans, a perennial desire that all other needs depended upon. The conference reports pinpointed specific remedies, including providing qualified teachers in every school; a longer school term; higher salaries to attract qualified teachers, especially in rural districts; and properly constructed and furnished schools. Determined to promote these concerns aggressively, the conference appointed a committee to petition the new governor, Robert A. Cooper, who had been elected in the final weeks of the war and inaugurated in January 1919. Chappelle chaired the committee that called on Cooper to appoint black citizens to local boards of trustees that supervised any type of African American education. The committee wanted black trustees on these school boards because many current white trustees never visited black schools and remained ignorant of their problems. African American representation on these boards, the committee argued, would lead to improved conditions for black students.[5]

Richard Carroll, a longtime African American Baptist minister who curried favor with white power, was often at odds with forward-looking black reformers, like those at the Columbia conference, who challenged prevailing standards and encouraged political solutions. Carroll had worked on interracial cooperation since the early twentieth century. A tireless speaker and self-promoter, Carroll traveled frequently across South Carolina and throughout the South constantly informing local newspapers of his engagements and itinerary. Carroll proudly stayed out of politics and encouraged black South Carolinians to follow his example. Such an approach made him a popular black leader with white South Carolinians but far less admired by black reformers. Carroll wasted no time ingratiating himself with the new governor. Within days of the Columbia conference where African Americans had openly called for increased and widespread political participation, Carroll furnished Cooper with names of African American reformers whom he characterized as plotting to divide the white people of South Carolina.

At the top of Carroll's list of black troublemakers was the man he deemed the "most officious," Bishop W. D. Chappelle. The AME bishop took a prominent role in most of the public activities that African American reformers had planned and executed. Of course, he was the leader at the February conference who openly advocated a strategy to divide white voters. Other black reformers from Columbia named by Carroll included Joseph C. White, minister of Zion Baptist Church; W. W. Herbert; Nathaniel F. Haygood, pastor of Sydney Park Methodist Church; and Robert W. Mance, president of Allen University. Additionally, he named Rev. E. H. Coit from Charleston; Mr. Nance from Newberry; and Rev. Irving E. Lowery, a journalist originally from Sumter. The men Carroll identified as most troublesome were primarily ministers. He also identified several business reformers from Columbia on his list of troublesome black reformers. The list included Lillian Rhodes, proprietor of Good Samaritan Hospital, passionate advocate for health-care reforms and the only woman on Carroll's list; I. S. Leevy, businessman and ubiquitous community leader; Harry E. Lindsay, grocer and chair of the Emancipation Day committee and the Lincoln Memorial Association; Jasper Duncan, director of the War Camp Community Service; Butler W. Nance, attorney and president of the NAACP chapter; Nathaniel J. Frederick, lawyer, editor of the *Southern Indicator*, and secretary of the State Colored Fair Association; and Hardy and Pinckney, undertakers. Carroll assured Governor Cooper that as one called to "preach the gospel of Jesus Christ" he had no interest in politics. Carroll furnished Cooper with names of white leaders who could vouch for his political virginity and who would verify that his work was consistent with whites' desires. Critical of African Americans who advocated political participation, Carroll characterized these black reformers to Cooper as "Negro political leaders who are running the underground railroad," an implication that they operated as covert agents working to usurp the current racial system. Further insinuating that he had valuable but sensitive information, Carroll urged the governor to keep these names to himself and "just watch the 'wireless telegraphy.'"[6]

Despite Carroll's disapproval and surreptitious warnings, calls for voter registration among African Americans did not remain simply rhetorical. The Charleston NAACP formed the Cosmopolitan Club to register new voters. The registrar's office only opened the first Monday of each month. Edwin Harleston, the NAACP chapter president, bragged that on that day black men lined up half way around the block waiting to enter the registration office, even though only forty or fifty men would manage to enter and register. Columbia NAACP members actively recruited new voters through a subcommittee chaired by attorney Green Jackson. The first Monday of each month, beginning in February, Jackson and three other NAACP members assisted new voters with the complex registration procedures and reading skills if needed. In preparation for the literacy test, branch president Butler Nance explained, "we put the constitution in their hands and . . . we teach them." The first Monday in February, which was the first Monday following the Columbia conference, these men registered one hundred new voters. The first Monday in March, they registered eight-seven voters; in April, seventy-five voters; and in May, sixty-two more voters. Proud of this accomplishment, Nance touted the new voters to the national office and assured New York that African Americans in Columbia intended to "fight until every man of color in this southland has a vote."[7]

Alarmed by this persistent voter registration effort, Graydon, a white attorney from Columbia, informed the governor of increased African American voter registration. He expressed much outrage that Richland County Board of Registration allowed this. Increasing his sense of indignation, Graydon noted, "I do not mean the intelligent classes but anyone who appears they register."[8] Graydon's comments to Cooper demonstrate white reformers' steadfast resolve to monitor black behavior and assess its appropriateness.

Increased agitation for voting among black South Carolinians, accompanied by a loss of white control and influence over African Americans, also worried low-country resident Philip Palmer of Summerville. Palmer worried, as many whites had, that young black men who had served in the U.S. Army had returned home with heightened expectations. Those who had served in combat in France were especially assertive, arguing that they were now entitled to vote and serve as jurors. Additionally, Palmer sensed that whites' control of politics, confidently managed before the war, was rapidly slipping.

He claimed to have heard literate black men, whom he identified as "conservative elderly colored men," express dissatisfaction about being unable to vote.[9]

The anxiety of whites like Graydon and Palmer typified white reaction to African Americans' assertion of their political rights. A sense of panic greeted these assertions. Maintaining white supremacy in South Carolina demanded white political control. Evidence of political participation from any African Americans other than the elite few threatened white control. It was in this atmosphere of postwar anxiety that white reformers across the South launched the interracial-cooperation movement that became the Committee on Interracial Cooperation (CIC). Born in crisis, the CIC touted the rhetoric of mutual fairness, "trust and good will," but the white reformers, at least the South Carolinians, who gathered several times in 1919 to organize the CIC wanted cooperation on their terms and consistent with white supremacy. The committee's name indicated that it was interracial, but black leaders were not allowed at the initial meetings because whites wanted to develop broader support for the organization before it became identified with black leaders. While the original organizers explicitly stated their purpose was to help black soldiers adjust to civilian life, whites no doubt used the CIC as a tool for serving their interest. White reformers anticipated that their efforts would tone down African Americans' heightened desire for change, push back the sense of urgency black reformers expressed, and restore harmony under white control.[10] Self-proclaimed white reformers, men and women otherwise supportive of black-uplift efforts, responded bitterly to any suggestion that the political structure be altered to allow increased black voting, as the following incident illustrates.

In Charleston, E. L. Baskervill, a black archdeacon in the Episcopal Church, sent Thomas R. Waring, editor of the *Charleston Evening Post*, an essay expressing his desire for improved race relations and social justice. In Baskervill's plea for social justice, he carefully distinguished this idea from social equality. "The negro is not seeking the white man's parlor or his dining room," he emphasized.

> What is the negro seeking? His rights as a true and loyal American citizen—a fair distribution of the public school funds, a man's chance before the civil and criminal courts, to vote as a citizen of

this great Republic and an opportunity for public improvement in general. The negro is not pleading to be Mayor or Governor of any city or State in the South, yet every qualified negro should be allowed to vote for the Mayor or the Governor and the qualification for the white man to vote should be the same for the negro. This plea of the negro is not radical, but conservative, sane and right, and under God, it should be made until it is heard and granted.[11]

Baskervill's rationale for black voting and his list of citizenship rights insulted and distressed Waring, who refused to publish Baskervill's letter. Instead Waring sought the advice of G. Croft Williams, a South Carolina leader in the postwar effort to improve race relations. Waring insisted that the archdeacon's views were "not conservative" but rather demonstrated an "aggressive note" and revealed a disconcerting "lack of judgment." Seeking confirmation in his judgment, Waring sent a copy of Baskervill's letter to Williams stating, "If Baskervill is running with or toward the extremists, it ought to be possible to set him right by good counsel, along the lines you and Prof. Morse have in mind for treatment of the question." Croft Williams and Josiah Morse were both professors at South Carolina College, Williams a sociology professor and Morse a philosophy and psychology professor. Both men represented South Carolina in the new postwar, regional interracial-cooperation effort that became the CIC. Waring no doubt had Williams's and Morse's interracial activities in mind when he consulted Williams, believing that the mission of the developing CIC was consistent with his desire to quell Baskervill's notion of expanding citizenship rights. Waring cast his refusal to publish Baskervill's comments as a defense of the Episcopal Church's reputation "for sanity and conservative thought." Knowing the influence black religious leaders had in their community, Waring did not want a black church leader espousing ideas that contradicted and challenged the white establishment.[12]

Croft Williams granted the *Charleston Evening Post* editor the affirmation he sought. Agreeing with Waring's decision not to publish Baskervill's letter because he believed it would create a tremendously negative reaction, Williams added that he believed Baskervill was "treading on very dangerous ground." He promised to speak with Bishop William A. Guerry about Baskervill and "see what can be done to either bring him into a different state of mind or [to dispose] of his leadership under the aegis of the Episcopal name."[13] Apparently the "state of mind" that so offended these two white reformers was Baskervill's straightforward insistence that voting restrictions not be based on race, a simple restatement of the Fifteenth Amendment.

This exchange between Waring and Williams illustrates the paternalism of white supremacy that white progressives embraced. Resolutely these men exercised white domination over Baskervill by silencing his views, questioning his character, and influencing his supervisor in the name of keeping peace and order. Williams's active leadership in the emerging regional interracial-cooperation movement also testifies to the paternalism underpinning this movement. The presence of a black majority in South Carolina caused white reformers, like Waring and Williams, to perceive any African American voting as a threat to white political control. If rival white factions divided and formed a voting coalition with black voters, they reasoned, white control would end. Such a scenario, they feared, would hand the balance of political power to a small group of black swing voters. So whites constantly used white supremacy to exclude blacks and warn other whites against the temptation to fracture white solidarity. As turmoil mounted in the immediate postwar era, William W. Ball, editor of *The State*, concluded that with increased black activism and protest for political rights, it was "highly necessary that white solidarity be unbroken." Moreover, Ball concluded expectantly, "when the time of quiet returns, as it will return some day, division will not be so menacing."[14]

As Baskervill's letter, which he attempted to make public, demonstrated, black reformers wanted a public hearing for their demands. Rather than continuing to suffer silently or talking only among themselves, African American reformers organized forums to present their frustrations to white officials. In July 1919, Nathaniel F. Haygood opened his church, Sydney Park, for one of these meetings, billed as an interracial conference. Haygood, a prominent Columbia minister, had addressed the February gathering that followed the welcome-home parade of the 371st Infantry Regiment. At that public event celebrating black soldiers' battlefield contribution to the war, Haygood asserted that African Americans wanted democracy at home just as they had fought for it in Europe. Evidence of expanding democracy, he insisted, would be blacks serving on juries and in the local police departments.[15] Just a few months later, Haygood again asserted his leadership by bringing the community to his church. Filled to overflowing, the Sydney Park Church hosted its congregation and other interested community members. Columbia's black reformers planned the conference, invited prominent white leaders including Governor Cooper, and promoted the event as an opportunity for the races to learn more about each other. I. S. Leevy chaired the meeting, which was characterized by "utter frankness" and "plain speaking."[16] As the organization of this event demonstrated, black reformers initiated most of the interracial-cooperation events where whites often responded with lukewarm indifference.

African Americans who gathered to be heard raised a broad spectrum of concerns. Bethel AME Church's new pastor, Turner H. Wiseman, immediately became a voice for change. Given Bethel's prominence in the Seventh AME District (South Carolina), the bishop had selected an experienced leader to pastor Bethel after the previous minister, Dr. A. W. Timmons, died in the influenza epidemic of 1918. A Spanish-American War veteran and native of Missouri, Wiseman had most recently lived in Oklahoma City, where he took an active leadership role in Oklahoma's civilian war effort. Wiseman served as treasurer of his county council of defense and the federal food administrator for Oklahoma's black population. At the July meeting in Columbia, Wiseman voiced concern about a perennial problem, police brutality. Wiseman detailed the common problem African Americans confronted when dealing with the police: the assumption of their guilt. He explained that the most law-abiding black citizen could not turn to local law enforcement for help when victimized by crime for fear of becoming the accused.[17]

A white participant, Judge Kimball, responded defensively to Wiseman's concerns, justifying the police actions and suggesting the police used force only when necessary. Rather than discuss seriously the long-term problem that Wiseman highlighted, Kimball countered that any problems between blacks and the Columbia police were generated by former black soldiers who returned with "foolish notions in their heads." Just that week, Kimball insisted, three or four former soldiers had been arrested for carrying and showing "obscene pictures." Other African Americans drew white reformers' attention to problems of inadequate black schools, health and sanitation problems, and inadequate accommodation on segregated streetcars and in Union Station. Although highlighting the problems did not solve them and white reformers generally only lectured African Americans about how they could solve these perceived problems with improved moral behavior, the meeting exemplified African Americans' optimism. The large attendance and black reformers' willingness to directly confront indifferent white leaders confirmed their hope and belief in the possibility of change. Many black reformers who organized and attended this conference had been included on Richard Carroll's troublemaker list that he had sent to Governor Cooper months earlier.[18]

Limiting black aspirations and controlling black reformers were key to facilitating white minority rule. African Americans' new, bold and public assertions, the signal of their increased political aspirations, shocked whites, who feared that they might be losing control of traditional African American community leaders. One black leader whom white business and religious leaders had long respected and confidently controlled was Richard Carroll. Carroll began an annual race conference in South Carolina in the early twentieth century. Gradually, the number of race conferences expanded to include one in each area of the state. Carroll imagined that by bringing together the "better element of both races," the annual conferences provided a forum for improving race relations. He always invited religious and business leaders, both black and white, as well as leading elected officials. He often invited the governor and usually a mayor. Carroll envisioned these conferences as opportunities for whites and blacks to express their concerns to each other and learn from each other. He always prided himself on hosting a conference that whites felt comfortable attending. He chose safe topics such as improved agricultural techniques, prohibition, evangelism, and stopping the migration tide. Yet Carroll never discussed politics—consistently reminded whites that he never discussed politics.

No doubt Carroll anticipated that his annual race conference in 1919 would fit the usual cautious pattern, with an agenda devoted to topics that steered clear of controversy. On January 22, the race conference in Columbia commenced with more than one thousand in attendance. Rev. D. F. Thompson, one of the ministers who had protested the showing of *Birth of a Nation* in Columbia, delivered the keynote address. Thompson had been an avid supporter of the war, serving as the chair of Columbia's United War Work Campaign. White reformers had praised Thompson's persuasive tactics in selling war bonds to African Americans, but they were decidedly less enthusiastic about his attempt to rouse the black community with his address "Grievances of the Negro" now that the war had ended.[19]

Thompson's list of grievances, which he shared with the interracial crowd, was long. It included dismal education, inadequate accommodation on segregated rail- and streetcars, labor coercion in response to the labor shortage and out-migration, and injustices of the courts, especially being excluded from serving as jurors. Thompson bemoaned lynching as the "lowest form of barbarism." He insisted that it must be completely eliminated "if the democracy for which the negro fought is made safe." Thompson concluded his grievance list on the most sensitive issue. "We will not be satisfied until we can vote," Thompson pronounced emphatically.[20] The content and tone of Thompson's speech, while consistent with the concerns of most African American reformers, violated Carroll's central purpose for the race conference: promoting racial harmony and fostering goodwill with white leaders. Clearly the hope that generated black reformers' postwar momentum in 1919 overrode Carroll's usual controlling influence. Consequently, Carroll's conservative and cautious race conference became a source of controversy among whites in 1919. This is further evidence of how the war had changed interactions among black reformers and between white and black reformers.

When Carroll had his public opportunity, he clearly dissented from Thompson's insistence, contended that "we can't win by making demands." At the Greenwood race conference in March, Carroll adapted his address because of his expressed frustrations with black South Carolinians who continually looked to politics for answers. "Colored people are expecting too much from the victories in Europe," he lamented. He offered a Washingtonian refrain about looking inward to solve problems rather than looking outward. "We get our rights by evolution and not by revolution," Carroll believed. He advocated that African Americans solve their problems by obeying the laws, being honest and patient, and praying rather than pointing to the "faults and shortcomings" of whites.[21] Carroll's forceful denunciation of the other black reformers' message and tactics testifies to their frequency and potency.

Whites, accustomed to praising Carroll's race conferences, instead responded with alarm. T. D. Wood, cottonseed-oil mill owner from Fountain Inn, monitored the current circulating ideas and attitudes among black South Carolinians by attending Carroll's race conferences, even addressing one. After attending the February conference in Darlington and the March conference in Greenwood, Wood concluded that African American ministers were advocating "a very dangerous policy" by becoming interested in politics. Moreover, gauging their activity as significant, Wood noted that these ministers were enthusiastically received by large black audiences. He referred to them as "fire-eating fools," and he especially feared what might happen if the rhetoric about rights and opportunities persisted until black soldiers returned from the war. His proposed solution revealed that whites perceived this new burst of African American optimism as a threat to their control. With expected tenacity, Wood's proposal also divulged the strategy many whites envisioned using to reassert their control if needed.[22]

Convinced that African Americans' mounting bravado would lead to violent racial clashes, Wood insisted that South Carolina develop a state militia to protect white communities across the state. Revealing white supremacist attitudes of both paternalism and intolerance, he remarked that "we white people of SC owe both to ourselves and the negro to point to him the right road to travel." He also insisted, "when the wisdom of fools prevails" whites have every right to protect their economic interests and "teach them a lesson that will be very lasting."[23] If racial violence were to erupt, Wood had already anticipated its proximate cause would have been African Americans' challenge to the existing white supremacy rules. Therefore, he had already resolved to fend off any such challenge with violence.

Throughout 1919, rumors circulated widely that South Carolina needed to prepare for inevitable racial uprisings. Contemporaries used the term "race riot" to label a broad array of racial violence that erupted during and immediately after the war. Following demobilization of soldiers in 1919, the nation witnessed the outbreak of racial violence in more than twenty-five cities across the country. Several of these violent incidents captured national headlines when African Americans began defending themselves against white mobs who perpetrated the violence. The NAACP termed the summer of 1919 "the Red Summer" as violence erupted in Washington, D.C., Chicago, Charleston, South Carolina, Knoxville, Omaha, Elaine, Arkansas, and elsewhere. The South Carolina press covered these stories extensively.[24]

Editorial pages conveyed whites' anxiety and fueled their speculation that black soldiers returning to South Carolina, emboldened by their war experiences in France, would soon incite violence at home. Psychology professor Josiah Morse publicly articulated whites' central fear concerning returning black soldiers. In France these young men had all their "notions and habits concerning social equality contradicted and completely overturned," Morse lamented. Whites became consumed with restoring these soldiers to their prewar culture of segregation, acculturating them to a subordinate status, and destroying their pictures of French women; pictures that served as more "dangerous excitants than strong drink," Morse feared. Privately he emphasized that the tensions between blacks and whites could not be exaggerated. "The war has advanced and aroused the negro much farther and more rapidly than the whites are willing to adapt themselves," Morse, South Carolina's CIC representative, explained. Mounting tension between returning black soldiers and white civilians sparked incidents in several cities including Washington, D.C., where violence broke out in mid-July.[25]

In the midst of the rumored violence and heightened frustrations following the news of racial turmoil in the nation's capital, Turner H. Wiseman, pastor of Bethel AME Church in Columbia, preached a sermon to dissipate the tension. With his sermon Wiseman pursued seemingly contradictory ends, attempting to calm emotionally charged people without extinguishing their eagerness for change. Wiseman reminded his congregation that African Americans were living in a "crucial period" of their history, a time when black aspirations for greater equality and opportunity were meeting determined white resistance. He reasoned that because whites had a strong tendency to judge all blacks by the actions of a few, the careless action of one black man could lead to widespread violence and chaos. This flawed and stereotypical thinking by whites, he explained, demanded that all African Americans act with special care not to offend.[26]

Fearful that the crime of one black man would lead to indiscriminate white retribution against all African Americans, Wiseman advised his congregation, for their own safety, to abide by the segregation laws on the streetcars. He encouraged returning soldiers to destroy their souvenir photos of French women. Wiseman's sermon reveals that black reformers at times felt compelled to temper more strident challenges to white supremacy with realistic survival strategies. The white reporter monitoring the sermon understood Wiseman's advice as an endorsement of segregation that encouraged black subjugation to white rule. Yet listeners with a more sophisticated ear for theological tension and congregants attuned to the nuances of a message delivered to two audiences simultaneously understood his words less as an endorsement of segregation and more as a muted acknowledgment of its existing power. Wiseman wove into his cautious message of warning a prophetic word of encouragement to those who labored continually under the weight of racial oppression. "Somewhere all injustice is paid for," the minister assured his parishioners. Also, Wiseman reminded all in attendance that Sunday that there was only one standard for justice, and it applied to whites and blacks alike.[27]

Ironically, he delivered this sermon July 27 just hours before whites in Chicago attacked young black swimmers, drowning one boy and sparking even more deadly violence than in Washington. South Carolina newspapers widely reported the weeklong racial mayhem in Chicago that left twenty-three blacks and fifteen whites dead. As news from Chicago unfolded, fear and alarming rumors of violent racial confrontation escalated in South Carolina. Governor Cooper confirmed that racial tensions ran highest in Columbia in late July. Psychology professor Morse likened Columbia to a movie theater where someone had yelled "Fire!" Panic had replaced reason, and he cautioned that a stampede would soon trample everyone if cooler heads did not prevail. Not only were whites panicked by widely circulated rumors that African Americans were arming themselves, but many also became convinced that African Americans were trained, equipped, and actively preparing for a race war. Graydon, a

Columbia attorney, invited Cooper to come see for himself that returning black soldiers drilled daily in July at Allen University.[28]

Publicly, white and black reformers pleaded for calm. A group of black and white ministers met in late July and sought to reassure everyone that the racial cooperation that characterized the war effort could calm the existing unrest. The ministers published a joint resolution July 30 calling for "patience and forbearance under all circumstances." In another effort to bring order to increased chaos a self-appointed group of white reformers formed the Citizens' Committee. On August 1 these white leaders publicly proclaimed that, while alarmed by threatening rumors, they had investigated every allegation and offered whites assurances that blacks had no "organized attack" planned. Also they warned African Americans against allowing "incendiary speakers" from outside the state to address their gatherings. Despite public displays of calm and control, whites and blacks privately developed strategies for the anticipated violence. The Citizens' Committee knew hundreds of whites were arming themselves, and they neglected to publicize the developing plans for hiding white women and children in designated safe places if violence began. Graydon, who offered the governor evidence of black soldiers' preparation for a race war, provided this information to persuade state government to step in and arm the capital city's white population with a machine-gun battalion. Reflecting on the summer of 1919 half a century later, Modjeska Simkins, a young teacher at the time, reported that African Americans prepared to defend themselves by purchasing arms and ammunition from Charlotte and Atlanta. Fearful that whites would attack them, blacks held regular target practice in the residential community of Liberty Hill.[29]

Similar rumors of pending racial violence emerged from the South Carolina Piedmont, the predominantly white portion of the state. W. W. Klugh of Clemson College believed that African Americans in the area were actively compiling an arsenal. Perhaps African Americans' strategy for armed self-defense was dangerous, but it was legal. Since most local white dealers refused to sell black South Carolinians arms and ammunition, mail-order was their most viable means of purchase. Consequently, Klugh urgently wanted South Carolina, in cooperation with the federal postal authorities, to close this avenue of weapons supply to African Americans. John Gary Evans, a Spartanburg lawyer and former governor, pleaded with Cooper in late July 1919 to organize a state militia in preparation for potential racial violence. Agreeing that military preparation was desirable, Cooper worked with Washington to reestablish the National Guard and increase South Carolina's quota of soldiers.[30]

Into the fall, whites continued to complain about blacks' purchasing weapons. Within two months of Klugh's protest, local law enforcement from Oconee, a Piedmont county in the westernmost corner of the state, lodged similar complaints. The complaints demonstrated whites' expectation of racial violence and their fear of African Americans' armed resistance. W. H. Mattress, an African American man who owned a "good farm" two miles from Seneca, in Oconee County, ordered two rifles and ammunition from Sears, Roebuck in the fall of 1919. Mattress's family had recently experienced trouble with whites in Anderson, so he planned to help his family by securing weapons. He had also purchased a .45 Colt revolver from a black soldier. Anxious for the guns' arrival, Mattress visited the post office every day. His impatience caught the attention of local law enforcement, who prevented delivery of the package. Frustrated with the delay, Mattress left for Atlanta. Some Oconee residents believed his hurried trip was to purchase weapons and ammunition that he could not secure through the mail. While he was gone, the sheriff raided Mattress's home and seized a rifle and a shotgun—not exactly evidence of an arsenal. Convinced, however, that Mattress was preparing for an organized black assault on whites, Sheriff W. M. Alexander and Special Officer B. R. Moss contacted Cooper to obtain legal authority to seize the ammunition at the post office and banish Mattress from South Carolina. Cooper advised the Oconee officials to solicit support from within their community for Mattress's removal. Magistrate J. N. Todd drafted a resolution demanding that Mattress leave the county and had five whites and five black community members sign it. Sheriff Alexander met Mattress at the train station with the resolution and a show of force. Mattress left Oconee.[31] While whites across South Carolina begged the state to approve whites' armed self defense, they would not tolerate African Americans' armed defense and employed the state to sanction disarming blacks.

Rumors of a racial uprising, which had spiked in July and August in the immediate aftermath of violent racial turmoil in Washington, D.C., and Chicago, boiled over in October when racial violence in Elaine, Arkansas, captured national headlines. Violence in the rural Mississippi Delta community erupted when local law enforcement disturbed a private meeting of the Progressive Farmers and Household Union on September 30. This secretly organized union of black farmers sought a greater share of the profits for cotton tenant farmers and fairer, more open debt terms for sharecroppers. Chaos ensued, and the local sheriff panicked and issued a call for help to whites in surrounding Delta counties in Arkansas and Mississippi. By sunset October 1, six hundred to a thousand whites had arrived armed and ready to kill any African American who moved. For two days whites hunted and killed African Americans. They also captured, interrogated, and forced false confessions from terrified blacks. Once the violence subsided, official reports acknowledged twenty-five black and five white deaths. The widely circulated unofficial accounts, however, revealed that white mobs had killed many more blacks. The reported estimates ranged from scores to hundreds. The white power structure immediately began constructing a narrative that blamed African Americans for the riots by alleging that blacks were plotting to kill their white landowners, thus justifying whites' initial intervention. Although no evidence ever emerged to support this alleged plot, when the killing stopped, the arrests began, but only of the alleged killers of the few white victims.[32]

Daily the Arkansas massacre received front-page coverage in South Carolina newspapers and doubtless generated racial anxiety in the state. Coinciding with this coverage of unfolding racial violence in Arkansas, attorney M. L. Bonham and Sheriff P. K. McCully, both local white leaders from Anderson County, reported to Cooper in early October that they believed an undercurrent of fear and anxiety was about to erupt into violence. These allegations by Bonham and McCully were strikingly similar to the concerns white leaders Graydon and Evans had expressed in July, as though they were following the same script. In separate but complementary pleas, the men emphasized that African Americans in Anderson were well organized. The sheriff explained that Anderson's black residents were well prepared and ready to resist "any real or imaginary infringement of their rights." McCully complained that whites were unorganized and in need of state help and requested that Camp Jackson send them equipment. Bonham specifically requested a machine gun and assured the governor that Anderson had enough discharged white soldiers who could handle it.[33]

In October, allegations that African Americans were gathering arms accompanied rumors of pending violence. McCully relayed a story with all the appropriate villainous attributes: an influential minister, an outsider causing trouble, organized black soldiers, weapons, and ammunition. The Anderson sheriff's narrative indicated that a local hardware store refused to sell a black minister from Brooklyn any cartridges. Angered by the refusal, the minister allegedly pulled ammunition from his pocket, announcing he had plenty more, and boasted that he had five hundred black soldiers organizing for an emergency. Were returning black soldiers as intent upon and organized for a race war as numerous whites asserted? Were white communities as vulnerable and unorganized as these whites claimed? A measure of exaggeration, especially about the defenselessness and victimization of whites, likely accompanied the requests to the governor for military equipment. Nonetheless whites clearly felt their control was threatened. Their willingness to advocate state-sanctioned violence and military force to quell African Americans' expressed frustrations over injustice and inequity reveals both how severely whites felt that threat and how determined they were to curtail it.[34]

Although South Carolina did not erupt into violence in the summer and fall, as many anticipated, the concern that violence would break out was palpable. Throughout 1919, Cooper regularly received reports from across the state warning of possible violence. T. R. Waring, editor of the *Charleston Evening Post*, confessed privately that he was most terrified because whites had lost control of the situation and did not know what, if anything, blacks might be plotting. To remedy their ignorance Waring wanted every investigative power of the government, state and national, at whites' disposal, as well as a "drastic suppression of the organs of irritation [the black press]."[35] White leaders blamed influences outside the region as the catalyst for potential trouble. Influences they held most culpable included "outsiders," especially African Americans from New York; ideas that black soldiers brought home from France, especially notions of social equality; and the black press, particularly publications that advocated expanding democracy. Concerns that reached the governor universally blamed at least one of these outside sources. When white reformers speculated publicly and privately about potential racial violence, they blamed anyone other than black South Carolinians. Perhaps they imagined that if resistance, especially violent resistance, had local origins, they had failed as practitioners of paternalistic racial control. Moreover, black South Carolinians' direct assault against whites would have demonstrated defiance and independence, attributes inconsistent with the system of white supremacy.

Despite the fears, rumors, and speculation, the only racial violence in South Carolina in 1919 was initiated and perpetrated by white "outsiders" upon African American victims. On Saturday night, May 10, in Charleston, white sailors stationed at the Charleston Navy Yard rioted, killing three black men and seriously injuring dozens more with indiscriminate shooting and beatings. Conflict began around 9:30 at Harry Police's pool hall near the corner of Market and Charles streets in downtown Charleston. The mayhem was sparked by an exchange of harsh words between white sailors and black Charlestonians that escalated to shoving. The owner reported that all involved grabbed pool sticks and headed to the street. When the altercation moved outside, two sailors were injured, and Isaac Doctor, a local black man, soon lay dead in the street from a gunshot wound. All witnesses agreed that hundreds of sailors began the rampage after this. As the rioters moved south on King and Meeting streets, major downtown arteries, the mob grew and indiscriminate violence escalated. No one disputed that black residents and black property owners became the sailors' sole targets.[36]

Reports on Sunday morning, May 11, indicated that after most readers had gone to sleep Saturday night, more than two thousand white sailors rioted unrestrained through Charleston streets using weapons of every type. White witnesses stated that white sailors raided two shooting galleries (one on King Street and one on Market Street) soon after the pool hall incident and then used the small-caliber rifles and ammunition they stole against unsuspecting black civilians. They chased victims into alleys and shot them, and pulled others from streetcars and cabs. A white Charlestonian reported being traumatized by having to watch rampaging sailors board a trolley, take a black man off, beat him, and then shoot him. Sailors pulled William Brown, a chauffeur, from his car and shot him. Brown died a week later of his wounds. The third fatality was James Talbert, who died from multiple, close-range gunshot wounds. The youngest known victim appeared to be Peter Irving, a thirteen-year-old left paralyzed by a gunshot wound to the back. The severely injured black victims who sought medical treatment at nearby Roper Hospital also suffered from gunshot wounds. Yet many injuries went unreported because, as later reports confirmed, many others sought safety and treatment from family, friends, and neighbors.[37]

Around midnight the mob attacked Fredie's Central Shaving Parlor, a black-owned barbershop that served white customers. Powerless to halt the violence against civilians and private property for several hours, the Charleston police brought the Marines in soon after this destruction with orders to apprehend the navy personnel and restore order in the city, which they did by early morning. The aftermath of the vicious assault by returning white sailors on local black civilians did not lead to the same hand-wringing anxiety or finger pointing that had accompanied the fear that black soldiers would initiate violence. By contrast, *The State* diminished the significance of this particular mayhem. While all witnesses reported that white sailors had targeted blacks for their unprovoked, violent rampage, W. W. Ball, editor of *The State*, rejected the label "Charleston riot." The murderous pandemonium did not merit the serious label "riot," Ball reasoned, because the perpetrators were visitors and few local whites participated. Such an "unfortunate incident" could have occurred anywhere, he remarked dismissively.[38] When violence erupted in Charleston with white "outsiders" and black victims, the reporting and editorializing in South Carolina newspapers did not last for weeks as had been the case when white civilians died in racial conflicts outside the state.

The Charleston NAACP reacted against the indifference shown by whites. Harleston, president of the chapter, led a committee that conducted a separate investigation. Pushing the Navy to punish the perpetrators and compensate black businesses, Harleston shared the results of his investigation with Secretary of the Navy Josephus Daniels and Archibald Grimké, president of the Washington, D.C., NAACP and a Charleston native. Locally, the NAACP drew Mayor

140

Tristram Hyde's attention to the pervasive problems the black community faced and petitioned for long-term solutions. Charleston's black reformers called for the city to address some of the systemic problems and hire black police officers, improve housing and sanitation, and expand educational opportunities for African Americans. Nationally, Grimké pressured naval leaders to pay attention. Speaking personally to Adm. George Clark, Judge Advocate General for the U.S. Navy, Grimké highlighted the irony that the Charleston riot received so little attention when the Houston riot resulted in nineteen hangings and at least forty soldiers imprisoned for life. In Houston, two years earlier, the rioters were black and the civilian victims white. Until Grimké approached Admiral Clark, the judge was unfamiliar with the Charleston travesty. Ultimately, the navy punished six sailors and Charleston reimbursed Fredie's, the business that suffered the greatest damage.[39]

When racial violence victimized black South Carolinians, public discussion was wanting, but the frenzy that enveloped white South Carolinians in the summer and fall of 1919, of course, derived from fear that whites would be victims of racial violence. In addition to fears about blacks from outside the region and returning black soldiers, whites also were panicked by reading materials offered by the black press, particularly the *Crisis*, the *Messenger*, and the *Chicago Defender*. Philip Palmer, a white resident of Dorchester, the county adjacent to Charleston, worried that African Americans in the low country had been influenced by newspapers and magazines from outside the region with the "most incendiary appeals."[40]

The *Crisis*, the official magazine of the NAACP, was founded and edited by W. E. B. DuBois, who made the monthly part of his crusade for equality and racial justice. His strategy for using World War I to expand democracy at home was deeply embedded in the *Crisis* because he controlled its contents and wrote the editorials. This magazine, feared by whites, reached South Carolina because it accompanied NAACP membership. South Carolina experienced its greatest NAACP membership expansion in 1919 with the organization of several new branches. Columbia and Charleston, which had effectively organized by 1917, significantly increased their membership in 1919. The Charleston branch campaigned vigorously to meet its enrollment goal of one thousand. In the fall of 1918, Darlington began a branch. In 1919, Anderson, Beaufort, Orangeburg, and Florence chartered new branches. Rapid expansion reflected the organization's national effort to increase membership, especially in the South. Formal chartering of NAACP branches took great courage, since whites viewed them as unacceptable.[41]

Josiah Morse, who had developed a regional reputation as a key white advocate for "interracial cooperation" and a strong opponent of racial violence, viewed the NAACP as unacceptable and wished it would disappear. He regarded the NAACP as a hindrance to racial harmony that fostered white resistance. "The South is not going to be coerced or directed by a hostile organization that confines its effort almost exclusively to the Negro, and puts notions into his head," he explained to a colleague during the height of the 1919 racial tensions. Morse's reasoning reveals the commitment of white reformers to white supremacy. Morse, like other whites, refused to accept independent black leadership and political power. Nonetheless, he was an outspoken public leader against lynching, and he supported a greater state commitment to the education, welfare, and safety of African Americans. He expressed these views in his leadership positions on the board of the University Commission on Southern Race Questions and as a South Carolina leader of the CIC. Morse, who saw no inconsistency in embracing white supremacy and advocating black progress, often complained that his leadership and "mildly liberal" views attracted scorn from fellow South Carolinians and accusations that he was a communist.[42]

Morse merely loathed the NAACP and resented its presence and influence; other whites went further, threatening those who joined the NAACP and exacting retribution against those who exercised leadership in the organization. Professor M. H. Gassaway of Anderson came to understand the risk that accompanied NAACP leadership. Gassaway, homeowner, educator, husband, and father, understood the frustration and despair of living what many considered an "exemplary life" only to experience the powerful intimidation whites levied against African Americans whose success threatened white supremacy. For thirty years he had been principal of an African American school in Anderson, his lifelong home. He and his wife, who taught at the school, had seven children. Gassaway boasted that the children had never been in any trouble.

Three of their sons served in the army, one son serving as a radio sergeant in France. Later, one son went to study law at Howard University, another attended Morehouse College, and one remained in Anderson to operate a broom factory. Gassaway's economic and professional success attracted the resentment of whites, who found an outlet for expressing their frustration when Gassaway became president of the local branch of the NAACP.[43]

After the Anderson NAACP became officially chartered in March 1919, a process Gassaway initiated soon after the war ended, members began securing private funds for the local black schools. Their efforts lengthened the school term and created fifteen summer classes for illiterate adults. The local NAACP also helped returning soldiers in their transition to civilian life. Specifically, they fought against Anderson's efforts to compel the labor of newly released black soldiers by issuing them work cards and exploiting vagrancy ordinances. Gassaway appealed to whites' economic self-interest and explained that the city's aggressive efforts to compel labor would simply lead the young men to leave the area permanently. From the chapter's inception, however, Vick Cheshire, editor of the *Anderson Daily Tribune*, resented the Anderson NAACP and fomented antipathy against it and against Gassaway, who otherwise enjoyed the respect of Anderson's mayor, superintendent, and chief of police.[44]

Cheshire was a virulent racist who actively supported Cole Blease, political champion of South Carolina's white working class. As a self-proclaimed spokesman for white laborers, Cheshire resented Gassaway and used black informants to uncover his NAACP connection and activities. Also, Cheshire used his editorial column to galvanize community resentment against Gassaway by warning that he challenged the principles of white supremacy and threatened to undermine white control. The editor revealed that Gassaway had organized and served as president of the Anderson NAACP, which had invited a black New York minister, S. W. Blatcher, to speak in the fall of 1919, when anxiety about "outside" black influences ran high. Confronted with this information, Gassaway acknowledged it but refused to resign and disband the Anderson NAACP as Cheshire expected.[45]

The frustrated editor increased the pressure on Gassaway by asking the school board to fire him, arguing that as a principal he influenced the entire black community with unacceptable ideas.

When the board refused to yield to Cheshire's pressure and remove a long-term principal with a successful record, he escalated the intimidation. Cheshire harassed Gassaway for two months but came to realize that, because Gassaway had the support of local white leaders, he could not prevail with quiet, behind-the-scenes maneuvering alone. So the editor resorted to inflammatory rhetoric and threats of violence. On the *Tribune*'s editorial page Cheshire charged Gassaway with teaching social equality and advocating for blacks' political rights. To incite whites' anger, Cheshire claimed this meant Gassaway advocated black men's right to sit beside a white man's daughter on a passenger coach, eat at the table in a Pullman dining car with a white man's sister, and occupy the sleeping car of a white man's daughter and wife.

Gassaway denied these inflammatory accusations but admitted he had spoken out for the rights of his people. He said that Cheshire's efforts succeeded in inflaming the "poor class of whites," and death threats against the principal followed. Gassaway's superintendent pleaded with him to leave South Carolina, revealing that Cheshire had personally approached him with dire warnings. Cheshire threatened to kill Gassaway if he did not leave or if a mob did not kill him first. Gassaway's friends and family, who believed he faced imminent danger, begged him to leave, and he did, fleeing to Cleveland, Ohio, for refuge. Later, from the safe distance of Cleveland, Gassaway told a reporter that he wanted the "whole country to know how the whites of Anderson, S.C., treat her respectable colored citizens."[46]

Gassaway epitomized the values white reformers advocated; he was hardworking, self-sufficient, educated, a homeowner who had raised responsible and independent children, and had a long-term marriage to one woman. Yet the commitment of Morse and other white reformers to white dominance privileged the value of white supremacy over all others, diminishing Gassaway's accomplishments and jeopardizing his life. While reformers abhorred the threats and violence that Cheshire and others used, they shared with them the foundational value of white supremacy, which minimized the influence of their objections to how white supremacy could be expressed. In this case, white supremacy empowered Cheshire to exploit the resentment of Anderson whites who had fewer accomplishments than a successful, well-educated black leader like Gassaway. Moreover, it emphasized why Gassaway and other black reformers had turned to the NAACP and the ballot. Edwin Harleston, president of the Charleston NAACP, emphasized this strategy at the Tenth Anniversary Conference of the NAACP in Cleveland during the summer of 1919. Of all the NAACP's activities, Harleston explained, "extension of the franchise" offered the most promise. "After all methods have been tried, and after all the plans that we have devised have been used, it all reverts back to the ballot for our salvation," he concluded.[47]

White reformers' rage against the NAACP found national expression with South Carolina representative James F. Byrnes. In an August congressional speech, Byrnes forcefully signaled an end to white reformers' wartime cooperative attitude. From the floor of the U.S. House, Byrnes declared, "This is a white man's country, and will always remain a white man's country." He railed against African American magazines and newspapers published by organizations headquartered outside the South for questioning white supremacy and fomenting violence that had threatened social stability following the armistice. He blamed the circulation of material from the *Crisis*, the *Messenger*, and black newspapers from northern cities for every perceived problem in the South. He claimed that W. E. B. DuBois's editorial "Returning Soldiers," in the May 1919 issue of the *Crisis*, violated the Espionage Act because the renowned intellectual challenged his readers to democratize their own government—a government, DuBois argued, that had turned a blind eye to lynching, disfranchised its citizens, promoted ignorance, and stolen from its citizens. The congressman from Aiken argued that such language deserved the attention of the attorney general, from whom Byrnes requested a formal judgment to determine if DuBois's confrontational language constituted a provocation for resisting the U.S. government. Byrnes constructed an argument that blamed the black press in Washington and Chicago for inciting riots in those cities, claiming that "negro leaders had deliberately planned a campaign of violence."[48]

In addition to claiming that the black press promoted radicalism, cooperated with communists, and plotted violent resistance, Byrnes was also outraged that editors like DuBois and A. Philip Randolph, editor of the *Messenger*, had drawn a connection between African Americans' wartime patriotic service and citizenship rights that included political and social equality. Byrnes emphasized that nothing about the recent war experience had persuaded whites that they should accept racial equality. If African Americans thought their participation in the war entitled them to political and social equality, then, Byrnes concluded, they should leave the country, and their departure would be "facilitated by the white people." If that defense of white supremacy was not clear enough, Byrnes continued with a thinly veiled threat that ninety million white people were determined to withhold racial equality from ten million blacks. Byrnes claimed that the South had neither employment nor room for blacks who had been "inoculated with the desire for political equality or social equality." As he concluded his provocative rant, Byrnes asserted, "as to social equality, God Almighty never intended" it; therefore, "that which the Creator did not intend man can not make possible."[49]

Byrnes's vitriolic speech before his colleagues in Congress served both as a figurative and literal announcement that wartime cooperation, tepid though it was, with black reformers had ended. During the war, whites had accepted African American reformers' initiatives either reluctantly, as affirmative expressions of patriotism, or grudgingly, as rewards earned for services that white reformers wanted them to render. At the war's conclusion, whites no longer needed cooperative black reformers as collaborators. Since African Americans never conceived of their war-related activism as a subservient response to appease whites, they did not terminate their push for full citizenship rights when the war ended and whites quit asking for help. Divergent expectations quickly emerged among white and black reformers as war demobilization proceeded. Whites anticipated a return to the prewar status, where they felt comfortably in control. They did not expect to continue the wartime "appeasement" with black reformers.

In contrast, African Americans anticipated pushing forward not stopping or looking back. For their patriotism and sacrifice, they expected compensation, and they frequently articulated the specifics: improved education, job opportunities, transportation facilities, health care, and housing; justice from the police and courts; and, most importantly, political rights to make the other goals possible. The clash of reformers' expectations became most evident when black reformers' call for voting rights met whites' escalating fear of racial violence. The harder African Americans pushed to realize their hopes, the more resolute whites' resistance became. Simultaneously, whites reasserted their dedication to white supremacy's ideals and its practical structure of white political, economic, and social control over the state's black majority. For African Americans in the Palmetto State, the restraints imposed by white supremacy prevailed against the short-lived war-related opportunities.

Racial violence that erupted across the nation, although usually initiated by whites, galvanized white Americans against black aspirations, leading them to conflate all forms of resistance with their heightened anxiety over socialism and communism exhibited in the Red Scare. Substantial improvement in African Americans' economic condition would be difficult as long as South Carolina's influential and wealthy elite benefited from African Americans' abundant and cheap labor. Determined to retain white dominance and further their own economic self-interest, elite whites exercised their political power to keep black labor plentiful and inexpensive. Their commitment to and dependence upon a "cheap labor" economic strategy, however, once again offered African Americans some leverage. During the war and long afterward, African Americans exercised another approach to dealing with their subordination: migration out of the state and region. White South Carolinians' reaction to the black migration north revealed the depth of whites' preoccupation with preserving cheap labor.

Chapter 6

The Great Migration

White reformers welcomed economic opportunities generated by the nation's mobilization for World War I. Yet, by eroding white supremacy's insularity, wartime opportunities also spawned a new, and less welcomed, instability. Among other things, the interjection of the federal government into local issues disturbed white domination of existing racial relationships. Complicating whites' ability to control political, economic, and social relationships, the wartime threats to white supremacy deeply troubled white South Carolinians. Black Carolinians emerged as agents of change and, during wartime, obtained needed leverage, despite the structural impediments of segregation and disfranchisement. Such a reconfiguration of power relations contradicted white supremacy's basic premise of white control. Between World War I and the Great Depression, hundreds of thousands of African Americans offered another challenge to white supremacy. They exercised control over themselves in open defiance of many white southerners' wishes and left the South.

Stimulated by wartime circumstances, black migration continued and accelerated during the decade of peace that followed. By the simple act of leaving, black southerners put whites in the defensive and very uncomfortable posture of reacting to change rather than initiating it. The war-stimulated economic opportunities for African Americans outside the South empowered blacks to erode whites' economic control scheme. Migration especially threatened whites whose economic prosperity rested on low wages made possible by maintaining an abundant, undereducated labor force. Thus, black migration challenged white supremacy fundamentally because it revealed that African Americans had a means of escaping white control.

This loomed as an especially crucial issue in South Carolina, where whites labored to control a black majority. The precarious control held by South Carolina's white minority made whites sensitive to changes that altered the racial status quo. Collectively, white South Carolinians shared a desire to regain control, assert their authority, and restore the "appropriate" social hierarchy, but they disagreed with each other on precisely how to do this.[1] Consequently the debate among whites over black migration became a public dispute about restoring white control over a situation that whites believed had been created by outside market forces and blacks' initiative. While whites shared an impulse to assert their prerogative in reestablishing their racial control, this collective desire did not unite them in a common strategy or a mutually agreed-upon outcome. Whites' unifying commitment to white supremacy created a misleading consensus by rhetorically blurring the tangible economic and class divisions among whites. Black migration provoked a crisis among white South Carolinians that exposed conflicting economic interests and revealed social strains that the white supremacy consensus attempted to conceal. Whites' differing judgments about black migration emerged from their conflicting class interests. Although reluctant to defend their economic interests openly, all whites readily promoted solutions to the perceived migration crisis that bolstered their own interests while concealing their self-interested justifications behind the shared rhetoric of white supremacy.

Large white landowners, especially cotton planters who relied on black sharecroppers, and the merchants who served this agricultural interest, had the most forceful and immediate response. Dependent on a surplus of black laborers, landowners panicked at the specter of financial losses they feared black migration would produce. They desperately hoped to slow, if not completely stop, the out-migration of blacks from South Carolina. Therefore, one facet of whites' debate about migration included a search for the root cause of the exodus of tens of thousands of African Americans. Whites who hoped that retaining black laborers would further their own economic interests imagined that by identifying the cause of migration they could promptly control and severely limit the flow of blacks leaving the Palmetto State. Numerous possibilities surfaced to explain black migration. White reformers, on the other hand, seized upon the black migration debate as an opportunity to promote their larger reform agenda. Reformers argued that they could affirm white control with a better strategy. By rejoicing at black migration rather than lamenting it, reformers anticipated South Carolina losing its black majority and becoming a whiter state. Thus they took a position on migration that opposed the landowners' interests. As white reformers and agricultural interests debated black migration, the discourse emerged as a question over how best to defend white supremacy. Advocating two conflicting solutions—slowing or stopping migration versus encouraging migration to produce a whiter state— differing groups of whites debated their positions in terms of white supremacy.

Embedded within the debate about whether to discourage or promote black out-migration was an extensive discussion about its causes. Disagreement over the precise reason African Americans left the state and region led to sharp disagreement about the appropriate response to the exodus. Some whites reasoned that an accurate assessment was a prerequisite for finding a resolution to the perceived crisis. Yet whites' range of explanations for the migration served more as suppositions bolstering their relative positions in the ongoing racial dialogue among whites than as reasoned conclusions. Interest in understanding the black migration, of course, extended far beyond white South Carolinians' narrow interests. The federal government, other southerners, residents of recipient northern cities, and African American reformers at the state and national level expressed a keen interest in understanding the impetus for black migration. South Carolinian black reformers who engaged in this public debate asserted their interpretations of the black migration as a means toward achieving their own central purpose: equality and justice.

Following emancipation, some freed people left the South to start new lives in other regions, particularly the West, but 90 percent of all African Americans remained in the South, moving only within counties and states. For half a century after the Civil War, migration of African Americans from the South steadily continued, but the overall proportion of black southerners who left the region remained small.[2] Unique circumstances ushered in by World War I, however, created exceptional opportunities in northern industries that unprecedented numbers of black southerners explored. The Great War had the twin effects of abruptly halting immigration from Europe and stimulating demand for labor because of America's drive for military preparedness.

By 1916, serious labor shortages persuaded northern industrial employers to recruit black southerners, an option ignored in the past because European immigration had provided ample, cheap white labor. War-related migration, occurring from 1916 to 1919, launched the Great Migration, the twentieth-century population movement that redistributed significant portions of the African American population from the rural South to industrial northern cities. Exact figures on the migration of black southerners to the North are not available for the war years, but scholars of the migration as well as casual observers agree that the numbers were substantial. From 1916 to 1919, approximately a half million African Americans migrated from the rural South. The stream of migration that began during the war continued and escalated during the 1920s. Between the end of World War I and the beginning of the Great Depression the number of black migrants doubled to one million.[3]

From 1910 to 1920, approximately 74,500 African Americans migrated from South Carolina. Migration from the Palmetto State peaked during the war and tapered off at its conclusion. But the agricultural devastation created by the boll weevil's arrival in South Carolina renewed the migration again in the early 1920s. South Carolina State Agricultural College conducted a study that revealed that 50,000 black South Carolinians migrated from forty-one of the state's forty-six counties during the six months between November 1922 and May 1923. One county reported losing 3,600 African Americans, 22 percent of its entire population, in the rapid exodus. Moreover, the *New York Times* reported that 3 percent of South Carolina's black farm population left the state in early 1923. During the 1920s, approximately 204,300 black South Carolinians moved north, about three times the number that had left the previous decade. The individual and collective decisions of African Americans to leave South Carolina for opportunities outside the region provoked an economic and social crisis among whites.[4]

In South Carolina, where whites intentionally excluded African Americans from formal positions of power, blacks, as a general rule, could not command the respect of the state's white power brokers or readily effect change in the larger society. But blacks physically leaving the South ignited a passionate controversy among whites and focused much attention on the African American community. White South Carolinians not only viewed African Americans' migration as a defiant challenge to white supremacy but also recognized the adverse economic consequences of migration, since African American laborers remained essential to the production of cotton, the South's chief economic pursuit and the source of white landowners' profits. South Carolina's postwar governor, Robert A. Cooper, confessed that to a "considerable extent the economic prosperity of the South depends upon negro labor." Moreover, the Georgia Bankers Association considered the migration more costly than "General Sherman on his march to the sea."[5] African Americans comprised two-thirds of South Carolina's agricultural labor force. Thus significant disruptions in that labor market meant serious difficulty or even financial ruin for white landowners, especially large landowners who depended heavily on black laborers. The economic loss from black laborers' leaving the region compounded problems inherent in the structure of the southern economy, which depended on an abundant supply of laborers to keep labor costs very low. Blacks' migration from the region significantly reduced the supply of agricultural laborers available to white landowners, fundamentally threatening their cheap labor strategy.[6]

African Americans' migration from the South captured the attention not only of white southern landowners who relied on African American labor but also of Americans everywhere. Residents of the urban industrial centers where black southerners began moving were especially aware of this unprecedented movement of people. Since the migration coincided with World War I, the federal government also became interested in understanding the dynamics of this internal population redistribution, which many policymakers feared would impinge on war-mobilization efforts. Before the United States entered the war, northern laborers complained about competition from African Americans, fearing their willingness to work for lower wages would drive all wages down. Such complaints drew the Department of Labor into an investigation of both the causes and the probable consequences of the migration. The magnitude of African

American migration led Woodrow Wilson's secretary of labor, William B. Wilson, to create a Division of Negro Economics within the Labor Department. Secretary Wilson appointed George E. Haynes, professor of economics and sociology at Fisk University, director of the new division. During 1917, Haynes supervised an investigation of the migration and published a sweeping report, *Negro Migration in 1916–17.* Concurrent with Haynes's federally sanctioned study was another study funded by a private foundation, the Carnegie Endowment for International Peace. As part of a larger series on social issues sponsored by the endowment, the Carnegie study, *Negro Migration during the War,* was spearheaded by Emmett J. Scott, secretary-treasurer of Howard University and special adviser to the secretary of war on matters relating to the interest of African Americans.[7]

Both of these contemporary studies addressed the central question of why African Americans were leaving the South. Both studies identified economic motives as the principal cause of the wartime migration. The labor markets in the North, which suffered from wartime labor shortages, provided the pull of higher wages while workers in the South simultaneously felt the push from the region's depressed cotton prices in 1914–1915, the destruction of the cotton crop by the boll weevil in parts of the South, the unusual flood destruction in 1915, and tight credit. In the Carnegie study, Scott concluded that the confluence of these two divergent labor markets, one thriving and one depressed, explained why African Americans left the South for the North and why World War I became the impetus for their departure. "The economic motive," Scott argued, "stands among the foremost reasons for the decision of the group [African Americans] to leave the South."[8]

Charles S. Johnson, a young black sociologist, researched and wrote extensively on the labor movement as a graduate student at the University of Chicago and as research director for the Chicago Urban League. Johnson stressed economic motivations as the cause of the Great Migration even more emphatically than Scott and Haynes. Yet while all three major contemporary studies of the Great Migration emphasized economic issues, these black scholars also identified a range of social factors, including inadequate education, poor housing, lack of justice in the courts, Jim Crow laws, cruel treatment from law enforcement officers, disfranchisement, and lynching as contributing factors to the African American impulse for northward migration. Central to the social, often termed "secondary," causes of migration was the racial oppression that African Americans suffered in the South. Yet Johnson accurately stressed, and others readily agreed, that racial oppression had always characterized black southerners' experience. Therefore, these experts argued, white oppression could not explain the timing of African Americans' migration from the South.[9]

Historical scholarship on the black migration, while acknowledging the validity of these contemporaries' emphasis on economic factors as a cause of the migration, has reconsidered the relative importance of social factors. James Grossman, in his seminal study of black migration, argues for a more complex analysis of the impetus for black migration. While agreeing that changing wartime labor markets help explain both the timing of new economic opportunities that became available during World War I and the enthusiasm African Americans demonstrated by so readily pursuing them, Grossman insists that understanding African Americans' motivations for moving north also requires an examination of noneconomic factors. Social motives, which scholars of the period and other analysts who drew heavily from their studies called secondary, were perhaps not as ancillary as the original research suggested. When the long lists of social or secondary factors are woven together, they become more than a compendium of independent reasons some blacks were dissatisfied. Taken together, the numerous social factors identify a pervasive and oppressive social and economic system that drove many African Americans to pursue opportunities elsewhere. In an analysis of the migration, published in *The State*, one correspondent agreed that economic opportunity largely explained the migration, but the writer also recognized that African Americans pursued the opportunities because "in the breast of so many there [was] a rankling sense of the injustices to which they [had] been subjected for so many years." Thus the migration of African Americans from the South caused contemporary observers and later historians to examine the source of black southerners' underlying dissatisfaction.[10]

William T. Andrews, an African American lawyer, real estate broker, and editor of the *Sumter Defender*, spoke at Richard Carroll's eleventh annual race conference in February 1917. Andrews forcefully and directly delineated reasons African Americans migrated from the South. As a graduate of both Fisk University and Howard Law School and one of a dozen or fewer black lawyers in South Carolina, Andrews demonstrated an exceptionalism that contributed to his boldness as he addressed a racially mixed audience. The audience included Governor Richard Manning and other white leaders who attended expecting deferential black speakers at the annual conference known for its conservatism. Unwilling to tailor his remarks to appease the audience, Andrews began by stating that blacks left South Carolina because of the "destruction of [their] political privileges and curtailment of [their] civil rights." His audience probably did not want the history lesson he offered. Nonetheless, Andrews recounted the brief era of black enfranchisement during Reconstruction that offered the African American a hope that dissolved into discontent when the "suffrage was rudely and violently wrested from him, his political rights destroyed." Andrews also lamented the rise of segregation and the restriction of blacks' civil rights as "statute after statute [was] passed to curtail the rights of the Negro." The courts failed to provide justice for African Americans, Andrews emphasized, so they were at the mercy of individual, lawless white citizens as well as the police and magistrates. "In tragic truth it must be confessed," Andrews explained of whites' response to lynch mobs, that no blacks enjoyed any protection when in the hands of the "bloody minded white man."[11]

As if his speech were a brief before the courts, Andrews continued with his well-organized presentation. He supported his assertions with detailed evidence of "almost unendurable conditions" in the Jim Crow railcars, residential restrictions, and the deplorable conditions of public schools. Andrews elaborated on the condition of public schools by citing the inadequate funding that drove away competent teachers, provided only a three-month school term on average, and created dangerously overcrowded schools. Underlying every problem, economic hardships, particularly the low wages agricultural laborers received, contributed to the black migration. For decades, blacks had worked for wages that provided inadequately for life's necessities. Moreover, as Andrews explained, continually receiving poor compensation encouraged the behaviors whites complained about incessantly: "no stimulus to develop greater efficiency

. . . [and] habits of indifference, shiftlessness and heedless spending."
Andrews understood that higher wages and opportunity incentives
could easily remedy these concerns. Whites, by contrast, insisted
that black laborers were "inefficient, lazy and unreliable," attributes
they believed provided evidence of blacks' racial inferiority and lack
of moral character. Andrews also pointed out that state law prohibited blacks and whites from working together in textile mills, eliminating alternative employment for black workers. He warned that
this trend would continue as long as white politicians would "pose as
champions of the poor, white working man" and make similar promises to white workers in other businesses. Such promises would eventually abolish all job opportunities for blacks where whites wanted
the jobs. Consequently, Andrews concluded, the enticing possibilities that lured blacks outside the region offered not only higher
wages but also "opportunity, a man's change and real freedom."[12]

The State covered Richard Carroll's 1917 race conference extensively, publishing Carroll's speech on migration but omitting any
coverage of Andrews's candid speech beyond mentioning the title
and place in the program. Andrews's speech became public because
the *Nashville Globe*, a black weekly, published the complete text. Before the war ended, Andrews moved to Baltimore. No doubt Andrews
had a personal understanding of the reasons African Americans migrated. In the 1920s he moved to New York, where he joined the
national staff of the NAACP.

Although their presentation styles varied greatly, Carroll fundamentally agreed with Andrews's thesis. Carroll spoke on the same
topic at the conference and also emphasized that blacks migrated
because of inadequate protection of life and property, inadequate access to a satisfactory public education, substandard wages, and poor
housing. Carroll also denounced white politicians who consistently
exploited white supremacy and "[rode] the negro into office." Yet
Carroll employed a cautious tone that never accused whites in general. Rather he "pleaded with the white people to give the negro
justice where merited." He denied that there was any appropriate
role for blacks in politics, suggested that only a portion of whites
perpetrated these injustices, and told blacks that they could solve
many of these problems by obeying the law, improving their home
life, and giving more attention to "moral and religious uplift." More-

over, Carroll always linked his discussion of migration to a strong recommendation that blacks stay in the South, where he claimed they were better off.[13]

As a black minister employed as a missionary for the Southern Baptist Convention, a white denomination, Carroll traveled across the state preaching the virtues of the South as the land of hope for blacks. "This wholesale movement of the negroes to the North is sad," he proclaimed. "It is a terrible blow to the white South as well as to the black South at this time."[14] Accusations abounded within the black community that Carroll was on the white man's payroll and acting in the interest of wealthy white landowners. William Sinclair, financial secretary for the Frederick Douglass Hospital in Philadelphia, had informed the leadership of the NAACP that Carroll was on "bad terms with the whole colored population of the State." In his conference speech, Carroll directly addressed other blacks' mistrust of him. "My own race has not treated me right," Carroll acknowledged. "They have called me a traitor, Democrat, bootlicker and trimmer." He of course denied the charges and emphasized that while he proclaimed the benefits of staying in the South, he had also pleaded with whites to grant justice to blacks.[15]

Carroll was not alone in strongly discouraging black migration. Delegates to the Twenty-Eighth Annual Tuskegee Negro Conference in January 1917, just weeks before Carroll's own conference, trumpeted the same message. The Tuskegee conference resolved that blacks should remain in the South and cooperate with whites for the betterment of their own future.[16] Yet as T. J. Wise, an African American from Greenwood, expressed eloquently in a letter to *The State*, cooperating with whites was difficult since most whites ignored or rejected African Americans' reasoning about migrating. Wise warned the concerned white South Carolinians that "not ten out of a 100 negroes will tell any white man why they are going North" because the truth indicted whites. Expressing his interpretation of the black migration to a white audience, Wise suggested that blacks were leaving the South because they wanted "protection of person and property." Furthermore, he insisted, "They say they are tired of hearing continually, 'This is a white man's country,' . . . They say they are tired of their ignorance; not even getting the amount of school tax for their enlightenment they are forced to pay. . . . They say they are tired of being pointed out in court houses as scullions by barristers who might not win their cause without this cheap appeal to prejudice." Wise continued his list of grievances against the white-dominated social order by recounting African Americans' frustration with being used as scapegoats for all the South's ills. Politicians become popular, Wise lamented, with their "unabridged vocabulary for abusing negroes," and white men who love justice are labeled "negro lover[s]." Wise believed this accounted for the public silence of whites and private whispers of, "'Do the best you can. I will be ostracized if I (speak in your favor) espouse justice.'" In addition to explaining why African Americans willingly left a society that offered them a poor quality of life, Wise reiterated the most obvious reason that African Americans migrated to the North: they wanted better wages. Wise concluded his letter with a humble refrain whose connotations of equality carried thundering challenges to the South's social structure of inequality. Ultimately, Wise surmised, a black man leaves the South because "he wants something of this world, since his Father created it. It's natural to seek."[17]

Other black reformers authenticated Wise's account of oppression and injustice. For example, Turner H. Wiseman, pastor of the Bethel AME Church in Columbia, was known for working during the summer of 1919 to relieve heightened racial tensions that characterized the postwar months. When questioned about his knowledge of African Americans' motives for migrating, Wiseman replied that "better wages and better living conditions and better schools are the drawing cards." Moreover, he indicated, some members of the Bethel congregation left South Carolina because they "want[ed] to vote and want[ed] to be men."[18] Lazarus A. Hawkins, an African American real estate broker and an officer in Columbia's NAACP, confirmed that better housing conditions enticed black South Carolinians to migrate because home ownership was so difficult for African Americans to obtain in the state. Hawkins claimed that it was "almost impossible for a negro to buy a three or five room house" in Columbia. Instead, homes in African American neighborhoods were owned by groups of five, six, and sometimes twenty families per house.[19]

An African American physician, John H. Goodwin, argued that blacks migrated north because of low wages, poor housing conditions, inferior schools, and intimidation in South Carolina. Goodwin, also an officer in the Columbia NAACP, supported his assertion with an account of two prominent black farmers from Edgefield who attended a Republican convention and then became objects of whites' threats and intimidation until they left the county. Goodwin claimed this led other, less prosperous African American tenants of Edgefield who worked for white landowners to leave as well. "If negro farmers, who were fairly well to do, had to leave the county because they attended a Republican convention, what chance would they, tenants have?" Goodwin asked.[20]

The NAACP, another voice for black South Carolinians, endeavored to shape public opinion and arouse concern among Americans in other regions who were barely familiar with the plight of African Americans in the South. The NAACP regularly drew attention to atrocities and injustices experienced by African Americans, especially in the South. During the Great Migration, the NAACP linked these injustices to the rapid black exodus from the region. The NAACP recognized that the economic losses created by the migration of African American workers, the South's main source of cheap labor, had captured many white southerners' attention. The NAACP worked to broaden the vision of moderate white southerners and help them recognize the clear relationship between African Americans' poor quality of life in the South and their desire to leave. African American leaders, of course, hoped that enlightened self-interest would then motivate whites to seek amelioration of some of the harsher injustices of southern society. An NAACP press release in November 1923 was entitled, "Another Reason Why Negroes Leave the South: South Carolina's Expenditures on Educating White and Colored Children Show Glaring Inequalities." Statistics from the South Carolina Department of Education revealed that the state spent ten times more money on white children than on black children even though the majority of students were black. Across the entire state only $53 was made available to transport black students to school while white children had access to $88,903 for the same purpose. Six months later, in May 1924, the NAACP issued another press release detailing a different type of racial injustice in South Carolina. This report gave an account of Alice Thomas, a black woman who had been flogged by six white men in Orangeburg. Following the beating, Thomas's attackers, whom she knew, bellowed, "Now I guess you will keep your damn mouth shut." Senseless violence like this, the NAACP asserted, provided "additional evidence on the reasons for the Northward migration of Negroes from the South."[21]

Although African Americans had a shared experiential understanding of oppression and injustice, they were hardly a monolithic community. Their common experience as victims of white oppression instilled in African Americans a common goal of justice and equality, but it did not unite them in a collective strategy for improving their economic, social, and political status. Like Andrews, Carroll, Wise, and others, black reformers in South Carolina discussed migration, with a focus on the numerous facets of injustice that explained why African Americans migrated. Most black reformers, however, did not engage in Carroll's style of ingratiating flattery that referred to some whites as the "better element of the white race, the thinking element, the justice loving element, the God fearing people."[22] Moreover, unlike Carroll, most black reformers articulated the specific reasons that blacks left South Carolina, hoping to ameliorate the harsh conditions that spurred migration rather than supporting schemes to stop blacks' migration. They also understood that political rights were an essential tool for attaining their goals, whereas Carroll accepted whites' dubious promise to protect blacks' rights if they accepted disfranchisement. Despite these crucial differences, Carroll also promoted improvements in education, health care, the criminal justice system, and economic opportunities. He emphasized to critics that he had traveled across South Carolina for twenty years "preaching the doctrine of justice and mercy and helpful relations between the two races." Yet Carroll always addressed blacks' need for justice in the context of honoring whites' desire for control. Undeniably, part of what whites wanted was to maintain white supremacy. This was incompatible with blacks' achieving justice and equality. So Carroll's insistence that every southern community had "some of the best white people in the world" rang hollow for most African Americans, especially when even Carroll acknowledged that "while they are not saying much for the negroes' protection and justice, they are friends to the race."[23]

While white reformers clearly had a different agenda than black reformers, their explanation for the black exodus from South Carolina supplemented and agreed with African Americans' reasoning. Yet white reformers used black reformers' rationale for blacks' fleeing to northern cities as fodder for their arguments with other whites. W. W. Ball, editor of *The State*, commented frequently on various aspects of migration. He casually admitted that justice in South Carolina was not color blind. "It is true that a white man who has killed a negro often receives less than justice," he wrote. Ball's editorials also corroborated other criticisms black reformers expressed, especially concerning education. "That the rudimentary education of the negro is sadly neglected in South Carolina is universally acknowledged," he admitted. He also thought limited educational opportunities distressed African Americans more than other injustices. "The Southern negro is not seriously disturbed about an occasional lynching," Ball callously suggested, but African Americans were "discontented because the negro schools are few and inferior. He is beginning to resent the fact that his children are taught by semi-literate teachers paid from $15 to $25 a month and that this degraded school is open only a few weeks in the year." Moreover, Ball believed, the average black South Carolinian was "beginning to desire a more comfortable house to live in and better sanitary surroundings."[24]

Lynching appeared on everyone's list of injustices experienced by black southerners. But analysts of the Great Migration disagree about its importance as a factor in migration. Unlike Ball, black South Carolinians readily acknowledged lynching and racial violence as causes of black migration.[25] In 1916, the lynching of Anthony Crawford, a wealthy black landowner in Abbeville, terrorized African Americans in that community. While all lynching was outrageous, Crawford's lynching evoked special terror because it revealed the extent of some whites' penchant for enforcing white dominance. As the proud owner of $25,000 worth of prime cotton acreage, Crawford attracted the envy of whites. His excessive confidence and independence challenged white supremacy's insistence on African Americans' submission. Ultimately, Crawford's self-assurance cost him his life when he publicly cursed a white merchant who offered to buy his cottonseed below market value.[26]

On one Saturday in October, Crawford's assertion of his manhood as a peer of the white man and his determination to protect his economic self-interest provoked whites' rage. The verbal altercation became physical when Crawford defended himself against the cotton-gin clerk who had attacked him with an ax handle. The Abbeville chief of police arrested Crawford, who quickly posted bail and returned to the gin to secure his cotton. Awaiting his return, a mob of more than two hundred whites had gathered. Crawford fled for safety to the gin's boiler room, where he found a hammer. Vigorously defending himself, Crawford swung the hammer at one attacker, crushing his skull. The mob then descended on Crawford, smashed his head with a rock, and repeatedly kicked him, knocking out his teeth and inflicting other injuries. Crawford resisted until he was stabbed in the back with a knife. The sheriff intervened, jailing the semiconscious and nearly dead Crawford before the mob finished him off. Yet the mob grew restless and determined. By late afternoon angry whites stormed the jail, justifying their actions on the basis of rumors that the sheriff planned to move Crawford. After the mob kicked Crawford down the jail's three flights of stairs, its brutality mounted as drunken participants cheered the ensuing beating and mutilation. The street theater proceeded as Crawford was dragged through the black district as a warning to others. At the fair grounds, the mob finally hung Crawford and fired several hundred rounds of ammunition into his lifeless body.[27]

William P. Beard, editor of the *Abbeville Scimitar*, excused Crawford's lynchers, claiming that Crawford had flagrantly violated the white supremacy implication that the "LOWEST white man in the social scale is above the negro who stands HIGHEST by the same measurement." Crawford's lynching clearly demonstrated the use of violence in sustaining white supremacy, and it also refuted white contemporaries' frequently asserted justification of lynching as a protection of white womanhood. Roy Nash, an NAACP officer from New York, reported after an investigation that Crawford lost his life because he refused to bow his head and embody the "humility becoming a 'nigger.'" Within a week of Crawford's lynching, reports indicated that one thousand African Americans left Abbeville with the cry, "Go north, where there is some humanity, some justice and fairness." Unsatisfied by its lynching of Crawford, the mob attempted to force his family to leave; the ensuing terror temporarily closed all black businesses in Abbeville. Only after aggressive intervention by elite whites did the intimidation stop, two weeks later. By 1920, the census revealed that more than 30 percent of Abbeville's black population had left the county, a much greater population decrease than anywhere else in South Carolina.[28]

As was discussed in the last chapter, M. H. Gassaway, an African American educator and president of the NAACP in Anderson, also ran afoul of Beard's maxim about successful blacks. Gassaway's personal and professional success made him a target for the frustration and anger of working-class whites of this Piedmont county. Vick Cheshire, a Cole Blease supporter and editor of the *Anderson Tribune*, used his newspaper and personal influence to galvanize white resentment of Gassaway's leadership of the local NAACP. After an extensive intimidation campaign, Gassaway moved to Cleveland, Ohio, for refuge.[29] Both Beard and Cheshire edited Bleaseite newspapers whose views reflected those of the white working class. Their comments on Anthony Crawford's lynching and Gassaway's intimidation reflected the beliefs of whites, especially rural and working-class whites, who advocated enforcing and extending white dominance through lynching and other forms of extralegal violence.

By contrast, white reformers denounced violence and intimidation, deeming them unacceptable means for enforcing white supremacy. Hunter A. Gibbes, an attorney from Columbia, referred to lynching as the "fury of an irresponsible mob, often visited upon a wretched, defenseless negro for a trivial offense" in which few doubted his innocence. Further, Gibbes excoriated South Carolina's judicial system for tolerating it, especially juries who failed to convict the perpetrators. "This spirit of lawlessness among juries is so great," Gibbes lamented, "that it is often practically impossible to get a conviction in a common ordinary case of plain murder."[30] Violence and intimidation directed at successful men like Crawford and Gassaway particularly troubled reformers because education, hard work, and property ownership, the qualities that cost Crawford his life and caused Gassaway to flee to save his, were the qualities white reformers admired and encouraged. They used the anxiety surrounding migration as an opportunity to assert their opposition to the brutality of lynching.

Some reformers scoffed at complaints pertaining to black migration. They noted the irony of whites who mistreated blacks and yet complained about their departure. Without disclosing the author's identity, W. W. Ball quoted, on the editorial page, directly from a private letter discussing migration. The correspondent wrote: "Our economists have not yet learned that one can't lynch one's 'nigger' and work him too. As a rule, the loudest protestants against his going away are those who have given him the least consideration." Ball's editorial reiterated the point, declaring, "The plain fact is that no man will stay in a land where he or members of his family may be lynched. . . . Whenever the lynching of white men shall come to be as common in the South as the lynching of negroes has been, there will be an exodus of white men, too."[31] This suggestion that middle-class whites sympathized with blacks and also opposed lynching made them vulnerable to the charge of violating white supremacy. But reformers distinguished violence from white supremacy, while other whites often linked them. Reformers could cling to white supremacy and, without any inconsistency, boldly denounce an injustice like lynching because the essence of white supremacy for them meant whites' maintaining political, economic, and social control. White reformers simply believed that white dominance was maintained most effectively through laws and courts.[32]

The dispute among whites over the appropriateness of intimidation, violence, and lynching as acceptable means of enforcing white hegemony reveals an important fissure. Broad adherence to white supremacy masked the reality of serious disputes among whites over interpretations of the tenets of white supremacy. In 1928, Harry Watson, longtime influential editor of the *Greenwood Index Journal*, explained this tension to Rev. E. O. Watson, editor of the *Southern Christian Advocate*. Watson stated: "I was taught that while this was a white man's country and all good must be kept in the white man's hand, that this carried with it a tremendous responsibility in the matter of strictest justice and fair dealing with the negro. The first part of this is generally accepted, but the second not so generally. Upholding this doctrine has not been always easy for me, just as it gave my father many days of trouble, and down right persecution at times."[33] Watson's frustration with whites who rejected the noblesse oblige of white privilege, which white reformers accepted, emphasizes class tension among whites. Whites, who otherwise shared a belief in their inherent superiority, disagreed about whether their perceived supremacy carried paternalistic obligations to care for and protect those they deemed inferior or whether it included the prerogative to inflict violence against them. That dispute, however, did not abrogate whites' shared desire for white supremacy to prevail.

White reformers' opposition to lynching and other forms of violent intimidation revealed a cleavage among whites about their understandings of white supremacy. But reformers intended their opposition to lynching, in the context of the migration debate, to be a criticism of whites who tolerated or promoted things white reformers opposed. As the critic who wrote to W. W. Ball crudely explained, one cannot both lynch and work black laborers.

Eugene W. Dabbs, a college-educated farmer from Salem, South Carolina, who regularly engaged in public policy debates, used the migration debate as an opportunity to criticize the exploitive credit system. Dabbs rejected the suggestion that blacks primarily migrated because of either lynching or the pursuit of higher wages. Instead, Dabbs argued publicly and privately that valuable African American tenants fled South Carolina because of the state's terrible credit system, which exploited labor by allowing criminal prosecution for debt. In addition to the landlord's lien on his tenant's crop, the law enabled the tenant to be subject to a lien by a third party, most often a town merchant. Because the law allowed criminal prosecution for unpaid debt, Dabbs believed, merchants made irresponsible loans. "Our rural police are collectors for merchants who know when they make the advances that the violation of some statute constitutes their best security," he charged. He claimed that rural police and magistrates in this heavily rural center of the state's cotton production spent 90 percent of their time collecting debts from tenants and sharecroppers through the criminal process. He apparently witnessed debt collection, compelled through threats of jail time, drive off a good farm tenant who later encouraged his entire extended family to leave the area. Dabbs asserted that other prominent farmers agreed with his analysis of the credit system and its role as a cause of black migration.[34]

While white reformers used the migration debate to criticize their opponents, their critics pushed back, rejecting the argument that African Americans in the South suffered any injustice, whether from the courts, lynch mobs, or employers. These whites detested public declarations from white reformers about such injustices. Ben S. Williams, a landowner from Hampton, a low-country, black-majority county, expressed his mounting frustration with white reformers whose discussion of black migration revealed that they had accepted what he perceived as a carpetbagger premise: that white men of the South treated African Americans harshly and denied them fundamental rights. "The plea of denial of rights and injustices is false and unjust," Williams asserted. Moreover, he wondered, which rights did black southerners think had been denied them? If they longed for "social equality and conjugal felicity," then Williams welcomed their departure. He believed that "when the negro becomes too great for his place in citizenship here let him seek loftier places elsewhere and good riddance." White men who engaged in such "hypocritical palaver and cowardly concessions," Williams said, have sacrificed "principle, dignity, honor and ideals of true manhood."[35] He challenged white reformers' masculinity as well as their commitment to white supremacy. Disagreements among whites always occurred as a racial dialogue of accusations, with each faction declaring that its opponents violated white supremacy and presenting itself as the true defender of white dominance.

Consistent with the white supremacy premise that African Americans should always follow and never lead, many whites reasoned that African Americans' migration to northern industries for higher wages could not have been initiated by black South Carolinians themselves. The notion that higher wages enticed African Americans to move north suggested black ambition and self-reliance, qualities inconsistent with whites' assessment of blacks as lazy and requiring constant white guidance. Therefore, such reasoning followed, an analysis of African Americans' motivation for migrating was unnecessary. Whites commonly believed that blacks had no independent motivation, being docile creatures led by whites. According to this reasoning, African Americans' behavior was best explained, not by investigating their motives, but by scrutinizing the character of the whites who directly influenced them. From this perspective, determining the provocation for migration meant ferreting out the alleged instigator: the labor agent.

In March 1917, Columbia employers who depended on African American laborers complained to Mayor Lewis A. Griffith that the exodus of black laborers had created a serious labor shortage in the city. By inquiring about recent ticket sales with the Seaboard railroad ticket agent, one Columbia employer learned that eighty African Americans had recently purchased tickets for Philadelphia. Although the Seaboard ticket agent indicated that each man had purchased his own ticket, the business owner nevertheless concluded that "there must be some solicitor in town getting them together." He demanded that the city investigate the matter, determine who the labor agents were, and immediately stop them from luring away his much-needed labor.[36]

This business owner represented one segment of the white population that feared black migration. Other white opponents of migration included large landowners, merchants who supplied the agriculture trade or provided crop liens, bankers who extended credit to landowners and merchants, and employers who depended on cheap black labor. They were immediately threatened by the loss of black labor because it translated into personal economic loss. They wanted to stop migration or severely reduce it, and they wanted immediate action toward this end. Their continued access to cheap labor depended on the state's maintaining an abundant supply of surplus labor, and migration steadily drained the surplus. Determined to survive economically, large agricultural landowners saw no solution to the problem except to keep African Americans in the South. One affluent planter confessed his determination to keep blacks from leaving by claiming, "When the last train-load of darkies leaves, d—d if I won't be swinging to the back platform!"[37] United by their mutual desire to stop further black migration, whites with a strong interest in cheap agricultural labor disagreed among themselves over the best means of stopping it. To some extent, these disagreements followed from different analyses of the cause of migration. Some portion of this group of whites assumed that force was the only disincentive African Americans understood. Others relied on the power and authority of state and local law. Some whites among this constituency preferred to use leaders inside the African American community to halt migration. Still others resorted to economic leverage. Regardless of the method they advocated, whites used the tenets of white supremacy as a justification.

South Carolinians who wanted to curb migration with state and local government authority turned to South Carolina's labor laws. In an effort to curtail the activities of labor agents, who solicited laborers to leave the state for higher wages, white landowners urged enforcement of a South Carolina statute that required labor agents to pay an annual license fee of $2,000 in each county they visited. Although not enforced by statute, South Carolina's public policy prohibited newspapers and other publications from advertising employment opportunities for African Americans in other states. Drawing upon this policy, Paul Sanders of Ritter, South Carolina, complained bitterly to state representative Turner Logan about an advertisement for wheat harvesters displayed in the post office. When Logan learned that the Farm Labor Bureau of the U.S. Employment Service sponsored the announcement, he explained to C. W. Pugsey, acting U.S. secretary of agriculture, South Carolina's policy and the concern his constituents, like Sanders, had expressed about losing their African American laborers. Pugsey assured Logan that the Farm Labor Bureau had not intended to recruit many African Americans with the posters because most of them, as cotton laborers, lacked the necessary skills to help with the wheat harvest in the Midwest. Nevertheless, Logan told the U.S. postmaster general to remove the posters, and he insisted "that action be taken at once to suppress all such posters here."[38]

Dissatisfied that both statutes and informal policies assisted opponents of migration, *The State* ridiculed South Carolina's public policy that prohibited newspapers from publishing out-of-state employment advertisements aimed at African Americans. White reformers disapproved of this policy because they disagreed with its objective of keeping blacks in South Carolina. Ball, *The State*'s editor, couched his criticism of the policy in terms of white supremacy. Attempting to shame opponents of advertising for black laborers, the editor claimed this policy "places a higher valuation on negroes than on white men" in South Carolina because it allowed out-of-state recruiting for whites but prohibited all advertisement for black laborers. Moreover, South Carolina's policy "has driven ten white men out of the State for every black man that it has kept at home."[39] The effort to align every criticism with white supremacy illustrates this doctrine's power to dictate the terms of debate and ultimately to shape policies.

Migration opponents not only looked for state assistance in retaining black laborers, but they also turned to key businesses for help. The Southern Railway, sympathetic with landowners' reported inability to retain sufficient agricultural labor, adopted a company policy against transporting African Americans who were migrating north. The railroad company pledged to "discourage the negro exodus from the South in every legitimate manner." Southern Railway's management ordered its employees to discontinue the company's long-standing practice of using extra space in baggage cars to carry black passengers. In exchange for committing the railway to the "promotion of a campaign to induce the negro to remain in the South," Southern Railway asked that bankers and other business owners support its efforts by employing surplus black labor in their communities.[40]

Other white South Carolinians who wanted desperately to retain the black labor force employed a range of deceptive tactics to conceal from public view their leadership role in discouraging blacks' migration. The most efficient method, some whites believed, was convincing others to lead the charge, and who better, they reasoned, than African Americans themselves? African Americans' criticism of outmigration would not only reduce whites' visibility in the controversy but also enhance the legitimacy of the antimigration message among blacks. Southern Railway encouraged every community to have someone "make it his special business to interest the negro preachers and have them take strong ground against the people of their race being lured away by promise of higher wages in other sections."[41] Recognizing the leadership role that black ministers played in African American communities, white leaders attempted to either influence or control their message. Moreover, whites exploited the differences among African Americans to serve their interest, as the struggle between Richard Carroll and other black reformers demonstrated. Whites always preferred black leaders who parroted their message, especially if those leaders had broad influence. Either because of his personal convictions or the coercive influence of white leaders, Carroll opposed migration and strongly encouraged blacks to stay in the South.

Other white opponents of migration grew frustrated with indirect methods and resorted to open intimidation. In May 1917, Sumter

County police arrested a prominent black minister, Rev. J. W. Moultrie of Immanuel Methodist Church, one of the oldest and largest congregations in Sumter, for being a labor agent who enticed black laborers to leave South Carolina. Based on an anonymous tip, rural police officer Sam Newman arrested Moultrie on a Sunday afternoon at the Atlantic Coast Line railroad station before a large crowd of African Americans. Outraged and shocked at what seemed like a terrible miscarriage of justice, Moultrie's friends questioned city officials about the arrest. Though reluctant to discuss the details, a local magistrate and Newman eventually indicated that they had acted on an anonymous tip from a black man. Under pressure, Newman soon confessed he had misunderstood the informant and arrested the wrong man. Newman surmised that the real labor agent must have been standing near Moultrie and he confused the two. Moultrie was released. Not content to let Moultrie's arrest end as a case of mistaken identity, Emmett J. Baxter of Sumter wrote a letter to *The State* suggesting that Moultrie's arrest had been calculated both to humiliate Moultrie and to intimidate prospective black emigrants. After all, Moultrie was a well-known Sumter resident and unlikely to be mistaken for an out-of-state labor agent. Baxter not only questioned Newman's motives but asserted a probable link to the real instigators of the arrest: "We [black Sumter residents] do believe that [a] policeman who is being paid by the taxes of all the people allowed himself to be used as the tool of some farming interests that have been hard hit by the migration of the negroes."[42] These Sumter residents well understood that whites used their power to manipulate the law enforcement system to serve their personal economic interests.

Diversity of viewpoints among whites on black migration extended well beyond disagreement over the most effective method of stemming the tide of African American laborers leaving the South. White reformers who did not depend economically on black labor were much less anxious to thwart black migration. Much of the discourse among South Carolinians appeared as a pragmatic discussion of how to minimize the seemingly endless flow of black laborers from the South. Yet the deliberations more accurately resembled a debate among whites about the future of South Carolina. Black migration revealed a cleavage in whites' vision for the state. White planters, merchants, and others economically dependent on black laborers pictured the future as essentially a continuation of the past. As beneficiaries of this labor-intensive agricultural economy, they wanted to retain the system that helped them prosper. Halting the exodus of valuable African American laborers seemed essential for maintaining the existing economic system. In a private missive, one white reformer lamented southerners' enthusiasm for terminating migration. Unfortunately, he surmised, too many whites exhibited the disposition of the "ancient Egyptians—they would chase the negroes to the Red Sea to bring them back."[43]

While white reformers never spoke with one voice, many of them envisioned a different future for South Carolina. They wanted to diversify the economy, making it less dependent on cheap labor. One reformer explained that if the state's farmers would plant more acreage in hay and grain crops and use more machinery, they could "afford to lose 50,000 negroes."[44] Reformers also understood that poverty was the companion of cheap labor and that pervasive poverty impeded progress. Reform advocates wanted to reverse the racial demography of the state, increasing the proportion of whites either by attracting whites to the state or by encouraging the black exodus. Proposing more white immigration to the South was a time-honored idea throughout the region. Duncan Clinch Heyward had supported a scheme for recruiting white immigrants during his term as governor at the turn of the century, but little effort was actually devoted to implementing the idea. With reformers' enthusiasm running high at the end of the war, Heyward reintroduced the idea of white immigration in February 1919. Emphasizing that South Carolina's black majority hung over the state like a "pall and hinders us from progress in every direction," he supported black migration coupled with encouraging white immigration into the areas that blacks left. Based on the can-do spirit of the war and the government's willingness to tackle any problem, Heyward suggested, the federal government might help South Carolina implement this proposal.[45]

In addition to reducing the size of the black population, South Carolina reformers longed to decrease illiteracy and improve the overall quality of life for South Carolinians. White reformers blamed the presence of hundreds of thousands of impoverished and uneducated African Americans in part for adverse conditions in South Carolina. Therefore, they deplored large landowners' efforts to halt blacks' mass departure. Instead, they promoted this seeming calamity as the South's unexpected good fortune. As J. J. Cantey, a Summerton native, pleaded: "In the name of God . . . In the name of all that the white race holds sacred, in the name of Anglo-Saxon democracy, in the name of the bloody battlefields where Washington and Lee fought to hold high and clean the banner of liberty for the white and all other races, . . . let the negro emigrate."[46] With his public statement, Cantey employed all the touchstones of white supremacy—divine sanction, patriotism, military sacrifice, and political liberty—to justify not stopping migration. Since many whites used white supremacy to justify their opposition to black migration, Cantey knew that to support black migration he had to forthrightly defend his position by linking it directly with the canon of white supremacy.

South Carolina's white reformers embraced black migration as an opportunity to further their progressive vision on two fronts. First, the migration of African Americans from South Carolina had the obvious effect of reducing the state's black population. They placed great emphasis on creating a whiter South Carolina because they perceived that the state's large African American population contributed to the state's many problems and was an obstacle to virtually all reforms. J. T. Williams, a white reformer from Greenville, questioned whether South Carolina could make the same progress "half white and half black that we could make with a total white population." Moreover, Williams rhetorically inquired, "Is not a white South the dream of every Southern patriot?"[47]

Second, as African Americans left South Carolina, white reformers envisioned that problems would leave with them, resulting in a better opportunity for their reform agenda in South Carolina. White reformers had long realized that the state was incapable of sustained progress as long as the majority of its population remained poor and undereducated. Reformers also knew that ameliorating the adverse consequences of ignorance and poverty was made even more difficult by the fact that so many of its victims were black. White South Carolinians, deeply imbued with the value of white dominance, would not readily advocate expensive measures to raise living conditions, improve education, or expand economic opportunities for African Americans. Consequently, the combination of a highly impoverished black population and a white population committed to white dominance confounded reform efforts because white supremacy prevented significant improvements to the conditions of that impoverished population. Thus white reformers seized upon the black out-migration as a solution to their long-standing dilemma of how to substantially improve economic and social conditions in the state in the face of South Carolinians' intense opposition to measures that could benefit blacks.

Realizing, of course, that not all African Americans would leave, white reformers had to devise some method for improving the living conditions of black South Carolinians that would not be so costly to the state and would not arouse strong opposition from most whites. This was the second opportunity white reformers saw in black migration. They used the incessant complaining of white agricultural interests about the black exodus to garner support for improved treatment of African Americans within the state's segregated social order. Editor Ball told white employers who expressed concern about black migration that "the way to check it [black migration] is in the hands of the employers themselves."[48] *The State*'s editor explained this reasoning: "If white employers in the South wish to retain their supply of negro labor, the hour has come when they must show an interest in its welfare." Bell unfavorably compared black laborers' employers to textile mill owners who, he argued, cared for their white operatives.[49] As the editor's comments suggested, white reformers also recognized in the migration panic the opportunity to make African Americans' employers pay for some of the improvements. In 1919, A. T. Gerrans made this same argument to Governor Cooper. "The Manufacturers and Farmers, who are dependent on colored labor," Gerrans insisted, "must join hands and heads and devise plans for the economic welfare of this labor, with a view of not only educating it to work consistently and persistently but to live better in every way."[50] White reformers insisted that if agricultural landlords wanted to persuade their laborers to remain in South Carolina, they needed to contribute financially to improving the conditions of African Americans. Reformers hoped to position themselves in a win-win situation either by forcing planters to accept black migration or by convincing them to use their own resources to help with the "uplift" of blacks who stayed. White reformers understood that raising African Americans' standard of living and enhancing their educational opportunities were essential for the overall progress of the state.

White reformers appealed to white supremacy as a tactic for amassing broad political support for improving adverse conditions that prompted blacks to leave South Carolina. Persuading a majority of white residents that African Americans' plight needed improvement was a difficult challenge for reformers, but actually alleviating these conditions proved even more daunting. Rather than emphasizing African Americans' adversity, which would have garnered little sympathy, white reformers attempted to persuade whites that black poverty was undesirable because it also hurt whites. Those advocating black emigration to the North used the labor-shortage crisis as an opportunity to criticize the various interests, headed by large planters, whose policies had created many of the state's problems. These problems affected poorer whites as well as African Americans. "Neglect to train the negro has held the South back," Taylor Kennerly, a migration observer, argued. Moreover, he continued, the "low scale of wages and standard of living of the blacks have been a mill-stone about the neck of the poor white man as well."[51] Because of white supremacy, white leaders were only willing to underscore problems that the state's economic system created for blacks by illustrating that whites also suffered.

Migration debates also provided white reformers with a forum for criticizing the low-wage economy. Large landowners offered the most forceful opposition to migration. The abundance of labor available to plant and harvest cotton held agricultural wages down and maximized owners' profits. Those paying the wages wanted to keep them low, and those receiving the wages wanted them higher. Yet as long as a majority of the low-wage workers were African Americans, few whites complained. Keeping blacks poor and dependent helped the large landowners. As Gavin Wright has pointed out, however, low wages for African Americans also helped to keep white laborers' wages low.[52] *The State* explained that white landowners regularly paid $1 per day to the "unspoiled white man," the same wage they paid black farm laborers.[53] White reformers who wanted to move the state away from dependence on low wages argued that blacks' leaving the state benefited whites. But to challenge the low-wage economy was to challenge both the business and planter elites of South Carolina head-on. Rather than directly assault these elites and their economic strategies, reformers used white supremacy to emphasize the consequences of this economic strategy. One editorial proclaimed that the "southern oppressors of negroes" were actually the "enemies of all labor, regardless of color. If they can hold the negroes in semi-bondage, the poor whites will be scarcely less their slaves. In the final reckoning it must be seen that economic laws draw no color line."[54] Thus, white reformers suggested that the planters' economic interests threatened one key aspect of white supremacy: its implication of white equality and independence.

Close analysis reveals that white South Carolinians seldom spoke with a unified voice about black migration. Instead they offered a range of responses to migration, even though they agreed that the exodus posed a challenge to white supremacy since it enhanced the independence of African Americans and, consequently, limited whites' leverage over blacks. The defense of white supremacy was a unifying theme. White reformers and their opponents similarly approached the black migration issue by asking how whites were hurt or helped by the demographic shift. All whites pledged their commitment to preserving the supremacy of whites, but their competing class and economic interests motivated them to employ white supremacy in pursuit of contrary ends. Discussions of black migration in a variety of public forums and private conversations revealed antagonism among whites as these classes struggled on behalf of competing visions of South Carolina's future while masking that conflict with a defense of white supremacy. Whether white South Carolinians responded to the migration crisis by reasserting heavy-handed white control and employing whatever means necessary to ensure the preservation of cheap labor, or by defending white supremacy through a renewed vision for a white majority and a plea for stronger commitment to paternalism, all whites were committed to resolving the crisis to benefit some group of whites. Challenging white supremacy remained unthinkable, so white reformers sought new and creative ways of interpreting its tenets. They recognized that in the public debate over black migration, as in almost all public debates in early twentieth-century South Carolina, the side that most persuasively linked its case to the future of white supremacy was likely to prevail.

Part 2

The Politics of White Supremacy

Chapter 7

A Reform Coalition

In the era of World War I, South Carolina's political system operated in a culture shaped by the dictates of white supremacy and white South Carolinians' fixation on defending them. William Watts Ball, a keen political analyst in early twentieth-century South Carolina and editor of *The State*, commented before one election that despite intense anti-Catholic sentiment among southerners, "the South on election day would vote for the Pope himself rather than share the post offices with the 'niggers.'"[1] In order to ensure white rule in a black-majority state, white South Carolinians constructed and carefully guarded the 1895 constitutional voting restrictions and the all-white Democratic primary, both components of their antidemocratic political scheme that disfranchised African Americans. Thus, African American reformers, inspired by World War I, fought for state action in a context of political exclusion, which would make their task impossible if they worked alone. Obviously a political system constructed by whites to embody white supremacy had debilitating consequences for African American reformers who struggled outside and against the centers of power. Yet this political system also constrained white reformers, political insiders who did not resist white supremacy but rather pledged unwavering support for it as they pursued their moderately progressive agenda for economic and educational reform.

Shaped by white supremacy, South Carolina's political structure, with its statewide white primary and constitutional restrictions on voting, had been in place for two decades prior to World War I. With both suffrage restrictions and the white primary in place, intensely competitive factions within the Democratic Party vied for influence and political office in the white primary, the only real political contest in an essentially one-party political system.[2] The Democratic Party consisted of factions that reflected a complex array of class differences, competing economic and business interests, political rivalries from an earlier era, personalities, and long-standing regional rivalries. Some factions were cohesive, self-identifying, and quasi-permanent, while others were fluid, forming loose coalitions that changed from election to election and issue to issue. In this political environment, constructed by white supremacy considerations, reformers pursued agendas that required greater state activism.

South Carolina's white reformers represented only a small portion of the state's white citizens. They came primarily from the town-centered middle class. Collectively, their agenda included improving the state's educational system, economic infrastructure, tax system, and humanitarian institutions; implementing scientific agriculture; and curbing crime and violence. As only one faction in the political arena, they could not command winning majorities alone so they had to find allies and forge political coalitions to accomplish their goals. Yet South Carolina's political system, constructed to guarantee white dominance, hindered reformers' ability to forge effective coalitions. Within South Carolina's narrowly construed democracy, white supremacy's rhetoric and logic pervaded the political landscape. All political factions in the Democratic Party maneuvered behind the unifying facade of white supremacy. Yet white supremacy, the common denominator and shared allegiance among white South Carolinians, thwarted potential progressive coalitions and strengthened the state's tendency to accept the status quo. As one reformer aptly described the struggle for reform in South Carolina, "We can't afford to be 'forward-looking,' we are too busy trying to keep the back wheels from skidding into the ditch."[3]

In imagining a progressive coalition, white reformers might logically have found allies among working-class whites and tenant farmers, industrial and agricultural workers who, reformers believed, stood to benefit directly from the programs reformers advocated. Additionally, since these workers owned little or no property, they would have had minimal concern about funding these reforms with increased property taxes, the primary source of state revenue. Yet these mill workers and landless farmers did not share the middle-class reformers' worldview of methodical and reasoned progress. Instead, they formed the core of a faction that consistently opposed reformers and their agenda. Class differences existed among whites about the appropriate enforcement of white supremacy. While all white South Carolinians agreed that whites and not blacks should hold political and economic power and dominate all aspects of the culture, they had different understandings about structuring and enforcing white supremacy. Working-class and poor agricultural laborers preferred enforcing racial order with harsh rhetoric and extralegal violence. By contrast, reformers preferred the systematic order of segregation, a formal system of racial etiquette and racial order enforced through law. White reformers, who supported a paternalistic style of securing white supremacy, advocated a measure of educational, economic, and social uplift of African Americans, while their opponents viewed such assistance as an affront to white supremacy.

The disagreement that emerged about the appropriate means for whites to control blacks, restrain their aspirations, and regulate racial interaction also created class tension about how white supremacy should structure relationships among whites. Laborers emphasized that white supremacy meant simply two categories: white and black. As whites, no matter how marginal their economic standing, they asserted their full entitlement to white privileges. White reformers, by contrast, recognized an expanding and changing world that valued education, diverse economic skills, expertise, and order. While agreeing that whites should rule society, they rejected the assertion that all whites were equally capable of exercising control. White laborers rejected reformers' paternalistic arrogance when they, rather than blacks, became the target of control schemes that encroached upon their independence. Consequently, laborers preferred political rhetoric and leadership that respected their manhood and white equality. As Bryant Simon emphasizes, as white laborers' economic independence, evidenced by property ownership, slipped away in the late nineteenth and early twentieth centuries, the identity of these white men who valued independence rested more heavily on racial entitlement and patriarchy. Without economic independence, they vigilantly guarded against the slightest perceived challenge to either their white or male privileges.[4] Coleman L. "Coley" Blease provided the colorful and controversial political style they craved as he led

South Carolina's largest, most cohesive, and self-identifying faction of the World War I era.

Mill operatives, concentrated in the up-country counties, formed the core of the Blease faction. This faction cohered in the early twentieth century as the textile industry expanded rapidly across the Piedmont, creating a critical mass of white working-class male voters. These industrial wage earners, along with white tenant farmers, sharecroppers, and some small landowners, faithfully delivered 40 to 50 percent of the vote to Blease and his political lieutenants in every election since 1888. A onetime legislative leader for Benjamin Tillman, Blease considered himself an heir to the Tillman movement's political philosophy of white supremacy and white male authority. Tillman and Blease both exploited class antagonisms and railed against the elites, promoting the political ideal of white equality rather than economic prowess that linked a man's worth to his wealth and income. Blease's support, however, centered much more than agrarian leader Tillman's on mill workers. Blease never commanded the loyalty of large numbers of yeoman farmers who identified themselves overwhelmingly as Tillmanites. Blease's two terms as governor from 1911 to 1914 proved to be a graveyard for reform proposals.[5]

As governor, the flamboyant Newberry attorney outraged progressive South Carolinians, dismissing them as "fool theorists" and members of the "holier than thou crowd."[6] As his supporters desired, Blease consistently opposed all progressive reforms, especially those that affected the working class, even though workers in other parts of the country insisted on them. For example, in the early twentieth century, reformers promoted health inspection for children to detect disease and physical defects. In 1912, the legislature passed a bill to guarantee the benefit of medical inspections to all children across the state. Blease promptly vetoed this bill, insisting that he was protecting the virtue of young girls and the dignity of working parents from public ridicule when their child's "problem" became public record. Decreasing illiteracy and improving education had long been promoted by South Carolina reformers. White reformers wanted a compulsory school attendance law as one means of attacking the state's many educational problems. Blease adamantly opposed compelling parents to send their children to school, and during his second term as governor, he vetoed four compulsory school attendance bills. Blease claimed that he was trying to preserve the rights of parents to control children in South Carolina. Aware that mill parents preferred that their children work rather than attend school, reformers linked compulsory school attendance to child labor restrictions. Yet the minimum age for workers in South Carolina remained at twelve during Blease's administration despite reformers' efforts to raise the minimum to fourteen or sixteen.[7] Mill operatives perceived the reformers' proposed health and education legislation as an assault against their authority that revealed reformers' disrespect for workers' status as independent white men. Thus they applauded Blease's obstinacy.

Blease's opposition to child labor laws, compulsory school attendance, and school health inspections made him the foremost nemesis of South Carolina reformers. But Blease's audacious move to pardon 1,743 prisoners during his final term as governor reflected a tolerance for crime and violence that deeply offended white reformers. The infamous pardons reinforced reformers' opposition to Blease and caused a permanent division between white reformers and Bleaseites. W. W. Ball often referred angrily to Blease's indiscriminate pardons. "Presumably the vicious class, the bootleggers, and moonshiners and the men who may want pardons and commutations will vote for him [Blease] as always they have done," Ball complained during one campaign. C. P. Hodges of Marlboro expressed the outrage that reformers directed at Blease's seeming indifference to crime when he observed, "Were Blease governor [again] don't you know that a thug or ruffian might feel secure in shooting you or me or any other decent man down if in his way?"[8] Reformers equally loathed Blease's popular and public defense of lynching. At a national governors' conference in 1912 Blease proclaimed, "Whenever the constitution of my state steps between me and the defense of the virtue of the white woman, then I say to hell with the Constitution!" He consistently justified lynching black men as an appropriate response to rape allegations. When white reformers protested his advocacy of vigilante justice, Blease simply demeaned them as the enemy of white womanly virtue.[9]

Blease's cavalier opposition to white reformers and their goals drove J. M. DesChamps, a former Tillmanite, to criticize Blease severely for linking his movement to the earlier reform movement.

DesChamps argued that Tillmanism looked forward and Bleaseism looked backward. According to DesChamps, Bleaseism had no principle but was defined by its "lack of principle." He declared that Bleaseism was "anti-progress to the core. It is worse than non-progress" and ran headlong from "civilization toward barbarism."[10] Many historians have echoed contemporaries' assessment of Blease as a colorful demagogue who railed against reform to no real end and failed to advocate the positive measures his constituents needed. David Carlton has persuasively argued, however, that Blease's constant opposition to reform appealed to South Carolina's white working class because white workers resented the paternalism of reformers, whose advocacy of mandatory school attendance, child labor restrictions, and health inspections offended workers' traditional desire for independence.[11] Blease effectively defended their white manhood and served as a constant reminder to educated, middle-class reformers that an essential tenet of white supremacy was white equality that transcended education and economic status.

The bitter gulf between white reformers and Bleaseites illustrates one way that white supremacy constrained reform. White supremacy drove political discourse. As a consensus ideal no one could ignore it and survive in the public arena. Every class and economic group perceived its own interests as being furthered by white supremacy, because its precise meaning remained intentionally undefined. Blease masterfully used the white supremacy consensus, regardless of the shallow agreement, for his own ends. Working-class whites, poor tenant farmers, and sharecroppers, who experienced the same marginal economic status as many blacks, clung to the idea that white supremacy connoted white equality. Blease knew that this tenet of white supremacy mattered most to his constituents. He also knew white reformers' style, proposed policies, and broader goals violated this tenet. Yet these rifts over specific understandings of white supremacy remained buried beneath the ambiguous consensus, which was essential to all whites who believed it was not worth the risk of publicly airing precise differences. Such public disclosures might have weakened the potency of the absolutely agreed-upon idea of white control and black inferiority. Thus poor and working-class whites derived from white supremacy a self-identity based upon race. Armed with this identity that elevated the importance of white manhood, they embraced a political style and values that prevented cooperation with white reformers.

Bleaseite opposition to reform stemmed from a confluence of race, class, and gender ideals that valued white male superiority instead of educational achievement and economic power. Blease campaigned like a zealous racial demagogue. His overt and colorful defense of white supremacy appealed to working-class voters more than the subdued techniques of middle-class politicians. The contrast between Blease and other politicians of the era was neither that Blease advocated white supremacy while others did not, nor that the white working class was more amenable than other classes to racist appeals, but rather that Blease found the fitting class expression of white supremacy that others had not. As an anti-Blease leader, Ball recognized the genius of Blease's political rhetoric. By contrast, he lamented, thousands of Bleaseites followed Blease because his opponents didn't "give them a strong stimulating candid leader" and were "always slow at recognizing what appeals to the common people." Thus the powerful allure of white supremacy cemented the working class's political allegiance to Blease and cast them against reform. In a private reflection, W. W. Ball remarked as early as 1916 that poor whites hindered the state's progress with their votes against reform. "Their race prejudice is used to neutralize their power," Ball complained. "The exploiters of white labor use white supremacy and persuade labor to vote against their economic interest."[12] Yet Ball was less cognizant that reformers' commitment to white supremacy also neutralized their power.

With harsh opposition from the working class, white reformers were left to form coalitions with other factions in the state, not only to advance their agenda but also to keep Bleaseites from dismantling their accomplishments. The remainder of the non-Blease factions in South Carolina's Democratic Party formed a loose, ad hoc anti-Blease coalition—it did not rise to the level of a faction—its name standing as testimony to the power of Blease and his movement to define the terms of political campaigns in World War I–era South Carolina.[13] These voters did not work together to elect candidates to office, nor did they share a legislative agenda. They formed a single-issue coalition, drawn together by a mutual desire to defeat Blease and Bleaseite candidates. South Carolina's reform faction spear-

headed this coalition because of its complete inability to achieve reform goals for the state if Blease prevailed. White reformers
provided much of the coalition's leadership, ideas, and energy, but
they did not dominate it numerically or completely control it. Instead, they continually guided, cajoled, and compromised with other
factions and interests.

In addition to the reformers, the anti-Blease coalition at various
times included industrialists, merchants, business owners, professionals, bankers, investors, most agricultural landowners from modest yeomen to large plantation owners, and even some tenants.
Obviously, these various anti-Blease factions held competing economic and class interests that thwarted cooperation. Many of the
anti-Bleaseites had been affiliated with the competing Conservative
and Tillmanite factions in earlier years. Their alliance against Blease
required constant negotiation around sensitive issues and legacies of
past allegiances so as not to offend a group whose support was needed. This historic division among members of the anti-Blease coalition also limited the opportunity to rally their constituents with
strong rhetorical appeals to the past. Contemporary southern historian U. B. Phillips encouraged W. W. Ball to publish his book manuscript about the Tillman movement in South Carolina. Ball expressed
reservations about publishing it because of the tumultuous factional
rivalry in South Carolina politics. "Former Tillmanites and Conservatives [are] now pulling together in our factional affairs against
Bleaseism," Ball explained to Phillips, thus Blease's opponents "cannot afford to fight over the Flaccid tissues of long dead issues."[14]

Within the factional Democratic Party that housed the solid
Blease faction and a loose anti-Blease coalition, most statewide elections in World War I South Carolina followed a readily discernible
pattern. A number of candidates ran for a single office in the first
primary. The field generally included Blease or one of his allies and
several anti-Blease candidates. Blease usually drew a strong plurality
but seldom a majority in the first primary, necessitating a runoff. In
the runoff primaries, Blease generally maintained his support from
the first primary, and most of the remaining factions rallied together,
delivering a majority vote and the political office to the lone remaining anti-Blease candidate. Yet the coalition that rallied to defeat

Blease in the second primary cohered for that purpose only. Thus the anti-Blease candidate took office with majority support but with a very tepid endorsement and without any legislative or policy mandate. The anti-Blease voting coalition usually fizzled, at least temporarily, shortly after the election victory. The following analysis of three war-era election campaigns, featuring Cole Blease against the anti-Blease coalition, explains why white reformers had difficulty electing candidates who would enthusiastically endorse their reform agenda and aggressively push it when elected. Moreover, these three campaigns—Blease's attempt to thwart reform governor Richard Manning's reelection in 1916, his run in the 1918 election for the U.S. Senate seat that became vacant following Ben Tillman's death, and Blease's run in the 1922 gubernatorial election—illustrate white reformers' strategic manipulation of white supremacy to oppose Blease and elect their candidates.

As the United States anticipated involvement in World War I, South Carolina faced another of its bitter political contests between two warring portions of the Democratic Party. As Manning concluded his first two-year term as governor, he announced his reelection intentions in the spring of 1916. During his first administration, Manning led the general assembly to enact a host of progressive legislation that nudged the state in the direction reformers hoped to continue moving. The legislature created several new state agencies, including the Board of Charities and Corrections, the Tax Commission, and the Board of Arbitration and Conciliation. With white reformers' leadership, the state adopted its first compulsory school attendance law, increased state aid for public education, and raised the minimum age for workers to fourteen, all measures they had found impossible to pass during Blease's two previous administrations. Additionally, pro-labor measures that regulated when and how wage laborers were paid were adopted to minimize mill owner exploitation and rationalize an otherwise chaotic compensation system. Although none of the modest labor reforms developed during his first administration fundamentally altered labor relations or economic life in South Carolina, Manning received the accolades of supporters and the scorn of critics during one of the most activist legislative sessions in the state's history.[15] The unprecedented state activism invited challenges to Manning's reelection bid from laborers and textile mill owners, who both resented state intrusion, although perhaps for different reasons.

Manning expected a challenge from Blease. Bitter rivals, Manning and Blease represented the two extremes of the pro-reform and antireform spectrum in South Carolina. As the governor who succeeded Blease, Manning had eagerly embraced reforms that Blease had blocked for four years. The unexpected challenge to Manning came from Robert A. Cooper, who shared most of Manning's agenda. Cooper's challenge of Manning was encouraged by mill owners and their supporters. They resented the new labor regulations and also resented Manning's refusal to take a pro-company position on a few strikes and labor disputes. Other economic elites also expressed enthusiasm for Cooper's candidacy because they opposed the new Tax Commission, which threatened, in the name of equalization, to increase their taxes.[16] These political challenges from opposite ends of the economic spectrum, represented by Blease and Cooper, demonstrated the fundamental obstacle to attaining white reformers' progressive agenda. Blease's challenge represented the entrenched opposition to the reform agenda from the white working class, which resented progressives' paternalistic intrusiveness. Cooper's challenge represented the difficulty of forming strong and dependable coalitions with economic conservatives and business elites, who opposed the increased regulation and taxes that were inherent in progressive reforms. The depth of the Bleaseites' class antipathy toward reformers, expressed in every election, negated any cooperation, leaving reformers to look to their less-malicious opponents for allies. The reformers' need for political support from economic conservatives limited their strategy and narrowed the scope of their vision.

In the bitter contest of 1916, Blease received a plurality in the first primary vote. With approximately 64,000 votes, Blease held an impressive lead over Manning's 41,000. Cooper ran third with almost 31,000 votes. Although Blease fell short of the required majority, consistent with the cyclical pattern, he polled 47 percent of the vote in the first primary. His solid, dependable support in every election exasperated white reformers. As often happened in runoff primaries, the anti-Blease coalition suppressed, at least momentarily, its differences. Two days after the first primary Cooper conceded his support to Manning and united with the progressive faction to defeat Blease. In the runoff primary, Manning dramatically increased his vote by 30,000 (most of the Cooper votes) while Blease gained only 3,000 additional votes. With less than a 5,000-vote margin, anti-Blease forces reelected Richard Manning to a second term as governor of South Carolina.[17]

Of course, the September runoff primary assured Manning's reelection because the November general election was meaningless without viable Republican opposition. One student of South Carolina politics referred to the white primary as a "gentlemen's agreement" that could be "sustained solely by the fear of the consequences of a division among the whites" and the "introduction of the negroes as a factor in the legal election."[18] To prevent any group of disgruntled Democrats from opposing the party's nominee because its candidate lost in the primary, the party mandated that members take a loyalty oath, swearing their support for the party's nominee in the general election. All observers recognized that success of the oath depended on the social stigma associated with bolting or aligning with African Americans. A compelling reason for the success of one-party rule in South Carolina lay in the perceived imperative of maintaining white supremacy, something white South Carolinians felt deeply because of their state's black majority. Maintaining white supremacy within South Carolina's political system of intense and bitter competition among factions proved possible only as long as all whites agreed to support the Democratic primary winner no matter how bitter the primary contest had been.

White South Carolinians regularly criticized anything that might possibly resurrect the horrors they imagined stemming from Reconstruction. Their fear of black political influence, however, extended beyond the unlikely possibility of a return of black political rule to the state. Instead, whites feared a far more likely alternative: that African Americans might gain political influence by becoming the balance of power between competitive white factions. If the South Carolina electorate divided into roughly equal factions, a small number of voters, uncommitted to any faction, could become a powerful swing vote, enjoying political power disproportionate to their numbers and handing victory to whichever faction they supported. In South Carolina, a relatively small proportion of black voters constituted a significant fraction of the overall electorate because African Americans were in the majority. Any disaffected white faction needed support from only a small percentage of black voters in order to form a viable and potentially winning coalition. The potential for a successful biracial political coalition, which a disaffected white faction would dominate, both heightened whites' temptation to attempt such a gambit and intensified whites' efforts to stigmatize any appeals to African American voters. Allowing a small portion of black voters to hold the balance of power between competing white political factions was anathema to most whites.[19]

After the September runoff Blease grudgingly accepted Manning's victory but began openly complaining of corruption in the primary. Blease soon flirted with the unimaginable. In October 1916, just three weeks after Blease's narrow defeat in the primary runoff and one month before the general election, a bitter Blease accepted an invitation to address an all-black audience at Allen University, an African Methodist Episcopal college in Columbia. While being generally moderate and guarded in his language, Blease used his opportunity at Allen, before a Republican audience, to attack the integrity of the recent Democratic primary and to suggest he was an appropriate political ally for black South Carolinians.[20]

The irony of Allen University inviting Cole Blease, one of the most notorious racial demagogues in South Carolina politics, to deliver the keynote address at the opening ceremony of its academic year was not lost on many African Americans, who protested Blease's invitation. Alumni and students petitioned Allen's president, Dr. Robert W. Mance, to withdraw the invitation, pointing out that Blease's presence on the campus "will greatly embarrass our wives and daughters," since Blease had spoken so "harshly in the courts and on the stump against the virtues of the negro women and the respect and decency of negroes in general." Blease had frequently and publicly justified lynching black men who allegedly raped white women, and he had also suggested that raping black women was not a crime. Yet Bishop W. D. Chappelle of the South Carolina AME church, who envisioned the economic and political potential of African American voters allying with Blease, attempted to mitigate the controversy among African Americans. In his flattering introduction of Blease, Chappelle dismissed Blease's infamous comments as "harsh things said on the stump." The bishop suggested Blease intended his rhetoric "only to tickle the ears of the voters and thereby gain their support."[21]

In Blease's speech to approximately four hundred African American students, the former governor suggested that he had been cheated in the 1916 gubernatorial primary. Blease further intimated that if he were South Carolina's next governor, he would provide "justice to the negro." Attempting to associate Manning and his administration with South Carolina's historic injustices against African Americans, Blease accused his political opponents of denying black South Carolinians the privilege of serving on juries, the opportunity for adequate education, a fair return for the taxes they paid, and justice in the courts.[22] At the least, Blease's address at Allen University testified to the bitterness he felt after his defeat by Manning. It also demonstrates the opportunism of Blease and black reformers, both of whom needed political allies and in their desperation considered making strange bedfellows.

Later, Blease's political opponents charged that his decision to address an all-black Republican audience at Allen University proved that he was both entertaining the idea of a bolt from the Democratic Party and also, flirting with the unthinkable, considering a direct appeal to black voters in the general election. Opponents claimed that in addition to his speech at Allen, there was other evidence that Blease was planning a general election bolt. John McLaurin, one-time Blease supporter, reported that Blease was negotiating with the Republican Party even before he accepted the invitation to speak at Allen. Moreover, the *Scimitar*, a Bleaseite newspaper, had reported that Blease was a candidate for governor in the November general election. Blease lost to Manning in the 1916 primary by less than five thousand votes. Had he entered the general election with all his usual supporters he would have only needed a relatively small number of African American voters to deny Manning reelection. If Blease had indeed contemplated a challenge to Manning in the general election of 1916 and an appeal to black voters to bridge the few-thousand-vote gap, he never followed through with the plan. Knowing that Democratic voters swore an oath to support the primary winner in the general election, Blease doubtless realized he could not possibly count on all of his supporters to violate a sacred pledge closely associated with white South Carolinians' ability to maintain white supremacy within their black-majority state.[23] Blease's decision not to run in the 1916 general election, however, did not prevent his opponents from highlighting the potential dangers that his flirtation with such a heresy posed for white Democratic control of South Carolina.

Whites' shared commitment to white supremacy allowed competing white factions to use white supremacy both to challenge opponents and to protect their own interests. White reformers were certainly willing to exploit whites' allegiance to white supremacy to enhance their prospects for political victory. The anti-Blease coalition walked away with its narrow victory in 1916 determined to avoid depending on such slim margins to defeat Blease in the future. In 1912, he won reelection to a second term as governor by garnering 51 percent of the vote in the first and only primary. When Blease challenged "Cotton Ed" Smith for his U.S. Senate seat in 1914, Blease received 43 percent of the vote in the first primary against the popular, sitting senator. In 1916, when Blease challenged Manning, the incumbent governor, he picked up 47 percent of the vote in the first primary.[24] Frustrated by its inability to dissuade white working-class voters from supporting Blease, the progressive core of the anti-Blease coalition decided to pursue a strategy to reduce Blease's voting strength through careful disfranchisement of as many of his likely supporters as possible. Not surprisingly, white reformers cloaked their white working-class disfranchisement strategy as a crucial protection for white supremacy.

Clamors for election reform followed on the heels of the 1916 gubernatorial election. Immediately after the election, *The State*, the newspaper edited by W. W. Ball, mounted a campaign for suffrage restrictions designed to defeat the Blease faction. Concealed under the banner of white supremacy, the suffrage-restriction campaign began with a call for sweeping reform of election practices and strict enforcement of South Carolina's existing election laws, which required all voters to present a poll-tax receipt and a registration certificate.[25] Strict enforcement of these laws, of course, threatened to disfranchise thousands of illiterate and marginally literate white voters who did not own the requisite property. Such a willingness to disfranchise illiterate whites, although within the state's constitutional bounds, violated one of white supremacy's tenets, white equality in the public sphere. Reports regularly circulated in South Carolina political circles that precinct managers refused to enforce election laws against white men because the officials believed such restrictions would "belittle" the whites in question.[26] In an effort to convince legislators and a majority of white voters to accept an idea as unpopular as disfranchising some white voters, reformers raised the specter of revived African American political power. Champions of suffrage restrictions argued that unless new draconian measures were adopted, South Carolina could never be safe from the return of black rule.

Since white reformers believed that most propertyless, illiterate voters strongly supported Blease, disfranchisement was an attractive strategy, but suffrage restriction advocates skirted dangerously close to flagrant violations of a cherished tenet of white supremacy. To disguise their own blatant class manipulation designed to advance their coalition's cause, progressive leaders invoked white supremacy. White reformers argued that if South Carolina did not enforce its own laws, federal intervention would soon follow, leading eventually to a restoration of African American voting on a large scale, white South Carolinians' greatest political fear. White reformers argued that resurgent black political power posed a far greater threat to white supremacy than the disfranchisement of a relatively small proportion of white voters. "THE NOTION THAT A WHITE SKIN AND NOTHING ELSE SHALL BE A SUFFICIENT QUALIFICATION FOR VOTING WILL HAVE TO BE ABANDONED," *The State* insisted. "IF THE PEOPLE OF SOUTH CAROLINA LACK THE COURAGE AND THE CONSCIENCE TO DISFRANCHISE AN ILLITERATE WHITE MAN THEN THEY WOULD BETTER CEASE TO TALK ABOUT KEEPING THE NEGROES OR EVEN THE MAJORITY OF THEM PERMANENTLY OUT OF POLITICS IN THE COMING YEARS."[27] Such a bold and direct assault on the Bleaseites' core claim to white privilege in the name of white supremacy demonstrates the volatility of a political system that rested on the illusion of white unity as a common principle.

White reformers supported their argument that black South Carolinians might regain voting rights unless illiterate whites were disfranchised by pointing to recent congressional attempts to craft a new "force bill." Through the legislation, also known as the Lodge election bill, originally proposed by Republican senator Henry Cabot Lodge of Massachusetts in 1890, Congress threatened southern states with federal investigations into their election laws and practices. The 1890 bill had failed, but Republican senator Jacob Gallinger of New Hampshire submitted a new, similar bill in 1916. Such an investigation of southern states' election practices, *The State* declared, would enable outsiders to observe the extent to which South Carolinians ignored their own election laws by allowing white illiterates to vote while disfranchising black illiterates. Doubtless white Democrats feared that congressional Republicans could acquire ample evidence, in the proposed investigation, to support their assertion that whites selectively enforced the voting restrictions, thus consistently violating African Americans' constitutional right to vote.[28] Therefore, white reformers, advocating suffrage restriction as a progressive reform, concluded that South Carolinians' willingness to defend white supremacy at its margins by allowing illiterate whites to vote jeopardized the state's ability to maintain the core requirement of white supremacy: preventing African Americans from exercising the franchise.

Soon the general plea to enforce existing election laws turned to the specific summons for the Australian, or secret, ballot. In his annual address to the general assembly in January 1917, Manning called for the adoption of the Australian ballot to "safeguard elections" and to ensure that each voter could express his "independent will." Knowing the idea was very unpopular in rural districts, Manning specified that the Australian ballot was most needed in cities, towns, and large communities.[29] On its surface, the Australian ballot seemed a more politically palatable method of suffrage restriction than insisting on strict enforcement of the state constitutional requirements, but either method promised to disfranchise some illiterate white voters as well as many African Americans. Supporters of the Australian ballot anticipated that it would sufficiently intimidate illiterate voters to either keep them away from the polls or cause them to mark their ballots improperly. Poll managers could readily disqualify improperly marked ballots. One proponent argued that the Australian ballot would limit voting to persons with "some information and rudimentary education."[30] Moreover, by limiting the use of the Australian ballot to more densely populated areas, proponents of the secret ballot targeted Blease voters in the state's mill villages. To conceal their strategy, however, white reformers disguised their "reform" legislation as a defense of the white working man's liberty. After all, one proponent of the Australian ballot suggested, the expressed purpose of the secret ballot was the "protection of the poor man's freedom at the polls." Secret ballots, reformers publicly claimed, enabled wage laborers and tenants to exercise the franchise without fear of coercion from their employer or anyone with whom they had an economic obligation.[31] The legislature, controlled by anti-Blease forces, passed a limited version of the Australian ballot during the 1918 session.[32]

After the close and hard-fought 1916 election, reformers conceded that Cole Blease had a lock on nearly 40 percent of the state's vote. The 1918 wartime election generally confirmed the strength of Blease's base. Defeat at the polls, especially his narrow loss to Richard Manning in 1916, never discouraged Blease for long. Indeed, from 1888 to 1916, Blease ran for one political office or another in every election, even though his losses far outnumbered his wins. In 1918, Blease set his political sights on the U.S. Senate, as he planned to challenge his former mentor, Ben Tillman, who was seventy years old and rumored to be in poor health following a stroke. Tillman, an icon in South Carolina politics and a U.S. senator since 1894, was seeking reelection to his fifth term. His reelection was in question only because of his age and failing health. In 1917, Tillman had publicly suggested that he might not seek another term, but he changed his mind as the election drew near. Nathaniel B. Dial, a lawyer and banker from Laurens, also planned to challenge Tillman's reelection.[33]

Fearful that Blease had a reasonable chance of unseating the ailing senator and indifferent to the lawyer-banker conservatism of Dial, the progressive core of the anti-Blease coalition vowed to find a more vigorous candidate than Tillman to enter the race in an effort to fend off Blease's challenge. Manning and his progressive allies understood that the success of their political agenda and their larger economic development strategies depended on South Carolina's having a strong pro-war, pro–Wilson administration senator in Washington. A victory for Blease, an outspoken opponent of President Wilson and critic of the United States' involvement in the war, might seriously jeopardize their reform agenda.

Manning and the reformers privately turned to popular Columbia-area congressman Asbury Francis "Frank" Lever. As a nine-term representative and the chair of the House Committee on Agriculture, Lever had gained attention as a strong supporter of the Wilson administration and had proved instrumental in promoting wartime food-production legislation. Moreover, Lever's political strength as an agricultural spokesman in South Carolina, especially among Tillman's farmer constituency, made him seem like the perfect choice to oppose Blease. Lever declared his candidacy for Tillman's Senate seat on the final day of April 1918. Within weeks, however, Lever had withdrawn from the race. He coveted the U.S. Senate seat, but he was loath to cross Tillman. Once Lever announced his candidacy, Tillman angrily exposed the behind-the-scenes maneuvering of Manning and other reformers to get Lever into the race. Lever, damaged by Tillman's revelation, pulled out of the Senate race, claiming that his service to the Wilson administration as chairman of the House Committee on Agriculture would prove more valuable than his contributions as a freshman senator. Ironically, just as anti-Blease forces feared, Tillman died July 3, weeks before the Democratic primary. Had Lever remained in the race, white reformers could have rallied behind him. Instead reformers were left with only Dial, a staunch anti-Bleaseite but a poor campaigner with strong ties to the old Conservative faction, as a candidate.[34]

Once their strategy for recruiting a strong anti-Blease alternative candidate to Tillman failed, reformers fought Blease's bid for the Senate by uniting behind Dial and employing aggressive tactics to weaken Blease. During the summer campaign that led up to the August primary, white reformers exposed past Blease maneuvers that seemed the equivalent of political blasphemy in South Carolina. Anti-Bleaseites accused Blease, who avidly opposed the Wilson administration and World War I, of being disloyal to his country, the Democratic Party, and white supremacy. They charged that in the summer of 1917, after the United States issued its declaration of war and prepared to mobilize soldiers, Blease made two speeches, one at Pomeria and the other at Filbert, in which he criticized President Wilson for getting the nation involved in war. It was rumored that in his speech at Pomeria, Blease scoffed at Manning's sons in their "pretty uniforms" and encouraged recruits to shoot them in the back. (Manning had six sons who served in the war; one was killed in action a week before the armistice was signed.) These two speeches, and other comments from Blease, handed his opponents ammunition for their claims that he was unpatriotic and disloyal to the Democratic Party. While campaigning in Florence, a town in the eastern Pee Dee section of the state, Dial confronted Blease before the audience. He charged Blease with being "disloyal from the crown of his head to the sole of his feet." Blease's only response was to leave the meeting without giving his speech. Opponents asserted that Blease aligned himself with a pro-German newspaper and hampered the patriotic spirit of young recruits and soldiers. Throughout the 1918 campaign, the political energy of the anti-Blease coalition focused on electing candidates who demonstrated loyalty to the Wilson administration and support for American soldiers at war.[35]

Hoping that the charge of disloyalty had weakened Blease and provided white reformers their ace in the hole, the anti-Blease coalition played yet another card. Late in the campaign, appealing to voters' commitment to white supremacy, reformers charged Blease with betrayal of both his party and the sacred tenets of white supremacy. Blease's opponents revived the political overture Blease had made to African Americans in the 1916 election season when he complained bitterly to an all-black audience at Allen University about corruption in the Democratic primary. The October timing of Blease's appearance, just three weeks after his close defeat in the primary, suggested that Blease had contemplated violating the sacred pledge that all white voters made to support the primary winner in the general election. Blease had also appealed to black voters in the general election in November.[36]

On the stump, Dial read portions of Blease's October 1916 speech as reported in the *Samaritan Herald*, an African American newspaper. White reformers were certainly willing to exploit whites' commitment to white supremacy to enhance their prospects for political victory and to insure Blease's defeat. They emphasized that Blease's speech to an all-black Republican audience, assailing the integrity of white Democrats, violated their trust as well as white supremacy. As the result of these tactics, Blease's support fell to an all-time low as he captured only 40,456 votes, or 36.5 percent of South Carolina's electorate, in losing to Dial in the Democratic primary.[37] Dial quickly concluded that "we have buried this perennial menace so that he will never show his face as a candidate again." In 1918 the anti-Blease forces had succeeded in convincing more South Carolina voters than usual that Blease was a bad political bet. White reformers' resounding victory for the Wilson administration during the war, while the nation watched, greatly relieved their anxiety. Sloan L. Goldsmith, of Piedmont, informed Governor Manning that "the wool is being pulled off of some of the Bleaseites' eyes at last. I thank God I have lived to see some of the rankest in South Carolina change."[38]

But the 1918 Senate race, in which Blease handed his opponents the opportunity to challenge his patriotism and his commitment to the Democratic Party, illustrates the tenacity of Blease's core support. Even at his political nadir, Blease retained the loyalty of nearly two-fifths of South Carolina voters. Thus, the outcome of the 1918 election reinforced reformers' strategy of completely writing off this portion of the electorate as potential allies. Once reformers determined that white laborers' votes were beyond their reach, they embraced the strategy of minimizing the Blease vote through careful disfranchisement of his voters.

White reformers' hopes that Blease's poor showing in the 1918 wartime primary represented a permanent reduction in his support were dispelled as early as 1922, when Blease declared for the open governor's seat.[39] The wartime characterization of Blease as disloyal and unpatriotic had decreased his core support, but the charge carried less resonance as South Carolinians' memory of the war faded. South Carolina's 1922 campaign for governor, like the statewide elections of 1916 and 1918, illustrates white reformers' relentless exploitation of white supremacy as a political tactic for defeating Blease. Also, the 1922 gubernatorial election demonstrates how white supremacy functioned as a pervasive element of South Carolina politics by creating an enticing political strategy and constraining reform.

In the race, white reformers devoted their efforts largely to the campaign against Blease rather than to a concerted campaign in favor of a specific pro-reform candidate. As Ball complained in a post-election analysis, "Most of the energy and time of fairly self-respecting and intelligent South Carolinians in recent years has been absorbed in the effort to avoid felonious, not to obtain good, government."[40] In the campaign against Blease, reformers focused primarily on exploiting Blease's ties with Joe Tolbert, a white Republican, and suggesting that such ties posed a serious threat to white supremacy. White reformers fashioned such a defensive political strategy for two reasons. First, as previous elections had demonstrated, Blease's base was solid, substantial, and relatively unshakable. The anti-Blease coalition had only about 55 to 60 percent of the electorate from which to forge their needed majority, so they had little margin for error. Thus reform champions had to minimize the Bleaseite vote and aggressively motivate largely apathetic anti-Blease voters. A bitter campaign claiming that white supremacy was at stake, they reasoned, was the best means of stirring voter enthusiasm.

Second, the fragmented nature of the anti-Blease coalition prevented aggressive support for any single anti-Blease candidate during the bulk of the campaign, waged largely over a six-week period before the first primary. Because the anti-Blease movement was a very loose coalition of disparate interests and former rivals, a strategy that backed one anti-Blease candidate against the other would not likely amass a winning majority in the first primary. Also, the strategy could possibly arouse enough bitterness among the losers to endanger cooperation against Blease in the runoff. For example, in 1922, some anti-Blease leaders felt that John Gary Evans, a strong Tillmanite during the 1890s, would make an effective candidate against Blease for governor. Naturally, some white reformers expressed concern about whether former Conservatives, with their lingering antipathy for Tillmanites, would support Evans. Ball recognized that because former governor Evans revived animosities between former Tillmanites and Conservatives, his candidacy was problematic. "In short," Ball reluctantly concluded, "the normal majority for conservative and progressive government in South Carolina is too small to admit indulgence in unnecessary contests within it."[41]

Despite the strategic need for cooperation, the large number of anti-Blease candidates demonstrates the coalition's fragmentation. Five anti-Blease candidates ran for the open governor's seat in 1922: Thomas G. McLeod of Bishopville, state senator George K. Laney of Chesterfield, John T. Duncan of Columbia, William Coleman of Union, and J. J. Cantey of Summerton. Neither Coleman nor Cantey had held public office before. Ball and many other state leaders consistently expressed frustration that the anti-Blease forces could not fully cooperate. Some within the anti-Blease movement even suggested that their coalition agree to hold a regular nominating convention. Such a convention would facilitate cooperation in advance of the election and produce a slate of nominees, possibly making it easier to elect a unified anti-Blease slate. Cantey, who shared white reformers' disdain for Blease, railed publicly against them for this behind-the-scenes maneuvering, calling the manipulation "as bad as Bleaseism." Reflecting on the election, Ball shared his frustrations over the large number of anti-Blease candidates with his friend and brother-in-law, Tom Waring. "We ran as usual," Ball lamented, "a mob against a machine."[42] In the first primary, "the machine"— Blease—polled almost 45 percent of the vote, leaving "the mob" to divide the remaining 55 percent.

As the 1922 campaign heated up, white reformers implemented their projected white supremacy strategy for fighting Blease. They reminded voters of Blease's political machinations from earlier years, when he addressed an all-black audience, and offered new allegations. They charged that after the 1920 presidential election Blease reached out to Joe Tolbert and the South Carolina Republican Party. These allegations openly questioned Blease's loyalty to the Democratic Party and suggested that his overtures to Republicans posed a direct threat to white supremacy in South Carolina. Calculating its potential damage with Blease's supporters and its capacity to rally their own supporters, the anti-Blease coalition had a letter from Blease to Tolbert published in newspapers across South Carolina. In the private communication, Blease confided to Tolbert, leader of Black and Tan Republicans in South Carolina, that he was a "Jeffersonian Democrat, who rejoiced at Harding's election." Besides this complete breach of southern Democratic etiquette, Blease offered an additional criticism of former president Wilson when he rejoiced at the "downfall of idealism," which Blease argued to Tolbert "gave us nothing but fresh-made graves, widows, orphans and billions of dollars [in] taxes, under the guise of liberty. We have less liberty now than we have ever had and fewer privileges as a result of Wilson and his henchmen."[43] Blease's own hand confirmed an overture to Tolbert, and reformers interpreted its meaning to fit their purposes.

With a Republican administration in Washington, white reformers speculated that Blease's overture to Tolbert was his attempt to benefit from the national Republican Party's rumored efforts to

strengthen the GOP in the South. Since 1900, Republicans had garnered only about 2,500 votes per election in South Carolina. The
national Republican Party indicated in 1922 that at least that many
votes were needed per congressional district if South Carolina
wanted to continue sending delegates to the national convention.
Moreover, speculation suggested that Tolbert might lose his position
as state Republican boss if he failed to garner significant numbers of
new voters. Sensing that Tolbert might be desperate in 1922, anti-
Bleaseites attempted to associate Blease with the Republicans' expansion efforts in the South.[44]

Hoping this association would alarm Bleaseites, reformers explicitly argued that Blease's flirtation with Republicans jeopardized
the privileges white supremacy extended to South Carolina's white
working class. Anxious to exploit the notion that Blease threatened
white supremacy, *The State* reminded white textile workers that "negroes are not allowed to work with white people in the cotton mills
and they should not be." Since working-class whites in South Carolina viewed keeping African Americans out of the mills as a vital
safeguard to their racial prerogative, reform strategists suggested
that Blease had threatened this guarantee. *The State* insisted that if
Republicans began polling a substantial number of votes in South
Carolina, the GOP would immediately move to "break down the
barriers that keep the negroes out of the Southern mills." Furthermore, *The State* argued, Republicans would seek the "abolition of all
racial discrimination in the industries."[45]

Wade F. Milam of Walhalla provides further evidence that reformers' primary campaign strategy for defeating Blease rested on
successful exploitation of white supremacy politics. Milam told reform leaders that he had some inside information about the connection between Blease and Tolbert. Milam claimed that with a little
time and extra assistance he could expose the Newberry lawyer's
dealings with Tolbert to Blease's strongest supporters, cotton-mill
workers. Milam thought he could spin the news so that "cotton mill
operatives would even 'itch' to get to the polls on the 29th," and vote
against Blease. After all, Milam asked, "Why not fight this matter
with circulars, billboards, and if you please the K.K.K.?"[46] Touting
Tolbert as his source, Milam made his supposedly damaging information public in a letter to *The State* just days before the first pri-

mary. Milam claimed that Blease told Tolbert, "I am sorry I did not stump South Carolina for Harding" in 1920. Milam argued that supporting a Republican presidential candidate, as Blease seemed willing to do, sowed the seeds for a return to "carpet bag rule" in South Carolina. The restoration of Republican rule in South Carolina, he surmised, would inevitably lead to the repeal of all segregation laws. "THINK OF IT!" Milam said, "A Pullman car running from Columbia to Jacksonville, Florida, occupied by 20 buck negro men and a few fair daughters of the South." Milam clearly intended these allusions to rape and miscegenation to offend white South Carolinians' sense of racial entitlement and appeal to the working class's notions of white manhood. Milam also contended that Republicans would inject "cheap negro labor" into the cotton mill and thus eliminate the whites-only textile labor force.[47]

Such political hyperbole offended a group of white Sumter Republicans, who immediately held a meeting and drafted a resolution to assure other white South Carolinians that their county's fledgling political organization had no plans for "any interference with white supremacy here."[48] The Sumter Republicans flashed their white supremacy credentials to defend themselves against a charge that a revival of their party threatened white rule in South Carolina. Regardless of the accuracy of their speculation or the improbability of a renewed Republican threat to white supremacy in South Carolina, anti-Blease candidates and strategists never tired of publicizing Blease's alleged enthusiasm for Harding and strongly suggested that Blease might have violated his Democratic loyalty oath in the general election. Privately, progressive strategists conceded that Tolbert probably had no serious interest in an alliance with Blease, but they congratulated themselves on exposing the Tolbert letter. "Something had to be done to arouse our people," Ball remarked to Harry Watson, another reform leader. Judging from the large number of letters the campaign received referencing the Blease-Tolbert relationship, Ball concluded it had "excited intense interest everywhere." Equally important, reform leaders believed that the "publication of them [the letters] chilled the ardor of his supporters."[49]

These private political discussions revealed how white reformers crassly manipulated white supremacy for political gain. When South Carolina's first-term junior senator, Nathaniel Dial, learned that

Harding had decided not to extend any patronage to African Americans in the South, he shared the information with Ball, the editor of *The State*, in strictest confidence. Dial realized that the information might allay some whites' fears about a new Republican challenge to white supremacy, so he and Ball agreed not to disclose the information. After all, Dial reminded Ball, "these fears may be a very good asset to our State."[50] Ball and Dial had also plotted the earlier strategy of exposing the Tolbert letter to South Carolinians. "If we could get these Republican flirtations of Mr. Blease ventilated in the Southern newspapers from Washington, I think it would be of greater assistance than for *The State* to bring them out first," Ball told Pat H. McGowan, an aide to Dial in Washington.[51]

The first primary result replicated the familiar pattern: no candidate received a majority so a runoff primary was necessary. Blease received a plurality with about 46 percent of the vote; Thomas G. McLeod, the Bishopville candidate who had served two previous terms as lieutenant governor, finished second with 38 percent of the total vote; George Laney, the long-term legislator from Chesterfield, garnered over 13 percent of the vote; and the two novice anti-Blease candidates, J. J. Cantey and William Coleman, shared just under 3 percent of the vote. In the second phase of the election, Blease faced the challenge of expanding his strong base into a voting majority. The anti-Blease coalition used the two weeks of the runoff campaign to unite their fractured forces behind McLeod. Since many voters had seen their first choice defeated and dropped from the ballot, white reformers' greatest challenge lay in motivating the anti-Blease vote to turn out in the second primary. This need for a strong anti-Blease turnout contributed to white reformers' heightened use of inflammatory rhetoric against Blease. Between the two primaries in 1922, a group identified as "Democrats of '76" ran a political advertisement highly critical of Blease and his relationship with Tolbert. The group laced the advertisement with rhetorical appeals to white supremacy that accused Blease of weakening the "firmness of the white man's government of this State." The advertisement asked, "Are the white people of South Carolina, the political heirs of Hampton and Tillman, prepared to entrust their government to a man who is the confessed approver, adviser and comforter of Joe Tolbert, the political heir of the Scalawags and Carpet-baggers?"[52] Although

Hampton and Tillman were leaders of rival white factions of the past, the anti-Blease campaign rhetoric linked the men against their agreed-upon enemy, whites who violated white supremacy.

McLeod benefited from the customary search for unity against Blease. The anti-Blease strategy worked as expected, and South Carolinians elected McLeod as their next governor in the runoff primary on September 12. Ball often lamented the weakness of the reform faction in the political culture of Blease-era South Carolina, arguing that the fragmented nature of the anti-Blease coalition produced weak leaders. Ball noted that McLeod's success in 1922 demonstrates that almost anyone could hold high political office in South Carolina provided that a "majority will form against Blease." Perceiving McLeod as a political mediocrity, Ball mused that any "man of force should have little difficulty in rallying a larger majority."[53]

In each of these war-era elections, broad acceptance of white supremacy among whites facilitated white unity and cooperation in support of their common goal of preventing or severely restricting African Americans' political participation. The shared allegiance among white South Carolinians to white supremacy also made racial appeals a potent—sometimes an omnipotent—political weapon used by competing white factions. In all political contests, factions framed their opposition to undesired candidates or proposed legislation as a needed defense of white supremacy, suggesting that the targeted opponent threatened the nonnegotiable principle. In these three elections, the near-universal appeal of white supremacy among whites invited reformers to employ this defensive strategy to prevent Blease's election, which they viewed as unacceptable to their reform agenda. The temptation to use this defensive tactic—accusing opponents of threatening white supremacy—was overwhelming because it worked so well. Yet white supremacy as a political weapon was a double-edged sword. White reformers, one faction of the Democratic Party, could brandish the sharpened tool against Bleaseites with predictable consequences, but white reformers' opponents could push back with the same potent instrument and produce the same lethal results.

The end to which political participants employed the tempting and successful tactic was simply a defense of the status quo: white supremacy. The politics of white supremacy encouraged an identity politics. All white participants asserted their claims to the mantle of white supremacy, trumpeted their qualifications, and challenged the authenticity of others' true identity. South Carolina reformers readily embraced the identity; however, they wanted more than a white identity. They wanted to reform the state's economic, educational, and social systems in the context of maintaining white dominance and a rigid racial hierarchy. Yet white supremacy militated against reformers electing strong, progressive leaders who could aggressively campaign for change. In order to defeat Blease, reformers needed allies from within the anti-Blease coalition, which was a diverse association of varying economic interests. Whites' collective adherence to white supremacy coalesced on the agreement to protect white dominance and to cooperate against threats to that dominance. But this limited consensus among whites with economic and class differences did not facilitate cooperation on other issues. Therefore, the anti-Blease coalition, which could rally in defense of white supremacy, could not collaborate to accomplish progressive ends. If progressive candidates or legislative reform initiatives offended conservative economic or social interests, these factions could, with ease, turn the defensive strategy against white reformers, accusing them of violating white supremacy. Since whites agreed to rally against threats to white supremacy, everyone simply crafted arguments that characterized unwanted candidates and initiatives as threats to that supremacy. Thus, white supremacy protected the status quo and impeded changes that threatened any entrenched interest.

Faced with weak coalitions, white reformers had difficulty electing candidates committed to their agenda. Moreover, they experienced significant difficulty garnering legislative support for their desired reform policies from this ineffective and weak coalition as the subsequent analyses of debates about woman suffrage, tax reform, and education reform will demonstrate. Had white supremacy not been so compelling, so broadly shared, so fundamental to the self-image of early twentieth-century white South Carolinians, racial appeals might not have been such effective weapons in the hands of obstructionists.

Chapter 8

Woman Suffrage

As their enthusiasm for suffrage restrictions indicated, South Carolina's white reformers preferred and sought control over the scope and character of the electorate. They favored restricting participation to the "better sort" whenever possible. Nationally, progressives endorsed the enfranchisement of women as a method for infusing the electorate with the better sort. National progressives believed that women, especially middle-class women, brought a wholesome, softening, and virtuous quality to the harsh realm of politics. However, the paramount concern over white supremacy, particularly in the midst of war-induced African American activism, placed South Carolina's white reformers in a precarious position on the woman suffrage issue. The usual reform opponents fought against woman suffrage with the customary weapon: a broad array of conservative factions that insisted that change threatened white supremacy. Unlike most other reforms, however, woman suffrage divided white reformers. The dictates of white supremacy influenced the positions of both supporters and opponents. Woman suffrage invited federal involvement, the volatile element that enhanced the division among white reformers. White reformers on both sides of the issue, as well as other opponents of woman suffrage, calculated how expanding the franchise to include women would affect strategies for maintaining white control.

In 1919, as individual states began ratification debates of the amendment to enlarge the franchise to include women, the South gained attention for its incessant opposition to the amendment.[1] The South's particular insistence on maintaining white supremacy and conserving traditional gender roles shaped the region's woman suffrage movement and explains its limited success.[2] Within the context of southern conservatism, South Carolina stood as an extreme case. Compared to other southern states, South Carolina had a small and weak suffrage movement. It was one of only a handful of states that never developed an antisuffrage movement, a further indication that suffrage advocates' demands posed only a minimal threat and did not warrant organized resistance. Moreover, South Carolina's legislature quickly and soundly defeated the proposed national woman suffrage amendment with a concurrent resolution, making the Palmetto State one of the ten states that rejected ratification.[3]

Why such a categorical rejection? After the sound defeat, a frustrated supporter of woman suffrage in South Carolina publicly pondered the same question: "Why do we [South Carolinians] always resist the current of progress?" This advocate for woman suffrage lamented the state legislature's sound rejection of the federal amendment and charged that the "principle of state rights is being used as an obstacle to impede the progress of an overwhelming sentiment in favor of extending the right of suffrage to women."[4] Debate over the amendment to give women the vote ignited fears among white southerners who loathed extending federal authority into issues currently controlled by the states. South Carolina's white progressive women who championed ratification experienced the frustration all white reform advocates confronted in South Carolina: continual resistance on the grounds that change might alter the delicate political balance that ensured white control. The woman suffrage debate in South Carolina, which occurred in the context of increased African American activism during World War I and its immediate aftermath, brings to light the complex relationship between race, class, and gender in a state where white control remained crucial to the state's empowered white minority.

Advocated by some Americans since the mid-nineteenth century in various contexts and at various levels of intensity, woman suffrage reemerged as a national political issue during the second decade of the twentieth century. By 1918, President Woodrow Wilson's administration and the national Democratic Party heartily endorsed woman suffrage as a reward to American women whose wartime efforts had been instrumental in the nation's preparedness campaign—much to the chagrin of southern Democrats who opposed all federal involvement in election reform. Although South Carolina suffrage advocates, who were overwhelmingly women, did not command the support of most South Carolinians, most women in the state, or even a majority of white reformers, these determined women labored to extend the franchise and to diminish gender inequalities in the Palmetto State.

When woman suffrage reemerged as a national political issue during the Progressive Era, South Carolina was slow to participate. By 1914 three urban centers—Spartanburg, Charleston, and Columbia—had each organized a city chapter of the National American Woman Suffrage Association (NAWSA) with approximately four hundred members collectively. Leaders from these city clubs; Emily Plume Evans, former governor John Gary Evans's wife; Hannah Hemphill Coleman; and Harriett Powe Lynch, along with other women, met on May 15, 1915, and formed a statewide organization, the South Carolina Equal Suffrage League. The white reformers who led South Carolina's suffrage movement were well educated and socially prominent. As patrician club women, participants in the suffrage movement also were active in state chapters of the Federation of Women's Clubs, the Federation of Labor, and the Woman's Christian Temperance Union. By 1917 South Carolina boasted twenty-five local NAWSA clubs, although Lynch, the league's president, acknowledged that some were inactive. These suffrage activists preferred educational strategies to awaken those South Carolinians indifferent or opposed to woman suffrage. Commentary in *The State*'s weekly Sunday "Club Women's Interests and Activities" column revealed that suffrage supporters overtly shunned militant strategies and readily accepted slow progress that focused on state-by-state extension of suffrage rather than federal action. These women held luncheons and invited national speakers, wrote letters, distributed literature, supplied debate literature for schools and clubs, and lobbied legislators. These progressive club women advocated woman suffrage as essential to other reforms to restrict child labor, secure an eight-hour workday, improve health and public safety standards, increase educational opportunities, and promote temperance. They also imagined that enfranchised women would restore virtue and elevate politics.[5]

Approximately one hundred South Carolina women belonged to

three state chapters (Charleston, Greenville, and Orangeburg) of the more militant National Woman's Party (NWP) led by Alice Paul. Susan Pringle Frost led the Charleston club after withdrawing from the South Carolina League, which she concluded was too risk averse. While the Charleston branch became the most active National Woman's Party chapter in the state, it garnered only fifty-three members, a fraction of the membership of the much larger six-hundred-member NAWSA affiliate in Charleston. Helen E. Vaughan led the Greenville chapter, which in 1918 renounced its NAWSA membership to join the NWP. While rhetorically these women endorsed the militancy of the national organizations, they practiced few radical tactics in South Carolina.[6]

The women who waged the suffrage campaign belonged to the South Carolina League and had pressed members of the South Carolina General Assembly regularly since 1915 for women's voting rights. Despite the consistent pressure, the state legislature dealt substantively with enfranchising women only in its 1917 session. On January 30 and 31 of that year the state senate debated a resolution to hold a referendum to amend the state constitution to allow woman suffrage.[7] This resolution reflected the state's rights approach woman suffrage strategists designed as a compromise measure to allay concerns about federal control of voting. Many white South Carolinians, regardless of faction, feared that a federal amendment would jeopardize the patchwork of disfranchising strategies southern states had erected to circumvent the Fifteenth Amendment.

During the January 1917 legislative debate, Senator James A. Banks of Calhoun spoke against the proposed state referendum, insisting that the majority of women did not want the vote. Another opponent of the resolution, Senator John F. Williams of Aiken, suggested that no more than twenty-five thousand "sissy men" favored the referendum and South Carolina would have "a terrible time getting rid of it once the good women saw their mistake." Williams's criticism challenged the masculinity of men who supported woman suffrage and ridiculed the notion that real men would partner with women to secure and maintain power. Attempting to link the woman suffrage movement with another unpopular cause, Williams called for a proviso to the suffrage referendum granting "divorces from the bonds of matrimony." Williams believed that the unpopularity of such a proviso would stigmatize woman suffrage in the eyes of many voters in South Carolina, the only state in the nation that proudly refused its citizens legal divorces.[8] During the debate, Senator Niels Christensen, a prominent reformer from Beaufort, emerged as the strongest advocate of woman suffrage in the senate. The women in Christensen's family were prominent suffrage activists. His mother, Abbie, had been active in the 1890s movement; his sister, Andrea, was vice president of her local chapter of the South Carolina League; and his wife, Nancy, supported Susan Pringle Frost, the militant Charlestonian suffrage leader. Despite Christensen's influence and stature among his colleagues, the senate failed by five votes to gain the two-thirds majority necessary for a state referendum. Even so, the 25–19 vote in favor of a referendum encouraged suffrage advocates who previously had failed to have the issue even considered.[9]

The 1917 general assembly session closed with suffrage advocates hoping for more progress next session, but by 1918 circumstances had dramatically changed because of both the United States' entry into World War I and recent national progress on a federal woman suffrage amendment. Following the U.S. House of Representatives' passage of the federal amendment in January, South Carolina women activists asked Congressman Alfred W. Horton of Spartanburg, a champion of woman suffrage, to withdraw the state referendum resolution, anticipating the amendment's passage in the U.S. Senate soon. With a federal amendment pending, the women leading South Carolina's suffrage movement decided that a strategy advocating a state referendum seemed unnecessary. The emphasis shifted from lobbying the state legislature to lobbying the U.S. Senate for passage of the federal amendment. Students and faculty from the state's women's colleges—Winthrop, Coker, Anderson, and Converse—petitioned South Carolina senator Benjamin Tillman demanding passage, but Tillman never deviated from his long-standing opposition to woman suffrage.[10]

Tillman died in July 1918, months before the Senate voted on the proposed federal amendment, opening a new opportunity. Not only did South Carolina have a new senator in Washington, but also the women supporting the suffrage amendment selected new leadership for the movement. The South Carolina Equal Suffrage League canceled its 1918 meeting because of women's endless civilian wartime responsibilities. However, just weeks after the armistice ended World War I, the South Carolina League held its annual meeting in January 1919 and elected a new president, Eulalie Chafe Salley of Aiken. A successful real estate broker, mother of two, and wife of a lawyer who did not support her activities, Salley led the league with energy. James Henry Rice characterized this independent businesswoman and political activist as a "woman of iron will and dauntless determination." In January 1919, Salley began a six-month, aggressive push for passage of the Susan B. Anthony amendment in the Senate. She energized the fight with improved organization, extensive letter writing, lobbying, and public speaking.[11] William P. Pollock, a lawyer from Cheraw, won a special election in November 1918 to complete Tillman's Senate term, which would end March 3, 1919. Suffrage advocates had more success lobbying Senator Pollock, who was the only congressional member from South Carolina ever to vote for woman suffrage, a vote he cast in February 1919, when the amendment failed in the Senate by only one vote. Pollock's short term had expired when the Senate finally passed the amendment in June. His successor, Nathaniel B. Dial, opposed woman suffrage.[12]

The opposition of so many white South Carolinians to woman suffrage revealed the depth and breadth of their commitment to both patriarchy and white supremacy. As the debate heated up in 1919, one South Carolinian insisted that woman suffrage advocates were nothing but a "gang of home destroyers and State wreckers." He reasoned that if women voted, so would African Americans. Reminiscent of the "sissy men" comment from the 1917 debate, this opponent expressed his equally rigid gender ideals when he concluded: "If our women would become home makers, let politics alone and devote themselves to the Christian religion, the Southland would blossom like the rose, but otherwise the future is not auspicious."[13] In addition to restricting women to a domestic and subservient status that denied them political influence, white men wanted to keep African Americans politically impotent, and they feared that the proposed federal suffrage amendment jeopardized their ability to control voter eligibility. Instead, they defended the state's right to decide voting questions since such control allowed South Carolina's white men the maximum leeway in disfranchising unwanted participants. Many white men opposed any measure that eroded their control of suffrage issues. A constitutional amendment that guaranteed voting rights to women, they reasoned, opened the constitutional door for "outsiders" to challenge existing racial restrictions. One outraged South Carolinian considered woman suffrage the *"most serious* question that has ever confronted our fair South land" because he perceived that it jeopardized black disfranchisement. This Charlestonian privately told South Carolina governor Robert A. Cooper in 1919: "We certainly know that the way to manage the negro is to keep him in his place and keep his hands off the government. We cannot discuss all those things through the newspapers or in public on account of making them too wise, but the white people of the South had better have their eyes open on this question. Eternal vigilance is the price of liberty. Will the South safeguard her liberty, or are we to witness her down fall?"[14]

James F. Byrnes, a U.S. representative from the Second Congressional District, expressed his opposition to the Anthony amendment in a letter to prominent South Carolina editor W. W. Ball. Byrnes detailed his concerns about the effects of the amendment on South Carolina's ability to maintain white supremacy. "Unfortunate, though it may be," Byrnes observed, "our consideration of every question must include the consideration of this race question." The proposed amendment to enfranchise women, Byrnes noted, granted Congress unprecedented constitutional authority to transfer control of suffrage requirements from the states to the federal government. "It is certain," Byrnes surmised "that if there was a fair registration they [African Americans] would have a slight majority of voters in our State." In addition to blacks' numerical strength, Byrnes believed, the pending amendment would give African Americans an additional advantage because black women would be more enthusiastic about voting than white women. Byrnes had read the *Crisis* and recognized the NAACP's plans to encourage African American voter registration among women once the amendment was ratified. Aware that the *Crisis* circulated in South Carolina, the congressman had unleashed a tirade against this publication on the House floor just weeks after the Senate passed the proposed amendment. Byrnes feared black women in his home state would respond to the NAACP's call to action.[15]

Ratification of the woman suffrage amendment, Byrnes reasoned, would not only endanger white supremacy by enfranchising African

American women, but it would also heighten the probability of federal control of voting legislation. Byrnes feared this proposed amendment would provide impeccable legal footing for Republicans who opposed the suffrage restrictions that southern states had enacted to disfranchise African Americans. He noted that without the woman's suffrage amendment advocates of African Americans' voting rights had to rely only on the Fifteenth Amendment, which Byrnes thought could never withstand the scrutiny of judicial review. The congressman's doubts about the Fifteenth Amendment's legitimacy were premised on the notion that southern Reconstruction state governments that ratified this amendment were illegitimate. While few prominent jurists shared Byrnes's doubts about the Fifteenth Amendment, the congressman clung tenaciously to his view. He also realized that if the Anthony-inspired amendment was ratified, its legitimacy would render his reservations about the Reconstruction-era amendment moot. Believing that the woman suffrage amendment would strengthen the hands of Republicans, Byrnes opposed its ratification.[16]

Byrnes was hardly the only white South Carolinian who opposed woman suffrage because he feared federal control might replace local and state control. While the Senate debated the proposed amendment in 1919, J. F. J. Caldwell of Newberry denounced it as a violation of state's rights. If Congress, rather than individual state legislatures, controlled laws governing the franchise, Caldwell reasoned, then South Carolina's white minority lay at the mercy of a congressional majority, which came from states "where there is no negro peril." Caldwell asked: "How shall we manage to prevent that [black] majority from ruling the State? By force? Or by fraud?" Raising the specter of the post–Civil War experiment that whites always remembered with dread, Caldwell emphasized that the last time the federal government violated state's rights it "brought upon us all the horrors and abominations of so called reconstruction." South Carolina's only salvation, he insisted, came with the restoration of state's rights "whose power enabled us to rescue government from barbarous negroes and plundering carpetbaggers." Caldwell invoked the menacing imagery of Reconstruction, and his argument reflected the views of many white men in South Carolina who interpreted the equal suffrage amendment as a direct threat to state's rights. White South Carolinians' anxieties about the possibility of blacks voting peaked in 1919 because African American reformers had begun demanding voting rights in the aftermath of the war.[17] In 1919, South Carolina governor Robert A. Cooper received correspondence from those worried that whites would lose control of the electoral process if woman suffrage passed. "I believe that welfare of the Negro is best served by the domination of an absolutely white government," Governor Ruffin G. Pleasant of Louisiana vented to Cooper, "and he should not be encouraged to enter political strife that after all will result in the white race asserting its superiority and its will to rule."[18] Pleasant's hand-wringing musings to Cooper suggested that he anticipated white violence against blacks if the political balance of power shifted.

While white South Carolinians generally agreed on the need to disfranchise virtually all African Americans, they were far from united in their opposition to woman suffrage. Speaking in opposition to the "reactionary forces against women voting in the democratic primary," former state senator William S. Hall of Cherokee County criticized the state's rights argument that was often used against woman suffrage. Hall insisted that the Constitution did not reserve powers to the states to be used as "instruments to obstruct the progress of democracy."[19] Equally frustrated with reasoning that suggested woman suffrage jeopardized white supremacy, J. S. Hartzell of Cheraw pointed out: "The negro 'bogey' is called from its grave whenever it can serve the purpose of two-by-four politicians. Are the negro men voting now? Will they vote any more if the suffrage bill is passed? Will the negro women vote if the men do not?" Hartzell concluded that southern states had "always taken care of such contingencies and can again."[20] Hartzell's reasoning demonstrates that suffrage supporters also rationalized their position's consistency with white supremacy.

Senator William Pollock made an unpopular stand by speaking in favor of woman suffrage on the floor of the U.S. Senate and voting for the amendment. But he noted that his support of woman suffrage did not defy white supremacy. State and national suffragists, as well as President Wilson, targeted the new senator as a potential supporter. They heavily lobbied Pollock to cast one of the two remaining votes needed for passage of the amendment.[21] In his speech before the February 10, 1919, vote, Pollock argued that the nation's professed faith in democracy during an international war rang hollow if the Senate denied the American people the right to settle the woman suffrage issue. Risking his reputation in conservative South Carolina by supporting woman suffrage, Pollock carefully assured white South Carolinians of his commitment to white supremacy while voting for the federal woman suffrage amendment. In concluding his speech, he warned opportunistic politicians outside the South, "You will not undertake to place in control over us a race of people that you would never allow to govern you. The white men have outvoted the negro men and that under trying conditions, and God helping us from this day forward the white man and the white women will outvote the negro men and the negro women."[22] He understood that in voting for woman suffrage he had to dispel accusations that the amendment threatened white supremacy. Even with Pollock's vote, enough other southern Democrats in the senate voted against the amendment to defeat it by one vote.

While the women who led South Carolina's suffrage fight praised and appreciated Pollock's bold vote, harsh criticism drowned out any positive sentiment.[23] After leaving Washington, Pollock continued his support of woman suffrage and carefully linked that support to white supremacy. He proposed that South Carolina impose an eligibility requirement that citizens demonstrate proof of "legitimacy" extending back three generations to ensure that black South Carolinians would not be enfranchised by this federal constitutional amendment. He argued that if such a requirement were incorporated into the state's constitution, it would not only solve the race question but also would stigmatize illegitimacy, encourage marriage, and keep "family relations sacred."[24] His insistence on displaying his white supremacy credentials illustrates white reformers' willingness to craft their rhetoric and shape their proposals to reassure whites that any proposed change would not undermine white control.

The continued disfranchisement of African Americans was hardly the only concern revealed in the debates over woman suffrage. Opponents began sensing that ratification of the amendment was inevitable, even if South Carolina rejected it. Consequently, they began calculating its consequences on factional rivalry within South Carolina politics. If the electorate was going to expand without their approval, then opponents of woman suffrage at least wanted to control its expansion. Publicly, the editor of *The State*, W. W. Ball, perhaps the architect of the reform coalition in South Carolina, suggested that women should demonstrate their desire to vote by first lobbying for election reforms like the Australian ballot, which would ensure privacy at the polls, a quality Ball deemed essential for women's safety at the polls. Ball claimed not to oppose giving women the vote, but he doubted that most women wanted it and he opposed a federal amendment granting woman suffrage. He frequently used the editorial page of *The State* to warn woman suffrage proponents about the potential dangers women faced if the measure succeeded. Since whites were a minority in South Carolina, if women became eligible to vote, Ball explained regularly, then white women would have a duty, rather than a right, to vote in order to offset the votes of literate black women. Ball feared that white women would not take this responsibility seriously, thus jeopardizing white control. Emma A. Dunovant of Edgefield, a leader in the South Carolina Equal Suffrage League, author of the league's weekly newspaper column, and close friend of Eulalie Salley, bitterly resented Ball's editorials. Publicly Dunovant challenged Ball's position by asking, "What is the right way to give women equal suffrage?" She told Salley, "I hope I can live to see the day when Ball can be made to eat every thought and word that has emanated from his cloudy brain on the subject of suffrage and women."[25]

Ball revealed privately that his paramount concern about expanding the franchise was the safety of the anti-Blease majority. As the 1916 and 1918 elections illustrated, political competition in this era occurred in the context of two discernible political organizations within South Carolina's Democratic Party: the Blease faction, with doggedly loyal supporters; and the anti-Blease coalition, a tentative coalition of progressive reformers, patrician conservatives, large landowners, and business elites that Ball had helped to stitch together. He openly expressed concerns that woman suffrage would endanger white supremacy, but, in all probability, he dreaded woman suffrage because he had calculated that it would aid the Blease faction. Ball remained exasperated that Blease, the obstructionist and determined opponent of progressive reform, had such a "hold on a class of people that no one else in this state has." White reformers in recent elections had joined with outright conservatives to limit the political obstruction of the Bleaseites.[26]

If women became enfranchised, Ball and other political observers in South Carolina anticipated that mill women, potential Bleaseites, would likely "vote much as their husbands and brothers do." Moreover, Ball feared that Blease could easily persuade mill-village women to go to the polls. By contrast, he doubted that the wives and daughters of planters, professionals, and businessmen would vote. Steeped in patrician and patriarchal notions, he reasoned that elite and middle-class women would treasure their "separate sphere" that allegedly protected them from the corrupting world of politics. At least he feared these women would not respond as enthusiastically as working-class women might respond because of their concern over sacrificing their gentility or socially accepted femininity.[27] As Ball and others privately calculated woman suffrage's effect on the strength of their political coalition, they anticipated a loss of political power. Fears of a shift in the relative strength of political factions lay at the core of some whites' opposition to woman suffrage. To mask their factional self-interest during public debates, they represented their opposition as a carefully calculated defense of white supremacy.

South Carolina's white reformers had for so long associated reform with suffrage restrictions that it became hard for many of them to see franchise expansion as a reform. Yet clearly some white reformers reached different conclusions on this issue, especially the women who led the suffrage fight and the smaller number of male reformers who supported them. These reformers instead calculated that extending suffrage to women would be the best way to foster reform. They anticipated that middle-class, reform-minded women would turn out in larger numbers to defeat antireform Bleaseites. Rather than uniting in support of woman suffrage, white reformers were divided, rendering success impossible. This split revealed that white reformers had to work together to pass future reforms because their opponents were so strong and their potential winning margin so narrow.

South Carolina's general assembly considered the Susan B. Anthony amendment when the legislature convened in January for its 1920 session. The debate was minimal and the defeat resounding.

The house opposed the amendment four to one, and only four state senators voted for it. While the house overwhelmingly rejected ratification of the amendment, one member could not resist a final opportunity to justify the maneuver with white supremacy rhetoric. William R. Bradford, the house sponsor of the joint resolution rejecting the amendment, reported that it saddened him to disappoint the women of South Carolina, but he had a public responsibility to "prevent the injection of the negroes into politics." Even as supporters experienced overwhelming defeat, Marion R. Cooper of Beaufort, one of the few house members who favored woman suffrage, made a final attempt to refute charges that woman suffrage endangered white supremacy. Cooper contended that opponents like Bradford exaggerated the concern about black voting, and he labeled the hyperbole "pure rot." He reasoned that whites had effortlessly controlled black voting "with a little tobacco and liquor" during Reconstruction and could do so again. Despite South Carolina's dogged opposition, ratification of the Nineteenth Amendment succeeded nationally in August 1920 when Tennessee ratified it.[28]

The concern so openly expressed by Byrnes and other white South Carolinians that the equal-suffrage amendment would prompt African American women to seek voting privileges were partially realized immediately following ratification, which created excitement and anticipation in South Carolina's African American community.[29] African American women acted as quickly as possible. On the first day of September registration, well-prepared women in Columbia lined up to register. Surprised by the black women's presence as well as their preparation—they brought their tax receipts and were willing to take the literacy test—the white registrars grudgingly registered those not discouraged by long waits. Employing a time-honored expression of white supremacy, the registrars served the white applicants first. At least one hundred African American women came that first day, and many of them reportedly waited in registration lines for six to eight hours. "Who stirred up all these colored women to come up here and register?" one white man asked in frustration.[30]

Butler Nance, president of Columbia's NAACP, "admired the courage and nerve" of the women, who lined up again the next day. After that first day, however, white registrars met these women with more than frustrating delays. A lawyer began "assisting" the registration procedures after the unexpected deluge of black registrants. He confronted the women with more than a test of their reading skills. White election officials badgered them with demands to read and explain long passages from the civil and criminal codes rather than the Constitution. Moreover, they were asked to explain how one appeals a court case, to define the meaning of civil code and *mandamus*, and to answer trick questions about the state budget. The women were also denied their voter registrations for allegedly mispronouncing words.[31]

Frustrated by the walls whites had erected, yet also expecting resistance, these women formed a temporary organization to fight the injustice. They worked with Columbia's NAACP and Nance, one of South Carolina's few black attorneys, who mounted a legal challenge. Nance filed an appeal for thirty-two of these African American women against the Board of Registration of Richland County for refusing to register them. The appeal stressed that college-educated women, with degrees from colleges such as Benedict, Allen, Shaw, South Carolina State, and Fisk, were told that they failed the required literacy test when instead many were inappropriately given other challenges. South Carolina's state constitution required potential voters to read and write any portion of the state constitution, but the Richland County registrar had asked these women to read from the civil and criminal law code. It was disclosed privately that the county registrar selected a passage that included "miscegenation, sodomy, incest, burglary, robbery, larceny," and, in an effort to humiliate the African American women, he asked them to explain the terms.[32]

William Pickens, an NAACP field secretary, visited Columbia during the excitement. While on a regional tour promoting the national organization and encouraging membership, Pickens observed the outrages in Columbia firsthand. He was excited that Nance and the women launched the legal challenge. The New York NAACP office supported the Columbia case and promoted it in numerous New York newspapers as evidence of South Carolina's defiance of the recently ratified Nineteenth Amendment. Pickens wrote an article for the *Nation* to draw national attention to South Carolina's immediate violation of the new amendment. Although the NAACP headquarters wanted to draw special attention to the incident, African American leaders in Columbia were divided between wanting national publicity of the injustices and fearing reprisals if white South Carolinians discovered a close connection between the Columbia NAACP and the organization's New York office. Moreover, the women planned to continue recruiting other women to register, and they feared that too much attention might jeopardize that effort. Nance said, "Let the world know the kind of 'DEMOCRACY' that our sons fought for on the battle fields of France." Yet the Columbia NAACP's secretary, Dixie B. Brooks, carefully denied that the registration of African American women had been an "organized effort." She specifically asked the national organization to "be careful not to irritate by publishing this—[it] may thwart our plans before election time."[33]

Whites in Beaufort handled African Americans' registration efforts with more stealth and deception, but with determination. Several hundred black women and men in Beaufort County attempted to register after ratification of the federal amendment. Rather than confront the potential voters directly, the local Beaufort registration board simply refused to meet in September. Women were not eligible until September, and the law prohibited registration thirty days before the election, so registering in October was irrelevant. Since few whites lived in this overwhelmingly black-majority county, this quiet foot-dragging almost worked without a problem. Yet eight white women who intended to register refused to acquiesce to the strategy. They petitioned against the board's refusal to meet, insisting on an opportunity to register before the election. Their confrontation led to more behind-the-scenes "handling." Niels Christensen, Beaufort's senator, who supported woman suffrage and sympathized with the women, confided to Governor Robert Cooper that if their petitions were honored, trouble would erupt in the low country. Christensen feared that if these eight women showed up to vote on Election Day, the black population would be outraged; murmurings of their discontent had already reached him. Two of the white petitioners taught in black schools on Saint Helena Island, an all-black island with six thousand residents. Christensen convinced the women that if they voted under these circumstances, "friction would be engendered" among the black population and the women's lives and work would

220

suffer. When confronted with the "sensitive issue" that Christensen revealed, the women dropped their petitions.[34] The courageous efforts of African American women to register to vote after ratification met whites' determined resistance, which prevented significant increases in African American voting in South Carolina. Ironically, however, this grassroots political activism among African Americans gave substance to Byrnes's fears.

Extending the franchise to women by federal amendment did not loosen the grip of white supremacy, as many feared or claimed to fear. Yet, the reaction against woman suffrage revealed that white South Carolinians who advocated reform, especially women, worked in the context of debilitating constraints: a consensus for white supremacy, class tension, and entrenched patriarchy. White supremacy tended to bolster the status quo and to operate as an obstacle to change. Since enfranchising women represented a dramatic change, woman suffrage advocates had to persuade wary politicians and white voters that such a fundamental political and social change would not alter or appreciably erode white control. Suffrage activist Jessie Clayton, assured that the failure of South Carolina to ratify the suffrage amendment was not her fault, concluded that "the race question is at the bottom of the failure of all these southern states to ratify. It is such a bugaboo to scare the ignorant voter, and so convenient for the scheming intelligent politician." Consequently, she recognized, "we have to combat both the misdirected intelligence and ignorance."[35]

In this political milieu, advocates of woman suffrage had to assuage racial fears and persuade opponents that the current racial hierarchy and political order that guaranteed white control would be maintained. Thus, defending white supremacy was equally essential to both suffrage amendment supporters and opponents. The nearly universal commitment of white South Carolinians to the nonnegotiable ideals of white supremacy invited opponents of reform to champion their interests by linking them to the existing order. Although advocates of woman suffrage aggressively and explicitly tried, they never fashioned an appeal that convincingly aligned their cause with the maintenance of white supremacy. Consequently, woman suffrage proponents found their appeals trumped when opponents played the race card. Opponents of woman suffrage used white supremacy to disguise and protect their own patriarchal, class, and factional interests in political struggles against this reform. National reforms like woman suffrage presented special difficulties for white reformers because of the need to accommodate the regional and local demands of white supremacy. South Carolina's resolute rejection of the national woman suffrage amendment illustrates that this pervasive fear among whites that any change might jeopardize the existing racial hierarchy permeated political discourse and shaped public policy. Such fears complicated all attempts to alter the status quo because quelling and dispelling fears proved far more difficult than exaggerating and exploiting them.

Chapter 9

Funding Reform

As South Carolina white reformers pursued their post–World War I agenda, they viewed tax reform as the most fundamental and challenging reform of the era. All other reforms—public education, paved highways, public health, a more humane criminal justice system, and improved social services for the poor, wayward youth, and the mentally ill—involved expanding state services and raising additional state revenue. But by 1920, calls for retrenchment of government spending had grown loud as a reaction to state spending increases that reformers had championed during Governor Richard Manning's administration, which coincided with the war years. From 1914 to 1919 the state spent more for education, the state mental hospital, highway development, and higher pensions for Confederate veterans (see table 1).[1] Since South Carolina's revenue came overwhelmingly from property taxes, increased spending meant higher property taxes. South Carolinians who experienced these escalating property taxes during the war years had begun to urge retrenchment. Reformers advocated tax reform to prevent a tax revolt. Without tax reform, state revenue might stagnate or even decline. To salvage recent improvements in education and other modest reforms and to pursue a broader progressive agenda, South Carolina needed a more diverse tax structure. The structure reformers promoted would shift the tax burden away from agricultural property, allow the state to tax property according to its income-generating capacity, and tax income not raised directly from property ownership.

Cognizant that tax reform was foundational for other reforms and convinced of the urgency to reform the tax system as a means of combating demands for tax reduction, reformers faced a daunting

Table 1. Appropriations from the South Carolina General Fund, 1914–1919

	1914	1915	1916	1917	1918	1919
Administration						
Executive	$125,270	$143,850	$161,855	$178,185	$205,448	$193,487
Judicial	107,545	106,920	112,395	130,295	124,836	155,208
Legislative	62,804	62,562	61,706	62,450	63,458	72,195
Tax	92,746	106,246	111,879	106,213	110,713	157,517
Debt Retirement	259,033	261,033	260,044	221,729	222,849	222,289
Confederate Pensions	261,600	300,000	300,000	300,000	299,800	400,000
Prohibition Enforcement				90,000	25,000	22,809
Education						
Higher	327,777	347,215	334,969	376,330	519,608	680,206
Public Schools	251,500	286,500	303,500	444,100	503,600	524,602
Smith-Lever Fund			31,382	41,843	54,919	67,995
Social Services						
Mental Hospital	312,881	459,700	418,000	575,000	616,496	695,402
Public Health	45,220	57,676	58,575	77,176	105,241	139,449
Institutions: Corrections and Humanitarian	113,751	110,155	116,533	134,304	261,115	358,652
Other Expenses	186,126	221,902	215,302	251,880	263,047	202,872
Total Appropriations	$2,146,253	$2,463,759	$2,486,140	$2,989,505	$3,376,130	$3,892,683

Source: Appropriation bills, *Acts and Resolutions of the General Assembly of the State of South Carolina, 1914–1919*.

challenge. South Carolina's tax system facilitated the undervaluing of assets, empowered local authorities to protect local wealth, and enabled some forms of wealth to escape taxation completely while the revenue burden mounted on others. Mustering political support to reform a system that so effectively protected entrenched interests would be difficult, especially since the proposed tax reforms would be reaching into the pockets of the most affluent and powerful South Carolinians, who would forcefully resist such intrusions. Reformers had to take on these powerful interests, many in their own political coalition, because wealth was neither abundant nor widespread in the state. Taken together, South Carolina's poorly educated population, its low per capita wealth, and its economy that heavily depended on cotton agriculture, textiles, and Charleston commerce left the state saddled with a small and slow-growing tax base. In the World War I era, South Carolina's economic and social problems, many of them interrelated, defied easy solutions because of their sheer magnitude. In addition to the barriers that reformers recognized, there was also the ubiquitous but less obvious obstacle of white supremacy.

As reformers undertook the challenge of enlarging the state coffers, they had not fully grasped that white supremacy, which they unequivocally supported, would complicate their tax reform goals. Indeed, white supremacy provided a subtext for all discussions about expanding state services and increasing state spending. In this black-majority state, whites sought assurance that their taxes would not fund services for African Americans. Their most reliable assurance that blacks had few public resources came from keeping all state services to a minimum and guarding local control of tax issues. Thus many whites fiercely resisted greater public spending and shifting any taxation authority to the state. White reformers reassured critics that the tax reform measures they proposed would produce more revenue for educational and public welfare improvements that would overwhelmingly benefit whites. Their opponents, nonetheless, asserted that any erosion of local authority threatened white supremacy, especially in black-majority counties, and they resisted all tax proposals as unnecessary if blacks stood to benefit, even minimally. In addition to becoming a justification for continued localism, white supremacy also imposed constraints on tax reform in less obvious ways. One of the most fundamental tax reforms desired by white reformers, the division of property into different classifications for tax purposes, required amending South Carolina's 1895 constitution, a document many whites perceived as the very foundation of white supremacy. As a result, tax opponents wielded white supremacy to deny tax reform advocates what they insisted was their most essential reform: amending the constitution.

By almost any measure, South Carolina's World War I–era tax system was inequitable because it violated the basic principle of taxation: ability to pay. The unfairness and inequity in the system resulted primarily from the state's excessive reliance on property taxes to shoulder an overwhelming share of the revenue burden. Edwin Seligman, the foremost national authority on tax policy in this era, declared the general property tax "beyond all doubt one of the worst taxes known in the civilized world." Beyond violating an abstract philosophical principle of fairness, heavy reliance on the property tax had practical political consequences. The existing tax system placed the fiscal burden disproportionately on landowning farmers, a significant voting constituency. Increases fell heavily on this group, and the increases had a multiplying effect because every government entity in South Carolina—state, county, and municipality—depended heavily on this tax. In 1919, state government derived approximately 83 percent of its revenue from property taxes. Annual corporate license fees contributed an additional 7 percent to the total state budget. The remaining 10 percent of state revenue came from a host of miscellaneous sources collected for specific purposes by individual state agencies, such as colleges and the state prison. Therefore, state government depended almost exclusively on property taxes and corporate license fees to finance the state's general budget. Revenue from corporate license fees increased only as corporations' wealth increased or as new corporations formed. Thus increases in state appropriations depended almost entirely on property tax increases. Each year, at the conclusion of the legislative session, the general assembly determined a property tax levy that promised to raise sufficient funds to meet the state's appropriation levels for that year. As state appropriations increased, property tax levies rose proportionately.[2]

County governments, which historically provided most of the funding for public education in South Carolina, also relied heavily on property taxes. Counties derived revenue from a constitutionally mandated three-mill property tax, levied exclusively for funding each county's public schools. In addition to the three-mill property tax levied for education, each county levied a property tax to raise additional funds for public schools and sufficient revenue for general county expenses. South Carolina's local taxing units, which included townships, school districts, municipalities, and special tax districts, also depended on property taxes for revenue. Most of the local levies on property met specific purposes such as schools, and the local district voted on these taxes. Local taxing districts also used the poll tax, which was a one dollar annual tax per male citizen between the ages of twenty-one and sixty; its proceeds directly benefited the school district that collected the tax.[3]

Nationally, reliance on the property tax as the major source of state and local revenue developed in an era when the young republic's population had been predominately rural and agricultural. Taxing property seemed equitable and expedient when farmland was the chief source of productive wealth in most areas of the country. But the economy that created a tax structure pegged almost exclusively to property values had grown more complex. Industrialization and urbanization shifted populations from farms to towns and consolidated wealth in industry and commerce rather than exclusively in land. With the development of industry, different types of property generated widely different amounts of income. Moreover, professionals and white-collar workers could earn large salaries without owning large amounts of productive property. Although the South experienced these economic and demographic changes later and at slower rates than other parts of the country, by the twentieth century, levies on property alone no longer were a fair and equitable means for taxing wealth in South Carolina.[4] Consequently, reformers envisioned a state tax system for South Carolina that could tax wealth created by industry and commerce and that could tax the incomes of professionals who might otherwise not own income-generating property.

States throughout the nation had already begun reforming their tax systems to reflect this fundamental economic evolution. South Carolina's continued reliance on property taxes indicated that the state trailed most of the nation in the tax reform movement. In 1920, among the forty-eight states, South Carolina derived the highest percentage of its state revenue from property taxes. With the exception of the corporate license fee, South Carolina had not taken significant steps, as other states had, toward taxing other forms of wealth. South Carolina was one of only five states without an inheritance tax. The state also lacked occupation, sales, consumption, and luxury taxes. As of 1919, South Carolina did not have an income tax. Although state government had derived a very small amount of revenue from a state income tax from 1898 to 1917, in 1918 legislators deemed the law unjust and repealed it. The income tax law had raised very little revenue and was ultimately found unjust because it functioned as a voluntary tax—only those whose conscience compelled them to report their incomes paid the tax. Seligman declared South Carolina's income tax law a "complete failure" because the state refused to enforce it. The legislature refused to appropriate money to collect the tax, so most South Carolinians responded by ignoring it completely. After the legislature repealed the law, former governor Clinch Heyward told friends that the "big planters were the class of people most reluctant to pay income taxes." Every year several counties paid nothing, suggesting no one in those counties had an income that exceeded $2,500. During the entire twenty years that the law remained in force, residents of Berkeley County paid only $29, and that occurred in 1909. Equally remiss was Saluda County, where the only tax collected in twenty years came in 1915, when one citizen paid $10.[5]

Reformers who criticized South Carolina's tax system claimed it was unfair in two ways. First and foremost, the state's extensive reliance on the property tax caused property to carry too much of the revenue burden, allowing other forms of wealth and income to escape taxation. Second, the administration of the property tax created a host of inequities among different classes of property as well as among individual owners of the same class of property. For tax purposes, property was broadly construed to mean all property, real and personal. Real property included all real estate from farms to town lots and all physical structures from barns to cotton mills. Real property included agricultural and commercial classes of property, as well as property owned by railroads, public utilities, and corporations. Personal property included intangible property like stocks, bonds, mortgages, cash, and savings accounts, as well as tangible property like jewelry, furniture, mules, and farm implements.[6]

These structural tax inequities were embedded in South Carolina's 1895 constitution that included two specific regulations on assessing property and levying taxes. It specified that "all taxes upon property, real and personal, shall be laid upon the actual value of the property." This meant, simply and quite literally, that all property would be assessed at its actual market value. Additionally, the constitution stated that "the General Assembly shall provide by law for a uniform and equal rate of assessment and taxation." This meant that the legislature had to impose the same tax rate on all classes of property, whether a thousand-acre plantation, a rural farm house, a savings account, a hydroelectric plant, factory machinery, or a family heirloom necklace. No rate distinctions, known as property classification, could be made between corporate and agricultural property, between income-generating property and non-income-producing property, or between tangible and intangible property.[7]

Although often portrayed as straightforward, simple, and fair, the constitutional mechanisms governing South Carolina's tax system compounded the inequity of the state's excessive reliance on property taxes. These constitutional provisions not only prohibited lawmakers from adapting the state's tax system to fit the state's changing economic needs, but also encouraged citizens to manipulate the system for their personal advantage. Because these tax regulations carried constitutional rather than merely statutory authority, these two brief constitutional statements set a high bar for reformers to scale in their struggle to reform South Carolina's tax system. Constitutional revision was not only procedurally difficult and only partially controlled by the legislature, but South Carolina's 1895 constitution represented the embodiment of white supremacy. Recommendations to revise the constitution could always be characterized by tax-reform opponents as challenges to white supremacy, a possibility that tempted tax reform opponents.

Although unambiguous in its wording and intent, the provision that all property should be assessed at its actual value invited every state official from local assessors to supreme court justices to ignore it consistently. Citizens and politicians alike scoffed at the legal requirement. Everyone familiar with the problems of South Carolina's tax system cited the universal practice of undervaluing property. In 1918, the U.S. Census Bureau estimated that the assessment for all property currently being taxed in South Carolina was about 25 percent of its actual value. South Carolina governor Robert A. Cooper told Missouri governor Frederick Gardner that South Carolina's most glaring tax defect was the undervaluation of property: "Our system of assessment is localized to the greatest extent possible, and there is no uniform rate of valuation through out the State. As a result of the absurdly low assessment, we have a relatively high levy. The per capita tax, however, is, I believe, lower than that of any other State," Cooper reported. In a special report to the general assembly, examiners who noted the blatant inconsistency between the constitutional mandate and the actual practice of tax assessment wrote, "The operation of the tax system of South Carolina is in point of fact as much of an outlaw business as the gentle art of cracking safes or of distilling moonshine whiskey."[8]

The undervaluation of property reinforced localism by empowering local authorities to protect local wealth. The administrative machinery that the state created to collect taxes facilitated the complicity of all taxpayers in the pervasive undervaluation of property. American history, from the Revolution forward, is replete with hostility toward taxation and laced with open tax revolts. Given the Americans' aversion toward paying taxes, it is hardly surprising that South Carolinians wanted to minimize their tax liability by keeping their property assessments low. Highly decentralized, South Carolina's tax system provided both incentive and opportunity for reaching that goal. First, assessment began, and often remained, with individual taxpayers. As prescribed by law, taxpayers reported and assessed their personal property annually, and every fourth year individuals, as well as businesses, did the same for their real estate. With each report to the local county auditor, taxpayers signed an oath swearing they had listed all their property—personal and real—and had returned it at its full market value, as the constitution mandated. By asking property owners to assess their own property, the process began with those most self-interested in low assessment. The county auditor took these individual reports and technically assessed the property, but customarily the auditor accepted the owner's assessment. Beyond simply lying, owners developed innovative techniques to hide their property's true value. The market value of property became most apparent at the moment of sale because the sale price was part of the public record. Thus assessors could easily determine the value of real estate by noting its price on the deed of conveyance. South Carolinians routinely circumvented the system by listing the selling price as "$5 and other considerations." Although generally "other considerations" meant additional sums of money, the use of this ambiguous phrase kept assessors from discovering the current market value.[9]

The second component encouraging low property assessments was the authority of the county auditor, which was limited in serving the state's interest and powerful in serving taxpayers' interests. As an elected official, the county auditor answered to no independent state authority. While county auditors could lower reported assessments, state law did not authorize them to increase any property valuation returned by taxpayers. Property assessment could only be increased if either the board of assessors (whose jurisdiction was a taxing unit within a county, such as a township, school district, or municipality) or the county board of equalization authorized the increase. Yet the law allowed the local board of assessors only three days per year to assess all the property in its tax district, heightening the probability of accepting most assessments as reported. The chairs of each county's many local boards of assessors, along with the county auditor, formed the final authority, the county board of equalization, which was responsible for equalizing the valuation among tax districts and ensuring equal assessment of all property within the county. This board could also adjust property valuation provided it assessed all county property in five days. Ultimately, these assessment officers were accountable to the county taxpayers whose property they assessed, increasing the opportunity for cronyism and corruption.[10]

This multilayered, highly decentralized system invited inefficiency, corruption, and inequality. It placed most of the assessment authority with the county auditor, a political official who was subjected to public pressure to keep assessments low and who had minimal authority to raise the assessments above what community pressure would allow. Moreover, members of the local boards of assessors represented the interests of their townships, and they sought primarily to ensure that assessed property values in their tax districts were not higher than in other parts of the county. Defenders of this local assessment scheme argued that property values varied widely across the state and that local residents who understood the local economy could best assess property values. Reformers countered that local assessors were too easily influenced by their neighbors and too reluctant to challenge values self-interested constituents presented, and that they had too little time to do anything other than accept owners' valuations. Moreover, local assessment meant that thousands of South Carolinians informally determined their own property values, which were then formalized by county officials, guaranteeing unequal assessments throughout the state. The state's tax system lacked a central, impartial authority that could impose uniform assessments across the state. Such a decentralized system that effectively served so many South Carolinians' perceived self-interest for paying minimal taxes resisted reform.[11]

Localism not only encouraged low property assessments, it also facilitated each county's rate of taxation. Although in principle county tax levies had to be approved by the general assembly, in practice each county's legislative delegation determined its county's tax levy. Each delegation recommended the annual levy to the legislature, which generally deferred to the county delegations as a matter of home-rule tradition. In every case, county tax levies were much higher than the state levy, placing most of the taxing and spending decisions in the hands of a few white men from each county. Reformers wanted to shift the spending decisions to the state level and de-emphasize the role of local government in public spending. As long as local governments controlled their revenues, South Carolina's unequal distribution of wealth intensified existing disparities so that large portions of the state remained poor while the few prosperous areas, like Charleston and Greenville, enhanced their prosperity. White reformers wanted the entire state to benefit from the wealth generated in selected areas of the state.

Steeped in localism, the state's tax and assessment systems motivated local officials to keep the property assessments in their districts low. The actual amount of taxes individual property owners paid depended on a formula involving two factors. One factor was the assessed value of any given property, and the other factor was the millage levy.[12] For example, a farm assessed at $1,000 and taxed at 12 mills owed $12 in taxes. But officials could raise the same $12 in tax revenue with 120 mills levied on property assessed at $100. Thus, from the standpoint of taxpayers, low assessments could offset high millage, and low millage could offset high assessments.

An accurate understanding of South Carolina's tax structure always depended on a consideration of both the assessment and the millage. In this system, inequities among taxpayers arose when either the assessment or the millage was inconsistently or unfairly applied. Since the legislature determined the millage levy for state taxes, the rate was consistent across the state. In the case of state taxes, disparities among property owners arose when property assessment rates varied widely across the state, as they often did. As discussed above, local officials notoriously undervalued property. A state tax official remarked, "Long experience has shown conclusively that values placed on property, particularly real estate and certain classes of personal property, by a board of appraisers, are more often than not ridiculously low."[13] Local assessors understood that the lower the property assessment in their district, the less state taxes their district would have to pay. Low property assessments, however, did not hinder a county's ability to raise sufficient revenue for its own expenses, since the legislative delegation determined the millage level for the county. Since the legislature, a central state body, determined the millage and local assessors determined the assessment, South Carolina's taxing system encouraged local political divisions to keep their assessments low and contribute as little as possible to the state treasury, retaining as much revenue as possible in the local district. Reformers realized local assessors had competing loyalties: a weak one to the state and a strong one to their local district or county. Reformers envisioned that successful tax reform would align assessors' loyalty with the state rather than with the county or township.[14]

The central role of white supremacy in South Carolina's tax policy stemmed from the antebellum tax code that taxed slave property, thereby empowering slave owners to control and constrain state government. White supremacy continued to shape the state's tax system after emancipation through South Carolina's segregated public schools, which maintained a separate and inferior school system for the state's African American children. The state tax for public schools, commonly known as the constitutional three-mill tax, enabled white supremacy to control tax policy and practice. Architects of South Carolina's 1895 constitution intended this mandatory property tax as a remedy for white illiteracy. They envisioned the revenue from this tax supporting the public school systems and consequently eradicating white illiteracy within one generation. The constitution's new literacy requirements for voting necessitated efforts to combat the high illiteracy rate among the state's white population. Even though these new voting requirements were designed to disfranchise black voters, an honest enforcement of these provisions would have disfranchised many white voters as well.[15]

From its inception the constitutional three-mill tax operated as a state-mandated local tax rather than as a true state tax. While the constitution fixed the levy at three mills, the actual amount of revenue the tax produced depended on the property assessment, which, as previously explained, was determined by county assessors. Revenue raised from this tax remained in the county where it was collected. Thus each county operated its public schools with revenue generated from property taxes in the county. With a consistent rate of three mills across the state but widely varying assessed property values among the counties, the three-mill tax created tremendous disparities across the state in available public school funds because wealth was unevenly distributed among the forty-six counties and property assessment rates also varied from county to county. The primary concern of elected and appointed county officials was raising sufficient revenue to support adequately the white school population in their counties. The three-mill tax could readily raise enough revenue to support the white schools in counties with few white children, even if property was severely undervalued. Therefore, South Carolina counties with proportionately fewer white children tended to keep their overall county property assessment low. In 1920, South Carolina counties with the highest educational spending per white child were the counties where whites represented less than one-third of the population. For example, counties where whites were a distinct minority, such as Sumter (29 percent), Allendale (22 percent), Jasper (28 percent), Fairfield (24 percent), Calhoun (31 percent), and Lee (33 percent), spent on average $46 to $61 per white child for education, whereas counties with white majorities such as Lexington (67 percent), Lancaster (55 percent), Pickens (83 percent), Horry (76 percent), and York (53 percent), spent less than $27 per white child.[16]

White illiteracy tended to be highest in counties with the highest proportion of white children. In order to raise sufficient revenue to serve the educational needs of all the white students in these counties, assessors had a motivation to raise property assessments, since the constitutional levy was fixed at three mills. However, if the local boards of assessors increased property assessments to generate additional funds needed for education, taxpayers in white-majority counties of the state would also pay more state taxes than black-majority counties, because the same property assessment was used to determine taxes owed to the state as well as the county. The constitutional three-mill tax, therefore, motivated whites in black-belt counties to keep property assessments very low. Reformers knew this and targeted this particular manipulation as an obstacle that must be overcome. J. F. Lyles declared, "We can never get on a sure footing until we call a constitutional convention and get rid of the specific three mill tax for school purposes." County retention of revenue from the constitutional three-mill tax compounded the tax system's inequalities. Because white South Carolinians demonstrated tremendous indifference to providing adequate educational opportunities for African American children and because the white population was unevenly distributed, the three-mill tax provided an additional incentive for assessors in black-majority counties to undervalue their county's property. Moreover, the white reformers' call to revise the 1895 constitution invited opponents to label reformers untrustworthy and charge that they intended to undermine white supremacy.[17]

Because the state's tax system included built-in incentives for local assessors to keep property assessments low in their jurisdictions, reformers fought for a centralized assessment authority. In 1915, under Richard Manning's administration, reformers made the first step in that direction with creation of the state tax commission, which approximated a statewide central tax-assessment agency. The legislature gave the state tax commission, composed of three members appointed by the governor to six-year terms, broad authority to supervise the administration of assessment and all the tax laws of the state. Nevertheless the commission operated under several serious limitations. First, it lacked explicit authority to regulate, discharge, or penalize local assessing officials. Thus local assessment boards and the tax commission possessed dual authority, and naturally, the weight of tradition tilted final authority toward the local boards. Second, the legislature never appropriated sufficient revenue to allow the tax commission to effectively supervise property assessment across the entire state. A shortage of funds effectively limited the commission's ambitions and accomplishments. Despite specific requests from the tax commission, the legislature refused to appropriate money for a state assessment survey of all real property in the state. The tremendous resistance to giving the commission authority to assess local property demonstrates that most property owners benefited from the local assessment system.[18]

The general assembly limited the tax commission's authority in a third way by creating the state tax board of review, an institution unique to South Carolina. Reformers prevailed in creating the state tax commission partly because the board of review, which checked the commission's power, had been created first in 1913. The board's only function was to hear appeals from property owners dissatisfied with the tax commission's assessments. The board of review undermined the tax commission's authority, since all the commission's decisions were subject to review. The tax commission devoted considerable time to defending its inherently unpopular assessments. Moreover, members of the board of review were political appointees who usually had little or no expertise in taxation. Independent efficiency experts hired to analyze South Carolina's tax system criticized the formation of this board and found that the board regularly lowered assessments on corporations without justification.[19]

Frustrated by the tax commission's limitations, reformers consistently pushed to expand its authority. The defense of T. Hagood Gooding, auditor from Hampton County, illustrates the vigor of some South Carolinians' resistance to the commission. The legislature continually denied the commission formal authority to dismiss county auditors, so the tax commission in 1919 decided to appeal to executive authority to remove Gooding, whom they viewed as particularly corrupt. The tax commission filed charges against Gooding with Governor Cooper, seeking to have him dismissed from his post because of egregious violations of his responsibilities. The tax commission documented fifteen charges, among them failure to furnish the commission with a list of merchants and their assessments; failure to send out notices to merchants of increased assessments the commission had made; disregard of the tax commission's guide for assessing automobiles; and failure to record the annual real estate assessments on individuals' property. With a full knowledge of these allegations, voters from Hampton County reelected Gooding county auditor in 1920. When Cooper attempted to remove him from office, residents flooded the governor with petitions to retain Gooding. The residents said that "charges now made against Mr. T. Hagood Gooding were heard and considered by the voters, and we deem it contrary to the expressed will of the democrats of Hampton County and contrary to the principles of the party to refuse the recognition of their choice."[20] Doubtless numerous Hampton County residents appreciated the obstructionist tactics Gooding used against the tax commission. The commission theoretically held oversight responsibility for the state's tax administration. In practice, however, its authority was limited to assessing public utility, commercial, and business property. Assessment of other real estate, especially agricultural property, remained under the authority of local county assessors.

Rebuffed in its efforts to conduct a statewide assessment survey of all property, the state tax commission focused more narrowly on equalizing commercial property. Predictably, the commission promptly grew unpopular with business and industry. Prior to the creation of the commission, corporate property, like agricultural property, had been systematically undervalued. Rather than invoke the obvious but radical solution of enforcing the constitutional stipulation to value all property at actual market value, the tax commission sought to determine a percentage of full value that would equalize assessments of all commercial property across the state. The commission eventually settled on an arbitrary assessment rate of 42 percent of full value. The commission's decision illustrated how the state's tax officials openly flouted the constitution by establishing a rate of less than 100 percent as a matter of public policy. While the tax commission assessed textile mills, banks, public utilities, railroads, insurance companies, and merchants at 42 percent of actual value, these commercial and industrial interests complained that they were taxed at higher rates than other property.[21]

The state constitution required the assessment of all property at actual market value and the taxation of all types of property, whether agricultural, commercial, tangible, intangible, rural, town, merchants' stock, farm implements, or household furniture, at a uniform rate. Yet tremendous inequality in tax assessment existed between different classes of property. Everyone knew the reality of South Carolina's taxing system directly violated the constitution. Prevailing sentiment was that strict enforcement of the provisions would drive capital out of the state, so officials at all levels, from the county auditor to the state tax commission, ignored the constitutional directives. While no one seriously advocated enforcing the provisions strictly, the reformers preferred amending the constitution and others preferred working within the existing system, employing a range of strategies to protect their interests. Reformers specifically wanted to authorize the state to classify property and to tax different classes at different rates so the tax burden could be distributed more evenly among those with the ability to pay and more revenue could be raised.

The fact that some classes of property completely escaped taxation further complicated an already complicated tax system, intensifying the inequality among different classes of property. While assessors knew that some real estate remained off the tax books, intangible property such as stock, bonds, mortgages, cash, and savings almost entirely escaped taxation. Unlike a farm, a cotton mill, or a merchant's stock, intangible property proved easy to hide from tax assessors. Moreover, if the state's tax law had been applied rigorously, owners of intangible property would have been taxed out of most of their property. For example, if an individual had $100 in a savings account, the law required the account holder to report the entire amount as property. If the total tax levy was seventy mills, he or she would owe $7 in taxes on the savings account, more than the account earned in interest. Everyone agreed that application of the law to intangible property would be so onerous that capital would flee the state. Thus tax officials did not expect South Carolinians to report intangible property and such property therefore generally escaped taxation, even though it was quite capable of paying its fair share. John J. McMahan, former state superintendent of education and a strong advocate of tax reform, recognized this injustice. "The man who owns mules and cows and hogs, enumerates them and pays on them. The man who owns mortgages or money in banks seldom gives them for taxes. Everything works to shift the burden to the poorer man and relieve the majority of the money-making men," McMahan lamented.[22] Unless South Carolina amended its constitution, prospects for taxing intangible property seemed slight.

Reformers had long understood that the structure of the state's tax system perpetuated inequities and raised insufficient revenue to pursue their reform goals. They also understood that tackling such an essential and foundational reform required a transformation from localism to state activism. Governor Cooper explained: "What the world needs is more vision. What South Carolina needs is more statemindedness." When emphasizing the need for tax reform, Cooper explained that South Carolinians needed a "state mind first and then our community mind." Minimal state government spending confirmed that South Carolinians lacked the statemindedness that Cooper advocated. Among states, South Carolina ranked at the bottom in per capita spending. In 1919, the average per capita cost for state government nationally was $6.05; South Carolina's per capita cost was $2.40.[23] While many South Carolinians complained about the extravagance of their state government, the evidence did not support their accusation. Reformers encouraged statewide thinking to counter the long-standing practice in South Carolina of encouraging each community, county, and town to attend to its own interest and to empower a few people with that responsibility. Such localism neglected statewide challenges, inadequately and inefficiently addressed county needs, and favored the interests of the few who were in control. Since taxes served as a surrogate for power and decision making authority, white reformers' proposal to shift tax and spending decisions from local to state government entailed not only a fundamental shift in power, but also a transformation in the purpose of government.

Reformers had few reliable allies in their quest to remake South Carolina's tax system. As a small faction that had encountered persistent opposition, tax reformers recognized the stubborn tax reform hurdles. Embedded in the identity of many South Carolinians was a knee-jerk resistance to increased taxes, making any progress difficult. Many tax reform opponents did not share the progressive desire to raise additional state revenue. Instead, they preferred keeping state government broke as a means of keeping it ineffective. In addition to the entrenched localism that benefited those who could exploit the existing tax laws, reform advocates confronted a myriad of narrow economic interests that calculated taxes in terms of their costs, not the state's benefit. Among South Carolinians who opposed tax reform were manufacturers, bankers, merchants, and corporate interests—taxpayers within the reformers' own loose political coalition who benefited from the existing tax inequities. These opponents knew they would pay significantly higher taxes if reformers succeeded. Other tax-reform opponents consisted primarily of Bleaseites who paid few taxes and would arguably have benefited from increased state spending but nevertheless voiced loud opposition to new taxes. Revenue empowered state government, which they perceived as an unwanted interference in their lives. Cole Blease, the flamboyant faction leader, often aimed his attacks at all state spending and spoke continually of extravagance and fraud. Blease's charges resonated with his followers, who resisted expanding the size and power of state government, believing that a larger and more powerful state government threatened their liberty. Moreover, Blease's rhetoric suggested that increased state spending would undermine white supremacy by benefiting African Americans. The details of the tax system were also quite complicated, so many South Carolinians had not considered how the structure promoted inequality by allowing certain classes of income to escape taxation. Simple indifference remained a valuable ally for tax reform opponents.[24]

Tax reformers obviously faced formidable obstacles. Prior to 1920 they had succeeded only in creating the state tax commission. In addition to equalizing assessment among the various commercial properties in the state, the commission had recommended several new sources of revenue that could help the state reduce its excessive reliance on the property tax, but the legislature had refused to pass any of them. As the commission proposed new taxes, it attracted bitter opposition from across the state. Opponents protested the very existence of the tax commission. At every legislative session since its creation, hostile legislators proposed its abolition. Although the commission managed to survive these challenges, the besieged agency lacked the clout to lead the monumental task of reform.

Ultimately, financial pressure from increased state appropriations eroded taxpayers' previous indifference, making tax reform a greater priority in South Carolina. Not only did state spending increase during the second decade of the twentieth century, as support for public education increased, local and county property levies rose simultaneously, since most state aid to education depended on matching local spending (see table 1). Property owners who regularly experienced these state, county, and local property tax increases joined reformers in the call for tax reform. Not surprisingly, cries for government retrenchment accompanied, and at times drowned out, the call for tax reform. But despite growing opposition to the expanding state government, reformers resisted the pressure to cut spending. They defended the appropriation increases as essential for the state's future. Rather than risk a rollback of the modest gains they had achieved in other areas, reformers insisted that South Carolina find new sources of revenue and relieve the tax burden on property with a fundamental overhaul of the tax system. Clearly, some South Carolinians' taxes had increased in recent years, but reformers believed significant wealth escaped taxation and that wealth had an obligation to support expanding state spending needs. Thus, in 1920, a few key reformers forged a political strategy and energetically pushed for tax reform. Such an ambitious proposal to shift financial resources and spending authority from local to state government invited formidable opposition from other white South Carolinians who readily employed white supremacy politics to protect their interests.[25]

Chapter 10

Taxing Wealth

When the general assembly convened in January 1920, South Carolina's white reformers greeted the new session with hopeful expectation. With World War I successfully concluded, reformers anticipated continuing the state-centered activism they had marshaled to meet wartime demands. Soon after the armistice, reformers' optimism received institutional expression through the organization of the South Carolina Development Board. This private, statewide organization promoted reformers' comprehensive postwar reforms, justifying the optimism and commitment to state-level reform that had been spawned by their wartime-mobilization experiences. Further buoying their confidence, Cole Blease's historically poor showing in the 1918 U.S. Senate race had signaled the weakening of their leading political nemesis. A final, significant factor explained their hopeful anticipation: the state's postwar prosperity was at its zenith. Encouraged by the wartime economic boom, Governor Robert A. Cooper touted South Carolinians' "unwonted prosperity" and "remarkable freedom from economic strife," in his 1920 annual address. Cooper hoped the new prosperity would prompt the state to "undertake greater constructive work than ever before."[1] White reformers intended to parlay Cooper's call for an aggressive reform agenda into passage of their long-desired changes, beginning with tax reform.

Niels Christensen Jr., state senator from Beaufort, quickly emerged as the most important leader of the tax reform movement. Owner and editor of the *Beaufort Gazette*, Christensen also worked in the family hardware, lumber, and building supply business, N. Christensen and Sons, and managed Christensen Realty. A longtime proponent of tax reform, Christensen entered the battle on several fronts. When the 1920 legislative session began, Christensen introduced a resolution to appoint a joint legislative committee to study the state's taxation system and guide proposed legislation to passage. As chairman of the finance committee, he hired outside experts to study South Carolina's tax system. Along with his legislative positions, the energetic senator used his leadership in the private sector to build support for tax reform. Christensen played an instrumental role in the formation of the South Carolina Development Board, a private organization of prominent business, industry, agriculture, and education leaders who planned to promote economic development in South Carolina. In March 1920, Christensen addressed the board's organizational meeting on how to get action from the legislature on tax reform. Christensen became the president of the board, which enthusiastically endorsed the legislature's willingness to tackle the issue of tax reform. Christensen's real estate and business interests might have influenced his passion for tax reform. With entrepreneurial vision and extensive ownership of undeveloped land in the South Carolina low country, Christensen perhaps envisioned long-term opportunities for himself and the state if he could erode the existing tax liability associated with holding unproductive land for future development.[2]

Just as Christensen had planned, the general assembly created a legislative committee to study South Carolina's tax system. Formally named the Joint Special Committee on Revenue and Taxation, the committee had six members—two senators and four representatives. The two senators were Christensen and John Marion of Chester. Marion chaired the committee, which became known as the Marion Committee. The committee conducted its study in the months following the 1920 legislative session and submitted its report, commonly known as the Marion Report, to the general assembly at the 1921 session.[3]

The committee conducted an extensive study and published an informed and exhaustive analysis of the state's tax structure that offered recommendations for future reform. After a detailed analysis of the state's cumbersome tax structure, the Marion Report summarized its findings in three broad conclusions. First, while endorsing the broadly shared and popular sentiment that property tax rates were too high, the committee dismissed the charge that extravagant appropriations and wasteful spending were the culprits. Second, the report concluded that in order for the state to operate efficiently and to support charitable and correctional institutions, public schools, institutions of higher learning, and public welfare more generously, state government needed more revenue. Third, the committee concluded that South Carolina's flawed administration of the general property tax reinforced and compounded the inequity of the existing tax system.[4]

Based on its analysis of these problems, the committee made a series of specific recommendations intended to overhaul the state's tax system. The Marion Report recommended that South Carolina create a radically different tax system based on a classified property tax, a personal income tax, business and corporate taxes, and an inheritance tax. The report strongly endorsed replacing the property tax, which treated all property—personal and business, agricultural and industrial, tangible and intangible—identically, with a property tax that would classify property by its income-earning capacity. This foundational reform—classification of property—would require amending the constitution, a recommendation that critics charged would jeopardize white supremacy. While the Marion Committee considered the potential benefits of a consumption or sales tax, the committee rejected this as either a permanent or stopgap method of taxation, recognizing the regressive nature of such taxes, which would fall heavily on tenants and small farmers.[5]

The Marion Committee developed a plan for implementation that committee members characterized as thoroughgoing and fundamental. The South Carolina press deemed it "radical" and "revolutionary." But it is probably best characterized as idealistic. Acknowledging that thoughtful people might disagree about the specific revenue recommendations, the committee insisted on "the validity of one conclusion that it desires to urge with all the earnestness at its command. That conclusion is—that there can be no sound, sane, thorough-going reform of the taxing system of South Carolina until the constitutional restrictions upon the power of the General Assembly in relation to the general property tax are removed." Reform that did not begin with constitutional reform, the committee indicated, was "mere tinkering." Convinced that amending the constitution was essential to reform, the Marion Committee staked its entire list of recommendations on this objective. The committee's gamble on this point invited opponents to disguise their self-interested opposition to tax reform as a defense of the constitution that many white South Carolinians viewed as the guardian of white supremacy.[6]

Based on the premise of constitutional reform, the committee outlined a four-year plan for achieving lasting and fundamental reformation of the state taxing system. According to the plan, in 1921 the general assembly would adopt a joint resolution to amend the constitution by removing the limitations on the general property tax. Simultaneously, the legislature would launch a massive statewide campaign to educate South Carolinians about the taxation problems and proposed solutions. In 1922, the people would adopt the proposed constitutional amendments at the general election in November. At the following legislative session, in 1923, the general assembly would pass the necessary legislation to conduct a complete reevaluation of all property in the state at full market value, as well as inventory all other taxable resources in the state. Once the constitution was amended, all property accurately assessed, and all wealth discovered and inventoried, the legislature would undertake the final and most important step in 1924: passage of a comprehensive revenue act including a remodeled property tax, an income tax, business tax, and inheritance tax.[7]

Christensen, the reformers' most vocal champion of tax revision, creatively secured the services of outside experts for the Marion Committee, although the legislature provided no funds. Concurrent with the Marion Committee's study of South Carolina's tax system in 1920, Griffenhagen and Associates, a Chicago firm of efficiency engineers, conducted a similar survey of the state's taxing problems. As chair of the senate finance committee and as ex officio member of the budget commission, Christensen requested that Griffenhagen and Associates survey the organization and administration of state government and then report its findings to the governor and budget commission. The general assembly appropriated an inadequate sum of $1,000 for the operation of the joint committee's study. Such a small appropriation seriously limited the committee's ability to conduct a comprehensive study and prohibited contracting with outside experts. Christensen's efforts to hire Griffenhagen and Associates as experts for the budget commission and paid from its budget, doubtless an intentional rather than a serendipitous effort to cope with the limited funds available for the study, made professional expertise available to the Marion Committee.[8]

In the end, the efficiency experts' report bore a remarkable resemblance to the Marion Report. It criticized severely the philosophy, as well as the administration, of the existing property tax system. It called for reducing inequity among taxpayers and recommended a classification system for taxable property. Just as the Marion Report had recommended new revenue sources, the Griffenhagen report endorsed an income tax and inheritance tax. As an out-of-state firm, Griffenhagen and Associates analyzed South Carolina's tax system in the context of other state tax systems. The Chicago efficiency experts praised the tax commission, still very unpopular among South Carolinians, and recommended that it be given even greater power. Each report reinforced the other's conclusions, providing both outside expertise and local endorsement. Together the two reports left no doubt that the system was in desperate need of reform.[9]

Both the Marion Committee and the Griffenhagen study, launched in a spirit of optimism about South Carolina's economic future, became public in a very different economic climate. Largely because of a collapse of cotton prices, reformers' anticipation of sustained prosperity rapidly evaporated in the months following the adjournment of the legislature in March 1920. Since the early years of World War I, enhanced cotton demand had increased prices. South Carolina farmers had enjoyed record profits during and immediately following the war. High cotton prices, however, had encouraged farmers to expand their cotton acreage, leading to an overproduction that many farmers had borrowed to create. Overproduction of cotton coincided with the onset of the national agricultural depression. Indeed, cotton prices plummeted in the brief period between the commissioning of these studies and the publication of their reports. By late summer of 1920, South Carolina farmers had begun to panic. South Carolina agricultural commissioner B. F. Harris declared the "calamity that befell the cotton producers was as unexpected as war itself, and as dreadful as the epidemic of the flu." Cotton sold for at least thirty-seven cents per pound in the spring of 1920. But by the end of the year, the market value of cotton had fallen to fourteen cents per pound. Such a significant price drop devastated cotton farmers and other business interests that depended on cotton sales, especially banks. That fall, Chas Peple, deputy governor of the Federal Reserve, indicated that South Carolina banks had overextended their credit against cotton. Farmers and agricultural leaders focused on the cotton crisis, suggesting acreage reduction schemes, cooperative marketing, warehousing the cotton until prices rebounded, and delaying tax payments as possible methods of weathering the storm. The cotton-price collapse late in 1920 reduced the aggregate value of cotton for the entire year to $110,925,000, a disastrous drop from the 1919 aggregate value of $254,567,000.[10]

Just as the bottom fell out of cotton, the Marion Report and the Griffenhagen tax study's recommendations became public. Of course, these recommendations for new taxes, tailored for a more optimistic economic environment, landed with a thud in an economy mired in crisis. Simultaneously, reports surfaced that South Carolina's appropriation requests for 1921 would reach an unprecedented high of $10 million.[11] Predictably, South Carolinians rebelled. With farmers facing devastating losses, all suggestions of increasing state appropriations encountered tenacious opposition. Tax reformers were unprepared for the economic slump and their opponents regained the initiative. Before the general assembly convened for its 1921 session, Eugene W. Dabbs, a Maysville landowner, responded to the news of potential increases in state appropriations with a call for a statewide taxpayers' convention to protest such increases at a time when agriculture was suffering. Dabbs, owner of a three-thousand-acre farm in Sumter County, had sided with reformers on many issues. College educated himself, Dabbs had sent his sons and daughters to college, served as a school board trustee in Sumter, and supported education improvement at every level. He corresponded regularly with Clarence Poe, editor of the Raleigh, North Carolina–based *Progressive Farmer*, agricultural reformers, Pedigreed seed executive David Coker, and many other reformers. He regularly wrote letters to the editor to newspapers around the state. Fundamentally, Dabbs advocated passionately for agricultural reforms that would improve life for ordinary white farmers. He had pursued that end in many ways, including serving one term in the state legislature and as president of the South Carolina State Farmers' Union.[12]

Leading a call for a taxpayers' convention in December 1920, Dabbs rallied the tax-and-spending opposition. From across the state, proponents of reduced appropriations assured Dabbs of their full agreement with this cause and pledged their presence at a convention scheduled for January. Recognizing the shift of momentum to his opponents, Senator Marion contacted Dabbs and urged him to lead the tax opposition movement responsibly. Marion empathized with Dabbs's concern with the looming agricultural crisis, but explained that the current tax system worked against farm interests. As the senator who chaired the committee that had just spent months analyzing the tax problems, Marion sent Dabbs a copy of the committee's report. Marion emphasized that farmers suffered from the existing tax structure and that any remedy would require fundamental constitutional reform. Marion also highlighted that South Carolina behaved as an "outlaw administration" of state government's most important responsibility: administering a fair tax system. Consequently, South Carolina's tax system created "inequality, injustice and inadequate revenue." Dabbs made careful notes from the 175-page report. The report, together with Marion's communication, apparently encouraged Dabbs to nuance his plea for retrenchment. Dabbs's subsequent public promotion of the taxpayers' convention combined his demand for a halt on spending with a plea that legislators accept the premise of the Marion Report: that property carried an excessive taxation burden and that farmers should be provided with much-needed tax relief.[13]

Hailed as the South Carolina Taxpayers' Convention, this gathering of citizens in Columbia on the same day the legislature convened for it new session, January 11, 1921, essentially served as a forum for vocal opponents of state spending. Here they expressed their frustrations to a receptive audience. Drawn together by the agricultural crisis, the convention declared: "The conditions surrounding the taxpayers of South Carolina today are of a character without a parallel in our experience." However, John Rainey of York equated the taxpayers' convention to similar revolts staged between 1868 and 1876. Rainey compared recent appropriation increases to the "reckless extravagance and waste" of the Reconstruction government. Employing a time-honored tactic of white supremacy politics, Rainey intended his comparison as the ultimate criticism of state spending patterns. Emphasizing that he had never voted for Cole Blease, Rainey threatened that if the legislature remained unresponsive to the farmers' plight he was "ready to help clean out the stables" at the next election. Before adjourning, the convention solidified its protest with several resolutions calling broadly for retrenchment and economy in state government, an extension for payment of 1920 taxes due to economic distress, and modification of the constitutional provisions that created an unjust tax system.[14] The final resolution suggested that Marion's private attempt to educate Dabbs about tax reform had met some success. Sensitive to the public outcry and the economic difficulties confronting farmers who faced selling their annual cotton crop at a loss, legislators immediately began reconsidering appropriation increases and echoed the pleas for economy in state government. *The State* reported that "taxpayers have been more than usually outspoken in their demands for retrenchment."[15]

The severity of the economic downturn and pervasive citizen calls for tax relief caught reformers off guard. As opponents of state spending gained the upper hand, they effectively blocked any chance of comprehensive tax reform at the 1921 legislative session. The collapse of the cotton market sealed the fate of the Marion Committee's idealistic and systematic plan for sweeping tax reform. The legislature stopped short of debilitating cuts from the public budget, but the organized taxpayer protest had weakened lawmakers' resolve for substantial increases in state spending. Economic collapse and legislative failure forced reformers to develop a new strategy. They proposed studying the problem again, this time couching reform in the language of "economy and consolidation," and showing greater political sensitivity to the agriculture perspective.[16]

Christensen, who had masterminded the 1920 tax reform strategy, took the lead in making the adjustments. Now he knew that any strategy reformers employed to salvage the tax reform momentum had to seriously consider the criticism about spending extravagance. Thus Christensen proposed that the legislature create another committee, the Joint Legislative Committee on Economy and Consolidation, to analyze all agencies and departments of state government, discover inefficiency, and recommend changes to the state's fiscal system supporting permanent relief to overburdened taxpayers. Charged with a different emphasis from that of the Marion Committee's work, the new committee again hired Griffenhagen and Associates as the experts to assist the committee in its investigation. Once again, Christensen's fingerprints were all over tax reform attempts. When the committee began its work that summer, it elected Christensen chairman. Unlike the Marion Committee, the 1921 joint legislative committee did not exclusively examine the state tax system but conducted a broader investigation into state government. Its principal goal, however, remained a remedy for the inequitable distribution of the tax burden in South Carolina.[17]

Reformers were still deeply committed to state spending for education and other progressive programs. In 1921, Comptroller General Walter E. Duncan warned against cutting appropriations in South Carolina. Reductions in state spending, Duncan claimed, would be "destructive" and would "put South Carolina back into educational darkness, back into the sand ruts and the mudhole, back at the tail end of American civilization." Therefore, reformers were unwilling to sacrifice their long-term goals by yielding completely to taxpayers' complaints. Instead, they honored the calls for more efficiency by conducting an analysis of state government designed to probe its inefficiencies. While the committee publicly promised to conduct a thorough study of state government to ascertain its problems, its real purpose was to document again what the Marion Report had revealed and what most students of state government already understood: the tax burden needed to be shifted away from visible property. Only a substantial revision of the state tax system, which required amending the constitution, could accomplish that goal. Moreover, by hiring consultants who had studied other state governments, Christensen reasoned, as he had in 1920, that the Griffenhagen Report would add an impartial perspective and provide reformers with a stamp of authenticity for their reform agenda.[18]

Issuing a politically astute report when the general assembly convened in 1922, the Joint Legislative Committee on Economy and Consolidation attempted to encourage supporters and assuage critics. Overall, the report concluded, South Carolina's state government operated quite efficiently. Yet the committee identified areas that needed improvement. With limited criticism of state government operations, the committee hoped to pacify critics who clamored for spending reductions and complained of administrative duplication and waste, while indirectly defending an expanding state government. The committee made specific recommendations aimed at saving money, increasing efficiency, and reforming the tax system. First, it advocated postponing all construction and other capital improvements for one year. Second, it recommended improving the operation of state government through consolidation of some state agencies, better organization, central purchasing, and better operating procedures. The report's third and pivotal recommendation involved an overhaul of the tax system. The committee crafted its proposal with an eye toward agricultural interests, which wanted property tax reduction, as well as toward avid reformers concerned about systematic restructuring. No doubt Christensen envisioned that the winning tax reform strategy demanded a legislative coalition of reformers and farmers.[19]

In its tax recommendations, the committee reiterated its support for the Marion Report of the previous year, emphasizing that amending the constitution to allow property classification was "the most important single tax reform before the people of the state and the General Assembly." Further, the committee asserted that there could be "no complete remedy in sight without constitutional changes." As a substitute for the Marion Report's four-year plan, Christensen's committee proposed an accelerated plan with an immediate, two-pronged approach. First, it accommodated critics of state government with a proposal to reduce the state property levy two-thirds by lowering the levy from twelve mills to four mills. Second, the committee recommended a package of new taxes that included an income tax, inheritance tax, and gasoline and oil tax to help reformers find the revenue needed for their programs.[20]

Having learned from their failures in 1921, reformers prepared themselves for a political fight in 1922 by strategically attaching their overall tax reform measures to the farmers' demands for property tax reduction. When the general assembly began the 1922 session, Christensen's committee report, which carried the approval of Griffenhagen and Associates, became the blueprint for tax reform. Following two consecutive years in which the legislature financed formal studies of South Carolina's tax structure, progressive lawmakers, serious about reform, were determined to make tax reform, which included constitutional amendments, the paramount issue of the 1922 legislative session. Christensen, chairman of the senate finance committee, spearheaded the legislative tax reform package.

During the weeks before the 1922 legislative session opened, all parties interested in tax reform busied themselves with private and public meetings. On December 1, 1921, fifty to sixty prominent reformers across the state held a private conference on the pending tax issues. Those invited to attend the conference were asked not to inform the press, suggesting that reformers viewed this gathering as an opportunity for developing their political strategy.[21] Two weeks following the reformers' private meeting, a group of reformers caucused publicly, seizing a prominent place in the public debate on tax reform. The December 14 conference of taxpayers elected officers, developed a platform, and named itself the South Carolina Taxpayers' Association. Building on the taxpayers' convention that E. W. Dabbs had spearheaded the previous year, the taxpayers' association advocated systematic solutions to the state's tax quandary rather than simply demanding government retrenchment. Key reformers who were not in the legislature saw the taxpayers' association as a vehicle for advancing the tax reform cause. August Kohn, a close student of South Carolina's tax system and long-time advocate for reform, presided at the organizational meeting in Columbia, attended by more than two hundred men and women.[22] Kohn, son of a German immigrant, spoke regularly to organizations around the state, such as the Kosmos and Kiwanis clubs, advocating tax reform. Noting that Kohn had followed legislative issues closely for thirty years, the *News and Courier* touted Kohn as a citizen expert who had studied the tax issue and understood it better than anyone else.

The South Carolina Taxpayers' Association emerged from this meeting with a set of tax proposals remarkably similar to the recommendations reported from Christensen's committee. The association also supported passage of the constitutional amendments that had been proposed in the previous session. Many of the men and women who emerged as leaders of the taxpayers' association had a history of reform activism, and others vigorously promoted tax reform throughout the legislative session. The newly elected chair, Charles W. Coker of Hartsville, had previously been elected president of the

South Carolina Advancement Association, an organization founded by reformers in 1919 to promote "economic, industrial, social and moral progress of the state." E. W. Dabbs, elected to serve on the executive committee, nominated Mrs. Fred S. Munsell of Columbia to serve as vice chair. Just one year previously, women had gained voting rights with ratification of the Nineteenth Amendment, despite South Carolina's opposition. Thus for the first time men had to consider this expansion of the electorate in their political calculation. While no other women were elected to the executive committee, conference participants elected several women—Mrs. J. R. Salley, Mrs. William Darlington, and Mabel Montgomery—to serve on the publicity committee. As clubwomen, they had organizational experience. Montgomery, an experienced activist on behalf of the illiteracy commission and other education reform efforts, knew education improvement depended on increased revenue.

After the initial meeting in Columbia, the association called for meetings in every county. Reed Smith, a professor at the University of South Carolina, regularly offered his expertise on the state tax system at these county meetings. He published his analysis of the tax reform issues in the university bulletin series and also developed a pamphlet for high school debating teams that informed students of the key issues for debating tax reform. Charles Coker and Bright Williamson, leaders in the taxpayers' association, also held leadership roles on the South Carolina Development Board, demonstrating reformers' overlapping interests and coordination of private initiatives to underpin public efforts in enacting their overall reform agenda.[23] Thus, lawmakers interested in passing this agenda began with a significant degree of citizen support.

When the 1922 legislative session opened January 10, all observers anticipated that tax reform would emerge as the central issue. Currency deflation, crop failure, and price reductions had triggered an economic collapse across South Carolina, and the intensified demands from landowners for tax relief continued. The *Greenville News* noted that it had heard the "cry for tax reform for a long time" but complained that reform never came. This Piedmont daily recognized the entrenched interests of those who had always opposed new taxes and who likely would continue their opposition even in the face of the pressure for reform generated by the new agricultural crisis.

Thus, the *Greenville News* wondered if South Carolina had "enough men with moral stamina in the legislature and in public life to stand up and tell the dear people the truth about taxation."[24]

Christensen, speaking with the authority of the Joint Legislative Committee on Economy and Consolidation, secured broad support for the tax reform agenda before the session began. The reform agenda enjoyed the support of the new taxpayers' association and the South Carolina Tax Commission. John Atkinson of Spartanburg, speaker of the house, supported tax reform when the general assembly convened. Atkinson, who served on the Marion Committee, charged that the "cause of all the economic distress in South Carolina is to be laid at the door of the faulty tax system of the state." Governor Robert Cooper devoted his entire 1922 annual address to discussing the necessity of immediate tax reform "to strengthen the morale of the people and to stabilize the unsettled economic conditions." Cooper advocated adoption of all the proposed taxes and the constitutional amendment. Together, he argued, they would provide the state with a tax system that embodied the ability-to-pay principle, ending a "continuous source of irritation and injustice."[25]

With South Carolinians expressing almost universal dissatisfaction with the property levy, reformers seized this opportunity to channel voters' frustrations into support for a more equitable distribution of the tax burden. By contrast, tax reform opponents tried to turn public anger into broad support for spending reductions, which reformers realized could reverse previous gains and thwart future reform. Reformers, however, benefited from the timing of the crisis. The 1922 election would be the first one held since the agricultural crisis had crippled South Carolina's economy. Every member of the South Carolina House of Representatives and a significant portion of state senators seeking reelection had to face the people in the summer of 1922. South Carolina landowners, especially cotton farmers, demanded a reduction in the state property levy and threatened to defeat legislators who ignored their pleas. Moreover, in 1922 South Carolina would be electing a new governor, and W. W. Ball warned that "Blease plans to run in 1922 with 'high taxes' as his texts."[26] Landowners promised political retribution unless they received substantial tax relief. C. P. Hodges of Marlboro told Ball that farmers in South Carolina were in a desperate state of mind about taxation.

Even the "men of intelligence and information threaten to vote for Blease for Governor if the legislature does not radically reduce the tax levy and cut appropriations," Hodges reported. He mentioned three prominent men from Marlboro who were "talking in such a vein."[27] Thus, the pending election strengthened landowner threats and provided a powerful motivation for South Carolina legislators to support the tax reform as long as it included a reduction in the property levy.

The tax reform program of 1922 included a proposal to amend the constitution, a reduction in the property levy from twelve mills to four mills, and the new taxes (an income tax, inheritance tax, gasoline and oil tax, luxury tax, hydroelectric power tax, and a modest increase in the corporate license tax) proposed by the Joint Legislative Committee on Economy and Consolidation. Opposition to the tax reform proposal quickly surfaced. Legislative wrangling over the myriad tax proposals dominated the session. Most of the legislative debate took place in the senate, where the upper chamber quickly revealed it was far more reluctant than the house to support sweeping tax reform. South Carolina had forty-six state senators and senate districts coincided with county lines. Opponents of the various new taxes could lobby more effectively the one senator from their respective counties than to lobby the larger house delegations. Thus, senators generally proved more vulnerable to lobbying pressure than house members. Unlike the house, where tax legislation glided through, contentious debate erupted in the senate over every bill considered.[28]

The reformers' most significant defeat came early in the legislative session when legislators debated a joint resolution amending the constitution to permit property classification. When Claud Sapp, Columbia representative, led the fight for the proposed amendment in the house, S. J. Sellers, representative from Ruby, opposed any alteration in the constitution. "Instinct tells me," Sellers observed, "that there is danger concealed somewhere when we begin to fool with the constitution."[29] Early in the legislative session, the senate provoked significant opposition when it furiously debated the joint resolution for a constitutional amendment. An all-day debate lasted into the night of January 25 and ended without a vote, but not before Duncan D. McColl Jr., a banking and textile leader from Marlboro, and Glenn Ragsdale of Fairfield, both influential senators, warned that tampering with the constitution was "fraught with grave danger." Hiding behind the "dangers" of amending the constitution that represented the political security of white supremacy, these opponents demonstrated the pervasive power of white supremacy as a tool for maintaining and protecting the existing power structure. Christensen attempted to call the bluff of senators, who vigorously defended the sacredness of the constitution. Christensen threatened to pass a resolution calling for a strict enforcement of the constitutional provision that all property be taxed at 100 percent of market value unless the legislature agreed to consider constitutional reform. He recognized the hypocrisy of the opposition and knew that strict enforcement of the uniform taxation clause would be far more damaging to their interests than the proposed reforms. Reformers knew opponents did not resist this constitutional amendment because they feared an erosion of constitutional authority to limit black political participation. Rather, as George Laney of Chesterfield noted, the commercial and industrial interests of the state opposed classification of property because the state could then tax millions that currently escaped taxation. "Telegrams are coming from all over the state, to touch wealth lightly," Laney complained. "It all depends on whose ox is being gored. We have been goring the ox of the farmer for a long time, I hope and believe the present General Assembly will give him relief."[30]

The frustrations continued for Christensen, the leading architect of the tax reform package, when, on February 20, he exploded in anger on the senate floor and resigned as chairman of the finance committee. He cited his immense frustration with his senate colleagues after they defeated the hydroelectric tax, one of the more minor taxes.[31] The lobbying efforts of both Southern Power, the company expected to pay 80 percent of the tax, and the textile industry had succeeded in killing the bill. Senators from textile counties almost unanimously opposed it. Senator Johnson of Allendale, a low-country county without textile mills, accused the senate of bowing to the lobbying pressure and predicted that it would be "heralded all over South Carolina that capital has the senate by the throat."[32] From the senate floor Christensen declared: "Business has won in the senate against agriculture in a crisis when agriculture is in desperate straits." As a business owner, Christensen explained that he understood why business protested against the tax burden being shifted to them. Yet, he explained, the time had come "to ease up on those who are losing each year." Christensen's cogent characterization of the senate's response to the tax bills as a contest between agriculture and business created tremendous interest around the state in this legislative session and led Senator Proctor Bonham of Greenville, a leading industrial county, to call for formal censure of Christensen. Livid at Bonham, Christensen defended his remarks by recounting the businesses that appeared in the senate to cry, "Don't tax us." Christensen stated: "The captains of industry gathered here. Representatives of the great insurance companies came from their headquarters and their influential local connections joined them. Powerful cotton mill presidents of the Piedmont came . . . the able and experienced advocates of the Southern Power company came in force. Associations representing retail merchants came. Our committee rooms, our lobbies and this senate floor were alive with them for weeks." Privately, W. W. Ball questioned Christensen's dogmatism and wondered if it was politically astute in the long run. Yet Ball evaluated Christensen as "disinterested and clear headed" and deemed him "one of the few intelligent men we have in public life."[33]

Drawing class lines and reminding his fellow senators of the demand from farmers for property tax relief, Christensen refocused the reformers' strategy of linking their cause with the destitute farmers' plight. Christensen's theatrics, although deemed demagogy by his critics, brought enough public pressure to ensure that the senate would pass an income tax bill, although perhaps not one with rates Christensen and other reformers would have preferred.[34] After elaborate legislative maneuvering the senate passed an income tax bill that included markedly lower rates than those called for in the house version. Eventually, the two bodies agreed on a compromise income tax tied directly to the federal income tax structure and taxed South Carolinians' income for state purposes at 33.3 percent of federal income tax owed. The new law applied the income tax to corporations as well as individuals at the same rate. The defeated house bill had proposed a higher rate for corporations.[35] The income tax law stood as reformers' crowning achievement in the 1922 legislative session, which undertook more serious tax reform than previous sessions that had merely gestured toward it. Together the income tax, gasoline tax, inheritance tax, and increases in corporate license fees permitted the reduction of the state property levy from twelve mills to seven mills. Still the legislature fell far short of passing the complete tax package that would have reduced the property levy to the original goal of four mills.

More important, the reformers failed to persuade the legislature to initiate the cornerstone of all tax reform, constitutional revision. One South Carolinian noted that the "most important tax reform measure being considered by our lawmakers is the constitutional amendment allowing classification of property for purposes of assessment. It is not nearly so desirable that taxes be lowered as that they be equalized. It is almost unthinkable that in the agricultural crisis of South Carolina at the present real estate mortgages go untaxed."[36] Trumpeted by all serious analysts of South Carolina's tax problems as the most crucial area for reform, amendment of the state's constitution in the 1922 session met determined opposition. Christensen and others who advocated constitutional reform argued that an amendment allowing a just tax on mortgages, savings, bonds, stocks, and credits was necessary for equitable taxation in South Carolina.[37]

Classification of property would have been the easiest method of relieving the tax burden on agriculture property and shifting taxes more fairly to corporate and industrial income-producing property. Powerful corporate interests realized this and consequently opposed property classification with their most effective weapon: manipulation of white supremacy. Their stealth tactics of opposing constitutional reform as a defense of white supremacy effectively negated the need to expose their self-interested opposition of property classification. While corporate and industrial interests more openly defended their economic interests in the fight over the hydroelectric tax when the costs were much lower, they defended with more nuance against constitutional reform since the stakes were much higher. Thus, race and white supremacy figured less obviously in the public debate over tax reform, but they remained central and debilitating. Their less-overt tactics also concealed from subsequent historians the manipulative power of white supremacy to uphold the status quo and stifle change.

Corporate and industrial interests effectively halted reformers' most essential tax reform, amending the constitution, by arguing that the 1895 constitution could not be altered without endangering white supremacy. One of the main goals of the tax reform movement was revision of the constitution so the legislature could classify property and then tax different property classes at different rates. Every study of the tax system, by both insiders and outsiders, diagnosed the problem as stemming from the constitutional provisions governing taxes, and therefore recommended amending the constitution. Numerous governors, legislators, and newspaper editors had repeatedly trumpeted the need for either amending the current constitution or calling a constitutional convention. John Marion, chairman of the Marion Committee, said the constitutional regulations on property tax were the essence of South Carolina's tax problems, and he insisted that the elimination of constitutional restriction was essential for meaningful tax reform. "Altogether," Marion declared, "I am fully convinced that the friends of tax reform cannot put too much emphasis upon the passage of this constitutional amendment as the necessary first step." Moreover, Marion recognized that partial property relief would only serve to delay real reform.[38]

Despite a clear understanding among reform leaders that constitutional reform was essential, efforts to push amendments through the legislature failed. By the 1920s white South Carolinians had come to see the 1895 constitution as the bedrock of white supremacy. They tended to look at any change with skepticism. Commercial and industrial interests and wealthy capitalists feared property classification the most, and thus often hid behind white supremacy in their fight to defeat tax reform. They cloaked their opposition to constitutional reform as a defense of white supremacy, putting advocates of tax reform in the awkward political position of appearing to undermine one cornerstone of white supremacy in South Carolina, the 1895 constitution. Leading reformer William Ball lamented the popular and prevailing adage that "white supremacy is imbedded in and protected by the constitution of 1895."[39] Of course, many South Carolinians who opposed tax reform and the related constitutional amendments realized the constitution could be easily amended without endangering white supremacy, but these individuals represented interests that were willing to exploit the deep-seated racial fears other South Carolinians had in order to thwart reforms they perceived as hostile to their economic self-interests. Therefore, no matter how much tax reform was needed to secure additional revenue to support public education and a host of other measures, and no matter how dependent successful tax reform was on constitutional revision, South Carolinians as a whole were unwilling to alter the document they believed enshrined and preserved white supremacy. Thus tax reform opponents' political manipulation of white supremacy denied white reformers their most fundamental tax reform: property classification.

While progressive tax reform ambitions remained partial and incomplete, reformers made significant gains in 1922. The legislative fight that targeted business, industry, and high personal incomes had divided reformers' tenuous anti-Blease coalition. When the legislative session ended, the primary season was just months away. The reformers' political coalition had always been uneasy, and the tax debate made it even more fragile. In addition to facing an election season with their tattered coalition, reformers had to contend with gubernatorial candidate Cole Blease running against the new taxes. As Wade Milam, a reformer from Walhalla, explained, "Blease knows he has a walk-over for Governor this time. All he has to say is 'taxes' and even does not feel it necessary to work up a hot sweat." Reformers did not want the 1922 campaign to become a referendum on tax reform since members of their broad coalition might be tempted to side with Blease on this issue. Thus the 1922 tax debate further explains why reformers built their political strategy for the 1922 governor's race around accusing Blease of violating white supremacy by publicizing Blease' overtures to state Republican leader Joe Tolbert. They needed a bold preemptive strike against Blease, a diversion to defuse his campaign attacks on the new taxes.

In this era, when factions looked to broaden or firm up support, white supremacy politics presented a tempting and convenient strategy for rallying wayward allies against a common foe. White supremacy politics had defeated the reformers, but in the 1922 gubernatorial campaign, the reform faction proved unable to resist the temptation to turn white supremacy against one of its master practitioners, Cole Blease.[40]

Chapter 11

Financing Educational Reform

At the conclusion of World War I, South Carolina's population, with a 20 percent illiteracy rate, ranked as the second most illiterate in the nation. Moreover, three in four South Carolina adults lacked even an elementary school education. "South Carolina has been widely advertised as the most backward of all the states in public education," state superintendent of education John E. Swearingen lamented in 1921.[1] All reformers, black and white, agreed that South Carolina's proportionately large illiterate and undereducated population, coupled with its inadequate public school system, compounded the state's poverty, its excessive dependence on labor-intensive cotton agriculture, and its inadequate state services. Consequently, education reform remained central to the reformers' vision. Black reformers believed education could diminish poverty among African Americans and reduce their vulnerability to white exploitation. As educated black leaders, they believed that education would promote greater opportunity for African Americans' economic independence. White reformers believed that all other essential reforms such as attracting capital investment, implementing scientific agriculture, diversifying economic opportunities, raising the standard of living, expanding humanitarian institutions, and reforming the political system depended on dramatically reducing illiteracy and raising the education level of the general population. All reformers articulated a broadly shared vision of the transforming power and desirability of a significantly improved educational system.

Black reformers frequently asserted that they wanted a decent education system for black South Carolinians. At every public commencement, conference, and community celebration, black churches, colleges, businesses, fraternities, educators, professionals, and ministers called for improved educational opportunities. Benjamin F. Hubert, a prominent black educator at South Carolina State College, said in 1920 that black farmers, although they lacked formal education, understood the value of educating their children. Black farmers, Hubert explained, had discovered "that disease, crime, and poverty go hand in hand with illiteracy." Consequently, they wanted decent school buildings, longer school terms, and competent, well-paid teachers. Black reformers, however, stood outside the system, seemingly reliant on moral suasion alone because disfranchisement excluded them from formal power. African Americans in South Carolina were left at the mercy of whites, who perpetuated the racial disparities in public education; whites controlled district school boards, which hired the teachers, set the length of the school term, established policies, supervised the schools, and distributed public funds. James Asa Brown, a black minister in Orangeburg, concluded that the most important change needed to expand education for African Americans was that "white people speedily change their attitude toward the education of the Negro race. Continuous discrimination" Brown warned, "will result in great danger to the country." Marginal improvements in black public education had come only when black reformers petitioned and publicly pressured whites, as they had in 1919 to provide black teachers for Charleston's black public schools, or when black reformers negotiated privately with whites, as I. S. Leevy had a few years earlier, to obtain a new black public school, Booker T. Washington, in Columbia. With the fading of the war-mobilization demands that had briefly enhanced their influence with white leaders, black reformers' leverage had diminished, making even these incremental improvements difficult.[2]

By contrast, white reformers were much better poised to navigate the education-reform maze. It is tempting to see white reformers as omnipotent, but in the political context of white South Carolinians, they lacked sufficient influence to act alone. Having successfully weathered two political storms in 1922—one legislative, one electoral—white reformers felt emboldened to tackle education reform beginning in 1923. Although it was an incomplete victory, in 1922 white reformers had channeled the frustrations of a brewing tax revolt into a significant piece of tax-reform legislation that generated new revenue and facilitated some shift in the tax burden away from property owners. That same year reformers scored another win by once again defeating Cole Blease in his bid for the governorship. Even though some reformers thought Thomas G. McLeod would make a mediocre governor, they rejoiced at his victory over Blease, gladly celebrating mediocrity instead of obstinacy. A banking lawyer from Bishopville with ties to the utility industry, McLeod began his governorship in January 1923 with a commitment to continue the property-tax relief that had begun the previous year. Building upon the initial, limited, tax-reform successes, reformers tackled, during McLeod's first administration, the next major and foundational reform in their agenda: education.

By the third decade of the twentieth century, a state with such an undereducated population remained unprepared to contend with the rapid urbanization and industrialization that were transforming the nation economically and socially. Compounding the macroeconomic forces that had been at work in the nation for decades was the collapse of cotton prices in 1920, which precipitated an economic depression in agriculture. While many South Carolinians preferred to slow the pace of economic change and halt the erosion of the cotton-based economy, reformers embraced opportunities for expanding economic diversity and improving agricultural efficiency. They favored preparing South Carolina to participate in and benefit from the inevitable movement away from labor-intensive agriculture rather than be victimized by it. Reformers also believed that good government depended upon an educated citizenry. They imagined decreased ignorance in South Carolina could be gauged by a parallel reduction in the Bleaseite vote. Thus, white reformers prescribed education as the universal treatment for the state's ills. Yet transforming South Carolina's population into a literate and educated citizenry required an educational system very different from the existing one, which helped maintain white supremacy, making any change difficult.

As in the rest of the South, the dictates of white supremacy required that white South Carolinians should maintain a dual, segregated school system with unequal and extraordinarily inferior opportunities and resources for African Americans. In 1916, while statewide spending for white students totaled only $17.02 per child, state per capita spending for black students was a meager $1.90. The school year for African American students averaged just over three months statewide, less than half the length of the annual school term for white students. More than half of South Carolina's school population was black, but these students received barely a third of the teachers. While the disparity between the black and white school systems remained statewide, the funding gap was most pronounced in counties with the largest proportions of African Americans. For example, Beaufort, a low-country county with a nearly 80 percent African American population, spent on average $38.72 for each white child and a mere $3.13 per black child. South Carolinians maintained this disparity through a system of local control and local financing. In each school district, an all-white board of trustees controlled both the white and African American schools. District trustees had sole control over school administration and financing. The trustees distributed the district's total revenues among the segregated schools. The firm commitment of white school board trustees to white schools first and foremost, coupled with the political exclusion of disfranchised African Americans, perpetuated systemic inequality.[3]

Although white supremacy advocates systematically used local control as a fail-safe measure to guarantee that South Carolina devoted only minimal resources to educating African Americans, the decentralized approach created an inefficient educational system that also hindered educational progress for most whites. Reporting to South Carolina's general assembly in 1900, state superintendent of education John J. McMahan persuasively explained that local control acted as an impediment to improving public education in South Carolina. He rejected the idea that a state school system existed since the county, the district, the school, and even the teacher operated independently without any governing authority. Each county supported its own schools. Each district operated the poorest schools its residents would tolerate. "Isolation reigns," McMahan proclaimed. His frustrations centered on the inadequacy of an educational system sustained exclusively by individual rural communities whose citizens were often poor and undereducated. As William A. Link has argued, "nowhere was the strength of localism more evident than in the rural South."[4] In South Carolina, local control of education entailed more than district school boards hiring their own teachers and choosing their own curricula. Local control meant that local communities bore virtually the entire financial responsibility for public schools.

The foundation for South Carolina's system of local funding for education was embedded in the state constitution and firmly entrenched in the state's political tradition. During the late nineteenth century, state support for public schools in most states, including South Carolina, generally involved little more than permitting local districts to levy their own taxes and perhaps contributing a modest sum to the schools' operation. Only a small percentage of school revenues came directly from general state appropriations.[5] The South Carolina constitution of 1895 initiated the illusion of state support for public schools by creating a state board of education and a mandatory three-mill property tax to support public schools. Designed to help eliminate white illiteracy, the three-mill tax provided the principal revenue for funding public schools in South Carolina after 1895. But the revenues that the property tax generated were neither collected nor distributed statewide. Instead, each county collected the three-mill tax and distributed the funds to the school districts on the basis of student enrollment.[6] In addition to the three-mill tax, public schools received revenue from three other taxes: the poll tax, the dog tax, and any special tax that districts voluntarily levied on themselves. Each local school district controlled the funds collected from these taxes. These special taxes, which were also property taxes, created some of the greatest education spending disparities. Town districts primarily levied these optional taxes to enhance their schools with longer terms and more and better-qualified teachers, and districts with a railroad, public utility, or a power plant benefited tremendously from levying the special taxes. But most of the nineteen-hundred-plus districts in the state, which were rural, levied only the mandatory taxes, leaving them with minimal resources.[7]

The educational inequities among white South Carolinians were far less glaring than the racial discrimination in public education. But public economic resources available to whites varied significantly. Funding schools with a state-mandated property tax whose funds remained in the local community obviously benefited counties with the largest tax base, while counties with less valuable property suffered. Widely varying assessed property values across the state created one form of education spending inequality. Not only did the uneven distribution of wealth in the state create broad discrepancies in educational opportunity among whites, but so did the uneven geographic distribution of the white population. Counties with the largest proportion of whites spent the least per capita on each white child. Conversely, counties with the smallest proportion of whites had the highest per capita spending for white students. In the school year 1911–1912, counties that were more than 75 percent white spent $5.34 per white child, but in counties in which whites made up less than 25 percent of the population, per capita spending on white children reached $14.79.[8] Counties with fewer whites could educate their small number of white children with revenue raised only by the county's three-mill property tax, whereas white-majority counties had many more white children to educate and the three-mill property tax funds were stretched thinner. Cognizant that extreme local control and local funding of public schools created unequal educational opportunities for whites, white reformers longed for a more centralized state education system.

Although white reformers never proposed to dismantle the segregated school system or significantly improve black schools, they wanted to replace the highly decentralized, locally controlled system with a state educational system. White reformers' willingness to accommodate the demands of white supremacy seriously restricted their progressive vision for education reform in South Carolina. Reformers tolerated a modicum of progress for black schools as long as that improvement did not outstrip white progress. They couched advocacy for modest improvement in black education in paternalistic language that recommended white guidance, but when it came to allocating resources, they insisted that African Americans first help themselves. Although not a homogeneous group, many white reformers knew that continuing the dismal public support for black schools would never move the state from the bottom of national rankings. Even so, political considerations stifled their willingness to advocate for even the limited level of improvement they knew was necessary.

White reformers accepted the goal of ensuring white control in a black-majority state, especially in the heavily black parts of the state. Yet they rejected the mechanism, local control, that facilitated that assurance, because relegating the financial responsibility for education to school boards in local districts also created inequity among whites. White reformers wanted a state system for funding education that would eliminate the disparity inherent in local funding so that all white children received the same opportunity for a quality public education. Yet reform opponents argued that a state system of education would jeopardize white control by replacing informal decision making with a uniform, bureaucratic rule that would make channeling resources primarily to whites more difficult. So reformers' proposal for a state-funded educational system invited opponents to resist the reform in defense of white supremacy.

Reformers began an education campaign for a state-funded system of public education in 1923. Once again, as this campaign demonstrated, every reform effort in South Carolina required navigating objections by opponents who charged that the proposed change threatened white supremacy. Consequently, reformers shaped their education reform efforts to assuage doubts, real and feigned, that white supremacy would be protected. Moreover, opponents' persistent charge that change would violate white supremacy dissuaded white reformers from overtly supporting needed improvement in black schools even when they privately and indirectly encouraged it.

The progressive ideal for education funding rested on centralization. The magnitude of the challenge and the improbability of success led reformers, prior to the post–World War I era, to work for gradual improvement in the context of the existing local-funding system. In 1907, South Carolina reformers made initial headway toward improving public education as they spearheaded a successful effort to create public high schools. With a $50,000 state appropriation for the High School Act, the general assembly provided a matching-funds incentive intended to foster local interest in establishing high schools. The law set specific criteria for high schools—length of term, number of credits, number of teachers, and so on—and then provided some state funds to districts that met the criteria, which included that the district levy a four-mill property tax. This principle of providing minimal state matching funds to districts that met state-legislated standards characterized reformers' initial approach to enhancing state funding of education. This approach reflected self-help reasoning: the state helped districts that helped themselves. While the High School Act was certainly an important milestone for educational funding, it did little to aid the state's many poor districts.[9]

In 1909, reformers made the first significant attempt to offer state aid to poorer districts with the passage of the Term Extension Act. This new legislation offered state matching grants to school districts unable to finance at least a hundred-day term with the three-mill constitutional tax and an additional two-mill district levy to help them lengthen the academic term.[10] Term extension proved merely the first in a series of important but specialized state reform measures enacted between 1909 and 1920 to assist disadvantaged districts. During this twelve-year stretch, many laws were enacted and revised, reflecting the experimental nature of reformers' approach to funding public schools. Moreover, this legislation reflected existing national education-finance theory, which emphasized the state's responsibility to equalize opportunity by rewarding local initiative.[11] By 1920, five significant state-aid laws had emerged from this flurry of legislation. These laws, enacted primarily during Governor Richard I. Manning's administration, offered state matching funds to local districts to help them meet specific goals.[12] Together, these laws and their revisions constituted the preponderance of white reformers' accomplishments in improving education. They facilitated the growth of high schools, promoted longer school terms, standardized and enhanced teachers' salaries and qualifications, and offered transportation for some students. All this state aid was allocated to white schools. (See table 2.)

Despite these small legislative successes, by the 1920s white reformers saw that South Carolina's public education system had not improved rapidly enough to overcome its long-standing deficiencies. In national rankings, South Carolina continued to find its place at or near the bottom. The federal census of 1920 revealed that South Carolina ranked forty-seventh out of forty-eight states in literacy. Compounding the negative attention South Carolina received from the 1920 census was the publication of the Russell Sage Foundation's educational ranking of states. The foundation developed a method of comparing the educational progress of states with each other and assessing each state's own progress over time. Derived from a statistical analysis of educational data gathered nationwide, an index number was calculated for each state on the basis of ten statistical measures of educational improvement. Six components of the index equation came from various attendance statistics, and the remaining four elements were related to the financial investment in public schools.

Table 2. State Aid Appropriations for South Carolina Public Schools

Year	High School	Term Extension	Rural Graded	Equalization	Over-crowding	Total
1909	$60,000	$20,000				$80,000
1910	60,000	60,000				120,000
1911	60,000	60,000				120,000
1912	60,000	60,000				120,000
1913	60,000	60,000	$15,000			135,000
1914	60,000	60,000	60,000			180,000
1915	60,000	60,000	82,000			202,000
1916	60,000	60,000	120,000			240,000
1917	75,000	60,000	187,500	$50,000		372,500
1918	75,000	60,000	187,500	100,000		422,500
1919	100,000	60,000	200,000	125,000		485,000
1920	175,000	70,000	275,000	150,000		670,000
1921	275,000	70,000	275,000	400,000	$75,000	1,095,000
1922	290,000	56,000	295,000	370,000	75,000	1,086,000
1923	325,000	56,000	290,000	553,910	150,000	1,552,569[1]
1924	872,000	55,000	315,000	750,000	300,000	2,572,000[2]

1. 1922 deficit appropriation ($177,659) included in total.
2. 1923 deficit appropriation ($280,000) included in total.

Note: Additional appropriations made in 1923 and 1924 for serious underestimations of funds needed the previous year.

Sources: *Annual Reports, State Superintendent of Education*, 1909–1924; *Annual Reports, Comptroller General of South Carolina to the General Assembly*, 1910–1925.

South Carolina's index number improved between 1890 and 1918, but because other states improved at a faster rate the state consistently hovered near the bottom of the rankings. In 1918, the final year of this analysis, South Carolina hit bottom: forty-eighth out of forty-eight states.[13]

Frustrated with the state's continued low educational rankings, white reformers mobilized private citizens to push the state to improve white schools. In May 1921, Dr. Robert Pell, president of Converse College, rallied local residents in Spartanburg in popular support for education reform. Those attending this conclave planned another meeting in July and invited all concerned white citizens to attend, making it clear whom they intended to assist. Attendees at this second meeting formed the South Carolina Citizens' Education Association, electing J. Rion McKissick, *Greenville Piedmont* editor and future head of the University of South Carolina, president.[14] The Citizens' Educational Association was formed with the expressed purpose of petitioning the legislature to conduct a survey to assess the state's educational weaknesses and recommend necessary changes. Elsewhere, educational surveys, along with emerging financial theories, served as important components of the national movement toward improving education. Three southern states—Kentucky, Alabama, and Virginia—had conducted educational surveys during the proceeding decade. State superintendent Swearingen, who was generally enthusiastic about the prospect of identifying solutions to long-standing problems in education, expressed reservations about outside participation in this search for flaws. Fearing that nonsoutherners might finger the segregated educational system as a source of inefficiency and waste, Swearingen railed that any "theorists who put Anglo Saxon standards second or who do not understand and recognize our paramount obligation to maintain white supremacy ought not to be allowed to touch anything here." As Swearingen's reservations demonstrate, the demands of white supremacy perpetually defined the boundaries of reform in South Carolina, even reform intended to benefit whites only.[15]

Beyond the specific goal of conducting an educational survey, Pell hoped that the Citizens' Educational Association would unite South Carolinians who wanted rapid educational reform. Pell envisioned the association as a vehicle for both promoting educational reform legislation and informing the general public on issues pertaining to education, much as the Taxpayers Association had pressured the legislature and rallied the public for tax reform. The Citizens' Educational Association operated as a loosely constructed organization rather than as a formally organized body. Members affiliated with approximately twenty-five other statewide, whites-only organizations, including the American Legion, American Legion Auxiliary, League of Women Voters, State Teachers' Association, Daughters of the American Revolution, State Federation of Women's Clubs, South

Carolina Sunday School Association, South Carolina Press Association, and alumni associations from every college in the state, comprised the majority of the association's membership.[16] Because the Citizens' Educational Association was already in place by 1921, it provided a network for helping renewed reform efforts that began in 1923. The association also heightened public awareness, especially among influential white business and political leaders, of the shortcomings of public education in South Carolina.

Before moving South Carolina closer toward a true state system of education and away from reliance on local control, reformers had to persuade others that the patchwork approach to funding education was inadequate and inefficient. Not only had the state-aid measures that white reformers pushed through the legislature between 1912 and 1920 failed to close the gap in educational quality among white schools, but the cumbersome collection of laws also too often compounded existing educational inequalities. The effect of rewarding local effort with matching state funds had the unintended consequence of benefiting wealthier school districts that readily levied the additional taxes to receive the matching state money, rather than the poorer ones that often did not. The counties in greatest need of aid often received little or no assistance because their residents lacked either the resources or the resolve to levy the required tax. Thus, their general state taxes aided the schools in wealthier counties. Additionally, since state aid for schools increased if the county's tax receipts for a given year fell below the previous year's collections, the existing matching-funds approach had the unintended consequence of placing a premium on tax evasion. One education official contended that some districts made concerted efforts not to collect either poll taxes or dog taxes because of this provision.[17]

In 1924 Power Bethea, rural school supervisor and state statistician, reported to Governor McLeod that the current laws regulating state aid for public schools were too complex. The numerous laws and modifications that had arisen to meet specific needs often demonstrated little coordination with previous legislation. Moreover, the requirements within the various laws often contradicted one another and confused administrators. For example, enrollment and attendance minimums varied with each new law and changed periodically. Expounding upon this confused policy, Bethea charged that very few county superintendents understood all the state-aid laws. Only the most experienced and knowledgeable superintendents could successfully negotiate the complex system and acquire all possible funds for their schools.[18]

By the early 1920s, apart from being inefficient and complex, the legislation that provided state assistance for South Carolina public education was also increasingly expensive. Each year, new laws demanded additional revenues, while existing measures required increased appropriations because more and more schools applied for aid. In 1909, the state appropriated $80,000 to assist local communities with public education expenses. The following year that figure increased by 50 percent. By 1917, in only five years, state appropriations had increased 137 percent.[19] With passage of the final state-aid law in 1920, South Carolina appropriations for assistance to weaker public schools had reached $670,000. The following year this figure escalated to $1,095,000—a 63 percent increase. Two years later, in 1923, state spending climbed another 41 percent, to $1,552,569. These annual escalations alarmed legislators and alerted them to the state's inability to continue funding indefinitely these unpredictable increases.[20] (See table 3.)

State costs were unpredictable because the amount of state aid needed correlated with the number of districts that applied for aid, which was difficult to estimate reliably. Receiving state aid under the system demanded not only that a school be eligible but also that it apply for assistance. Bethea complained that the tedious process of approving these applications occupied two months of his valuable time. Each year more districts applied, and the requests from eligible districts repeatedly surpassed appropriations. As the number of deserving districts requesting aid multiplied, the rewards to each school dwindled because the state's revenue did not keep pace with demands for its resources. In 1923, the legislature appropriated $150,000 to relieve overcrowded elementary grades, yet qualifying applications totaled $272,831. That same year deserving schools were eligible for $663,310 in aid based on the criteria of the law that guaranteed a seven-month term, but the legislature capped appropriations at $553,910. The state superintendent resolved this problem by granting awards on a prorated basis so that all eligible schools received something.[21]

Table 3. Annual Percentage Increase in
State Appropriations for Public Schools

	Current Dollars		Constant Dollars*	
Year	Total	% Increase	Total	% Increase
1909	$80,000		$296,296	
1910	120,000	50%	428,571	45%
1911	120,000	0	428,571	0
1912	120,000	0	413,793	-3
1913	135,000	13	450,000	9
1914	180,000	33	600,000	33
1915	202,000	12	673,333	12
1916	240,000	19	727,273	8
1917	372,500	55	980,263	35
1918	422,500	13	938,889	-4
1919	485,000	15	932,692	-1
1920	670,000	38	1,116,667	20
1921	1,095,000	63	2,027,778	82
1922	1,086,000	-1	2,172,000	7
1923	1,552,569	43	3,044,253	40
1924	2,572,000	66	5,043,137	66

* Adjusted for inflation, expressed in constant 1967 dollars. U.S. Bureau of the Census, *Historical Statistics of the United States, Colonial Times to 1970*, 2 vols. (Washington, D.C.: Government Printing Office, 1975), 210–11.

Sources: *Annual Reports, State Superintendent of Education*, 1909–1924; *Annual Reports, Comptroller General of South Carolina to the General Assembly*, 1910–1925.

Thus, by the early 1920s, the inadequacy of white reformers' prewar piecemeal approach to education reform, which provided narrow remedies for systemic problems, had become apparent. The time had arrived to abandon a system that operated under the philosophy that the district should remain the primary unit for funding and administering public education. Drawing upon their wartime experiences that relied much more on statewide coordination and state action, reformers looked for new political leadership as an impetus for a new approach. In the fall election of 1922, James H. Hope challenged the incumbent, John E. Swearingen, in the race for state superintendent of education. Swearingen, an Edgefield native who had lost his sight in a childhood hunting accident, had held the post since 1909, the year the Term Extension Act passed. Swearingen's tenure as superintendent paralleled the growth of reformers' early strategy, which promoted ad hoc state-aid laws designed to help poor white schools. Thus reason suggested that a new strategy needed a new state superintendent.[22]

Swearingen's own candidacy for reelection to his eighth term as state superintendent had been damaged by an aborted flirtation with the governor's race. Still, his defeat surprised many, especially since he was the long-term incumbent running against Hope, a challenger whom few seasoned educators knew. Swearingen complained that he lost his reelection bid because Hope ran for superintendent with countless promises, including cheaper and better books, higher salaries for teachers, longer school terms, more high schools, more professional supervision, personal visits to schools, greater appropriations from the legislature, and, ironically, lower taxes. "I would not like to describe these promises because the word I should have to use would not look well in print," Swearingen confided to a friend.[23] Regardless of why Swearingen lost, his defeat enhanced the cause of educational reform in South Carolina. While genuinely committed to improving educational opportunities for white students, Swearingen, the architect of the existing funding system, remained an avid adherent of the philosophy that the state should help only those districts that first helped themselves. As the smallest administrative unit and the one closest to the people, the district, he reasoned, could most effectively encourage responsible participation from local residents. Swearingen's departure from the state superintendent's office doubtless expedited a reconsideration of this logic and the state's commitment to rewarding local initiative at the expense of equalization.[24]

In sum, South Carolina stood at the threshold of significant educational reform in 1923. A host of factors contributed to the growing momentum for change. Public concern about the state's national ranking in education had precipitated formation of the Citizens' Educational Association. There was a growing awareness of the incoherence of existing programs for state funding that left economic control of education in the hands of 1,936 district school boards. The legislature had become convinced of its need to control seemingly unpredictable increases in appropriations. Together, the new leadership at the state department of education combined with these factors to create an atmosphere conducive to systemic reform.

Taking the helm of the state department of education early in 1923, James H. Hope proved determined to lead the state rapidly in a direction it had been hesitantly inching toward for a long time. Hope's first publication as superintendent identified rural schools' lagging development as a major problem for South Carolina's white public schools. Moreover, he promptly asked state statistician Bethea to develop a comprehensive plan for financing schools to replace the existing hodgepodge of legislation with a simplified system that could stabilize escalating and unpredictable costs and equalize distribution of state aid. Bethea's compliance launched a new phase of debate in South Carolina's journey toward educational reform.[25]

Bethea enthusiastically accepted Hope's directive to create a new financial plan for funding South Carolina's public schools. Bethea, a graduate of Wofford College, had joined the professional staff of the department of education as a rural school supervisor in 1921. The following year, he acquired the additional responsibility of state statistician. Eager to distinguish himself, the youthful Bethea pursued Hope's assignment with vigor, developing a proposal entitled the *Suggested Plan for Financing the State School System*, which Hope published in October 1923 and promptly circulated among influential educators and politicians. As a young education administrator and graduate student at the University of South Carolina, where he received his master of arts in education in 1925, Bethea kept abreast of current literature in the field. Armed with the expertise that reformers deemed essential, Bethea devised a plan that reflected contemporary trends in educational theory. His introductory comments in the *Suggested Plan* explained the purpose of the proposed reform and confirmed that his intentions were "to harmonize [South Carolina's] school system with the leading educational state systems in the nation."[26]

Bethea's proposal, embodying the idea of shifting the principal financial burden to the state, introduced what became known as the 5-2-0 plan, under which the state would provide funds sufficient to pay teachers' salaries for five months, the county would fund two months of salaries, and the district would pay for any additional days that it wanted beyond seven months, but extension of the school term beyond seven months was not mandatory. To pay for the state's five-month share of teachers' salaries, Bethea proposed that the state levy an additional twelve-mill property tax. He fashioned this twelve-mill tax as a true state tax administered by the state department of education. Each county would continue to use the constitutional three-mill tax and levy any additional taxes necessary to ensure its two months of salaries. Poll taxes, dog taxes, and other special taxes remained available to each district, both for miscellaneous expenses and for optional extension of the school term beyond seven months. Bethea's plan also included salary schedules for principals and teachers based on professional experience as well as sizes and types of schools. The salary schedules, however, were applicable only to the state's white educators. African American teachers were to receive one-half the amount designated for their white counterparts.[27]

Before Hope distributed his plan to county superintendents and legislators, Bethea sought early endorsements from key leaders in the state. Eager to solicit gubernatorial support for his plan, Bethea sent McLeod a copy of his plan and requested the governor's endorsement. McLeod recognized the value of the proposed plan and deemed it worthy of serious consideration. Understandably delighted with the governor's assessment, Bethea requested permission to quote McLeod in subsequent promotions.[28]

Careful not to exclude the legislative branch from his preliminary lobbying, Bethea discussed the 5-2-0 plan's merits with Claud Sapp, chairman of the house ways and means committee. Sapp, a native of Lancaster County, one of the state's heavily rural white-majority counties, attended law school at the University of South Carolina and later became a permanent resident of Columbia. After serving as state representative for Richland County from 1913 until 1915, Sapp continued his career in state government as the assistant attorney general from 1916 until he returned to the house in 1921. Two years later he became the new chairman of the house ways and means committee. Consistent with his progressive reputation, Sapp embraced Bethea's effort to reform educational funding and proclaimed that the *Suggested Plan* was "one hundred percent better than the current method of school support." He became a key champion of improving education for the rural white population.[29]

Encouraged by this preliminary support from McLeod and Sapp, Bethea cultivated broader public support. Recognizing the influential position Robert Pell held as president of the Citizens' Educational Association, Bethea sent Pell a copy of the *Suggested Plan*, requesting that the association endorse his plan and include it in the association's legislative agenda slated for discussion during American Education Week in November.[30] Pell agreed to support Bethea's plan and joined him in promoting it. Pell lobbied McLeod to give serious consideration to a public endorsement of Bethea's plan in his annual "State of the State" address to the general assembly in January. Pell also agreed to publicize Bethea's plan during the American Education Week's activities coordinated by the Citizens' Educational Association.[31]

As part of South Carolina's observance of American Education Week, the association requested that each county hold a mass meeting on the Saturday (November 24) of American Education Week and that each county superintendent inform citizens about Bethea's plan, the educational survey, and other nationally oriented legislation. While it was important to inform local residents, the county superintendents' most significant responsibility was to secure their constituents' support for the plan. Twenty-five of South Carolina's forty-six counties held these requested meetings. Twenty-one of these counties endorsed Bethea's plan. The remaining four counties that held rallies did not take a vote, but no county went on record in opposition to the plan. Pleased with the success of American Education Week, Bethea reported the positive results to the governor, asserting that the majority of the white population favored his plan and asking again for McLeod's endorsement in the governor's annual message to the legislature in early January.[32]

The overwhelming endorsement of Bethea's 5-2-0 plan emanating from those county rallies, however, did not emerge from lengthy or serious debate. Despite Bethea's efforts to use that information to suggest the existence of a white consensus, this endorsement cannot be viewed as a gauge of popular support for the 5-2-0 plan simply because the majority of the state's white population resided in these twenty-one counties.[33] Few South Carolinians were involved in these well-orchestrated but largely ceremonial Saturday afternoon gatherings. Widespread endorsement of the *Suggested Plan* at those county rallies instead signified white reformers' determination to reform South Carolina's method of financing public education. Although it would be presumptuous to conclude from their persistence and enthusiasm that reformers understood the details and accepted the implications of Bethea's plan, their candid support for the *Suggested Plan* confirmed their desire that public school funding change and change soon.

As the new year dawned, the groundwork for the promotion of Bethea's *Suggested Plan* had been laid. When the 1924 South Carolina General Assembly session opened January 8 with McLeod's annual address, the governor praised the progress of education in the state and lauded efforts to provide equal educational opportunities for rural white children. Yet Bethea's three months of lobbying apparently fell on barren soil. Despite his initial positive reception of the *Suggested Plan*, McLeod disappointed Bethea and others by neglecting the school financing issue in his speech. He made no public statement against Bethea's plan, but privately he expressed reservations to both Bethea and Pell. The governor scolded the reform advocates for focusing excessively on the state's neglect and "backwardness." He preferred an upbeat emphasis that stressed progress already made. More praise and less disparagement, McLeod admonished, would garner "added inspiration and impetus to further development." More to the point, McLeod explained that while he favored improvements in state financing of education, his commitment to tax reform assumed a higher priority than his support for education finance reform. Since being elected in 1922, McLeod had worked to develop a system of indirect taxation, involving some type of sales tax, to replace the general property tax that still buttressed the state revenue base in 1924. McLeod told Bethea and Pell that he was unwilling to sacrifice the progress made in tax reform for any purpose. Since Bethea's program was funded with precisely the kind of property tax the governor was trying to convince the legislature to move away from, McLeod felt that he had no choice except to oppose it.[34] Niels Christensen, the ardent tax reform senator from Beaufort, encouraged McLeod to oppose the proposed educational funding reform specifically because it included a direct increase in property taxes.[35]

As the general assembly session opened on January 8, the legislature voted for a special recess to expedite the budget process, enabling legislators to focus exclusively on the appropriation bill without the added distractions of regular legislative business. During this recess the joint appropriations committee, composed of the house ways and means and the senate finance committees, met frequently and extensively as members negotiated with state agencies about their funding.[36] On January 14, state superintendent James Hope and state high school inspector J. D. Fulp met with the joint appropriations committee to discuss the department of education's budget requests. Shocking many committee members, Hope and Fulp submitted a proposed budget for the department totaling $2,645,154, a 43 percent increase from 1923's $1,851,716 appropriation, which the legislature had regarded as generous. Within this budget recommendation was an $872,074 request for aid to fund the creation and maintenance of high schools, representing a 155 percent increase from the $341,901 spent in 1923. Additionally, the department also requested $750,000 to fund equalization, up from $604,736 the previous year.[37]

While these spending increases were not unprecedented in the department of education's recent history and could easily be justified by the fact that applications for state aid annually exceeded available funds, Hope apparently intended his request for such a substantial increase to facilitate the adoption of Bethea's new financing plan. Requesting these funding increases while the existing laws remained in effect added credibility to the argument that these ad hoc laws created an unpredictable variable in public school financing. Moreover, Hope apparently believed that if he requested, and perhaps secured, these funds before Bethea's reform plan became a hotly debated piece of legislation, he might avoid the potentially dangerous political perception that the proposed financing plan would prompt a huge increase in state spending for education.

During the joint appropriations committee meeting with Hope, Senator Herbert H. Gross from Dorchester, chairman of the senate finance committee, registered his dissatisfaction with the current state-aid system, pointing out that poorer counties paid more in taxes than they received in aid while richer counties received the bulk of state aid. Declaring that "every white child in the state should be given the opportunity to be educated," house ways and means chair Claud Sapp asserted that the only way that equal educational opportunity could be achieved would be to "tax all the property of the state for that purpose, eradicate the county lines, and make the state the unit of education."[38] Enough other members in the legislature agreed with Sapp's assessment to ensure that the general assembly would give Bethea's plan full consideration in the 1924 session.[39]

When the general assembly reconvened on January 23, it began consideration of the joint appropriations committee report that suggested full funding of Hope's spending requests for the department of education's 1924–1925 budget of $2,645,154.[40] The committee's approval of this proposal suggested that Bethea had succeeded in raising committee members' awareness of the urgent need for public school financing reform. Achieving consensus on the need for reform, however, did not produce an agreement on how to accomplish that goal. The difficult task of devising a bill that could fulfill everyone's expectations, alleviate everyone's fears, and pass both houses of the legislature lay ahead. Four major obstacles jeopardized successful completion of this task.

One, disagreement abounded about the appropriate proportion of financial support the various government units should furnish. Who should bear most of the financial responsibility, the district, the county, or the state? Bethea's recommendation that the state fund teacher salaries for five months while the county fund them for only two violated a long-standing assumption among many South Carolinians, legislators and private citizens alike, that primary financial responsibility for education was rightly vested with local communities. Sharp disagreement over this basic principle dominated subsequent legislative debates. Two, if the legislature approved the new increases for education, what would be the primary source of additional revenue to fund the increases? Complicating the debate was the ongoing controversy over enacting a general state sales tax, which McLeod favored. Consistent with his general commitment to restructure and enhance the revenue base in South Carolina, McLeod strongly supported a state sales tax that would reduce the state's dependence on the general property tax. Much of the expected revenue from the sales tax proposed in 1924 was pledged to supporting educational needs without levying additional property taxes, which Bethea's plan proposed to do.

Three, what funding method would most equitably distribute revenue among white schools? Even if the legislature reached an agreement on what portion of support each government unit (district, county, state) would contribute and also agreed on how the taxes would be levied to generate this additional revenue, the legislature still had to devise an acceptable method of distributing the new funds. Redistribution of state resources was a crucial concern, especially for residents of counties and districts that could furnish adequate educational opportunities for the white students in their jurisdictions with their own local taxes. Many citizens and legislators questioned whether the tax revenues raised in one district should cross district lines to be redistributed throughout the county. For example, such redistribution would require Greenville mill owners to subsidize poorer sections of Greenville County. Others worried that shifting the responsibility for funding public schools from the district to the state could entail redistribution of taxes across county lines, creating a situation where property owners in Greenville or Charleston would be taxed to support schools outside their counties.

Finally, how might any proposed changes in funding education threaten white supremacy? Beyond fiscal concerns lurked a problem central to every reform initiative in the state. Within South Carolina, a black-majority state governed by a white minority factiously committed to maintaining white dominance, no issue threatening the entrenched system of white control could escape careful scrutiny of how any potential change might affect white supremacy. Whites demanded assurance that any changes in funding for public education would not generate new taxes for expanding black education or alter whites' legal ability to keep African American schools inferior. Together these four questions shaped the debate and influenced the compromises surrounding education reform in 1924.

Chapter 12

Legacy of Reform

Understanding the power of white supremacy requires scrutinizing the ways that whites exercised power. Additionally, it requires identifying the multifaceted and contradictory ways that they employed white supremacy's manipulative potential. The legislative debate over funding education that dominated the 1924 session reveals the pervasiveness and complexity of white supremacy. Within the banal routine of committee decisions, debated amendments, behind-the-scenes lobbying, and obscure procedural maneuvers, white supremacy's hidden power was revealed. Therefore, it is best seen with a keen eye for subtlety, to spot legislative machinations contemporaries employed to conceal their motives and strategies from their rivals. Beneath the detailed questions of who bore the greatest responsibility for funding education, what funding formula best balanced principles of local initiative and statewide equity, and what revenue source would raise adequate funds fairly lay whites' fundamental concern about whether the existing funding mechanism could be reformed while protecting white supremacy.

White reformers demonstrated creativity and determination in establishing a state system for funding education that required negotiating their way across rough white supremacy terrain where reformers both created obstacles and became entangled by them. White supremacy's influence in the debate was complicated: obvious and concealed, intentional yet also unanticipated. The most obvious expression of white supremacy was the segregated school system that whites operated with intended restrictions on spending for black schools. While reformers defended these spending limitations, whites' determination to keep the majority of South Carolinians minimally educated remained an essential reason the state lagged behind in education. White supremacy complicated and restricted reform. Yet, it also pervaded the educational funding debate as a stealth strategy that both reformers and their opponents exploited. Since both groups used white supremacy to achieve their contradictory ends, the outcome could not readily be predicted.

Reform opponents charged that white reformers threatened white supremacy with their proposed funding reforms, challenging reformers to placate the alleged concerns and counter with allegations of their own. Only by doing so could reformers achieve even their modest reform goal—greater educational opportunity for white South Carolinians.

During the first two weeks of the reconvened 1924 legislative session, both the house and senate committees on education held extensive hearings, and each formulated bills reflecting the growing desire to reform South Carolina's method of financing public education. Each committee posited different solutions to the problem. Lawmakers from the wealthier counties—John Evans of Spartanburg, Claud Sapp of Richland, Joseph Bryson of Greenville, and James S. Whaley of Charleston—expressed their willingness to assist poorer counties, prompting the lower chamber to pass a resolution on February 11, 1924, advocating reform. The following day, the bill popularly known as the 4-2-1 plan was introduced in the house. This formula proposed that four months of teacher salary assistance come directly from the state; the county would fund two months, and the district would fund an additional month's salary, totaling seven required months for all schools in the state. Aside from this minor modification, the House 4-2-1 bill was very similar to Bethea's 5-2-0 plan. The constitutional three-mill tax was to remain available for county use, while poll taxes, dog taxes, and special levies remained reserved for the districts. To fund the state's four-month portion of teacher salaries, however, the house bill proposed that the money come from general state appropriations rather than the property tax included in Bethea's 5-2-0 plan.[1] Apparently the house expected to pass a sales tax during the session and planned to use the additional general budget revenue for education. Receipts from the proposed sales tax would furnish enough new revenue to fund the 4-2-1 legislation without raising property taxes.

Meanwhile, the senate education committee devised an alternate bill that would substitute for Bethea's *Suggested Plan* and simplify the house 4-2-1 plan. Two days later, on February 14, the senate education committee submitted a bill that represented a more drastic departure from the existing funding system than either Bethea's 5-2-0 plan or the 4-2-1 plan submitted in the house earlier that week. The senate bill, known as the 6-0-0 plan, proposed that the state pay for six months of teacher salaries. In turn, the counties and districts could extend the school term to any length they wanted beyond six months. Besides increasing the state's share of financial support to six months, which no previous plan had suggested, and not requiring any local assistance as a prerequisite for the state subsidy, the 6-0-0 bill included another important provision that differed from the other proposals. This senate plan recommended that the constitutional three-mill property tax, which had always been a county tax, be converted to a state tax to assist in paying for the state's six-month salary obligation. General appropriation funds would provide the remainder of the state's responsibility for six months of teacher salaries.[2]

Obviously more radical than either of the previous schemes, the senate plan implicitly asserted that financial responsibility resided solely with the state and consequently the constitutional three-mill tax should be treated as a true state tax rather than as a state-mandated county tax. The radicalism of the senate plan stemmed from the background and inclinations of its coauthors, Senators Robert S. Rodgers of Dillon County and James Spruill of Chesterfield County. Both men were junior senators, beginning their terms in 1923, representing areas with large numbers of white children and relatively little taxable wealth. As young lawmakers they were more receptive to new ideas and less invested in conventional practices. Moreover, Rodgers had a particular professional interest in education. Before embarking upon his political career, he had served as county superintendent of education in Dillon, where he exhibited a determination to provide his home county with one of the best school systems in the state. Recognized for his diligence, he was elected by his colleagues as president of the South Carolina Teachers Association.[3]

With two bills circulating in the legislature, serious lobbying began. Wil Lou Gray, executive secretary of the Illiteracy Commission and supervisor of adult schools, joined the movement to make the state the primary unit responsible for funding education. Just a few years earlier, Gray, a prominent advocate for educational uplift in the state, spearheaded the campaign that women reformers waged to create the Illiteracy Commission. Passionate about reducing adult illiteracy among whites in rural communities and mill villages, she had been the impetus behind the state's recently created adult education program. Gray mailed copies of the House 4-2-1 bill to friends and colleagues within her network, requesting that each recipient inform five others of the need to support this legislation. The 4-2-1 plan appealed to Gray because of its general promise to guarantee rural white children equal educational opportunities. She justified her support for this bill on this point alone and did not become personally engaged in the debates regarding strengths and weaknesses of the two competing bills.[4]

The introduction of two separate pieces of legislation from the two houses elicited a less innocuous response from Bethea. Delighted with the House 4-2-1 bill, Bethea expressed outrage at the Senate 6-0-0 bill. He immediately shared his concern with Governor McLeod, touting the virtues of the 4-2-1 plan while emphasizing the liabilities he detected in the 6-0-0 plan. Passage of the 4-2-1 bill was essential, Bethea argued, because it, like his 5-2-0 plan, would replace the confusing conglomeration of school aid legislation and simplify procedures for funding public education. Eliminating this ad hoc legislation that lacked a cohesive goal, Bethea maintained, would enable the state consistently to guarantee a seven-month school term for all white schools rather than just the schools that met the prerequisites for receiving state aid under the previous legislation. Schools could easily calculate their share of state aid by simply multiplying four months of the assigned salary by their number of teachers. This would facilitate local planning, significantly reduce paperwork, and allow schools to depend on this money coming without having to wade through the lengthy application and approval process that slowed receipt of funds under the existing system. The 4-2-1 reform measure would also tighten the reins on the dramatic appropriation increases the legislature had experienced in recent years. Since state aid would directly correlate to teacher salaries defined by a fixed schedule, costs would increase only if the legislature raised salaries or if expanding enrollment required hiring more teachers. Not only would the 4-2-1 finance plan curtail the state's escalating annual expenditures for education, but also the cost of funding public schools could become predictable, making budget planning easier. Like his initial plan, the 4-2-1 proposal required local support, an imperative Bethea enthusiastically embraced.[5]

The senate 6-0-0 plan offered many of the same advantages of simplification and predictability that Bethea attributed to the 4-2-1 plan, although he refused to acknowledge that point. Instead of supporting the 6-0-0 plan, however, Bethea railed about the hazards to which he believed it exposed the state. Making the state responsible for more than 50 percent of educational cost was unwise, Bethea warned. It was particularly irresponsible, he declared, not to require any fiscal commitment from the counties or districts. Freed of funding responsibility, local interest in education would evaporate, he asserted, and South Carolina's educational system would decline as surely as Rome had fallen and government "fed everyone from a public trough." Bethea also expressed concern about the 6-0-0 bill's recommendation to transform the constitutional three-mill tax into a state tax because of its centralizing tendency. South Carolina's school system would become "as autocratic as Germany or Russia," he lamented, since the county superintendent would be relegated to a clerk. Moreover, Bethea believed that conversion of the three-mill tax to a state tax stood on shaky grounds constitutionally.[6]

Employing the criticism whites consistently used against their opponents, Bethea criticized the 6-0-0 plan as a threat to white supremacy. He noted that the senate plan did not include a mechanism for limiting the school term for African American schools. Under the senate plan, Bethea explained, there would be "no way to escape giving the negro less than six months." Under the existing system, district boards of trustees retained the power to establish the length of the school term, and these trustees consistently held blacks' school terms well below whites.' The 4-2-1 bill also did not contain a limiting clause, but since it required the state to fund only four months, the district reserved the authority to limit the term of black schools. Under the 6-0-0 plan the district was powerless to make the term length shorter than six months. Bethea warned that if the state required that black schools operate a six-month term, then it would deny whites the necessary resources for a seven-month term, a clear but absurd implication that the senate plan prioritized blacks' education over whites' opportunities. Bethea's warning to the governor illustrates the common, reflexive defense, so often employed, of claiming that the opponents' proposed change inadequately protected white supremacy.[7]

Despite Bethea's concerns, the senate moved quickly to discuss the 6-0-0 bill. Debate began in earnest on February 20 and continued for two days. Many senators praised the bill as a progressive attempt to remedy the shortcomings of the present system. Senator Luther Funderburk, a farmer from Kershaw County, favored making the state the principal unit of education funding. "Let the property of the state educate the children of the state, no matter where the property is located nor where the child comes into existence," Funderburk declared.[8] Senator Niels Christensen of Beaufort, however, opposed the bill. Christensen had been a fervent leader of progressive reform, but he did not support this education finance reform. Arguing that the present laws stimulated local interest and initiative, he asserted that the new method of funding education would stifle the self-help spirit, which he contended worked very well. He made this politically palatable argument because he refused to support any measure that might jeopardize tax reform, his personal priority. Of course, he also represented Beaufort, a low-country county whose nominal local taxes served its small white population adequately. Another senator, Alan Johnstone of Newberry County, also lamented the absence of some local fiscal obligation in the 6-0-0 bill's provisions. In addition to this reservation, Johnstone shared McLeod's reservation about a new funding program based on a property tax rather than the concept of indirect taxation. Despite opposition from several prominent senators, the 6-0-0 bill passed the senate overwhelmingly, 34–5. The five dissenters were Christensen, Johnstone, William Lightsey (Hampton), Samuel Ward (Georgetown), and George Wightman (Saluda). Christensen and Johnstone were adamant tax reformers and remained skeptical of any major reform that levied a property tax. The latter three senators were among the upper chamber's most consistent conservatives.[9]

Although the Senate had acted quickly and passed its 6-0-0 bill on February 21, the House 4-2-1 plan had remained dormant since its first reading on February 12. For the next few weeks the issue reached a legislative stalemate, although debate continued within private circles and in newspaper editorials. On March 6, the proposed general sales tax died in a voice vote, complicating the education finance reform issue, since the house had devised its 4-2-1 plan with the expectation that the sales tax would provide the additional revenue needed to meet the state's expanded share of education funding.

Fearful that one of the new school financing plans would pass without a sales tax to lessen the property tax burden, three Greenville school district boards—Greenville City, Parker, and Simpsonville—convened the next day to discuss the pending school legislation. Together they agreed that supporting either financial reform measure conflicted with their financial interest.[10] Without a sales tax, passage of either bill would require an increase in local property taxes. Since Greenville had a larger property-tax base than most counties, any change in funding procedures would likely result in a net transfer of tax revenue from Greenville to poorer counties. Death of the sales tax influenced these Greenville school board trustees to aggressively oppose reform legislation. Following their Friday night meeting, James L. Mann, superintendent of Greenville City schools, and L. P. "Pete" Hollis, superintendent of Parker School District, held an early Saturday morning conclave with the Greenville legislative delegation. There, Mann and Hollis presented legislators with a resolution expressing the trustees' reservations about both proposed financing reform plans in the absence of sales tax revenue. The superintendents readily persuaded local lawmakers that reform, without a sales tax, was ill advised. Next, the Greenville City and Parker school boards sent Mann to Columbia to lobby the entire legislature against both financial reform bills. They hoped the articulate Greenville superintendent could dampen whatever enthusiasm remained for the proposed bills.[11]

As Mann headed to Columbia that second week in March, the probability that significant reform of public school financing would emerge in South Carolina during the 1924 legislative session seemed remote. The senate had approved its 6-0-0 bill and sent it to the house for consideration, but the house had neither discussed the senate bill nor passed its own 4-2-1 proposal to second reading. Frustrated by the lack of time and surrounded by confused constituents, advocates of public school funding reform faced bleak prospects as the legislative session neared completion and fundamental disagreements still existed between the house and senate bills. Moreover, the sales tax defeat dashed their hopes for an indirect method of funding either of the proposed reform measures.

As Mann arrived in Columbia to lobby, the rival house and senate proposals prompted first confusion and later an impasse during the closing weeks of the 1924 legislative session. As the session wound down, however, the South Carolina Teachers Association, a chapter of the National Educational Association, assembled for its thirty-eighth annual meeting in Columbia on March 13–15. With more than twenty-five hundred participants from across the state, the 1924 convention set a new record for attendance. After an extensive membership drive in 1924, 48 percent of South Carolina's white teachers belonged to this association, which promoted professionalism among educators.[12] Cognizant that educators found public school funding especially important, the association held an information session about the pending legislation. On opening day of the convention, March 13, state superintendent of education James Hope addressed the superintendents' session on the provisions of the house and senate bills. Robert S. Rodgers, one of the senators who crafted the 6-0-0 plan and a former county superintendent, also spoke.[13]

That evening, Mann appeared before a joint meeting of the house and senate education committees to speak against the proposed bills. Not a participant in the South Carolina Teachers Association meetings, he came to address these legislative committees as a representative of the Greenville City and Parker school districts. He conveyed each district's opposition to both plans and articulated Greenville's reservations about both bills on three grounds, philosophical, racial, and economic. First, he reiterated the argument that local financial support and local control of schools served education best. Both bills, but especially the senate 6-0-0 plan, represented a movement toward consolidating management of education at the state level in an effort to equalize opportunities for all white children in South Carolina. Shifting authority from the district to the state alarmed Mann and the Greenville school board trustees, who feared that the 6-0-0 bill would centralize power in the hands of the state superintendent, an elected official. Any amalgamation between politics and education,

Mann contended, would destroy the latter. "The weak spots in our present system are spots where politics touch the schools," he alleged. If local districts lost their authority, he reasoned, community interest would immediately evaporate. He believed that local pride in and support for public schools stimulated educational advancement more than any other factor. Local support for public schools worked well in Greenville County, and residents were not anxious to change a system that they perceived operated effectively.[14]

Mann led with this philosophical argument about the inherent superiority of local initiative and local control in guaranteeing quality education. Yet his seemingly philosophical ideas about funding education served primarily as a smoke screen to conceal why the trustees and Greenville residents so cherished the ideal of local control. A relatively wealthy town district, Greenville already provided certified high schools at a time when most districts did not, and it provided a nine-month school term, far longer than that of most South Carolina schools. Greenville did not want to use its resources to fund education elsewhere. Since Mann was defending the status quo, he used the popular strategy that all defenders of the status quo employed, white supremacy. In addition to undermining local initiative, Mann alleged that the new funding proposals would benefit black schools more than white schools. Lawmakers could not ignore such an inflammatory charge. If Mann's allegations were true, the pending legislation violated white supremacy. Since white legislators never intended that, the charge served more as a rhetorical swipe designed to stigmatize the proposals. Under the existing system of financing, each district board and county superintendent could set the length of the school term, thus giving them the power to limit the term for African American schools. In 1923, the average school term for white children in South Carolina was 144 days, versus 80 days for black students. Both proposed reform measures guaranteed either a six- or seven-month term for all schools in the state, longer than black schools presently operated. Mann acknowledged that African Americans deserved some education, but he questioned the wisdom of redistributing to black schools tax money that had previously been spent for white schools.[15] He calculated that his accusation would bolster reform opposition.

Playing to what he perceived as a receptive audience, Mann initially appealed to lawmakers with these philosophical and racial arguments, hoping they shared his perspective on local control and knowing they shared his commitment to maintaining white dominance. After couching his opposition to school finance reform in terms of shared interests, he then explained Greenville's crucial reason for opposing this legislation so vehemently: economic self-interest. He argued that the cost of implementing the 6-0-0 plan would fall too heavily on Greenville. Greenville City and Parker school districts had recently built new schools, levying special property taxes to pay for them. Additional state-mandated property taxes could hinder their ability to retire this debt. He estimated that the legislature's enactment of this measure would increase Greenville's current property tax by eight mills simply to maintain its policy of paying higher-than-average teacher salaries and providing a longer school term than the state stipulated. Mann pronounced the additional costs too high for districts that had already built an excellent school system. The *Greenville News* labeled the 6-0-0 proposal an "unjust burden" on Greenville.[16]

Following Mann's fervent address, committee members discussed Greenville's objections. Persuaded by Mann's argument, Greenville's own representative, James Walter Moon, proposed delaying both bills until the next session. In the subsequent vote, twenty-one of the twenty-two members from both education committees approved the motion. Mann clearly had aroused considerable doubt about the wisdom of continued deliberation on either of the plans during the 1924 term. Tom Hamer, chair of the house committee on education, hesitantly accepted the joint committee's decision.[17] After this meeting the committee announced that it had agreed to delay action on the proposals until completion of a survey to examine South Carolina's educational system, identify problems, and recommend carefully considered solutions.[18]

The *Charleston News and Courier*, which had denounced both plans as "wholly unjust and inequitable" and "very dangerous," hailed the joint education committee's decision as wise and timely.[19] The newspaper knew that if either bill passed, Charleston would lose its lucrative state aid from the existing legislation. Since Charleston was the wealthiest county in South Carolina, the 6-0-0 reform measure would have terminated the county's eligibility for state aid because the required property levies would have raised sufficient revenue for Charleston schools to pay teacher salaries for six months. Instead of receiving aid, the county, like Greenville, would see portions of its increased property tax go to support education in rural and poorer parts of the state.

While the joint committee's decision to abandon reform pleased Charleston and Greenville, others were infuriated with these closed-door negotiations. News of this decision, which ended months of effort to reform public school financing, traveled quickly. Leaders in the South Carolina Teachers Association, who were meeting at the time in Columbia, refused to let this crucial issue fade without a confrontation. Instead, the association seized what appeared to be a dead issue and revived it. Mann's leadership in opposing finance reform incited outrage among the association membership. His failure to attend the association's annual meetings and his refusal to allow teachers in his districts to participate in the convention further alienated the group. One reporter characterized Mann's effect on the association as "setting fire to powder." Moreover, when the South Carolina Teachers Association learned that Greenville and Charleston's opposition had persuaded lawmakers to kill the reform bills, it grew more determined to revive them.[20] Unsympathetic to the two counties' complaints that the cost of reform would fall most heavily on the wealthier counties, these educators responded that "Greenville Textiles and Charleston's Standard Oil are able to pay so let them do it."[21] The teachers thought it reasonable that profitable businesses in South Carolina should contribute financial support for educating the state's future work force. Joseph M. Moorer, a Walterboro attorney, viewed Charleston's reasoning as obviously selfish and illogical. Such reasoning, he argued, assumed that all children educated in Charleston remained in Charleston and all children educated in "Rum Gully" stayed there. People move, Moorer pointed out, and their inadequate education affected all parts of South Carolina.[22]

The final session of the South Carolina Teachers Association on Friday, March 14, provided the teachers with a forum for action. Claud Sapp, one of the house's strongest supporters of educational reform, gave a special address entitled "What Teachers Should Know about Financing Public Education." In this appeal, he urged teachers to learn how South Carolina financed education so they could effectively lobby their representatives and elect reform-minded legislators. Sapp declared: "We have been waiting, waiting, waiting in South Carolina, since I was born. There is not a better time than now to guarantee every child an equal number of months in school." He complained that poorer counties were now paying taxes into the general state fund that benefited richer counties like Greenville and Spartanburg. Due to the matching-fund laws, districts with more financial resources levied the required taxes and benefited from the state tax subsidy, creating greater inequities than when the state provided nothing. South Carolina's problem, Sapp argued, was that rural white children received an inadequate education and remained unprepared to attend the colleges their fathers paid taxes to support. He subtly aroused regional resentments and evoked white supremacy's implication of white equality, asserting that rural whites deserved the same opportunities that white students in the state's wealthier districts already enjoyed. Following Sapp's impassioned speech, Richard C. Burts, supervisor of Rock Hill city schools and a longtime advocate for improved education, proposed a resolution calling for passage of either the 4-2-1 or the 6-0-0 bill that session. Swayed by Sapp's appeal, the teachers' association took a standing vote that resulted in such overwhelming support of the resolution that there was no need to call for opposition votes. To emphasize its determination, the association also authorized association president W. J. McGarity to appoint a committee that would present the resolution directly to the house and senate appropriations committees.[23]

The teachers' committee apparently had an astonishing influence on the membership of both committees. Tom Hamer, chairman of the house education committee, reversed the earlier decision, made after Mann's address, to allow the funding reform bills to die. After conferring with Burts and his associates from the teachers' association, Hamer had the pending 6-0-0 bill made a special order for March 19. Sketchy accounts of this meeting between the joint appropriations committee and the association's representatives indicated that Senators Robert Rodgers and James Spruill were decisive in reviving the 6-0-0 bill.[24]

Rodgers and Spruill played important roles in shaping the senate bill. These young senators represented Dillon and Chesterfield respectively, two counties with significant rural white populations that bordered North Carolina. A Charleston reporter noted that these counties' proximity to North Carolina prompted Rodgers and Spruill to turn to that neighboring state for assistance in formulating their legislation. Another bit of evidence suggests that this reporter's assertion was accurate. Coinciding with South Carolina's struggle to reform educational financing for the public schools was a study of North Carolina's school-finance policies. The researcher conducting North Carolina's study was Fred Morrison, a Columbia University graduate student who employed his mentor's cutting-edge theory on public education financing that emphasized the state's role in equalization. This idea competed with the earlier theory, which emphasized the value of matching state funds as a reward for local effort.[25] Undoubtedly Morrison's ideas caught South Carolina lawmakers' attention. A distinct departure from Bethea's 5-2-0 plan and the house's 4-2-1 plan, which emphasized reward for effort, the 6-0-0 plan resembled more closely the new theory of equalization promoted by Morrison. Thus, Morrison's study in North Carolina could explain how this newer theory of equalization came to South Carolina.

Having resurrected the issue for further consideration, the house chose to debate the senate 6-0-0 version of reform rather than its own 4-2-1 bill. Debate began on Wednesday, March 19. Immediately, Representative James Moon from Greenville, the legislator who originally moved to allow the education reform bill to die in committee, once again attempted to block consideration of the bill. But Hamer tabled Moon's motion to postpone debate. With a motion to kill the legislation, Charleston's William T. Harper launched a lengthy, heated discussion among his peers. Hamer countered Harper's motion with a defense of the bill, specifically praising its attempt to equalize educational opportunities for South Carolina's white children regardless of their county of residence. He stressed that distributing state aid by need and not as matching funds remained essential to the equalization principle. John B. Duffie, representative from Sumter and reform bill supporter, reminded house members of the state's inadequate and inequitable approach to funding schools. Conceding Duffie's characterization of the present public school financing system as lacking equality, Harper countered that South Carolina needed to demonstrate patience for one more year until completion of the public education survey commissioned by the legislature after pressure from the Citizens' Education Association. Moon, who had consistently opposed funding reform since Mann's address to the Greenville delegation on March 8, reiterated the need for caution and urged representatives to postpone consideration of the 6-0-0 bill until the next session.[26]

Harper and Moon stood as the lone dissenters in this house debate. After these two men concluded their commentary, several other members spoke in favor of the 6-0-0 measure, arguing that South Carolina's leadership needed to move beyond the provincial notion of districts and counties as self-sufficient entities. Instead, legislators embraced the policy of "taxing the property where it may be found and educating the children where they are."[27] Sapp, an outspoken supporter of reform from the start, joined the debate with an analogy that highlighted the inconsistency of Moon and Harper's territorial reasoning. When the draft commenced across South Carolina during the World War, state leaders did not rank potential soldiers according to the opportunities they had enjoyed, Sapp asserted. Rather, the state secured men as they needed them, expecting these young South Carolinians to fulfill their obligation to protect property. Now, he argued, it was time for the state to fulfill its obligation and support the cost of educating all of South Carolina's white children according to their need. Following Sapp's war analogy, Representative Paul Murph of Spartanburg addressed opponents' fiscal apprehension. He attempted to alleviate their fears by pointing out that the 6-0-0 bill would stabilize future appropriations. If apprehension about the bill stemmed from concern about increased state spending, then lawmakers had more to fear from the existing school laws, he implied. Following Murph's comments the house voted on Harper's motion to kill the bill, defeating the motion by a vote of 87–18 and guaranteeing that the bill would receive legislative consideration. The eighteen representatives who voted to shelve the bill included the entire delegations from Greenville and Charleston, with the exception of Greenville representative Arthur Marshall.[28]

Throughout the legislative session, reform opponents seemingly commanded the winning strategy, but this test vote revealed that the education finance reformers ultimately held a trump card. When debate began in earnest, house members made considerable progress in solving the problems that had impeded a compromise. The house proposed and accepted five amendments to the original senate 6-0-0 bill. Accepting the senate proposal that the constitutional three-mill tax pay a portion of the state's share of teacher salaries, the house education committee recommended that an additional four-mill tax be levied statewide to supplement the three-mill tax. This four-mill tax would also be a mandatory county tax credited to the state's share of education support. Each county would collect this combined seven-mill tax and distribute it within that same county. Disbursement of the seven-mill tax within the county was an effort to equalize funding among the many districts of any given county. There were more than 1,900 districts and forty-six counties. Because the taxes would be collected according to property values and distributed according to enrollment, districts that had low tax bases would receive revenue from wealthier districts. A second avenue of revenue redistribution, made possible with this bill, involved shifting tax revenues from county to county. If the seven-mill tax was insufficient to pay teacher salaries for a six-month term—and it would be insufficient in every county except Charleston—the state would make up the shortage from general state revenues.[29] Since property taxes furnished approximately 45 percent of South Carolina's general budget in 1924, counties with more valuable property contributed heavily to the state budget and would be indirectly assisting poorer counties through these supplemental appropriations.[30]

Chairman Hamer prepared the committee's second recommendation, which called for each district to provide one additional month of teacher salaries as a prerequisite for receiving the state's six-month appropriation. Largely an attempt to appease those concerned that the 6-0-0 bill eliminated all local responsibility, this minor concession also assured doubters that a seven-month school term would become a statewide requirement. One of the reformers' broad goals had been guaranteeing a seven-month school term for all white schools. The senate bill had not met that objective. This amendment altered the bill from the 6-0-0 to the 6-0-1 plan. A third amendment, offered by Representative Henry C. Jennings of Lee County, enabled the county as well as the district to provide additional funds for either extended school terms or higher teacher salaries, a responsibility assigned solely to the district in the original bill.[31] John

Duffie of Sumter proposed a fourth amendment addressing the high school problem. Because all districts did not have high schools, the state allowed students to attend high schools outside their district and county. Counties with established high schools expressed concern that this reform measure would cause overcrowding in their schools at their expense. To relieve this worry, Duffie's amendment required that the student's county of residence pay a subsidy to the receiving high school to cover any costs not paid by state-provided funds.[32]

These four amendments at least partially addressed the philosophical and economic objections that had arisen. But the final alteration to the bill dealt with that ever-present question of white supremacy. Throughout the legislative session, Bethea, Mann, and the editors of the *Greenville News* and the *Charleston News and Courier* had continually asserted that proposed reforms would significantly increase support for African American schools at the expense of white South Carolinians. These objections illustrate how the dictates of white supremacy complicated reform efforts. Reformers never contemplated undermining white control of public education funds, and opponents understood this. Yet any reform could be held hostage by the charge that the proposed change would erode white supremacy, no matter how absurd or improbable the alleged charge and no matter how minor the proposed change. Reform opponents strategically raised such objections to disguise more self-serving reservations. The intense and nearly universal appeal of white supremacy among white South Carolinians with an array of conflicting class and economic interests invited exploitation of the shared beliefs. Ironically, black reformers' activism strengthened reform opponents' seemingly absurd charges. Although black reformers lacked any formal state power, the nominal inroads they had made during the World War I era and their continued public assertions that African Americans needed better education made the allegations believable to white South Carolinians who wanted a thread of plausibility to justify their opposition to reform.

To provide statutory assurance that white schools, and not black schools, would benefit from the state-guaranteed seven-month school term, an amendment was inserted creating a prerequisite for receiving state funds that stated, "provided, however, That no school in any school district shall continue open for a longer period of time than that fixed by the board of trustees in the district where such school is located." Although vaguely worded to obscure its meaning, this clause was specifically designed to allow local school boards to legally limit school terms for African American schools. Few white reformers publicly uttered any desire to improve African American schools significantly, although they expressed their implied understanding of the overwhelming need. Moreover, the private consensus among legislators on this issue was that whites should maintain the authority to control the segregated system in a discreet manner. Richard A. Meares, Fairfield County candidate for the state senate in 1924, boasted in his campaign literature that this amendment meant that local school districts were not obligated to extend the term for African American schools.[33]

Acceptance of these five amendments concluded the debate on the public school finance reform that had now become the 6-0-1 bill. At the conclusion of this protracted discussion the house approved the measure and advanced it to a third reading. Still hoping to obstruct reform at the eleventh hour, Moon moved that the bill be postponed when it appeared for third reading on March 20. But his last-gasp attempt failed, and the 6-0-1 bill passed the house. The following day the Senate received the revised bill, accepted the amendments without discussion, and passed it without a recorded vote.[34]

After both houses of the legislature passed the bill, concerned citizens urged Governor McLeod to veto it. J. C. Moore, a physician from McColl, appealed to McLeod for a veto, insisting that the bill was "entirely too radical."[35] Several local district boards of trustees and county superintendents wrote McLeod objecting to the 6-0-1 bill. These local school officials thought the law would create negative repercussions for their district or county. Much of their anxiety, however, stemmed from either inadequate information or an abundance of misinformation. The *Charleston News and Courier* published a veto plea to McLeod, claiming that "enactment of a half-baked plan of this kind is no act of friendship to the schools of South Carolina." Reiterating the philosophical, racial, and economic arguments that opponents of reform had made again and again, the *News and Courier* warned that McLeod's veto remained the final hope for saving the state educational system from "disaster."[36] Despite these desperate appeals, McLeod signed the bill into law on March 22, 1924.[37]

James Mann immediately responded with a letter to the *Greenville News* that defended his opposition to finance reform. Pleased with Mann's argument, the *Charleston News and Courier* republished the same letter.[38] Because Mann's letter identified the South Carolina Teachers Association as the party responsible for reviving the reform debate that he had originally helped stifle, Senator James Spruill of Chesterfield asked B. L. Parkinson, the association's new president, for an explanation of the association's support. Parkinson suggested that the association supported the bill because it reflected the principle of equalization, the most recent theory of education funding, embraced across the country, that the state provides at least 50 percent of the revenue needed to operate public schools. Frustrated with the inequalities in South Carolina's educational system that allowed school terms for white students to range from four to nine months, the teachers' association readily embraced any measure that promised to tax "wealth where it is found and educate children where they are found."[39]

Having lost the fight to prevent the bill from passing, key opponents recruited Cole Blease to run for governor in 1924, urging him to make opposition to the new law the central component of his campaign platform. Moreover, evidence suggests that critics of the law who attempted to recruit Blease were not mill workers, the Newberry lawyer's traditional constituency, but rather his traditional political opponents, including mill owners. Knowing that Blease had rallied opposition to compulsory education earlier, these opponents hoped Blease would help them repeal the 6-0-1 law. Reform opponents encouraged Blease to assault the reform on grounds that it violated the white supremacy creed. They charged that already-overtaxed whites would soon be required to pay an additional $1 million per year to improve black schools because of the law. Despite the inaccuracy of this assertion, racial polarization had proven repeatedly an effective political tool in South Carolina. Informed in April about this alleged election strategy, McLeod realized that reformers needed to prevent an anomalous coalition between Blease and the industrialists. The attempt to orchestrate opposition never materialized, as Blease ran for the U.S. Senate rather than the governorship in

1924. But the effort indicated that the law's opponents had resolved to continue their fight and to wage it on the inflammatory stage of white supremacy.[40]

Early in 1925 McLeod proudly proclaimed in his reelection inaugural address that the 6-0-1 law was "the most progressive step the state of South Carolina had taken on educational lines since the establishment of the public school system."[41] While the term "progressive" accurately characterized some aspects of the 6-0-1 law, white South Carolinians' commitment to white supremacy and a segregated school system limited its claim on progress. Opponents of the education finance reform continually objected to any measure that significantly improved African American schools. Yet enactment of the measure exposed this objection as either a misplaced fear or a hollow attempt to alarm. Reform advocates never intended the law to benefit black South Carolinians substantially. If the legislation itself was ambiguous, South Carolina Department of Education officials quickly clarified any lingering uncertainties about the state's intentions. In a circular to county superintendents on the procedures for implementing the 6-0-1 law, state statistician and rural school supervisor Power Bethea explained: "It is the opinion of the State Superintendent of Education that the expenditure for negro schools under this act should remain in *status quo*. There should be no increase in the length of term, number of teaching corps, or salaries in the negro schools except the normal increase occasioned by increased enrollment and better building facilities."[42] Hope also established a formula for distributing the four-mill tax within the county that effectively favored white schools. The 6-0-1 law only stipulated that the new four-mill tax remain in the county but included no specific method of distribution. Hope decided that while the constitution required that the three-mill tax be distributed according to enrollment, the four-mill tax would be apportioned according to the number of white teachers, ensuring that white students were the prime beneficiaries. Moreover, African American teachers were paid below the salary standards established by the 6-0-1 law even though the law made no provision for this practice. The pervasive use of white supremacy politics by various white interests also demonstrates the seemingly insurmountable challenge black reformers faced. Even the small number of white reformers who favored improving black education operated in a political system that required that they constantly assert their opposition to aiding African Americans.[43]

Hailed as a landmark educational reform, the 6-0-1 law accomplished much of what it promised and some of what it did not. The law extended the school term for rural white children, who lagged behind their urban counterparts. During the first year after implementation of the law, rural white school terms increased statewide an average of 23 days, lengthening the average school term from 142 to 165 days—a 16 percent jump from the previous year. By comparison, town school terms experienced a modest gain of only 3 days, making their year still longer, however, at 175 days per school year. Ironically, the 6-0-1 reform also benefited African American students, despite every effort to prevent it, but to a much lesser degree. Rural black school terms increased 17 days, bringing the state average up from 80 to 97 days. Moreover, the 6-0-1 reform lengthened African American town schools' terms to 153 days, a 14-day increase from the 1923–1924 to the 1924–1925 school year.[44] No whites touted this improvement—quite the opposite. But this improvement that came quietly and indirectly through standardization was about the only way that black schools experienced incremental improvement. Rural school supervisor D. L. Lewis indicated that the state guarantee of a seven-month term across the state, informally understood to apply only to white schools, paved the way for standardization of curriculum and achievement goals. Previously, while school terms ranged from 40 to 180 days, curriculum and achievement goals had been difficult to establish.[45]

Extending the school term had been one of the reformers' primary objectives for enhancing the quality of education. Short school terms, however, were not the only problem that South Carolina schools experienced. Another of the state's lingering educational problems was the persistence of one-teacher schools. In general, rural children did not receive an adequate education from these schools because of the obvious difficulties one teacher would have teaching all levels of students. In 1919–1920 South Carolina supported 1,008 one-teacher schools. Many of these teachers had poor qualifications. The better-qualified teachers sought positions in consolidated rural schools or in town schools with higher pay. The 6-0-1 law accelerated the pace of school consolidation by establishing a minimum

Table 4. Taxes Levied by Local Districts for Public Schools

1923	$5,927,619
1924	5,912,523
1925	5,580,870
1926	6,342,560
1927	6,738,461
1928	7,222,648
1929	7,624,200
1930	7,936,189

Source: *Annual Report of the Comptroller General of South Carolina to the General Assembly*, Columbia, S.C.: Gonzales and Bryan, 1924–1931.

enrollment of fifteen students and an average attendance of ten students as a prerequisite for one-teacher schools' receiving state funds. During the 6-0-1 law's first year of operation 285 one-teacher schools consolidated.[46]

Thus the 6-0-1 law extended the school term and expedited consolidation of one-teacher schools for whites as proponents had claimed, but it did not dampen local community support for education as critics had alleged. During the year preceding passage of the law, taxes raised from special school district levies throughout South Carolina totaled $5,912,523. This figure constantly increased over the next several years, indicating that the law had not stifled local initiative but stimulated local support for public schools (see table 4).[47]

Beyond taking these steps to enhance equality among white schools, advocates hailed the 6-0-1 law as a reform that would bring stability and predictability to the state's education appropriations. On this claim, 6-0-1 delivered as promised. As expected, the appropriations necessary for implementing the reform the first year were significant and represented a substantial commitment from the legislature to improve public schools. In 1923 state appropriations for public schools represented approximately 18 percent of South Carolina's total budget. In 1925, following two years of steep increases in state spending for education because of the 6-0-1 reform, public school appropriations commanded 37 percent of the state's budget.

Table 5. Annual Percentage Increase in State Appropriations after Enactment of the 6-0-1 Law

Year	Current Dollars		Constant Dollars*	
	Total	% Increase	Total	% Increase
1923	$1,552,569	43%	$3,044,253	40%
1924	2,572,000	66	5,043,137	66
1925	3,046,000	18	5,857,692	16
1926	2,989,423	-2	5,640,421	-4
1927	3,250,000	9	6,250,000	11
1928	3,100,000	-5	6,078,431	-3
1929	3,375,000	9	6,617,647	9
1930	3,500,000	4	7,000,000	6

* Adjusted for inflation, expressed in constant 1967 dollars. *U.S. Bureau of the Census, Historical Statistics of the United States, Colonial Times to 1970*, 2 vol. (Washington, D.C.: Government Printing Office, 1975), 210–11.

Sources: *Annual Report of the State Superintendent of Education of the State of South Carolina*, 1923–1930; *Annual Report of the Comptroller General of South Carolina to the General Assembly*, 1924–1931.

The general assembly's unprecedented 66 percent escalation of education appropriations in 1924 anticipated the bill's passage, and the additional spending in 1925 came as a direct result of the law. Yet, after these landmark increases, state appropriations for public schools remained essentially constant at the 1925 spending level, as reformers promised. (See table 5.)[48]

Finally, the 6-0-1 law moved toward accomplishing the essence of its purpose: equalization of educational opportunity for white children. In the fullest sense, this goal was unattainable because individual districts could always increase spending and taxes to improve their local schools, but the law established a state-prescribed minimum for all districts across the state. Moreover, it created a measure of equality through tax redistribution. The constitutional three-mill tax and the additional four-mill tax worked to redistribute revenue from richer districts to poorer districts within each county. Additionally, general state appropriations redistributed revenue from richer to poorer counties. Under the previous system of state aid, each school that qualified for aid received the same amount, but the 6-0-1 law enabled districts with greater needs to receive greater assistance.

While South Carolina's educational finance law of 1924 introduced important reforms, the 6-0-1 law passed largely because, despite assertions to the contrary, it was not revolutionary. The law took the bold step of redistributing state resources across district lines and even some county lines, but it did not take the revolutionary step of pooling all state taxes into a general fund and redistributing them according to need. A revolutionary law would have provided equal provisions for African American schools, but the 6-0-1 law intended to improve opportunities for white children in poorer school districts. Moreover, to garner enough support for passage in the complicated milieu of white supremacy, reformers readily distanced themselves from any intention to help black schools. Rather than a revolution, the 6-0-1 law represented a long stride in an evolutionary march toward educational reform for whites.

On the whole, the 6-0-1 law of 1924 was the crowning achievement of South Carolina's white reformers during World War I and its aftermath. It fostered substantial progress in an area close to the heart of white reformers and central to their vision for a better South Carolina. But just as the law reflected the best that white reformers had to offer, it also revealed the limits of their vision, the treacherous environment in which they operated, and the ever-present grip of white supremacy in South Carolina. White reformers were primarily concerned with equalizing educational opportunities for whites. Some white reformers advocated modest improvement for black schools because they understood South Carolina would never improve overall without raising the educational level of African Americans, who were the majority of South Carolinians. Therefore, the politics of white supremacy doomed to failure any direct or consistent promotion for improving black schools. This pervasive political tactic magnified black reformers' challenge because they could not rely on white reformers who agreed with their cause. Throughout the reform crusade, South Carolina reformers battled a localism born in part of racism and the need for white control. Reform opponents cloaked their resistance to education finance reform as a defense of white supremacy. They had designed their opposition strategy, which played on whites' fears that racial dominance hung by a precarious thread, to conceal the centrality of their primary objection, economic self-interest. Reformers ignored the disguise and exposed the wealth that opponents coyly hid. Employing white supremacy toward a different end and with an alternate strategy, reformers emphasized the allure of white supremacy to connote rough equality among whites. Rather than arousing fear that a change might precipitate loss of white control, reformers emphasized the failure of the existing funding formula to extend the privileges of white supremacy to all whites. In this debate, reformers used white supremacy to a more persuasive end than their opponents had, convincing enough legislators that the time-honored local-funding approach victimized too many ordinary whites simply because of their rural location. Ultimately, 6-0-1 represented a slow and conservative outcome of white reformers' attempt to create a centralized state system of education. Like most of their goals, it fell short, and the compromised achievement occurred only after real, perceived, and contrived threats to white supremacy had been successfully negotiated.

Conclusion

African Americans' World War I–related activism is a reminder of historical contingency. From the vantage point of hindsight historians can see that African Americans' direct and aggressive challenge to white supremacy did not significantly loosen its grip, which remained stifling for decades after World War I. The war-era activists, however, did not live with the sense of certainty that white supremacy would retain its power for the remainder of their lives and well beyond. Every rumor, race conference, petition, voter registration, NAACP activity, and gesture of pride and confidence expressed by African American reformers aroused fear, anxiety, resentment, and hatred among some white South Carolinians. In response to each threat, whites explained how these activities threatened the methodically constructed white dominance of political, economic, and social institutions. African Americans' activism, which whites deemed threatening, initiated public and private discussions with and among elected officials (local, state, and national), in the state's newspapers, and among white South Carolinians generally. White South Carolinians defended the existing racial order with a wide spectrum of countermoves, each calculated to meet differently perceived intensities of danger. While black activism provoked diverse responses, all whites girded themselves to meet the challenge. Some whites appealed to authority for solutions and reassurance; some conferred with colleagues; some paternalistically offered tepid support to benign appeals; other whites plotted reprisals, opposed resistance, exploited division among African Americans, threatened racial violence, and used violence and intimidation against blacks. Whites' reactions validated African Americans' actions as mindful, overt strikes against the established racial order that whites considered essential.

As African Americans welcomed home black soldiers in February 1919 and black reformers anticipated that their return would accelerate progress toward greater freedom and equality, they could not foresee that most of their war-related gains had already been made. The success of the American Expeditionary Forces in France, which helped bring the war to a successful conclusion fairly quickly, limited the duration of the mobilization effort and stopped the brief burst of momentum that first signaled significant change. The war's conclusion abruptly halted the federal government's activism, which had intruded on traditional racial relationships during the war, an intrusion that occasionally aided African Americans in their struggle. The war's conclusion also ended black reformers' temporary influence with whites, so the reformers confronted stern resistance in 1919. Yet African American reformers continued to hope that progress was at hand, and whites continued to perceive that black reformers were constantly poised to seize any opportunity. Viewing African American activism as a constant and challenging presence, white South Carolinians defended white supremacy unrelentingly.

The hope that propelled black reformers' wartime and immediate postwar activism dissipated in the early 1920s. Black reformers' desire and call for change did not cease, but the urgency diminished. The nearly dozen local NAACP chapters, which had organized across the state between 1917 and 1919, expanded membership rapidly, and initiated much of the war-era activism, had become inactive by the early 1920s. As small chapters throughout South Carolina folded, the membership rolls at Columbia's NAACP, one of the state's strongest, also dwindled. By 1922, it struggled to pay the $50 annual branch dues to remain active. Butler Nance, the president, planned to launch a membership drive in 1923, but he died suddenly in his law office one afternoon in February of that year. The immediate efforts to revive the Columbia branch died with Nance. Columbia and Charleston officially maintained their charters, but the organizations lost their earlier vitality. A passionate Charlestonian, committed to the struggle, publicly pondered this question in the mid-1920s:

"What has become of our local Branch of the N.A.A.C.P.?" The struggle for freedom did not end, but the hope and pervasive sense that accelerated progress was imminent had evaporated.[1]

Black reformers' anticipation of success faded largely because the postwar depression zapped the economic momentum that had helped fuel their hope. During the economically depressed 1920s, obstacles for African Americans only mounted. Bank failures became commonplace in the 1920s, but when Edward James Sawyer's Bennettsville bank collapsed, the dreams and means of many African Americans vanished. Reputed to be one of the wealthiest African Americans in South Carolina, Sawyer owned extensive farmland and rental property in Marlboro County valued at $125,000. Exceptionally talented, Sawyer had also been one of the few African Americans who attended South Carolina College during Reconstruction. A lawyer, realtor, principal, postmaster, state representative, Republican Party activist, and editor of Bennettsville's *Pee Dee Educator*, he enjoyed unusual prominence. Confident and trusting of Sawyer, black professionals, farmers, business owners, benevolent societies, and secret fraternal orders in his Pee Dee region and across the state invested in Sawyer's bank, one of the few black-owned financial institutions in the state.[2]

During the war Sawyer advised African Americans to "invest heavily in Liberty bonds and Southern farms, for both are certain to enhance in value after the war, and those who possess them will be honored and respected." But the postwar era did not unfold as Sawyer and others expected. The deposits in Sawyer's bank represented collective wealth among black South Carolinians. Numerous secret fraternal orders, in several of which Sawyer had held leadership roles, lost everything. Reports indicated that, among others, the Knights of Pythias lost $80,000. Individuals' losses ranged from $100 to $10,000. This capital evaporation left disappointment, frustration, pain, and want in all quarters. The bank's collapse not only dissolved lifelong savings but also robbed many communities of limited resources, future opportunities, and hope.[3]

Before the economic downturn of the 1920s eclipsed war-era expectations, African Americans' wartime activism and the postwar memory of that activism, especially blacks' agitation for voting rights, permeated the political milieu in South Carolina and directly influenced whites' political strategies. Ironically, even though African Americans could not influence politics directly, they influenced politics as potential participants. Whites were always cognizant of black South Carolinians' power as potential voters in a black-majority state, and keeping that potential unrealized trumped every political strategy. The political machinations among whites revealed the lingering influence of black reformers' World War I–era activism.

As white reformers pursued their postwar agenda in the context of this heightened anxiety about blacks' potential political power, they formed several new organizations to rally progressive forces, articulate a shared agenda, and systematically develop practical strategies for reform. One of those organizations was the South Carolina Constructive League, which adopted a constitution in July 1919 that stated and prioritized the league's goals. After embracing the principles of good government, the Constructive League identified education and tax reform as its top two goals. Education reform, the league emphasized, necessitated "good schools in every section of the state." The 1924 6-0-1 law became the compromised embodiment of that goal: a state commitment to provide greater educational resources for white students in previously neglected, primarily rural, areas of the state. The league stated its tax reform goal as the creation of "an adequate and just system of taxation which shall raise sufficient funds to maintain an efficient and progressive government." The new income and inheritance taxes, created in 1922, nudged South Carolina in the direction reformers wanted, but the failure to amend the constitution to enable classification of property significantly thwarted the primarily goal of "an adequate and just system of taxation."[4]

In the Constructive League's constitution, reformers also articulated their commitment to white supremacy—the objective that complicated and limited their two foundational goals. As an expression of their paternalistic style, reformers stated that they wanted the "just treatment of the negro and the cultivation of harmony between the races, *but* at the same time the inculcation of the principle that our State shall be dominated by its white citizens." The caveat that white supremacy would be maintained constrained reform efforts because it favored opposition strategies that resisted change.[5] The systemic political weakness of reformers and the persistence of their opposition became evident in 1924.

Having narrowly defeated their leading nemesis, Cole Blease, in 1916, 1918, and 1922, reformers confronted him again in the 1924 race for one of South Carolina's U.S. Senate seats. In the context of the long-term struggle between Blease and anti-Blease forces, anti-Blease voters readily constituted a majority of South Carolina's electorate, but it was a slim and precarious majority vulnerable to the shift of only a small number of swing voters. Division among anti-Blease candidates was particularly bitter during the 1924 campaign, making a rapid reconciliation after the first primary more difficult. Consequently, the second primary proved a stunning disappointment for the anti-Blease coalition. By a margin of fewer than 2,500 votes, a majority of South Carolinians delivered Blease a narrow victory that awarded him a Senate seat for a full six-year term. Because the second primary vote was so close, 1,200 changed votes could have reversed the outcome, and contemporary observers touted any number of reasons as decisive.[6] But fundamentally the anti-Blease coalition handed the 1924 Senate race to Blease because it failed to successfully execute its essential and basic strategy: consolidating its forces after the first primary behind the leading anti-Blease candidate. Without effective organization, which the loose anti-Blease coalition within the Democratic Party lacked, reformers realized that electing candidates who would aggressively promote a progressive agenda remained virtually impossible. "The sum of it is that, factionalism or no factionalism, political fights cannot be made safely without organization—continuing organization," wrote reform leader and editor of *The State* W. W. Ball.[7] Yet, the obstacle to organization was the persistent refusal to entertain development of a two-party system. Thus white supremacy's demand for one-party politics thwarted development of a political structure that would have more readily facilitated reform.

Blease's election to the U.S. Senate in 1924 was an obvious setback for reform, signaling that the momentous opportunity reformers recognized a few years earlier had faded. With the onset of depressed agricultural prices that remained stagnant, South Carolina reformers enjoyed few subsequent successes until the unprecedented spending associated with World War II created new opportunities more than a decade later. While white reformers' war-era successes were limited, they were more tangible than those of black reformers, who could not easily measure their accomplishments when mired in the economic depression of the 1920s and 1930s. But their influence continued in obvious and direct ways through the young adults who came of age in the World War I era of struggle and anticipation.

Black reformers and their activism nurtured young adults who later made important contributions to African Americans' freedom struggle as they moved into leadership positions in South Carolina in the 1940s. Two young women, one from Columbia and one from Charleston, illustrate the direct link between World War I–era reformers and subsequent South Carolina activists. Modjeska Monteith Simkins, from Columbia, and Septima Poinsette Clark, from Charleston, were born near the close of the nineteenth century, Simkins in 1899, Clark in 1898. Both women received a formal, private education in the World War I era, pursued a teaching career, and had close mentors who actively participated in the budding NAACP. As a young woman of twenty-one, Simkins began teaching in 1920, the same career her mother began decades earlier. Her mother, Rachel Hull Monteith, modeled not only teaching, her lifelong career, but also political activism. Monteith was a charter member of Columbia's NAACP and held membership in the national organization before Columbia organized its branch in 1917. Simkins taught at Booker T. Washington in Columbia through the 1920s until she married in 1929 and then left teaching for other pursuits, including fundraising and health education with South Carolina's Tuberculosis Association. Clark began her teaching career at John's Island, where she taught during the turbulent war era (1916–1919), and then taught at Avery Institute in Charleston in 1919. Clark's activism began when she volunteered to collect signatures for the petitions in the NAACP campaign to allow black teachers in Charleston's public schools in 1919. Clark reported that Edwin Harleston and Thomas Miller, seasoned Charleston reformers who led the campaign, became her mentors, nurturing what would become her lifetime commitment to civil rights.[8]

The World War I campaign to allow black teachers in the Charleston public schools had a counterpart in World War II, the teachers' salary equalization campaign. Modjeska Simkins and Septima Clark both took leadership roles in local NAACP lawsuits that black teachers won in 1944 in Charleston and in 1945 in Columbia.

Clark taught in the Charleston public schools until she was fired in 1956 because of her membership in the Charleston NAACP, which she refused to cancel after the South Carolina legislature outlawed such membership for public employees. Simkins, following her mother's example, was an active member and leader in the NAACP, first in the Columbia branch and then in the new state chapter after its organization in 1939. Simkins was secretary of the state NAACP until 1957. Her lifelong activism made her one of South Carolina's most persistent twentieth-century civil rights leaders. Among Clark's many civil rights activities she developed the citizenship schools for the Highlander Folk School in Tennessee. Clark met Rosa Parks in 1955 when Parks attended one of the education programs at Highlander that Clark developed and taught. Simkins and Clark are two examples of the long and interconnected struggle of African Americans for freedom and equality.[9]

In 1920, a disappointed South Carolina reformer asked rhetorically, "Why must we always lag in great forward movements?" Voiced more with frustration than curiosity, the perennial question has been asked of South Carolina prior to and since 1920. Why? The answer, both obvious and elusive: progressive reform always became entangled by white supremacy. White South Carolinians had constructed a political labyrinth to trap African Americans at the bottom. White reformers, who contributed to its construction, unexpectedly became ensnarled by the tools used to maintain white domination while they simultaneously plied these tools in support of their political agenda. Ball understood the grip white supremacy held on his state. "The everlasting negro question! It will probably give trouble a century or centuries, after I am gone," Ball lamented privately.[10] Another South Carolinian expressed frustration and unusual insight into white supremacy's limitation of progress in South Carolina.

> I am aware of the menace of the race question. It is the stock argument. It was used against the reopening of the South Carolina college. It was used against free public schools. It was used against compulsory school attendance. It is largely responsible for the humiliating illiteracy among the whites of our state and for the fact that we are tagging at the foot of the educational procession. . . .

> Do you, Mr. Editor, never find it disheartening that the views of our people on great constructive movements are narrow and are kept narrow by this constant harping on the race question and the question of state's rights?[11]

As this observer noted and Ball sensed, white supremacy's destructiveness continually haunted South Carolina, denying African Americans an opportunity to develop their full human potential because whites jealously guarded their power to maintain white control. Yet whites did not have the power to distance themselves from the reverberating consequences of oppressing others. Whites clung tenaciously to white supremacy because they imagined its only victims were black—the intended ones. While white supremacy was the tool they used to dominate and control, it also entangled reformers in their own web. The shared commitment to white supremacy united whites but only to the end of maintaining white control. The whites it united had very real class differences. The shared desire of all whites to indulge the fantasy that they were inherently superior to other human beings established a powerful technique for sustaining the status quo, whether that was the existing voting system, traditional labor relationships, the taxation system, or the mechanism for funding schools. White South Carolinians' commitment to white supremacy unquestionably shaped how reformers thought about and created their reform policies and strategies to bring progress to the state. Nonetheless, white reformers remained steadfastly committed to white supremacy, regardless of its debilitating consequences for their own reform initiatives.

Notes

The following abbreviations are used throughout the notes.

CU	Clemson University, Clemson, South Carolina
DU	Duke University, Durham, North Carolina
LC	Library of Congress, Washington, D.C.
NA	National Archives, Washington, D.C.
NAACP	Papers of the National Association for the Advancement of Colored People, Microfilm
NAACP, LC	Papers of the National Association for the Advancement of Colored People, Library of Congress
SBCC	*State Board of Charities and Corrections*
SCCACI	*Commissioner of Agriculture, Commerce, and Industries of the State of South Carolina*
SCCG	*Comptroller General of South Carolina to the General Assembly*
SCDAH	South Carolina Department of Archives and History, Columbia
SCHS	South Carolina Historical Society, Charleston
SCL	South Caroliniana Library, University of South Carolina, Columbia
SCSSE	*State Superintendent of Education of the State of South Carolina*
SCST	*State Treasurer to the General Assembly of the State of South Carolina*
SCTC	*South Carolina Tax Commission to the General Assembly of the State of South Carolina*
SHC	Southern Historical Collection, University of North Carolina, Chapel Hill

Introduction

1. C. Vann Woodward frames the southern reform movement in the early twentieth century as the "paradoxical combination of white supremacy and progressivism," a progressivism constructed "for whites only." See his seminal *Origins of the New South*, 369–95, quotation on 373. Jack Temple Kirby's *Dark-*

ness at the Dawning provided the first synthesis of southern progressivism and argues that reformers embraced disfranchisement and segregation as essential reforms to facilitate their pursuit of a "whites only" progressive agenda. While Kirby rightly characterized the reformers' expectation that they could aggressively pursue white supremacy and progressivism simultaneously, my argument attempts to expose the flaw in white reformers' strategy and to explain how white supremacy did more to impede than to facilitate their reform agenda.

2. David Carlton offers an insightful analysis of white middle-class reformers in South Carolina. More than my study, Carlton's *Mill and Town* focuses on reforms in the pre–World War I era, particularly on the clash between white reformers and South Carolina's white laborers in the rapidly expanding textile industry. While Carlton rightly assumes the presence of white supremacy, he does not analyze it. I attempt to analyze the complicated relationship between reform and white supremacy.

3. Where Stephen Kantrowitz focuses on Ben "Pitchfork" Tillman's restoration of white supremacy and an analysis of its cultural hegemony evident in the use of racial and gendered rhetoric, this study examines the World War I–era challenges to the white supremacy that Tillman restored with more emphasis on the following: African Americans' activism in initiating this challenge, the use of white supremacy by all political factions, and the public policy debates sparked by Progressive Era reform. See Kantrowitz, *Ben Tillman*. J. Morgan Kousser's thorough study of disfranchisement emphasizes the elitist, conservative, and racist character of progressivism, see *Shaping of Southern Politics* and "Progressivism."

4. Jane Dailey, Glenda Gilmore, and Bryant Simon's edited collection, *Jumpin' Jim Crow*, includes contributions from each of the editors as well as a number of other fine historians on many facets of white supremacy from Reconstruction to civil rights. While none of the historians whose essays are included directly address the specific issues explored in my study or focus on the time frame of World War I, I share their interest in the complexity and contingency of white supremacy and the role of African Americans' resistance in the Jim Crow era. Gilmore's *Gender and Jim Crow* reframes the study of progressivism, placing African American women at the center of her study of Progressive Era North Carolina. African American women in South Carolina also engaged in the church, club, and community work that Gilmore describes. In this study of South Carolina, I discuss the active role that black men played in World War I–era reform efforts. For a recent study on the complexity of white supremacy in the rural South, see Schultz, *Rural Face of White Supremacy*, a study of Hancock County, Georgia, and the interpersonal dynamics of white supremacy in an interracial culture.

5. This study of South Carolina in some respects parallels J. Douglas Smith's *Managing White Supremacy*, a study of twentieth-century Virginia that examines the complexities and contradictions of whites who constructed and maintained white supremacy. Like Smith, I explore the complexities of white supremacy and how white supremacy shaped the political culture and whites'

exercise of power, although the issues and political culture in the two states were quite different. Smith argues that elite white Virginians managed white supremacy with paternalism in the early twentieth century. While supporting disfranchisement and segregation, Virginia's white elites eschewed violence and embraced interracial cooperation efforts that they could control and that did not threaten their power. Yet in the post–World War I era the Virginia elite faced challenges from whites who expressed more extreme views and wanted to draw a harsher and sharper color line and from African Americans who grew impatient and increasingly challenged Jim Crow. Smith explains the transformation in Virginia race relations from managed white supremacy to massive resistance and persuasively details how this transformation was a contested struggle among whites. While white reformers in South Carolina embraced the paternalism that Smith describes, neither they nor any other group of influential whites ever had as much uncontested control of race relations as the elite white Virginians that Smith examines. South Carolina's black majority, its sizable and politically active white working class, and the success of the Tillmanites in ousting the conservatives from political power in the late nineteenth century are all factors that made South Carolina different from Virginia and made the dynamics of white supremacy unpredictable.

6. William A. Link's *Paradox of Southern Progressivism* examines the clash between urban reformers seeking an active, bureaucratic state government and rural traditionalists who resisted southern reformers' paternalistic and interventionist strategy by clinging to localism and fierce individualism. I find this same struggle between reformers and traditionalists and examine the dynamic white supremacy played in the conflict.

7. Kantrowitz argues that white elites used white supremacy to manipulate nonelite whites to further class and gender hegemony. Bryant Simon argues that working-class whites used their "whiteness" as a claim to status and as a protection of their interests. While I agree with both, to interpret white supremacy manipulation as a tool exclusively of any particular class interests is to misunderstand how deeply committed all whites were to maintaining white supremacy. Thus, all classes and interests exploited the broadly shared commitment to white supremacy and could be entangled by others' skilled manipulation of it. See Simon, *Fabric of Defeat*; and Kantrowitz, *Ben Tillman*. For the broader works of whiteness scholarship, see Roediger, *Wages of Whiteness*; Ignatiev, *How the Irish Became White*; and Hale, *Making Whiteness*. As critics have charged, whiteness scholarship has become ubiquitous yet imprecise and overreaching in lumping all historical analysis of race into the category whiteness; see Arnesen, "Whiteness and the Historians' Imagination."

8. Traditional conservatives, planter elites, and their new allies among industrialists manipulated common whites' fears that racial solidarity was eroding as a strategy to preserve their economic privileges. Middle-class reformers defended white supremacy aggressively to guard against coarse charges from political champions of common whites that their reform programs threatened

white control. Working-class whites, white tenants, and small farmers drew upon the frequent emphasis on white unity, and guarded that tenet vigorously, to protect their status and resist attempts by middle-class reformers to marginalize and disfranchise them.

1. Black Hope

1. *The State*, 21, 22 February 1919.

2. When the war began, four all-black combat units already existed, the Ninth and Tenth Cavalry and the Twenty-fourth and Twenty-fifth Infantry, but these were never sent to Europe but instead to American-held territories. Responding to pressure from critics, the War Department created the Ninety-second and Ninety-third in 1917. The Ninety-third Division also included the 369th, 370th, and 372nd infantry regiments.

3. On African American soldiers in World War I, see Scott, *Official History;* Barbeau and Henri, *Unknown Soldiers;* Krawczynski, "World War I"; and Franklin, *From Slavery to Freedom.* For the names of soldiers, see Megginson, "Black South Carolinians in World War I." For a contemporary's assessment, see Heywood, *Negro Combat Troops.*

4. Scott, *Official History*, 231–38; Barbeau and Henri, *Unknown Soldiers*, 112, 134–36.

5. Scott, *Official History*, 231–38.

6. Ibid., 232–33.

7. *The State*, 21 February 1919.

8. *The State*, 22 February 1919.

9. *The State*, 26 February 1919.

10. *The State*, 1 March 1919.

11. Compiled from data in U.S. Bureau of the Census, *Fourteenth Census, 1920, Occupations*, 4:1013–16; *Agriculture*, vol. 6, pt. 2, 276–80.

12. Neil R. McMillen, *Dark Journey*, offers an insightful and thorough examination of Mississippi in this same period. For more on the oppression of African Americans in South Carolina, see Newby, *Black Carolinians;* Drago, *Initiative, Paternalism, and Race Relations;* Everett, "Race Relations in South Carolina"; Hemmingway, "Beneath the Yoke of Bondage"; Gordon, *Sketches of Negro Life;* Egerton, *Speak Now.* Dittmer, *Black Georgia*, offers an analysis of African Americans during this period in Georgia.

13. Kevin Gaines examines the racial-uplift ideology that influenced the strategies and discourse that black reformers of this era used in their struggle against white supremacy. These reformers represent a broad array of ideas and motivations. Not all of these reformers were co-opted by the white culture's dominant ideology; see Gaines, *Uplifting the Race.*

14. For a comprehensive examination of Reconstruction, see Foner, *Reconstruction.* For accounts of African Americans' role in Reconstruction in South Carolina, see Holt, *Black over White;* and Williamson, *After Slavery.*

15. On the Red Shirt campaign and restoration of Democratic rule, see Cooper, *Conservative Regime*, 21–44; Williamson, *After Slavery*, 266–73; and Kantrowitz, *Ben Tillman*, 53–79.

16. As Leon Litwack has demonstrated so thoroughly and persuasively, a new generation of young black southerners, born after Emancipation, clashed constantly with whites determined to enforce black subordination in the late nineteenth and early twentieth centuries. See Litwack, *Trouble in Mind*. For a thorough account of Tillman's rise to power, see Simpkins, *Pitchfork Ben Tillman*. For a more recent examination of Tillman's use of gendered rhetoric in his systematic restoration of white supremacy, see Kantrowitz, *Ben Tillman*.

17. Tindall, "Campaign for Disfranchisement," 212–16; Key, *Southern Politics*; and Kousser, *Shaping of Southern Politics*, 84–91, 145–52.

18. Black voter turnout reported in *The State*, 29 March 1917. Cole Blease quotation in *Crisis* 5, March 1913, 216. For World War I–era education statistics, see *SCSSE Annual Report*, 1916, 26, 131–32, 147–50. See Harlan, *Separate and Unequal*, who argues that the discrimination of the segregated schools intensified as southern states began spending more for public schools in this era. The federal government, in cooperation with several philanthropic organizations, published a study in 1917 highlighting the deficiencies in African American educational opportunities; see U.S. Bureau of Education, *Negro Education*, 1917.

19. For an excellent broad overview of African Americans and education, see Anderson, *Education of Blacks*; and Anderson, "Northern Foundations," 371–96.

20. Compiled from data in U.S. Bureau of the Census, *Fourteenth Census*, 1920, *Occupations*, 4:1013–16.

21. Statistical data on manufacturing is compiled from U.S. Bureau of the Census, *Fourteenth Census*, 1920, *Occupations*, 4:1013–16. For the development of an all-white textile industry, see Stokes, "Black and White Labor"; Carlton, *Mill and Town*; and Wright, *Old South, New South*. For the 1915 segregation statute for the textile industry, see *Acts and Joint Resolutions*, 1915, 79.

22. Compiled from data in U.S. Bureau of the Census, *Fourteenth Census*, 1920, *Occupations*, 4:1013–16. Lilla's and Lucile's stories are two of many found in the South Carolina Factory Schedules, 1920–21, Women's Bureau, Department of Labor, RG 86, NA.

23. "Report of the Directors and Superintendent of the South Carolina State Penitentiary, 1917," 28–36; "Third Annual Report of the State Board of Charities and Corrections, 1917."

24. "SBCC 4th Annual Report, 1918"; *The State*, 14 May 1917; "Report of Pardons, Paroles and Commutations," 1916; "SBCC 3rd Annual Report, 1917." For an extensive discussion of the State Federation of Colored Women's Clubs' efforts to support the Fairwold Home, see J. Johnson, *Southern Ladies, New Women*, 181–201; Hart, *War Program of South Carolina*, 43–44.

25. For a full discussion of DuBois's role, see David Lewis, *W. E. B. DuBois*.

26. These leaders and their activities will be discussed more fully in subsequent chapters. Organizers names, plans, and meeting places identified in *The*

State, 12, 13, 17 February 1919. These leaders also demonstrate that African Americans actively and self-consciously fought for their freedom long before the traditional emphasis on civil rights in the post–World War II era. See Payne, *Light of Freedom*, for his emphasis on the need for more studies that examine this earlier freedom struggle.

27. I. S. Leevy Jr. to I. S. Leevy, 7 March 1906; Personal Biography of Isaac Samuel Leevy, I. S. Leevy Papers, SCL. For a discussion of I. S. Leevy's life-long contributions, see C. L. Johnson, "Undertakings," 158–215.

28. Leevy Jr. to Leevy; Personal Biography. Leevy Department Store, opened in 1910, would be the first of many successful businesses Leevy owned, including Leevy's Funeral Home, Leevy Service Station, an automobile-repair garage, a real estate development company, a commercial hog-raising operation, a burial association, and Victory Savings Bank, which he helped organize and of which he served as vice president, president, and director. The list of other black-owned businesses is derived from advertisements in the *Palmetto Leader*.

29. Butler W. Nance to W. E. B. DuBois, 5 June 1915; enclosure, "An Address to the People of South Carolina, under the auspices of Capital City Civic League;" Mary Childs Nerney to B. W. Nance, 1 July 1915; Branch office in Columbia to Roy Nash, 1 May 1917; Selected Branch Files, South, pt. 12A, NAACP Papers. Leevy typified progressive black leaders in the World War I era who appealed to whites with political and economic powers for fairer treatment and expanded justice. Peter F. Lau discusses the NAACP's expansion into the South during World War I in *Democracy Rising*, an excellent monograph that examines African Americans' freedom struggle in South Carolina in the first half of the twentieth century. In the areas of our studies that overlap we used similar sources and independently reached similar conclusions.

30. Ball, *Sweet Hell Inside*, 80–89, 190–97; Drago, *Initiative, Paternalism, and Race Relations*, 172–76. David Lewis, *W. E. B. DuBois*, 527–38. Quotation from Harleston at Cleveland in Ball, *Sweet Hell Inside*, 196.

31. In 1922 Arthur Platt established a practice in Spartanburg. He was the only black attorney in the Piedmont in the first half of the twentieth century. Burke and Hine, "South Carolina State Law School," 18–26. A. Caldwell, *History of the Negro*, 265–67.

32. Nance to DuBois; Butler W. Nance to John R. Shillady, 24 January 1919, Select Branch Files, pt. 12A, NAACP Papers. "Butler Nance," SCL vertical file. Burke and Hine, "SC State Law School," 40–42; Mrs. R. T. Brooks to James W. Johnson, 18 March 1919, Select Branch Files, pt. 12A, NAACP Papers.

33. N. J. Frederick to Richard Carroll, 19 May 1915, Richard Carroll Papers, SCL. Nance to DuBois, 5 June 1915; Burke and Hine, "South Carolina State Law School," 40–42; Houston, "Need for Negro Lawyers," 49–52.

34. *Biographical Directory SC Senate*, 2:1114–16; Tindall, *South Carolina Negroes*, 100, 102, 112, 230–31, 272.

35. *Biographical Directory South Carolina Senate*, 2:1114–16; Tindall, *South*

Carolina Negroes, 100, 102, 112, 230–31, 272. The five other black delegates to the 1895 constitutional convention were Robert B. Anderson, I. R. Reed, Robert Smalls, William J. Whipper, and James Wigg.

36. Dr. C. C. Johnson, obituary, *Palmetto Leader*, 28 June 1928; A. Caldwell, *History of the Negro*, 3:131–33, 485–88; *The State*, 26 April 1917.

37. Henry H. Cooper married one of E. J. Sawyer's daughters, Ada Crosland Sawyer. Sawyer, the affluent and exceptional leader who lived in Bennettsville, sent Ada to Howard School in Columbia, the only public high school for blacks at the time. Although Cooper had seen Ada attending Howard, which was near his dental office on Washington Street, he and Ada were introduced by a mutual friend after she completed her education at Pratt Institute, a premier school of art and design in New York City, and returned to Bennettsville. Henry and Ada both had nine siblings and parents who had been born into slavery. Part of the first generation of black South Carolinians whose parents came of age after emancipation, this couple had three sons: H. H. Jr., Edward, and Noble. H. H. and Noble became dentists; Noble continued his father's practice in Columbia and H. H. practiced in New York City. Edward became a physician; professor of medicine at the University of Pennsylvania, which his father attended in the early twentieth century; and the first black president of the American Heart Association. The story of this one reformer's family provides a testimony to remarkable resilience, education against the odds, and determination through several generations. Author interview with Noble Cooper, Columbia, S.C., 17 February 2006.

38. Drago, *Initiative, Paternalism, and Race Relations*, 44.

39. Galloway-Wright, "Matilda Arabella Evans," 401–2. Other historians have also written extensively about Evans, including Darlene Clare Hine; see Hine, "Corporeal and Ocular Veil."

40. "Souvenir and Official Program of the Mid-winter session of the Bishops' Council of the AME Church," February 1923, Richard Carroll Papers, SCL; Brooks also appears in the NAACP correspondence as Mrs. R. T. Brooks. C. G. Garrett Jr. to Roy Nash, 1 May 1917; Mrs. R. T. Brooks to James W. Johnson, 8 March 1919, Selected Branch Files, pt. 12A, NAACP Papers.

41. *The State*, 17 February 1919; J. Johnson, *Southern Ladies, New Women*, 13–23. *40th Anniversary of the SCFCWC*, 6–9. For a recent work on multiracial women's activism, see Hewett, *Southern Discomfort*. Hewett examines black, white, and Latin women in Tampa.

42. J. Johnson, *Southern Ladies, New Women*, 50–53; *Charleston Messenger*, 5 July 1919.

43. Jenkins, "Marion Birnie Wilkinson," *Notable Black American Women*, 2:710–12. J. Johnson, *Southern Ladies, New Women*, 15–16.

44. C. L. Johnson, "Undertakings," 163–64.

45. Drago, *Initiative, Paternalism, and Race Relations*, 139–46, 169–72.

46. For a discussion of Allen University's independence compared with other private black institutions, see Gordon, *Sketches of Negro Life*, 92–97.

47. By the time of Chappelle's death in 1925 he had, as chancellor of Allen

University, paid off its $60,000 debt, restored it to financial respect, and built a new auditorium at the cost of $118,000. *Palmetto Leader*, 20, 27 June 1925.

48. *The State*, 21, 22 February 1919; Richard Carroll to Governor Robert A. Cooper, 8 February 1919, Robert A. Cooper Papers, SCDAH.

49. "Erasmus Lafayette Baskervill," in Boris, *Who's Who in Colored America*, 1:10–11; G. Croft Williams to T. R. Waring, 8 September 1919, Thomas R. Waring Papers, SCHS.

50. Drago, *Initiative, Paternalism, and Race Relations*, 134–36. For a full discussion of Daniel Jenkins's background and his clash with the Harlestons, see Ball, *Sweet Hell Inside*, 56–71.

51. Chappelle made these comments at the 1892 Republican Party state convention, Tindall, *South Carolina Negroes*, 49.

52. Richard Carroll to Booker T. Washington, 1 September 1914, 13:125–26; Richard Carroll to Booker T. Washington, 22 October 1906, 9: 99–100, Booker T. Washington Papers.

53. "Richard Carroll Dies," *Palmetto Leader*, 2 November 1929; letter of endorsement from Victor Masters, editorial secretary of Home Mission Board of the South Baptist Convention, 27 February 1915, Richard Carroll Papers, SCL; Newby, *Black Carolinians*, 169–84.

54. Booker T. Washington to Oswald Garrison Villard, 9 August 1910, 10:364, Booker T. Washington Papers.

55. Carroll's quotation from *The State*, 25 January 1907, cited in Newby, *Black Carolinians*, 176.

56. This article, published in a Southern Baptist newspaper after Carroll's death, illustrates whites' favorable attitude toward Carroll; see, "Death Silences Voice of Gifted Prophet of Racial Good Will," *Western Recorder*, 7 November 1929, in Richard Carroll Papers, SCL; *The State*, 15 April 1917; Reed Smith to David Coker, 22 November 1917, box 2, David R. Coker Papers, SCL.

57. McClellan quotation in A. Caldwell, *History of the Negro*, 190.

2. White Resolve

1. "On the Brink of Change," editorial, *The State*, 26 May 1917. William Watts Ball, editor of *The State*, was a vocal proponent of reform during this era. Although Ball is often remembered in South Carolina history for his reactionary opposition to the New Deal, in this era he very much accepted and promoted the reform agenda. For more on Ball, see Stark, *Damned Upcountryman*.

2. For an overview of progressivism nationwide, see Wiebe, *Search for Order*; and Rodgers, "In Search of Progressivism." South Carolina reformers were defined by what Rodgers referred to as the languages of humanitarianism and efficiency, but antimonopolism, the third language Rodgers identifies, was secondary if at all important. On the persistence of reform activity in the 1920s, see A. Link, "What Happened to the Progressive Movement?"

3. For more on overall progressive reforms in South Carolina, see Burts, *Manning and the Progressive Movement*; Duffy, "Charleston Politics in the Pro-

gressive Era"; Lupold, "Nature of South Carolina Progressives"; Cann, "The Morning After"; Mitchell, "Conservative Reform."

4. For South Carolina's inadequate road system, see Moore, *South Carolina Highway Department.*

5. For the status of poor health conditions and reform efforts, see Beardsley, *History of Neglect;* on lynching in South Carolina, see Mullins, "Lynching in South Carolina"; and Garris, "Decline of Lynching."

6. For a focus on progressive reform in the South, see Woodward, *Origins of the New South;* Kirby, *Darkness at the Dawning;* Grantham, *Southern Progressivism;* and W. Link, *Paradox of Southern Progressivism.* For more on the whites-only feature of southern progressivism, see Kousser, "Progressivism."

7. Here I define two premises of white supremacy so readers know how I use this concept throughout the book. There are other meanings of white supremacy, discussed later, about which all whites did not agree, but these are two that I have identified as commonly held by all whites. For a more thorough discussion of the historical development and theoretical underpinnings of white supremacy, see Hudson, "Maintaining White Supremacy," 1–33. My thinking about white supremacy has been influenced by George M. Fredrickson, *Racism: A Short History;* Fredrickson, *White Supremacy;* and Cell, *Highest Stage of White Supremacy.* Quotation in W. E. Smith, letter to the editor, *The State,* 22 April 1919.

8. Phillips presented these ideas at the 1928 American Historical Association meeting in Indianapolis; see Phillips, "Central Theme of Southern History"; quotation from 30–31. *The State,* 6 February 1922, 26 January 1919; *Anderson Farmer's Tribune,* 21 December 1915; U.S. Congress, *Congressional Record,* 57th Congress, 2nd sess., 24 February 1903, 2559–62. See Kantrowitz, *Ben Tillman,* for a thorough and provocative analysis of Ben Tillman's use of vicious racial rhetoric and advocacy of violence to firmly restore white supremacy and the cultural hegemony of patriarchy in South Carolina. Kantrowitz's analysis draws extensively from Tillman's rhetoric, especially its gendered dimensions.

9. This definition is drawn from George Fredrickson's discussion of racist ideology in "Social Origins of American Racism"; also, see Newby, *Jim Crow's Defense.*

10. Pro-slavery apologists, desiring to minimize cognitive dissonance that might arise in a culture that espoused a political philosophy of freedom and equality while sanctioning slavery, justified the South's slave-labor system as a paternalistic institution for racial and labor control designed to allow the inherently intellectually superior white race, as they conceived it, to shepherd the inferior, dependent Negro race. Invoking contemporary nineteenth-century scientific and social thought, whites rationalized Africans as biologically inferior to Anglo-Saxons. In addition to its economic benefits, pro-slavery theorists claimed, slavery also enshrined white supremacy as a lawful and legitimate social order for the antebellum South. G. Johnson, "Ideology of White Supremacy"; and Fredrickson, *Black Image,* 71–96.

11. Guion Johnson and George Fredrickson both discuss the literature and ideas nineteenth-century white Americans expressed about African Americans' basic nature, place in society, adjustment from slavery, religious and education potential, need for white supervision, etc., as the South moved toward institutional segregation and disfranchisement. Drawing upon contemporary theories of positivism, evolution, and progress, these journalists, politicians, polemicists, religious leaders, and business entrepreneurs ultimately justify white supremacy with these ideas. Many of the assumptions used to justify slavery were later used to justify the civil enslavement of blacks after emancipation. Both Johnson and Fredrickson discuss the development of white supremacy in terms of its development toward Jim Crow segregation and disfranchisement. For a thorough discussion of Reconstruction in South Carolina, see Holt, *Black over White;* Williamson, *After Slavery;* and Saville, *Work of Reconstruction.* For a recent analysis on an understudied group of whites, see Rubin, *South Carolina Scalawags.*

12. For a recent interpretation of the restoration of white supremacy, see Kantrowitz, *Ben Tillman;* and Tindall, *South Carolina Negroes.* For more on the desire of white southerners' use of suffrage restriction to strengthen their political power, see Kousser, *Shaping of Southern Politics.* For a broad examination of suffrage issues in the context of southern history, see Ayers, *Promise of the New South.*

13. U.S. Bureau of the Census, *Thirteenth Census,* 1910, *Population,* 1:41; U.S. Bureau of the Census, *Fourteenth Census,* 1920, *Population,* 1:45. States with a lower per capita wealth than South Carolina were Tennessee, at $864; North Carolina, $794; and Mississippi, $726. U.S. Bureau of the Census, *Wealth, Debt, and Taxation,* 1913, 26; data is from 1912. U.S. Bureau of the Census, *Thirteenth Census,* 1910, *Population,* 1:146–53.

14. Compiled from data in U.S. Bureau of the Census, *Fourteenth Census,* 1920, *Population,* 3:929–33. The internal variation in South Carolina's racial demography loosely fits the following pattern. The greatest concentration of black South Carolinians was found in the lower coastal and inner coastal plain regions, where African Americans constituted 60 percent to 80 percent of the population. Concentrations of African Americans diminished in the Pee Dee, located northeast of the lower coast, and in the upper and lower Piedmont, located in the northwest portion of the state, along the North Carolina boundary. Generally, the lower coastal and inner coastal plains had the highest percentage of African Americans, and the upper Piedmont had the highest percentage of whites. The percentage of African Americans in the Pee Dee, lower Piedmont, and midlands regions lay between these more extreme regions, but it was still quite high compared to other states, ranging from 49 percent to 69 percent. Several counties, however, are exceptions to this generalization. Horry County, in the Pee Dee, and Lexington County, in the mid region, were as white as the six upper Piedmont counties of Oconee, Pickens, Anderson, Greenville, Spartanburg, and Cherokee, whose African American populations were all less than 38 percent. Fairfield and Edgefield, counties in

the lower Piedmont, had black populations that exceeded 70 percent, proportionately just as high as numerous lower coastal and inner coastal counties. See South Carolina Racial Demography map on page 48.

15. Black-belt elites used this strategy of localism to serve their interests. Within a decade dynamics changed with new needs, especially pursuit of a state highway system. Elites then shifted their strategy to embrace a state solution of concentrating power in the general assembly, but only as long as they controlled it. The consistent element in both strategies was that they used power to serve their interests and thwart the majority, whether the majority was local blacks or whites statewide.

16. *The State*, 10 March 1920.

17. Rion McKissick became dean of the University of South Carolina School of Journalism in 1927 when W. W. Ball resigned that position. In 1936 McKissick became the university's nineteenth president, a position he held until his death in 1944. *Who's Who in South Carolina*, 137; Wardlaw, *Men and Women of Carolina*, 1–14; Burts, *Manning and the Progressive Movement*, 79; McNeely, *Fighting Words*, 97–98.

18. Wallace, *History of South Carolina*, 4:628; McNeely, *Fighting Words*, 84–85.

19. William Watts Ball was editor of the *Laurens Advertiser* (1890–1893), the *Columbia Journal* (1894), the *Charleston Evening Post* (1895–1897), and *Greenville Daily News* (1897); staff reporter for the *Philadelphia Press* (1898); city editor of the *Jacksonville Times Union* (1900–1902); assistant editor of the *Charleston News and Courier* (1904–1909); and managing editor of *The State* (1909–1913).

20. Stark, *Damned Upcountryman*, 3–5, 30–43.

21. For an alternate view of W. W. Ball, see Charles J. Holden, *In the Great Maelstrom*. Holden's analysis of Ball spans a much broader time frame than my analysis. Consequently, Ball rightly would not be considered a reformer in all parts of his life.

22. Ball kept a diary that chronicled his phone conversations, correspondence, and reflective commentary on current issues. Thomas Richard Waring, another influential journalist, was editor of the *Charleston Evening Post*, a position he assumed in 1897, when Ball left to become editor of the *Greenville News*. Waring remained editor until 1935, holding the position longer than anyone. He and Ball corresponded extensively. Quotations from William Ball to Nathaniel Dial, 12 May 1920, Ball Papers, DU.

23. McNeely, *Fighting Words*, 68–70; *Beaufort Gazette*, vol. 100, 1997, in McNeely; Wallace, *History of South Carolina*, 4:3–4. During World War I, Christensen joined the navy as an ensign and received a promotion to lieutenant. He was attached to the Sixth Naval District, located in Charleston, which enabled him to continue representing Beaufort in the state senate.

24. Tetzlaff, *Cultivating a New South*, 9–11, 70–72, 150–61; Wallace, *History of South Carolina*, 4:4.

25. *History of the Bar of Richland County.* Obituary, Claud N. Sapp, *The State*, 4 February 1947.

26. Burts, *Manning and the Progressive Movement,* 13–60.

27. *Biographical Directory of the American Congress 1774–1971,* 1285. Cyril Busbee, "Farm Tenancy in South Carolina," offers a contemporary's analysis of how farm tenancy had become an economic liability for the state and its citizens.

28. U.S. Bureau of the Census, *Fourteenth Census,* 1920, *Agriculture,* vol. 6, pt. 2, 276–80; *Agriculture,* 5:132. Pickens, Horry, Oconee, Greenville, Spartanburg, Cherokee, and Chesterfield were the seven counties where the majority of tenants were white.

29. "Declaration of the Conference of the Agricultural Commission of the American Bankers' Association and Representatives of 37 Bankers' State Associations, February 26–27, 1919, Washington, D.C.," Congressional Series, Asbury Francis Lever Papers, Special Collections, Strom Thurmond Institute, CU.

30. Parsons, "Lever's Great Act."

31. For a discussion of Coker's career, see Coclanis, "David R. Coker," 105–14; and his biography, Rogers, *Mr. D. R.*

32. Lander, *South Carolina 1865–1960,* 102–3.

33. Burts, *Manning and the Progressive Movement,* 165.

34. For a detailed analysis of the legislative struggle to pass compulsory school attendance, see Carlton, *Mill and Town,* 92–108. See chap. 11 for a more detailed discussion of South Carolina's educational finance laws. See William A. Link, *A Hard Country and a Lonely Place,* a study of education in Virginia that illustrates this same attitude of indifference toward education among many poor southerners. Margo, *Race and Schooling. Annual Report, SCACI,* "Labor Division," 1915, 510–11.

35. *Annual Report, SCSSE,* 1916, 127–50. A few up-country counties—Greenville, Lancaster, and Laurens—and several counties with large black majorities—Charleston, Georgetown, Beaufort, Berkeley, Fairfield, and Calhoun—fully funded nine months of school for white children. White students in counties with a black population that exceeded 70 percent benefited from the state's distribution of educational funds, which were allocated by population but spent at the discretion of white school boards.

36. *Annual Report, SCSSE,* 1916, 26, 131–32, 147–50. See Harlan, *Separate and Unequal;* Harlan argues that the disparity between black and white schools intensified as southern states began spending more for public schools in this era. The federal government, in cooperation with several philanthropic organizations, published a study in 1917 highlighting deficiencies in African American educational opportunities. U.S. Department of the Interior, Bureau of Education, *Negro Education.*

37. Swearingen, *Gallant Journey,* 31–32, 49, 100–107.

38. U.S. Bureau of the Census, *Thirteenth Census,* 1910, *Population,* 3:658–67; *Thirteenth Census,* 1910, *Abstract of the Census,* 245, 256–57. Louisiana had the highest illiteracy rate. Carlton, *Mill and Town,* 262–63.

39. E. Kohn, "Dr. Wil Lou Gray," 113–20; Montgomery, *South Carolina's Wil Lou Gray;* Carlton, *Mill and Town,* 263–64.

40. J. Johnson, *Southern Ladies, New Women,* 127–67.

41. For more on Cole Blease, see Burnside, "Governorship of Blease"; and Carlton, *Mill and Town,* 216–35. For the most thorough account of the Manning administration's reform efforts, see Burts, *Manning and the Progressive Movement.* David Carlton has argued persuasively that South Carolina's working class greatly resisted the paternalism of the reformers, who as middle-class Americans deemed it their responsibility to uplift others.

42. *Annual Report, SCCACI,* Labor Division, 1915, 444.

43. Compiled from data in U.S. Bureau of the Census, *Fourteenth Census,* 1920, *Agriculture,* vol. 6, pt. 2, 276; U.S. Bureau of the Census, *Wealth, Debt, and Taxation,* 1913, 26.

44. For general works on cotton dependence in the South and the credit problem that ensued, see Tindall, *Emergence of the New South;* Fite, *Cotton Fields No More;* Daniel, *Breaking the Land;* and Wright, *Old South, New South.* For an examination of the cyclical debt and credit problems, see Ford, "Rednecks and Merchants."

45. *Annual Report, SCCACI,* 1917 and 1918. Ebbie J. Watson, commissioner of agriculture, commerce, and industries died 27 October 1917, and A. C. Summers became commissioner, serving through 1918. In 1919 Harris became commissioner.

46. *Annual Report SCCACI,* Labor Division, 1919, 4–12.

47. *The State,* 5, 12 August 1917; 17 December 1918; Fraser, *Charleston! Charleston!* 359–61. South Carolina State Council of Defense, *Handbook for the War,* reveals the reformers' enthusiasm for the war.

48. *The State,* 5, 6, 10 July 1917. Governor D. Clinch Heyward promoted white migration in the early twentieth century, see Marcia G. Synnott, "Replacing 'Sambo,'" 77–89; Burts, *Manning and the Progressive Movement,* 41–42; Grossman, *Land of Hope,* 38–50. Migration and its role in developing a white South is discussed more in chap. 6.

49. Moore, *South Carolina Highway Department,* 44–49.

50. *The State,* 10 February, 7 June 1917, 11 February, 5 March, 22 December 1918.

51. U.S. Bureau of the Census, *Thirteenth Census,* 1910, *Population,* vol. III, 658–67; U.S. Bureau of the Census, *Thirteenth Census,* 1910, *Abstract of the Census,* 245, 256–57. For the entire population under age ten, South Carolina's illiteracy rate was 25.7 percent, and Louisiana's was 29 percent. The difference narrowed somewhat for illiteracy among voting-age males, with South Carolina's rate increasing to 27.1 percent and Louisiana's declining slightly to 28.6 percent. *Annual Report, SCSSE,* 1916, 78–80, 100–108. To be a certified high school, a school had to have a four-year curriculum, at least three teachers, at least a thirty-six-week school term, and fourteen units or courses. South Carolina did not adopt a twelfth grade for high school until 1944.

52. Williams, *Social Problems of South Carolina*, 58–64.

53. Burts, *Manning and the Progressive Movement*, 165–66.

54. "Some Notes on the SCDB," 1–4; *Columbia Record*, 5 November 1919; *The State*, 6 November 1919, 10 March 1920.

55. Josiah Morse to Samuel Chiles Mitchell, 5 June 1920, Mitchell Papers, SHC.

3. Mobilization for War

1. *The State*, 5 April 1917.

2. For a discussion of the range of national black leaders' responses to the war, see Ellis, *Race, War, and Surveillance*, 1–73; Ellis, "'Closing Ranks' and 'Seeking Honors'" explores thoroughly W. E. B. DuBois's controversial "Close Ranks" editorial in the May 1918 issue of the *Crisis*, where DuBois's critics charge him with reversing his historic boldness to advocate an accommodating silence on injustice during the war.

3. *The State*, 5, 6, 7 April 1917; *Charleston News and Courier*, 7 April 1917.

4. *Charleston News and Courier*, 18 April 1917.

5. E. L. Baskervill to *Charleston News and Courier*, 8 April 1917.

6. Thomas E. Miller to Governor Richard I. Manning and President Woodrow Wilson, in *Charleston News and Courier*, 9 April 1917.

7. For a discussion of African American leadership in South Carolina, see Newby, *Black Carolinians*, and Hemmingway, "Beneath the Yoke of Bondage." For general analysis of African Americans' struggles in this era, see Meier, *Negro Thought in America*.

8. For a full examination of blacks who resisted, see Kornweibel, "*Investigate Everything.*" Keith, *Rich Man's War*, examines opposition to the war among rural southerners, white and black. Yet Keith acknowledges that support for the war was strong among middle-class black leaders, 118–20.

9. *The State*, 5 April 1917. Another meeting was held on 11 April 1919 at Second Calvary Baptist in Waverly.

10. For a full discussion of the draft, see Chambers, *To Raise an Army*. For a discussion of how the World War I draft privileged white men, see Shenk, "*Work or Fight!*" which examines a range of variables in Georgia, Illinois, New Jersey, and California.

11. Entry, 13 January 1918, bk. 3, W. W. Ball Diary, Ball Papers, DU.

12. *The State*, 11, 12, 15 April 1917; Reed Smith to David R. Coker, 22 November 1917, David R. Coker Papers, SCL. The Commission for Civic Preparedness was the forerunner of the South Carolina State Council of Defense, formed later in 1917. Accounts in *The State* throughout 1917–1919 refer to the segregated African American war-preparation organizations. For more on David Coker, see Rogers, *Mr. D. R.*

13. J. Harry Foster to A. Frank Lever, 2 May 1917, Congressional Series, Asbury Frank Lever Papers, CU.

14. Charles L. Rhame to A. Frank Lever, 16 May 1917, Congressional Series, Lever Papers, CU.

15. S. L. Kransnoff to *The State*, 2 September 1917.

16. Frank S. Terry, W. M. Lesley, and M. Brabhau to A. Frank Lever, 25 April 1917, Congressional Series, Lever Papers, CU.

17. M. M. Mann to A. Frank Lever, 28 April 1917; J. Harry Foster to A. Frank Lever, 2 May 1917, Congressional Series, Lever Papers, CU.

18. Eugene Genovese develops the antebellum expression of paternalism and white supremacy in his interpretation of the master-slave relationship. J. Douglas Smith examines a twentieth-century manifestation of paternalism and white supremacy among elite white Virginians. See Genovese, *Roll, Jordan, Roll*; and J. D. Smith, *Managing White Supremacy*. Quotations in *The State*, 3 May 1917.

19. White southerners feared German subversion, and wild rumors of the black population's disloyalty circulated even before the United States entered the war. Throughout the war the federal government, through the Bureau of Investigation, worked with local police and sheriffs investigating accusations about German spies at work in the rural South. As Theodore Kornweibel Jr. argues in *"Investigate Everything,"* 37–75, these imagined German plots to stir African American discontent never existed. Blacks' discontent, expressed through opposition or disinterest in the war, was homegrown. Unwilling to acknowledge blacks' insightful understanding of their own oppression, whites preferred simply to believe that an outside enemy manipulated African Americans.

20. *The State*, 3 May 1917.

21. Ibid.

22. *The State*, 28 May, 9 August 1917.

23. Barbeau and Henri, *The Unknown Soldiers*, 36; Bright Williamson to David Coker, 14 June 1918, Coker Papers, SCL; *The State*, 11 September 1917.

24. Hemmingway, "Prelude to Change," 212–27.

25. *Charleston News and Courier*, 18–19 August 1917; Richard I. Manning to S. L. Kransnoff, 20 August 1917, Richard I. Manning Papers, SCL. Account of a conversation between Fitz McMaster and Leonard Woods reported by W. W. Ball, 9 June 1917, bk. 3, W. W. Ball Diary, Ball Papers, DU.

26. *The State*, 17 April, 20 May, 1917; Fort Jackson Museum, History of Fort Jackson, Chapter I—1917, http://www.jackson.army.mil.

27. *Charleston News and Courier*, 19 August 1917; Richard I. Manning to Acting Secretary of War, 12 September 1918, "Washington U.S. Officials and Congressmen Manning and Cooper" Section, Robert A. Cooper Papers, SCDAH.

28. *The State*, 1 August 1917.

29. *The State*, 21 August 1917.

30. Manning to Kransnoff; Manning to Judge Thomas E. Richardson, 24 August 1917, Richard I. Manning Papers, SCL. These letters were Manning's responses to the correspondents' complaints.

31. *The State*, 22 August 1917.

32. *Charleston News and Courier*, 19 August 1917.

33. *The State*, 19 August 1917; *Charleston News and Courier*, 20 August 1917.

34. Thomas E. Richardson to Richard I. Manning, 19 August 1917, Manning Papers, SCL.

35. *The State*, 23 August 1917.

36. Haynes, *Night of Violence*, 3–7.

37. Haynes, *Night of Violence*; C, Smith, "Houston Riot," 85–102.

38. Ibid.

39. Ibid.

40. Manning's quotation in *Charleston News and Courier*, 25 August 1917. Tillman's quotation in *The State*, 24 August 1917.

41. *New York Times*, 31 August 1917; E. Scott, *Official History*, 75–80.

42. *New York Times*, 31 August 1917.

43. *Charleston News and Courier*, 4 October 1917.

44. E. Scott, *Official History*, 77–81; for an analysis of the war experiences and contribution of the 369th, see Barbeau and Henri, *Unknown Soldiers*, 111–36.

45. E. Scott, *Official History*, 81.

46. *The State*, 21 August 1917.

47. Undated manuscript, cited in Burts, *Manning and the Progressive Movement*, 161.

48. T. C. Duncan to *The State*, 24 August 1917.

49. A. Frank Lever to J. Harry Foster, 5 May 1917, Congressional Series, Lever Papers, CU; J. F. Duggan to W. W. Long, who forwarded the letter with his own letter to David R. Coker, 30 May 1918, Coker Papers, SCL. For a case study of efforts to compel black labor during the war in Georgia, see Shenk, *"Work or Fight!"* 11–47.

50. James Henry Rice to Robert Ridgeway, 10 October 1919, box 3, James Henry Rice Jr. Papers, DU.

51. E. Julia Seldon, Spartanburg, to David Coker, 1 April 1918, Coker Papers, SCL.

52. R. Charlton Thomas to David Coker, 14 June 1918, Coker Papers, SCL.

53. *The State*, 3 January 1918.

4. Interracial Cooperation, 1917–1919

1. The Justice Department's Bureau of Investigation opened file 3057 in March 1917; the file later became part of the "Old German" series, investigation records of suspected German subversion of African Americans. Kornweibel, *"Investigate Everything,"* analyzes these voluminous records nationwide.

2. Kornweibel, *"Investigate Everything,"* 1–9, 37–75; E. Scott, *Official History*, 344–54. For an extensive analysis of rural southern dissent, see Keith, *Rich Man's War*.

3. B. F. McLeod to Department of Justice, 9 April 1917; Agent Branch Bocock reports, 10 May 1917, 23 May 1917; OG 3057, RG 65, Bureau of Investigation, reel 8, *Federal Surveillance*.

4. Quotation from Hart, *War Program*, 9. *Charleston News and Courier*, 18 April 1917.

5. The black civic-preparedness committee was the counterpart to the white committee. All served under the umbrella organization, the Commission for Civic Preparedness, which took the initial responsibility for civilian war-mobilization activities and was the forerunner of the South Carolina Council of Defense, which officially began in June 1917.

6. *The State*, 15, 16, 22, 24, 27, 28, 29 April; 2, 3 May 1917.

7. Other members were L. A. Ritchie of Abbeville and L. F. Percival of Greenwood. *The State* 15 April 1917. Short biographical sketches on Butler General of Marion, Jonas Thomas of Bennettsville, Jacob J. Durham of Columbia, and Ransom W. Westberry of Sumter available in A. Caldwell, *History of the Negro*, 3:90–91, 389–90, 490–93, 652–53.

8. Benjamin F. Hubert to *The State*, 5 April 1918; Hemmingway, "Prelude to Change," 216–17. *The State*, 22 June, 14 November 1918.

9. *Greenville News*, 9 November 1918; *The State*, 14 November 1918.

10. Early in the war a Committee on Soldier Life Activities organized entertainment activities. *The State*, 20 December 1917; 13, 14 November 1918; 22 January 1919.

11. For a discussion of the military's efforts to combat sexually transmitted diseases during World War I, see Odem, *Delinquent Daughters*, 121–27; Beardsley, "Allied against Sin," 189–202.

12. Statement of Mr. Alan Johnstone Jr. at the hearings before the Senate Committee on Military Affairs (18 June 1918), 65th Congress, 2nd Session, 89–91. *The State*, 30 April 1918; Odem, *Delinquent Daughters*, 125–26.

13. "40th Anniversary of the SCFCWC: 1909–1949," 7–9. J. Johnson, *Southern Ladies, New Women*, 181–83. In 1931 the state federation of colored women changed the name from the Fairwold Home for Delinquent Girls to the Marion Birnie Wilkinson Home for Underprivileged Orphans, to honor the longtime state federation president, Marion Wilkinson, who for decades led the effort to support the home.

14. For an examination of class tensions among African Americans, see Gaines, *Uplifting the Race*, and Greenwood, *Bittersweet Legacy*, which focuses on the complicated leadership strategies of the black middle class in Charlotte, N.C., before World War I. Quotations in A. Caldwell, *History of the Negro*, 3:441.

15. *The State*, 10 March 1918. The council members were Rev. N. F. Haygood, chair and minister of Sydney Park Church; Joseph J. Atwell, a member of the Columbia NAACP executive committee; Jacob J. Durham, minister of Second Calvary Baptist Church; Dr. John H. Goodwin, physician; Rev. C. A. Harrison; Rev. Rossie L. Brower; and Thomas L. Duckett, biology and chemistry professor at Benedict College.

16. Taylor's quotations in *Charleston News and Courier*, 9 May 1917; Agent Branch Bocock reports, 10–11 May 1917.

17. See chap. 1 for a more thorough discussion of the organization of these branches and its original members. Branch office in Columbia to Roy Nash, 1 May 1917, Selected Branch Files, South, NAACP Papers.

18. *Charleston News and Courier*, 9 May 1917; Committee of Colored Citizens (Richard H. Mickey, Secretary) to Charleston Chamber of Commerce, 10 May 1917, Branch Files, Group I, Charleston Branch, box G-196, NAACP Papers, LC.

19. Josephus Daniels to Carl C. VanDyke, 2 July 1917; Harold Knutson to R. Augustine Skinner, 6 July 1917, Clarence Miller to R. Augustine Skinner, 9 July 1917; Edwin A. Harleston to John R. Shillady, 2 November 1918, Branch Files, Group I, Charleston Branch, box G-196, NAACP Papers, LC.

20. For a discussion of the controversy surrounding *Birth of a Nation*'s initial release, see Cripps, "Reaction of the Negro." Richard Carroll lodged his protest in a letter to the editor, *The State*, 24 May 1918.

21. Carroll, letter to the editor, *The State*, 24 May 1918; *The State*, 10 March, 25 May 1918.

22. Other members of the delegation included Edward S. Willett; Mark G. Johnson, pastor of Ladson Presbyterian; A. W. Timmons; W. H. Thomas; and James A. Brigman, *Columbia Record*, 24 May 1918.

23. *Columbia Record*, 24 May 1918; *The State*, 25 May 1918.

24. Telegram from Reed Smith to Arthur H. Fleming, 24 May 1918; telegram from Arthur H. Fleming to State Council of Defense, 24 May 1918, in *The State*, 25 May 1918.

25. *The State*, 24, 25 May 1918; city council resolution and meeting report in *The State*, 25 May 1918.

26. *Greenville News*, 2, 9 October 1918.

27. On 17 May 1918 the Selective Service director, Enoch Crowder, modified the existing draft guidelines by issuing a "work or fight" order. Crowder intended the order to allay concerns about agricultural and war-industry productivity. John Chambers II, *To Raise an Army*, 192–96, explains that numerous state legislatures had already passed compulsory labor laws and pressured the federal government to follow their lead. After the issuance of the spring 1918 federal order, other states and local communities adopted additional "work or fight" ordinances that compelled labor more thoroughly. Whether federal, state, or local, these laws gave local draft boards great latitude in compelling labor. Many southern states used this authority to force black women to work domestic jobs, hardly essential for the war effort. For a discussion of the NAACP's campaign to curb southern states' enforcement of the "work or fight" laws only against black women, see Hunter, *To 'Joy My Freedom*, 227–32. No letters from South Carolina are included in the NAACP's "Work or Fight" file, but the problem clearly emerged in Greenville; see Group 1, Series C, Administrative Files, pt. 10, reel 23, NAACP Papers; *Greenville News*, 2, 9 October 1918.

28. For a discussion of whom the federal government identified as worthy of dependency status, see Hickel, "War, Region, and Social Welfare," *Greenville News*, 2, 9 October 1918; Richard I. Manning to Bernard Manning, 19 September 1917, Out Correspondence, reel 630, Richard Manning Papers, SCL.

29. Edwin A. Harleston to John R. Shillardy, 2 November 1918, Branch Files, Group I, Charleston Branch, box G-196, NAACP Papers, LC; *Charleston News and Courier*, 15 January 1919; *The State*, 17 January 1919.

30. *Charleston News and Courier*, 22 January 1919; *The State*, 17 January 1919; "Colored Teachers," 58–60; Michael Fultz's "Charleston, 1919–1920" provides a rich history of the circumstances that preceded the 1919 struggle and its context in the larger history of black education, but his study does not connect the activities of Charleston's African American leaders with World War I activism.

31. E. A. Harleston Address, Tenth Anniversary Conference of the NAACP, Report of Branches, June 28, 1919, pt. 1, reel 8, NAACP Papers.

32. "Colored Teachers," 58–60; *Charleston News and Courier*, 22 January 1919; *The State*, 7 February 1919.

33. "Colored Teachers," 58–60; *Charleston News and Courier*, 22 January 1919; *The State*, 7 February 1919.

34. A. Caldwell, *History of the Negro*, 3:57.

5. Interracial Tension, 1919

1. The committee members who drafted the Emancipation Day resolutions were Henry E. Lindsay (chair), Green Jackson, I. S. Leevy, John H. Goode, and H. P. Williams. *The State*, 2 January 1919.

2. *The State*, 5 February 1919.

3. Ibid.

4. *The State*, 5, 7 February 1919. A full discussion of the 1916 incident with Blease at Allen is included in chap. 7.

5. *The State*, 5 February 1919; Petition to Governor R. A. Cooper, February 1919, Robert A. Cooper Papers, SCDAH.

6. Richard Carroll to Robert A. Cooper, 8 February 1919, Cooper Papers, SCDAH. Names of the politically engaged African Americans are furnished in Carroll's letter; further identification comes from my research data base derived from many sources.

7. E. A. Harleston Address and Butler W. Nance Address, Tenth Anniversary Conference of the NAACP, Report of Branches, June 28, 1919, pt. 1, reel 8; Mrs. R. T. Brooks to James W. Johnson, 8 March 1919; Butler W. Nance, "Notes from the Columbia Branch," May 20, 1919, Part 12-A (Selected Branch Files), reel 18, NAACP Papers.

8. Graydon, attorney of Logan & Graydon, to Robert A. Cooper, 26 July 1919, Cooper Papers, SCDAH.

9. Philip G. Palmer to Robert A. Cooper, 3 October 1919, Cooper Papers, SCDAH.

10. Powell, "History of the Southern Commission," 1–3, 51.

11. E. L. Baskervill to T. R. Waring, 6 September 1919, Waring Papers, SCHS.

12. T. R. Waring to G. Croft Williams, 6 September 1919, Waring Papers, SCHS. The CIC did not become a permanent organization, with that name, until 1921.

13. G. Croft Williams to T. R. Waring, 8 September 1919, Waring Papers, SCHS.

14. T. R. Waring to G. Croft Williams, 6 September 1919, Waring Papers, SCHS; William Watts Ball to Barnwell, 20 January 1920, Ball Papers, DU.

15. See chap. 1 for a full discussion of the 21 February 1919 parade and Haygood's role in it.

16. *The State*, 11, 15 July 1919.

17. A. Caldwell, *History of the Negro*, 3:708–10; *The State* 15 July 1919.

18. *The State*, 11, 15 July 1919.

19. *The State*, 23 January 1919; 14 November 1918.

20. *The State*, 23 January 1919; 14 November 1918.

21. *The State*, 23 January 1919; "Race Conference Brings Big Crowd," 25 March 1919, unidentified clipping, Richard Carroll Papers, SCL.

22. T. D. Wood to Robert A. Cooper, 26 March 1919, Cooper Papers, SCDAH.

23. Ibid.

24. For a discussion of the national character of racial violence in 1919, see Schneider, *"We Return Fighting,"* 20–35.

25. Josiah Morse, letter to the editor, *The State*, 27 July 1919; Josiah Morse to Samuel Chiles Mitchell, 7 July 1919, Series A, folder 12, Mitchell Papers, SHC.

26. *The State*, 28 July 1919.

27. Ibid.

28. Robert A. Cooper to John Gary Evans, August 5, 1919, Cooper Papers, SCDAH; Morse, letter to the editor; Graydon to Cooper.

29. Graydon to Cooper; *The State*, 29, 30, 31 July, 1 August 1919. Historian David Duncan Wallace spoke privately to one of the Citizen Committee members, who reported information not published in the newspaper account; see *History of South Carolina*, 3:459; 1971 interview with Modjeska Simkins, Hemmingway, "Prelude to Change," 223.

30. W. W. Klugh to Robert A. Cooper, 5 August 1919; John Gary Evans to Robert A. Cooper, 31 July 1919; Robert A. Cooper to John Gary Evans, 5 August 1919, Cooper Papers, SCDAH. For a discussion of armed self-defense as a strategy African Americans used in fighting for their freedom, see Tyson, "Robert F. Williams."

31. *Keowee Courier*, 29 October 1919; telegram from W. M. Alexander to Robert A. Cooper, 15 October 1919; Robert A. Cooper to Sheriff W. M. Alexander, 18 October 1919, Sheriff W. M. Alexander and B. R. Moss to Robert Cooper, 20 October 1919, Cooper Papers, SCDAH.

32. For a thorough examination of the Elaine massacre, see Cortner, *Mob Intent on Death*; Stockley, *Blood in Their Eyes*; Whayne, "Low Villains and Wickedness," 285–313.

33. M. L. Bonham to Robert A. Cooper, 6 October 1919; P. K. McCully to Robert A. Cooper, 7 October 1919, Cooper Papers, SCDAH.

34. Bonham to Cooper; McCully to Cooper.

35. T. R. Waring to William W. Ball, 10 October 1919, Waring Papers, SCHS.

36. *Charleston News and Courier*, 11–13, 16–17 May 1919; *The State*, 11–12, 16 May 1919; Fraser, *Charleston, Charleston*, 363.

37. *Charleston News and Courier*, 11–13, 16–17 May 1919; Fraser, *Charleston, Charleston*, 363. The papers reported that seventeen injured blacks went to Roper Hospital. Harleston's subsequent investigation, from which Grimké reported, indicated that forty blacks had been injured.

38. *Charleston News and Courier*, 11–12, 17 May 1919; *The State*, 11, 16 May 1919.

39. E. A. Harleston Address and Mr. Grimké Address, Tenth Anniversary Conference of the NAACP, Report of Branches, June 28, 1919, pt. 1, reel 8, NAACP Papers; *Charleston News and Courier*, 25 May 1919; Fraser, *Charleston, Charleston*, 363.

40. Philip G. Palmer to Robert A. Cooper, 3 October 1919, Cooper Papers, SCDAH.

41. Branch Files, Group I, boxes G196-G197, NAACP Papers, LC.

42. Josiah Morse to Samuel Chiles Mitchell, 31 August 1919; Morse to Mitchell, 4 December 1919, Series A, box 2, folder 14, Mitchell Papers, SHC.

43. "Modern Exiles," 70–72; "Ordered to Leave or Pay with Life," from *Chicago Tribune*, in *The State*, 21 December 1919.

44. "Modern Exiles," 70–71.

45. "The Rev. Blatcher," n.d., *Anderson Tribune*, clipping in Richard Carroll Papers, SCL.

46. "Ordered to Leave or Pay with Life."

47. Harleston Address.

48. *Congressional Record*, 66th Congress, 1st Session, 25 August 1919, 4302–6; DuBois, "Returning Soldiers," 13–14.

49. *Congressional Record*, 66th Congress, 1st Session, 25 August 1919, 4302–6.

6. The Great Migration

1. Historians and contemporaries have noted the disparate responses from white southerners to black migration, but few have offered an analysis that adequately explains the variation. Some refer to a monolithic South that had first one reaction then another; see Goodwin, *Black Migration in America*, 12. Others have suggested that there were two white views on black migration from the South. According to this interpretation, one view emphasized the

economic detriment of black migration to the South and the other focused on the potential benefit to the South from black migration out of the region; see E. Scott, *Negro Migration*, 152–74. The most thorough analysis of white reaction to the Great Migration occurred in a symposium on that topic at Jackson State University in September 1989. Seven papers presented at that the conference are included in Harrison, *Black Exodus*. Joe Lewis Caldwell, "Any Place but Here," examines the effects of black migration on local politics; Grossman, *Land of Hope*, offers the most comprehensive examination of white reaction. J. William Harris, *Deep Souths*, also examines the region's response to national trends in World War I.

2. For an excellent study of the nineteenth-century migration, see Painter, *Exodusters*. Steven Hahn, *A Nation under Our Feet*, argues for migration as African Americans' expression of autonomy.

3. Grossman, "The White Man's Union," 84–86; Henri, *Black Migration*, 50–52. While the migration of African Americans from the South between 1940 and 1960 exceeded the migration from 1910 to 1930, the wartime exodus was the first massive migration of African Americans, and it laid a foundation for the later migration.

4. The migration figures were derived from the intercensal estimation of net internal migration, which is based on the survival-rate method of estimating, which subtracts the enumerated population at the end of the decennial period from the estimated survivors at the beginning of the decade. Intercensal estimations for both decades are found in U.S. Bureau of the Census, *Historical Statistics*, 1:87, 95; Shaffer, "A New South," 403–4; *New York Times*, 23 April 1923, clipping in pt. 10, NAACP Papers. South Carolina State study reported in "Information Service, Research Department Commission on the Church and Social Service, Federal Council of the Churches of Christ in America," 3 November 1923, pt. 10 (Migration), reel 13, NAACP Papers. For a more complete discussion of migration in South Carolina from Reconstruction to the Great Depression, see Devlin, "South Carolina and Black Migration"; and Newby, *Black Carolinians*, 193–200.

5. Robert A. Cooper to A. T. Gerrans, 1 April 1919, Robert A. Cooper Papers, SCDAH. Press Release, 2 November 1923, Notes, 23 November 1923, pt. 10, NAACP Papers.

6. U.S. Bureau of the Census, *Fourteenth Census*, 1920, *Occupations*, vol. 4, 1013–16.

7. U.S. Department of Labor, *Negro Migration*, 7–8; E. Scott, *Negro Migration*, introduction. Other contemporary analyses of the wartime migration include Work, "The Negro Migration," 202–12; Haynes, "Negroes Move North," 115–22; Woodson, *Century of Negro Migration*; Scott, "Letters of Negro Migrants," 290–340, 412–65.

8. U.S. Department of Labor, *Negro Migration*, 9–13; E. Scott, *Negro Migration*, 13–15.

9. As a graduate student at the University of Chicago, Charles S. Johnson

was one of the principal investigators in Scott's study; see C. S. Johnson, "Negro Migration"; Cohen, "Great Migration as Lever"; Grossman, *Land of Hope*, 13–16. Scholars of sociology, economics, and history have written extensively on the causes of the Great Migration. The earliest analyses drew from these contemporaries, who emphasized economic causes. Later studies focused on African Americans' destinations and their new lives as urban, industrial laborers, rather than on the reasons for their exodus. Two of the most synthetic works are James Grossman, *Land of Hope* and Nicholas Lemann, *The Promised Land*. Lemann's *Promised Land* is chiefly about the post-1940 migration, when agricultural mechanization played such an important role in motivating African Americans to leave the South. A journalistic interdisciplinary study of the United States' attempt to confront the pervasive problems of black poverty and oppression, it examines the migration from Mississippi to Chicago. For a historiographical review of the voluminous literature on the Great Migration, see Trotter, introduction to *Black Migration in Historical Perspective*, 1–21.

10. Grossman, *Land of Hope*, 1–9; Alan DeSantis, "Selling the American Dream," argues that the *Chicago Defender*, which circulated widely in southern states during the war, created discontent among black southern readers and encouraged their longing to pursue the American dream in Chicago, the "promised land." Special correspondent H. B. from the *New York Evening Post*, "Industry Lures Negro into Northern Cities," *The State*, 11 April 1923.

11. Lamon, "W. T. Andrews Explains," offers a brief introduction to W. T. Andrews, "The Causes of Negro Migration from the South," which is published in full as it originally appeared in the *Nashville Globe*, a black weekly, 23 February 1917.

12. Lamon, "W. T. Andrews Explains," 368–70.

13. Lamon, "W. T. Andrews Explains," 365–66; Burke, "School of Law," 10; *The State*, 8–9 February, 1 April, 6 July 1917. *The State* frequently published letters from Carroll discussing migration.

14. *The State*, 6 July 1917.

15. *The State*, 1 April, 6 July 1917; Carroll corresponded with numerous white leaders in South Carolina. Several letters from him or about him suggested that he cooperated with and received money from whites and that he was controversial within the African American community. Richard Carroll to R. A. Cooper, 8 February 1919, Cooper Papers, SCDAH; Reed Smith to David R. Coker, 22 November 1917, Richard Carroll to David R. Coker, 15 December 1915, Coker Papers, SCL; William A. Sinclair to Francis Blascoer, 29 August 1910, Part 8, NAACP Papers.

16. *The State*, 18 January 1917. For a thorough discussion of the classic debate between Booker T. Washington and W. E. B. DuBois, see T. Harris, *Analysis of the Clash.*

17. T. S. Wise, letter to the editor, *The State*, 15 April 1917.

18. *The State*, 2 December 1922.

19. *The State*, 7 December 1922.

20. *The State*, 30 November 1922.

21. NAACP press release, 9 November 1923; NAACP press release, 2 May 1924, pt. 10, NAACP Papers. For general information on the NAACP's purpose and strategy, see Kellogg, *NAACP: A History*.

22. *The State*, 8 February 1917.

23. *The State*, 8 February, 1 April 1917.

24. *The State*, 23 July 1917. William Ball wrote countless editorials on African Americans' migration from South Carolina.

25. For an early analysis of the relationship between violence and migration, see C. S. Johnson, "How Much Is Migration a Flight?" 272–74. Johnson concludes that violence, such as lynching, was a limited factor in northward migration. Neil Fligstein, *Going North*, tested violence in a statistical model to determine its significance as a cause of migration and concludes that it was not significant. Stewart E. Tolnay and E. M. Beck, "Rethinking the Role of Racial Violence," 20–35, challenge these conclusions by arguing that violence had a reciprocal relationship with black migration. That is, areas with high levels of violence experienced black out-migration, but the migration then motivated whites to improve conditions to stop the migration, so the net migration figures appear low or insignificant. *The State*, 4 May 1917.

26. Roy Nash drew national attention to the Anthony Crawford lynching with his article in the *Independent*; see Nash, "Lynching of Anthony Crawford," 456 ff. The NAACP became involved with the lynching, and Governor Richard Manning hired a private detective service to investigate it. For a detailed analysis, see Finnegan, "'Equal of Some White Men,'" 54–60.

27. Nash, "Lynching of Anthony Crawford"; Finnegan, "'Equal of Some White Men,'" 56–58.

28. Beard quotation in *Abbeville Scimitar*, 1 February 1917, cited in Finnegan, "'Equal of Some White Men,'" 54; Nash, "The Lynching of Anthony Crawford"; quotation in E. Scott, *Negro Migration*, 47.

29. See chap. 6 for a thorough discussion of Gassaway. "Ordered to Leave or Pay with Life."

30. Hunter A. Gibbes, letter to the editor, *The State*, 27 February 1918. Gibbes spoke against lynching again in 1926 in the high-profile Lowman lynching. Campbell, "Starkly Different Views."

31. W. W. Ball, editor of *The State*, published an extensive excerpt from a farmer's letter, 4 May 1917; *The State*, 26 March 1917.

32. Bryant Simon, "Appeal of Cole Blease," questions the unifying theme of white supremacy because of disagreement among whites about lynching as an acceptable means of enforcing white dominance. Yet I argue that disagreement about lynching, one means of enforcing white supremacy, does not negate the possibility that white southerners shared a common commitment to white supremacy. Disagreements among whites always occurred within the context of white supremacy. For an analysis of the antilynching campaign that demonstrates this disagreement, see Hall, *Revolt against Chivalry*.

33. Harry Watson to Rev. E. O. Watson, 25 September 1928, Harry Watson Papers, SCL.

34. E. W. Dabbs, letter to the editor, *The State*, 30 March 1917; E. W. Dabbs to David R. Coker, 2 January 1917, David R. Coker Papers, SCL. Clarence Poe, president and editor of the *Progressive Farmer* of North Carolina, recommended Dabbs to Governor Richard Manning for commissioner of agriculture after Ebbie J. Watson's death in 1917. Poe told Manning, "I don't need to tell you that Mr. Dabbs is a man of unusual ability, thoughtfulness and qualities of leadership." Clarence Poe to Richard I. Manning, 29 October 1917, Eugene W. Dabbs Papers, SCL. Dabbs had four children; his youngest son, James McBride Dabbs, became a minister and one of South Carolina's most notable white civil rights activists.

35. Ben S. Williams, letter to the editor, *The State*, 27 July 1917.

36. *The State*, 2 March 1917.

37. Ball recounts the response of a "well-to-do planter" when challenged on the South's need for cheap labor. William W. Ball to Clarence Poe, 5 May 1923, Ball Papers, DU.

38. Devlin, "South Carolina and Black Migration," 249–50; *The State*, 19 April 1917; *Columbia Record*, 17 April 1917; Henri, *Black Migration*, 62–63; Attorney General Thomas H. Peeples issued an opinion on a newspaper's right to publish advertisements for labor stating that it was not illegal but unadvised and not "patriotic"; *Annual Report of the Attorney General*, 1917, 88. Paul Sanders to Turner Logan, 21 May 1923; C. W. Pugsey to Turner Logan, 21 June 1923; Turner Logan to "Harry," the postmaster general, 9 June 1923, Turner Logan Papers, SCHA.

39. *The State*, 19 April 1917.

40. *The State*, 6 June 1917.

41. Ibid.

42. Emmett J. Baxter, letter to the editor, *The State*, 27 May 1917.

43. Ball to Poe.

44. *The State*, 4 May 1917.

45. See Marcia G. Synnott, "Replacing 'Sambo,'" 77–89; D. C. Heyward, letter to the editor, *The State*, 9 February 1919. In 1919 the idea formally reemerged with the formation of the South Carolina Landowners Association, a private effort of reformers to attract small landowners to South Carolina; see "South Carolina Landowners Association, pamphlet, 6 May 1919, Niels Christensen, President," Cooper Papers, SCDAH.

46. J. J. Cantey, letter to the editor, *The State*, 15 July 1917.

47. James T. Williams, letter to the editor, *The State*, 22 May 1923.

48. *The State*, 26 March 1917.

49. *The State*, 30 March 1917.

50. A. T. Gerrans to Robert A. Cooper, 21 March 1919, Cooper Papers, SCDAH.

51. Taylor Kennerly wrote a series in the *New York Evening Post*, "The Negro Exodus from the South," referenced in *The State*, 13 June 1917.

52. Wright, *Old South, New South*, 66–70.

53. *The State*, 21 July 1922.

54. *The State*, 5 July 1917.

7. A Reform Coalition

1. William W. Ball to Harry Watson, 15 July 1924, Harry Watson Papers, SCL; Ball made a very similar comment in postelection correspondence, William W. Ball to J. C. Derieux, 8 September 1924, Ball Papers, DU.

2. Carlton, *Mill and Town*, 215, estimates voter turnout in South Carolina at nearly 71 percent in 1900, 64 percent in 1910; and 80 percent in 1912. Understanding South Carolina's intraparty factionalism is often difficult because all voters and candidates wore the same label, Democrat.

3. William Ball to Thomas McDow, 17 August 1922, Ball Papers, DU.

4. Simon, *Fabric of Defeat*, 20–26.

5. Carlton, *Mill and Town*, 215–30; Simon, *Fabric of Defeat*, 11–35; Burnside, "Governorship of Blease"; Sloan, "Blease Movement in South Carolina"; Miller, "Coleman Livingston Blease"; Mixon, "Senatorial Career of Blease." For an explanation of the Tillman-Blease connection, see Kantrowitz, *Ben Tillman*, 296–300.

6. Simon, *Fabric of Defeat*, 27–28.

7. Carlton, *Mill and Town*, 181–86, 234–39.

8. Entry, 9 February 1922, W. W. "Billy" Ball recounts a conversation with C. P. Hodges; entry, 25 January 1922, bk. 5, Ball Diary, Ball Papers, DU. For a detailed account of Blease's pardons, see Brice, "Use of Executive Clemency."

9. Simon, *Fabric of Defeat*, 30–35.

10. J. M. DesChamps, letter to the editor, *The State*, 21 July 1917.

11. Carlton, *Mill and Town*, 221–35.

12. William Ball to C. P. Hodges, 18 September 1922, entry, 23 April 1916, bk. 1, Ball Diary, Ball Papers, DU.

13. Contemporaries referred to this as the anti-Blease faction. For clarity of conception, however, I will use the term *coalition* to indicate that the anti-Blease forces actually represented a host of interests whose common denominator was opposition to Blease.

14. William Ball to Worthington C. Ford, 13 December 1923; U. B. Phillips to William Ball, 9 December 1923, Ball Papers, DU.

15. For an expanded discussion of the reformers' legislative agenda during Manning's first administration, see Burts, *Manning and the Progressive Movement*, 83–113; David Carlton, *Mill and Town*, 258–60.

16. Burts, *Manning and the Progressive Movement*, 126–29.

17. *The State*, 31 August, 1, 12, 14 September, 1916. For more on the 1916 campaign, see Burts, *Manning and the Progressive Movement*, 126–32.

18. Quotation in *The State*, 23 October 1917; V. O. Key, *Southern Politics*.

19. In states where whites were a majority, an appeal to African American voters required much broader and larger-scale black participation to achieve success. Thus, in states without a black majority whites more willingly accepted black political participation on a very limited basis.

20. *The State*, 5 October 1916.

21. See chap. 6 for a discussion of Chappelle's explanation in 1919 of why he

would consider an alliance with Blease, whom he referred to as the "old devil himself." Ibid.

22. Ibid.

23. *The State* 6, 9, 22 July; 17, 19 August 1918; entry, 16 August 1918, vol. 13, Frederik Holmes Christensen Diary, SCL; Richard Manning to David R. Coker, 11 July 1918, Coker Papers, SCL. Hugh Haynesworth to Richard Manning, 26 July 1918; William Bank to C. W. B. Long, 15 August 1918; H. N. Edmonds to Richard Manning, 23 August 1918, Manning Papers, SCL.

24. Election returns, *The State*, 31 August 1912; election returns for 1914 U.S. Senate race reprinted in *The State*, 28 August 1918; election returns, *The State*, 1 September 1916.

25. Registration certificates were issued upon demonstration of literacy or proof of taxes paid on at least $300 of property. *The State*, 16–24 November 1916; Carlton examines the suffrage restriction attempted before the 1916 election in *Mill and Town*, 225–33.

26. *The State*, 22 August 1917.

27. *The State*, 18 November 1916.

28. *The State*, 10, 22 January, 20 February 1917.

29. *Annual Message of Governor Richard I. Manning, 9 January 1917*, 5–6.

30. *The State*, 23 October 1917.

31. *The State*, 6, 15 January 1917.

32. The bill that passed in 1918 enacted the secret ballot only in cities and towns, not in rural areas.

33. *The State*, 6 March 1918; Burts, *Manning and the Progressive Movement*, 190–97.

34. *The State*, 2, 4, 11, 17, 25 May; 14 June; 4 July 1918; A. Frank Lever to David R. Coker, 7 March 1918; Richard Manning to David R. Coker, 20 March 1918, David R. Coker Papers, SCL. Richard Manning to Robert Lathan, 8 March 1918; Ben Tillman to Richard Manning, 22 May 1918, A. Frank Lever to Richard Manning, 30 May 1918, C. J. Ranage to Richard Manning, 4 June 1918, James Adger Belton to Richard Manning, 3 July 1918, Manning Papers, SCL; Robertson, *Sly and Able*, 65–74. Dial had been in the race from the beginning.

35. *The State*, 13, 23 July 1918; 26 August 1918; Wallace, *History of South Carolina*, 450–52.

36. *The State*, 5 October 1916, reprinted in *The State*, 16 August 1918.

37. Leon Green to Richard Manning, 26 August 1918, Manning Papers, SCL; *The State*, 16 August 1918; official election returns in *The State*, 4 September 1918. Dial had 65,064 votes. James Francis Rice also ran but received only 5,317 votes.

38. *The State*, 17 August 1918; S. L. Goldsmith to Richard Manning, 20 August 1918, Manning Papers, SCL.

39. Robert A. Cooper had been elected to his second term in 1920 but resigned soon into the term to become a member of the National Farm Loan Board in Washington. Lieutenant Governor Wilson G. Harvey completed the term but did not seek election in 1922.

40. William Ball to U. B. Phillips, 4 December 1923, Ball Papers, DU.

41. Derived from an examination of Ball's diary from March to May 1922, especially 18 March, 10 April, 5 May, in which Ball recounts conversations with others and interjects his judgment; also entry, 31 August 1922, bk. 5, Ball Diary, Ball Papers, DU. Quotation from William Ball to Nathaniel Dial, 12 May 1920, Ball Papers, DU. Ball revealed personal concerns about the old Conservative-Tillmanites rivalry in 1923. William Ball to Worthington C. Ford, 13 December 1923, Ball Papers, DU.

42. *The State* 18, 28 August 1922; William Ball to Tom Waring, 12 September 1922, Ball Papers, DU.

43. Cole L. Blease to Joe Tolbert, 16 May 1921, in *The State*, 31 July 1922. In his diary Ball recounts conversations with former governor Heyward about Blease's overtures to Republicans. Ball and Heyward expressed concern that if South Carolinians elected Blease, the state would lose influence in the national Democratic Party because Blease had been such an outspoken critic of Wilson. Entry, 16 July 1922, bk. 5, Ball Diary, Ball Papers, DU.

44. *The State*, 7, 22, July 1922; *Charlotte Observer* editorial reprinted in *The State*, 25 July 1922.

45. *The State*, 7, 22 July 1922.

46. W. F. Milam to William Ball, 18 August 1922, Ball papers, DU.

47. Wade Milam, letter to the editor, *The State*, 26 August 1922.

48. George D. Shore, Sumter County Republican Club, letter to the editor, *The State*, 31 July 1922. Shore's suggestions were accurate. But the extreme weakness of the Republican Party in South Carolina, combined with white South Carolinians' willingness to accept all characterizations of Republicans as champions of African Americans' rights because of Reconstruction, meant Democrats could irresponsibly tar Republicans as threats to white supremacy with little retaliation at the polls.

49. William W. Ball to Harry Watson, 24 January 1923, Watson Papers, SCL.

50. Nathaniel Dial to William Ball, 9 August 1922, Ball Papers, DU.

51. *The State* published the *Charlotte Observer*'s reporting of the Tolbert letter before the Columbia paper printed the letter. William Ball to P. H. McGowan, 20 July 1922, William Ball to Nathaniel Dial, 17 July 1922, Ball Papers, DU.

52. *The State*, 4 September 1922.

53. Entry, 13 Sept 1922, bk. 5, Ball Diary, Ball Papers, DU.

8. Woman Suffrage

1. For a history of the national woman suffrage movement, see Catt and Shuler, *Woman Suffrage and Politics*; Kraditor, *Ideas of the Woman Suffrage Movement*; A. Scott and A. Scott, *One Half the People*; Morgan, *Suffragists and Democrats*.

2. Historians A. Elizabeth Taylor, Anne Firor Scott, Marjorie Julian Spruill, Suzanne Lebsock, Elna Green, Glenda Gilmore, and many others

have made the narrative of the woman suffrage movement in southern states a familiar one. See Wheeler, *New Women*; A. Scott, *The Southern Lady*; Lebsock, "Woman Suffrage and White Supremacy"; Green, *Southern Strategies*; Gilmore, *Gender and Jim Crow*. Ironically, ratification by one southern state—Tennessee—proved decisive as the final state needed for ratification.

3. Green, *Southern Strategies*, 106–25. The general assembly voted in January 1920 to reject the federal amendment. *The State*, 23, 29 January 1920.

4. W. S. Hall, letter to the editor, *The State*, 26 May 1920.

5. Herndon, "Woman Suffrage in South Carolina"; Taylor, "South Carolina," 298–310; Bland, "Fighting the Odds," 32–43.

6. Taylor, "South Carolina," 301–3; Bland, "Fighting the Odds," 32–37.

7. *Senate Journal*, 1917, 30.

8. *The State*, 31 January 1917. For a complete discussion of the divorce issue, see Hudson, "From Constitution to Constitution."

9. Tetzlaff, *Cultivating a New South*, 198–200. Defeated in the Senate, the resolution lay in the House until the next session. *The State*, 1, 4 February 1917.

10. Taylor, "South Carolina," 306–8; Herndon, "Woman Suffrage," 56–66; Wheeler, *New Woman*, 29–30.

11. Farmer, "Eulalie Salley."

12. Christie Benet, who was appointed to Tillman's seat until the special election was held, also voted against the suffrage amendment.

13. E. C. Bailey letter to the editor, *The State*, 26 January 1919.

14. "A Friend of the South," Argyle, Inc., Charleston to Robert A. Cooper, 20 June 1919, Robert A. Cooper Papers, SCDAH.

15. James F. Byrnes to William W. Ball, 18 January 1920, Ball Papers, DU. See chap. 6 for a full discussion of Byrnes's speech; U.S. Congress, *Congressional Record*, 66th Congress, 1st Session, 25 August 1919, 4302–6.

16. James F. Byrnes to William W. Ball, 18 January 1920, Ball Papers, DU.

17. J. F. J. Caldwell, letter to the editor, *The State*, 6 January 1919. See chap. 6 for a complete discussion of African American reformers' postwar activism.

18. Telegram from R. G. Pleasant to Robert A. Cooper, 26 June 1919, Cooper Papers, SCDAH.

19. *The State*, 26 May 1920.

20. J. S. Hartzell to *The State*, 10 November 1918.

21. Catt and Shuler, *Woman Suffrage and Politics*, 334.

22. *The State*, 11 February 1919.

23. Catt and Shuler, *Woman Suffrage and Politics*, 334.

24. *The State*, 28 May 1919. Pollock's reasoning that three generations took African Americans back to their enslaved ancestors, whose marriages were not legally recognized, explains his peculiar proposal.

25. *The State*, 21 January 1920; E. A. Dunovant to Eulalie Chafee Salley, 1 February 1920, Eulalie Chafee Salley Papers, SCL.

26. For more on Cole Blease, see Burnside, "Governorship of Blease," 216–35; for the most thorough account of the Manning administration's reform

efforts, see Burts, *Manning and the Progressive Movement.* Quotation from entry, 5 September 1920, bk. 5, Ball Diary, Ball Papers, DU.

27. Entry, 9 February 1922, entry, 5 Sept 1920, bk. 5, Ball Diary, Ball Papers, DU.

28. The house adopted the Bradford-Hart concurrent resolution 93–21 to reject the federal amendment on 22 January, and the senate concurred with the resolution 32–4 on January 28. The substantive conflict centered on using a concurrent resolution rather than a joint resolution, which some legislators thought would have permitted more debate on the issue. *The State*, 23, 29 January 1920. Fifty years later, in 1969, the South Carolina legislature symbolically accepted a half-century reality by finally voting to ratify the woman suffrage amendment.

29. Richard Carroll, in a letter to the *Anderson Mail*, 1 October 1920, reported the atmosphere of anticipation but expressed his opposition to political aspiration for African Americans. Clipping in Branch Files, Group II, L267, NAACP Papers, LC.

30. D. B. Brooks to Miss Lealtad, 20 September 1920, pt. 12, Branch Files, series A, The South, NAACP Papers; Pickens, "Woman Voter Hits Color Line," 372–73.

31. Butler Nance to Walter White, 12 September 1920, pt. 12, Branch Files, series A, The South; Pickens, "Woman Voter Hits Color Line," 372–73; D. B. Brooks to Miss Lealtad, 20 September 1920, pt. 12, Branch Files, Series A The South, NAACP Papers.

32. Pickens, "Woman Voter Hits Color Line," 372–73; Brooks to Lealtad; Butler Nance to Moorfield Story, 17 September 1920; William Pickens to Walter White, 10 September 1920, pt. 4, Voting Rights Campaign, NAACP Papers.

33. William Pickens to Walter White, 10 September 1920, pt. 4, Voting Rights Campaign, NAACP Papers; acting secretary of NAACP, "To The Editors" of the New York newspapers, pt. 4, Voting Rights Campaign, NAACP Papers. William Pickens to Butler Nance, 23 September 1920, pt. 12, Branch Files, series A, The South; Butler Nance to James W. Johnson, 17 September 1920, pt. 4, Voting Rights Campaign; Brooks to Lealtad.

34. Niels Christensen to Robert Cooper, 27 October 1920, "Registration," Cooper Papers, SCDAH.

35. Jessie Clayton to Eulalie Chafee Salley, 16 February 1920, Salley Papers, SCL.

9. Funding Reform

1. *Annual Reports*, SCCG, 1915–1919.

2. Seligman, *Essays in Taxation*, 62. South Carolina's tax system is not systematically explained in any one source, but this composite is based on information found in the following: *Annual Reports*, SCTC, 1915–1919; *Annual Report SCCG*, 1915–1919; *Annual Reports*, SCST, 1915–1919. My understanding

of the state's tax policy is also informed by the *Report of the Joint Special Committee on Revenue and Taxation, 1920*, 14 (hereinafter cited as Marion Committee Report 1920) and the "Griffenhagen Report," *The State*, 25 November 1920.

3. *Constitution of the State of South Carolina, 1895*, art. IX, Sec. 6; *Annual Report, SCTC*, 1920; *Annual Reports, SCCG*, 1919–1920. In addition to the property taxes, counties shared some of the proceeds from state license taxes such as the automobile license and hunting and fishing licenses. After 1920, counties collected revenue from another specific property levy, the two-mill highway tax. The highway tax, collected and spent in each county for building and maintaining highways, increased further the mandatory property levy. Additionally, state statute mandated that local school districts collect a dog tax of 50 cents per dog to be used for the district's public schools. Municipalities could also levy municipal license taxes on theatrical shows and businesses. *Annual Report, SCTC*, 1915; *Annual Reports, SCCG*, 1917–19.

4. Seligman, *Essays in Taxation*, 56–62; Seligman wrote the standard text on taxation policy for this period. Benson, "General Property Tax," 31–63; Oliver Lee Barnes, "The Economics of Tax Reform in South Carolina," explores the state's tax system from the perspective of economic theory and how changes in the tax system in this decade affected the tax system of post–World War II South Carolina.

5. Sumner, "History of the Property Tax," 59–74; *Annual Reports, SCTC*, 1916–1918. South Carolina's 1897 income tax was on the following scale: $2,500–5,000 at 1 percent, $5,000–7,500 at 1.5 percent, $7,500–15,000 at 2 percent, $15,000 and over at 3 percent. Seligman, *The Income Tax*, 417; Heyward quotation, see entry, 3 March 1918, bk. 5, W. W. Ball Diary, William Watts Ball Papers, DU. For a history of income tax payments, see *Annual Report, SCCG*, 1917, 37–38.

6. Isaac Edwards, letter to the editor, *The State*, 13 December 1921; Marion Committee Report 1920, 35–40.

7. *Constitution of the State of South Carolina, 1895*, art. III, sec. 29, art. X, sec. 1; Marion Committee Report 1920, 17–20.

8. *Annual Report SCTC*, 1917–1918; Marion Committee Report 1920, 28, 42; Robert A. Cooper to Frederick D. Gardner, 23 March 1920, Robert A. Cooper Papers, SCDAH; final quotation in Marion Committee Report 1920, 25.

9. Every four years property owners accounted for any sale or purchase of real property since the last quadrennial assessment. Law required the reporting of property held on January 1 of any given year as well as all agricultural products on hand on the preceding August 1. Marion Committee Report 1920, 21–24. Theo D. Jervey to *The State*, 25 January 1918.

10. The county auditor served in a supervisory capacity on both boards. Each county had numerous tax districts, primarily townships, and each tax district had a board of assessors appointed by the governor at the recommendation of the county legislative delegation. The board of assessors reviewed the

assessments with the authority to accept, lower, or increase the valuation returned by the taxpayers. "Griffenhagen Report," *The State*, 25, 26 November 1920; Marion Committee Report 1920, 21–34.

11. "Land and the Tax," editorial, *The State*, 2 January 1917; Marion Committee Report 1920, 54–55; *The State*, 23, 28 January, 18 February 1919.

12. Millage is a unit for levying taxation, and one mill equals one-tenth of 1 percent (.001).

13. This comment was made when the state tax collector asked that McColl furnish the "actual value" for an estate. He reminded McColl that actual values should not be confused with assessed values. Treasury Department IRS Columbia to Duncan Donald McColl, 14 February 1923, Duncan Donald McColl Papers, SCL.

14. Marion Committee Report 1920, 53–57; "Griffenhagen Report," *The State*, 25 November 1920.

15. For more on the disfranchising convention of 1895, see Kousser, *Shaping of Southern Politics*; Tindall, *South Carolina Negroes*; Tindall, "Campaign for Disfranchisement," 212–34.

16. Calculations based on data from *Annual Report, SCSSE*, 1920, and U.S. Bureau of the Census, *Fourteenth Census*, 1920, *Population*, vol. 3, 929–33.

17. These inequalities in educational spending became the impetus for the development of a system of direct state assistance for public education to counties with larger numbers of white children. The egregious maldistribution of public revenue for educational spending between white and black schools in counties with African American majorities was possible because white district school boards had complete discretion in distributing county revenue for public schools. Lyles quotation from J. F. Lyles, letter to the editor, *The State*, 11 February 1919; *The State*, 17 February 1922.

18. *Annual Reports SCTC*, 1915–1919; "Griffenhagen Report," *The State*, 25 November 1920.

19. *Annual Report SCTC*; "Griffenhagen Report," *The State*, 25, 26 November 1920; Marion Committee Report 1920, 21–24.

20. "Petitions for Auditor of Hampton County," to Governor Robert A. Cooper, 1921, "Transcripts Re: Hearings on Auditor, Hampton County," 26 April 1921, Cooper Papers, SCDAH.

21. *Annual Reports, SCTC*, 1915–1918.

22. "Griffenhagen Report," *The State*, 25 November 1920; Marion Committee Report 1920, 35–45; *Greenville News*, 7 January 1922; *The State*, 26 November 1920; August Kohn addressed this problem in a speech at the South Carolina Conference of Social Work, at Hartsville, S.C., June 4–6, 1925, printed as a pamphlet, *Taxation in South Carolina Briefly Discussed*, in Edgar Brown Papers, Special Collections, Strom Thurmond Institute, CU. McMahan quotations in "Taxation and the Need for Reform," ca. 1913, John J. McMahan Papers, SCL.

23. Governor Robert A. Cooper's address to the South Carolina Develop-

ment Board, 9 March 1920, printed in *The State*, 10 March 1920; U.S. Bureau of the Census, "Financial Statistics of States, 1919," cited in Reed Smith, *Tax Reform in South Carolina*, 10.

24. *The State*, 26 February 1917; 12 January 1918; 2 November 1919; 4, 23 January 1919; 4 February 1919. Cooper, *Annual Address*, 1919, 1920.

25. *Annual Reports, SCST*, 1917–1919; *The State*, 4 January 1919, 25 November 1920.

10. Taxing Wealth

1. Cooper, *Annual Address*, 1920.

2. *The State*, 6 March 1920. The prominent South Carolinians who met in March 1920 and named their organization the South Carolina Development Board had previously organized themselves under the label South Carolina Landowners Association, which Christensen had also founded and of which he had been president. The connection between the two organizations was not publicized since organizers of the Development Board wanted a broader emphasis than the Landowners Association had acquired. The Landowners Association had been affiliated with the Southern Settlement and Development Organization. The Development Board retained the affiliation with the regional development organization. *South Carolina Landowners Association*, pamphlet, 6 May 1919; Niels Christensen to Robert A. Cooper, 28 February 1920, Robert A. Cooper Papers, SCDAH; *The State*, 10 March 1920.

3. The four representatives were Lanneau D. Lide of Marion, Joseph A. Berry (speaker pro tempore) of Orangeburg, John B. Atkinson of Spartanburg, and Eugene R. Buckingham of Aiken. Christensen was by far the most experienced legislator on the committee, serving his fifteenth consecutive year in the state senate. Berry had served two previous terms in the house; Atkinson had one previous term of experience; and Marion, Lide, and Buckingham were all first-term legislators. Marion Committee Report 1920, 2; *Biographical Dictionary of South Carolina House*, vol. 1, Session List 1673–1973.

4. Marion Committee Report 1920, 78–128.

5. Ibid., 129–31.

6. Ibid., 131.

7. Ibid., 131–35.

8. *The State*, 7 March, 22 April, 25 November 1920; "Griffenhagen Report," *The State*, 26 November 1920; T. W. Howard, Griffenhagen and Associates, Chicago, to Governor Cooper, 1 September 1920, Cooper Papers, SCDAH.

9. "Griffenhagen Report," *The State*, 26 November 1920.

10. *Annual Report SCCACI, 1920*, 28, 38–49, 122; Charles A. Peple to E. W. Dabbs, 1 September 1920, Eugene W. Dabbs Papers, SCL; Bright Williamson to Robert A. Cooper, 11 October 1920; J. S. Wannamaker to Robert A. Cooper, 15 November 1920, Cooper Papers, SCDAH.

11. *The State*, 21 December 1920.

12. This understanding of E. W. Dabbs comes from an examination of the Eugene W. Dabbs Papers; see specifically E. W. Dabbs to Robert M. Cooper, 19 January 1914; E. W. Dabbs to D. R. Coker, 23 July 1920; Clarence Poe to Richard I. Manning, 29 October 1917, Dabbs Papers, SCL.

13. John Hardin Marion to E. W. Dabbs, 21, 26 December 1920, Dabbs Papers, SCL; E. W. Dabbs, letter to the editor, *The State*, 10, 20, 30 December 1920.

14. John L. Rainey to E. W. Dabbs, 29 December 1920, Dabbs Papers, SCL; *The State*, 12 January 1921; "Memorial from Taxpayers," *House Journal, 1921*, 24–25.

15. *The State*, 7 February 1921.

16. Thomas Waring to William Ball, 1 January 1921, Ball Papers, DU. The general assembly passed a joint resolution for a new study on the economy and consolidation. *House Journal, 1921*.

17. Niels Christensen to William Ball, 25 March 1922, enclosing a copy of a letter from Niels Christensen to J. L. Glenn Jr., 24 March 1922, Ball Papers, DU. In these letters Christensen defended his decision to hire Griffenhagen and Associates, whom critics began to call the "Yankee experts," in light of the agricultural crisis and the need for expertise that was otherwise unavailable.

18. Duncan quotation is from a speech at a conference for county officials, *The State*, 22 September 1921. *Report on Economy and Consolidation, 1921*, 7–8.

19. The report estimated that postponing capital improvements would reduce expenditures by approximately $750,000 for 1922, and it predicted a cost savings of $500,000 annually from consolidation of state agencies. The report also suggested consolidation in three areas: state finances, corrections and charitable institutions, and higher education. *Report on Economy and Consolidation 1921*, 7–8.

20. The tax package also included a moderate increase in corporate license fees, a moderate tax on hydroelectric power, and a luxury tax on automobiles, soft drinks, admissions to amusements and exhibits, cigars, and cigarettes. The committee thought the luxury tax was particularly appropriate during a depression. All of these taxes had been proposed in the house during the 1921 session. *Report on Economy and Consolidation 1921*, 26–29.

21. G. Croft Williams to Richard I. Manning, 7 November 1921, Manning Papers, SCL.

22. An executive committee elected at that meeting met 30 December 1921.

23. *The State*, 15, 20 December 1921; *Charleston News and Courier*, 28 July 1921, 25 January 1922; R. Smith, *Tax Reform in South Carolina*, 184–85. Subsequent county meetings were held across the state with legislative delegations beginning 7 January 1922 to secure legislative support for the tax reform package. Some of the overlapping members of the South Carolina Development Board and the Taxpayers Association were Bright Williamson and C. W. Coker, *The State*, 10 March 1920.

24. *Greenville News*, 8, 13 January 1922.

25. *The State*, 11 January 1922; Cooper, *Annual Message*, 11 January 1922.

26. Entry, 24 August 1921, bk. 5, Ball Diary, Ball Papers, DU.

27. Ball recounted a discussion with C. P. Hodges, entry, 25 January 1922, bk. 5, Ball Diary, Ball Papers, DU.

28. For a detailed discussion of the legislative session, see Hudson, "Maintaining White Supremacy," 278–92.

29. *The State*, 8 February 1922.

30. *The State*, 26 January 1922; *Charleston News and Courier*, 26 January 1922.

31. Niels Christensen's brother, Frederik Christensen, conveyed in his diary Niels's frustration with the senate just days before he resigned, entry, 18 February 1922, vol. 13, Frederik Holmes Christensen Diary, SCL.

32. *The State*, 16 February 1922.

33. "Mr. Christensen Resigns," *Senate Journal*, 1922, 541–42; *The State*, 23 February 1922; W. W. Ball to T. R. Waring, March 21, 1922, Ball Papers, DU.

34. Tom Waring commented that it "looks as if Christensen attempted to out demagogue Blease." T. R. Waring to William Ball, 21 March 1922, Ball Papers, DU.

35. Income tax is discussed in *Greenville News*, 19, 28 February; 12, 13 March 1922. Passage of the new taxes, especially the income tax on corporations, led to endless complaints particularly by textile owners about South Carolina's inability to attract capital investment because of the state's excessive tax rate. In 1923, the legislature conducted a special investigation into these complaints about industrial development in South Carolina. The study, which compared South Carolina to Georgia and North Carolina, concluded that South Carolina did not have excessive corporate tax rates. Some thought that taxes were higher because the rates were higher, but the assessments were much lower. *Report of Special Committee on Industrial Investigation*, 1923, 3–13.

36. "Citizen" to *The State*, 24 February 1922.

37. *Charleston News and Courier*, 26 January 1922.

38. John Marion to Theo D. Jervey, 21 September 1921, Ball Papers, DU; Theo D. Jervey to Editor Waring, 10 January 1922, Thomas Waring Papers, SCHS.

39. Editorial, "The Law of the Medes and Persians?" *The State*, 12 February 1921.

40. Quotation from W. F. Milam to The Editor (Personal), 18 August 1922, Ball Papers, DU. See chap. 7 for a complete analysis of the 1922 election.

11. Financing Educational Reform

1. U.S. Bureau of the Census, *Fourteenth Census*, 1920, *Population*, vol. 3, 929; *Annual Report*, SCSSE 1916, 78–80. *Annual Report*, SCSSE 1921, 33–35.

2. Benjamin F. Hubert, letter to the editor, *The State*, 9 February 1920; A. Caldwell, *History of the Negro*, 3:110.

3. *Annual Report, SCSSE*, 1916, 26; *Annual Report, SCSSE*, 1910, 13; U.S. Bureau of the Census, *Thirteenth Census*, 1910, *Population*, 3:658. For more on the inferiority of African American schools, see Anderson, *Education of Blacks*. For a discussion of white North Carolinians' use of local control in education to ensure minimal support for African American schools, see Leloudis, "Schooling and the New South."

4. McMahan's quotation in *Annual Report, SCSSE*, 1900, 12–13. This emphasis on localism, William Link asserts, made the American educational system an anomaly in the western world dominated by the European model of centralization, see W. Link, *Hard Country*, 3–10, quotation on 7. Districts were subdivisions within, and sometimes across, counties that the state constitution stipulated should encompass no fewer than nine square miles and no more than forty-nine square miles. During the early 1920s, South Carolina accommodated 1,936 districts; 52 of these crossed county lines. *South Carolina State Constitution of 1895*, art. XI, sec. 5; *Annual Report, SCSSE*, 1923, 160.

5. For a thorough analysis of educational financing, see Margo, *Race and Schooling*.

6. Enrollment was defined as ten days of attendance per year.

7. Lander, *History of South Carolina*, 122–29; *Annual Report, SCSSE*, 1921, 26–29.

8. U.S. Bureau of Education, *Negro Education*, 2:471.

9. *South Carolina State Constitution of 1895*, art. XI, sec. 2; B. J. Wells, "Mr. Swearingen's Administration"; *South Carolina State Constitution of 1895*, art. XI, sec. 6.

10. *Acts and Joint Resolutions in 1909*, 165.

11. In 1906, Ellwood P. Cubberley published *School Funds and Their Apportionment*, the pioneering study of education finance; see Johns, et al., *Economics and Financing of Education*, 204–6; Mort and Reusser, *Public School Finance*, 379–81.

12. The laws were the Term Extension Act, Rural Graded School Act, Act to Establish and Maintain High Schools, Equalizing Act to Guarantee a Seven Months' Term, and the Law to Relieve Overcrowding in the Elementary Grades of Approved High Schools. Carter, "State Support for Public Schools," 18–21; *Annual Report, SCSSE*, 1923, 209–32.

13. L. Ayres, *Index Number for State School Systems*, 9–15, 43–49.

14. Pell, "Citizens' Educational Association," 3–4; *Spartanburg Herald*, 10, 11, 12, 13 May 1921.

15. Robert Pell to J. Rion McKissick, 12 January 1923; McKissick's handwritten draft of a speech, n.d., J. Rion McKissick Papers, SCL; Robert Pell to Thomas McLeod, 15 November 1923, Governor Thomas G. McLeod Papers, SCDAH; *Annual Report, SCSSE*, 1921, 41.

16. B. L. Parkinson to J. Rion McKissick, 27 September 1923, McKissick Papers, SCL.

17. *Annual Report, SCSSE*, 1923, 27–41.

18. *Annual Report, SCSSE*, 1923, 13–17.

19. This percentage is adjusted for inflation.

20. Based on a survey of the *Annual Reports, SCSSE* from 1909–1923.

21. *Annual Report, SCSSE*, 1921, 61–63; *Annual Report, SCSSE*, 1923, 209–12.

22. *The State*, 13 September 1922. Campaign leaflet by John E. Swearingen, 1922; J. E. Swearingen to H. H. McCarley, 14 September 1922; and J. E. Swearingen to Mrs. J. B. Rasor, 19 September 1922, Swearingen Papers, SCL.

23. John E. Swearingen, *Progress without Extravagance*, n.d.; J. B. Rasor to J. E. Swearingen, 16 September 1922; J. E. Swearingen to J. B. Rasor, 18 September 1922, Swearingen Papers, SCL.

24. *Annual Report, SCSSE*, 1922, 446–47. During the 1920s national theories of financing education had challenged Ellwood P. Cubberley's ideas about rewarding local initiative as a method of equalization. In 1923, George D. Strayer and Robert M. Haig published their theory of state school funding, which influenced thinking on educational finance for the next fifty years. Strayer and Haig argued that reward for effort undermined equalization and that, instead of offering aid to districts that taxed themselves, states should provide every child with some prescribed minimum state offering of education; see Strayer and Haig, *Financing of Education*, iii–iv.

25. Hope, "To the People of South Carolina," 3–4, 9; *Charleston News and Courier*, 19 February 1924.

26. Bethea, *Suggested Plan*, Thomas G. McLeod Papers, SCDAH.

27. Ibid.

28. Power Bethea to Thomas McLeod, 18 October 1923, 8 November 1923, McLeod Papers, SCDAH.

29. Power Bethea to Robert Pell, 13 October 1923, McKissick Papers, SCL; Gibbs, *Legislative Manual*, 79.

30. Power Bethea to Thomas McLeod, 15 October 1923, McLeod Papers, SCDAH.

31. Power Bethea to J. Rion McKissick, 13 October 1923, McKissick Papers, SCL.

32. B. L. Parkinson's editorial in *South Carolina Education*, 15 November 1923, 13; Power Bethea to Governor McLeod, 21 December 1923, McLeod Papers, SCDAH. The counties supporting the plan included Abbeville, Aiken, Allendale, Bamberg, Barnwell, Darlington, Dillon, Dorchester, Fairfield, Florence, Greenville, Hampton, Horry, Lancaster, Lauren, Lexington, Orangeburg, Richland, Saluda, Spartanburg, and Williamsburg. Beaufort and Clarendon counties' boards of education supported the plan but did not hold public meetings.

33. Bethea to McLeod, 21 December 1923.

34. McLeod, *Annual Message*, 8 January 1924; Thomas McLeod to Robert Pell, 20 November 1923; Thomas McLeod to Power Bethea, 10 January 1924, McLeod Papers, SCDAH.

35. Niels Christensen to Governor McLeod, 15 December 1923, McLeod Papers, SCDAH.

36. *Greenwood Index-Journal*, 9, 12, 16 January 1924; *Charleston News and*

Courier, 15 January 1924. The other two issues that required subcommittees were the indirect-taxation proposals and debate about funding for the school for the mentally ill in Clinton.

37. *Charleston News and Courier,* 15 January 1924.

38. Ibid.

39. Bethea to McKissick.

40. *Charleston News and Courier,* 24 January 1924.

12. Legacy of Reform

1. *Greenville News,* 15 February 1924; *Charleston News and Courier,* 12 February 1924; *House Journal,* 1924, 304, 654.

2. *Charleston News and Courier,* 14, 15 February 1924; *The State,* 15 February 1924; *Senate Journal,* 1924, 366.

3. *Dillon Herald,* 3 April 1924; *Charleston News and Courier,* 14 February 1924.

4. E. Kohn, "Dr. Wil Lou Gray," 113–20; Wil Lou Gray to Interested Friends of Education, 18 February 1924, Wil Lou Gray Papers, SCL.

5. Power Bethea to Thomas McLeod, 15 February 1924. Attached to this letter to McLeod were two outlines of Bethea's opinion of the two proposed bills, "Advantages of 4-2-1 Bill" and "Objections to Senate School Bill Which with 3-mill Tax Guarantees a Six Months' Term by the State," McLeod Papers, SCDAH.

6. Bethea to McLeod, 15 February 1924, "Advantages of 4-2-1 Bill," and "Objections to Senate School Bill."

7. Bethea to McLeod, 15 February 1924, "Objections to Senate School Bill."

8. *Senate Journal,* 1924, 485–86; *The State,* 21 February 1924.

9. *The State,* 21, 22 February 1924; *Charleston News and Courier,* 22 February 1924; *Greenville News,* 22 February 1924.

10. *The State,* 7 March 1924; *Greenville News,* 23 March 1924.

11. *Greenville News,* 8, 23 March 1924.

12. "Minutes of the 38th Annual Meeting," 3–4; "Should SC Teachers Support Official Organ," 12–13; "Public School Membership," 29.

13. *Columbia Record,* 14 March 1924; *The State,* 14 March 1924.

14. *Greenville News,* 22, 23 March 1924; *Charleston News and Courier,* 21 March 1924; J. L. Mann, letter to the editor, *Greenville News,* 25 March 1924. In Mann's editorial, published after the 6-0-1 law passed, he conveyed information about his meeting with the joint education committees that had been withheld earlier.

15. *Greenville News,* 24 March 1924; Mann to *Greenville News.*

16. *Greenville News,* 24 March 1924; Mann to *Greenville News.*

17. *Charleston News and Courier,* 14 March 1924; *Greenville News,* 14 March 1924; Mann to *Greenville News;* Robert Pell to J. Rion McKissick, 12 January 1923, J. Rion McKissick Papers, SCL.

18. *Greenwood Index-Journal*, 21 March 1924; Elbert Aull to Thomas McLeod, 21 March 1924, McLeod Papers, SCDAH; *Acts and Joint Resolutions 1924*, 1482–84. Although the general assembly passed the recommendation that McLeod appoint a five-person commission, composed of one teacher and four laypersons, to conduct this survey with a $10,000 appropriation, the committee reasoned that significant alterations in funding education should wait until completion of the survey. Yet the legislature neglected to appropriate the required funds. Following the conclusion of the session McLeod agreed to fund the survey from the state's contingency fund. When the legislature reconvened in 1925, however, McLeod indicated that the survey would not be funded at all. He would not appoint a commission to conduct the survey because the resolution did not permit trustees from either colleges or public schools to serve on the commission.

19. *Charleston News and Courier*, 15 March 1924.

20. *Greenville News*, 22 March 1924; Mann to *Greenville News*; *Charleston News and Courier*, 21 March 1924.

21. Mann to *Greenville News*.

22. J. M. Moorer to Thomas McLeod, 22 March 1924, McLeod Papers, SCDAH.

23. McGarity selected four city supervisors—Richard C. Burts of Rock Hill (chair), W. T. Taylor of Gaffney, O. B. Cannon of Newberry, and A. J. Thackston of Orangeburg—and one county superintendent, H. J. Crouch of Barnwell, to form the committee. *The State*, 15 March 1924.

24. *House Journal* 1924, 1264; *Greenville News*, 22 March 1924; *Charleston News and Courier*, 21 March 1924.

25. *Dillon Herald*, 3 April 1924; *Charleston News and Courier*, 14 February 1924; Morrison, *Equalization of Financial Burden*, acknowledgments, n.p., and, 1–3. Fred Morrison was a student of George Strayer who, along with Robert Haig, developed and promoted the equalization theory. The academics associated with the older theories of matching funds were Ellwood Cubberley and Harlan Updegraff.

26. *House Journal*, 1924, 1282–85; *The State*, 20 March 1924.

27. *House Journal*, 1924, 1284. The five representatives speaking against Harper's motion were William Gray (Laurens), William Peary (Dorchester), David Smith (Colleton), John Lanham (Spartanburg), and Eugene Dabbs (Sumter), but *The State* did not attribute the quotation directly to any member. *The State*, 20 March 1924.

28. *Greenville News*, 22 March 1924; *Charleston News and Courier*, 21 March 1924; *The State*, 20 March 1924; *House Journal*, 1924, 1283–84. The remaining five opponents were James Hanahan (Fairfield), Norman Richards (Kershaw), Arthur Westbrook (Chester), Albert Woods (Marion), and John Evans (Spartanburg).

29. Manuscript Act of the General Assembly, 1924, no. 539, SCDAH; *The State*, 20 March 1924; *House Journal*, 1924, 1284.

30. *Annual Report of the Comptroller General*, 1924, 8–9.

31. *House Journal*, 1924, 1284; Manuscript Act.

32. Manuscript Act.

33. *House Journal*, 1924, 1285. Representatives Eugene Blease of Newberry and Jubal O. Williams of Pickens proposed the amendment; Manuscript Act; *Charleston News and Courier*, 20 March 1924; *Greenville News*, 24 March 1924; R. A. Meares, "An Analysis of '6-0-1' School Law and Its Effect in Fairfield County," McLeod Papers, SCDAH. State superintendent Hope later emphasized in a memo to the county superintendents that, while this clause authorized boards of trustees to set the school term length, no school was to operate less than five months, implying that local school boards' control had limits; James Hope to County Superintendents, 26 June 1924, McLeod Papers, SCDAH.

34. *Charleston News and Courier*, 21 March 1924; *House Journal*, 1924, 1283; *Senate Journal*, 1924, 1174.

35. J. C. Moore to Governor Thomas McLeod, 22 March 1924, McLeod Papers, SCDAH.

36. *Charleston News and Courier*, 21 March 1924.

37. Trustee of Edisto Island to Thomas McLeod, 22 March 1924, McLeod Papers, SCDAH; *Charleston News and Courier*, 24 March 1924.

38. Mann to *Greenville News; Charleston News and Courier*, 26 March 1924.

39. *Charleston News and Courier*, 24 March 1924; Parkinson, "Why SCTA Supports New Law," 12–13.

40. B. F. McLeod to Thomas McLeod, 10 April 1924, McLeod Papers, SCDAH; Jordan, *The Primary State*, 68–69. Blease won the senate seat in 1924, defeating James Byrnes and Nathaniel Dial.

41. Thomas G. McLeod, *Inaugural Address*, 1925, McLeod Papers, SCDAH.

42. *Annual Report*, SCSSE, 1924, 23.

43. W. A. Shealy, "Procedures in Financing Schools," 16–17.

44. *Annual Reports*, SCSSE, 1923–1925.

45. D. L. Lewis, "Division of Rural Schools," 232.

46. *Annual Report*, SCSSE, 1924, 10–12. An exception to this minimum-enrollment standard was offered to areas with low enrollment that could not easily consolidate because of natural barriers, such as mountains, rivers, etc. *The 6-0-1 Law*, 4; *Annual Report*, SCSSE, 1925, 12–14, 20–21.

47. *Annual Reports, Comptroller General*, 1924–1930. See table 4.

48. Ibid. See table 5 for appropriation figures after passage of the 6-0-1 law.

Conclusion

1. Butler Nance to James W. Johnson, 4 July 1922, R. W. Jackson to Mrs. Hunton, 18 May 1923, R. W. Jackson to Robert W. Bagnall, 14 August 1923, pt. 12A, NAACP Papers; clipping from *Charleston Messenger*, "Busy Body on the Inactivity of the Local NAACP," 20 June 1925, Branch Files, G-196, NAACP Papers.

2. A. Caldwell, *History of the Negro*, 267–68. *Light*, 22 August 1925.

3. A. Caldwell, *History of the Negro*, 267–68; quotation on 268. *Light*, 22 August 1925.

4. "Constitution of the South Carolina Constructive League," 29 July 1919, James Heyward Gibbes Papers, SCL.

5. Ibid.

6. In Robertson, *Sly and Able*, 91–94, Robertson argues that the decisive factor in the campaign was an advertisement published only a few days before the election that attempted to play on South Carolinians' anti-Catholic prejudices by reminding voters that Byrnes had been reared Catholic although he had since become an Episcopalian. Just as W. W. Ball speculated, "anyone of a dozen factors account for the result" of the Byrnes upset, but the more egregious political fumble was Nathaniel Dial's refusal, as an anti-Blease candidate, to support Byrnes.

7. William Ball to William Egleston of Hartsville, 12 September 1924, Ball Papers, DU. Organizing against Blease in 1924 also proved more difficult because Ball, one of the anti-Blease coalition's principal political operatives and architect of the coalition's strategy as editor of *The State*, had resigned his influential post at the Columbia newspaper to join the faculty at the University of South Carolina.

8. Woods, "Modjeska Simkins," 99–108; McFadden, "Septima P. Clark," 85–90. See chap. 6 for a full discussion of the NAACP fight for Charleston teachers. Wim Roefs, "Impact of 1940s Civil Rights Activism," argues for a link between these and other 1940s activists and 1960s activism. Other historians of 1940s civil rights activists in South Carolina include Peter Lau, Barbara Woods, and Miles Richards.

9. Woods, "Modjeska Simkins," 108–16; McFadden, "Septima P. Clark," 85–90.

10. Entry, 6 July 1923, bk. 5, Ball Diary, Ball Papers, DU.

11. George B. Cromer, letter to the editor, *The State*, 8 June 1920.

Bibliography

Manuscript Collections

Library of Congress, Washington, D.C.

Papers of the National Association for the Advancement of Colored People

National Archives, Washington, D.C.

U.S. Department of Agriculture: Agricultural Extension Service Records RG 33; Office of the Secretary of Agriculture, RG 16
U.S. Department of Justice, RG 60
U.S. Department of Labor: Division of Negro Economics, RG 174; General Records, RG 174; Women's Bureau, RG 86

Perkins Library, Duke University, Durham, N.C.

William Watts Ball Papers
Nathaniel Barksdale Dial Papers
Hemphill Family Papers

South Carolina Department of Archives and History, Columbia

Governor Robert A. Cooper Papers
Governor Wilson Harvey Papers
Governor Thomas G. McLeod Papers
Governor John G. Richards Papers
Manuscript Act of the General Assembly, 1924, 539

South Carolina Historical Society, Charleston

Charleston News and Courier Papers
Turner Logan Papers
Thomas Waring Sr. Papers

South Caroliniana Library, University of South Carolina, Columbia

Richard Carroll Papers
Frederik Holmes Christensen Diary
David R. Coker Papers
Eugene W. Dabbs Papers
James Heyward Gibbs Papers
Wil Lou Gray Papers
James A. Hoyt Papers
I. S. Leevy Papers
Richard Irvine Manning Papers
Duncan Donald McColl Papers
J. Rion McKissick Papers
John Joseph McMahan Papers
Fitz Hugh McMaster Papers
James Henry Rice Jr. Papers
Eulalie Chafee Salley Papers
Mendel L. Smith Papers
Modern Political Collections: Modjeska M. Simkins Papers
William W. Smoak Papers
John Eldred Swearingen Papers
Harry Watson Papers

Southern Historical Collection, University of North Carolina, Chapel Hill

Samuel Chiles Mitchell Papers
William F. Stevenson Papers
Daniel A. Tompkins Papers
John Thomas Woodside Autobiography

Strom Thurmond Institute, Clemson University, Clemson, South Carolina

Edgar Brown Papers
James F. Byrnes Papers
Clifton Manufacturing Records
Cooperative Extension Service Field Operations
A. Frank Lever Papers

Manuscript Collections on Microfilm

Kornweibel, Theodore, Jr., ed. *Federal Surveillance of Afro-Americans (1917–1924): The First World War, the Red Scare, and the Garvey Movement*

Papers of the National Association of the Advancement of Colored People
(NAACP Papers)
Booker T. Washington Papers

Government Documents

Acts and Joint Resolutions of the General Assembly of the State of South Carolina.
Columbia, S.C.: Gonzales and Bryan, State Printers, 1909, 1912,
1916–1926.

"Annual Report of John L. McLaurin State Warehouse Commissioner to the
General Assembly of South Carolina, 1916." *Reports and Resolutions of the
General Assembly of the State of South Carolina.* Columbia, S.C.: Gonzales
and Bryan, 1916.

*Annual Report of the Attorney General to the General Assembly of the State of South
Carolina.* Columbia, S.C.: Gonzales and Bryan, 1917.

*Annual Report of the Commissioner of Agriculture, Commerce, and Industries of the State
of South Carolina.* Columbia, S.C.: Gonzales and Bryan, 1917–1919.

Annual Report of the Comptroller General of South Carolina to the General Assembly.
Columbia, S.C.: Gonzales and Bryan, State Printers, 1910–1926.

*Annual Report of the South Carolina Commissioner of Agriculture, Commerce, and
Industry, Labor Division, to the General Assembly of the State of South Carolina.*
Columbia, S.C.: Gonzales and Bryan, 1919–1921.

*Annual Reports of the South Carolina Tax Commission to the General Assembly of the
State of South Carolina.* Columbia, S.C.: Gonzales and Bryan, State Printers, 1915–1919.

Annual Report of the State Superintendent of Education of the State of South Carolina.
Columbia, S.C.: Gonzales and Bryan, State Printers, 1900, 1909–1926.

*Annual Report of the State Treasurer to the General Assembly of the State of South
Carolina,* Columbia, S.C.: Gonzales and Bryan, State Printers, 1915–1919.

"Fourth Annual Report of the State Board of Charities and Corrections, 1918."
Reports and Resolutions of the General Assembly of the State of South Carolina.
Columbia, S.C.: Gonzales and Bryan, 1919.

*Journal of the House of Representative of the General Assembly of the State of South
Carolina.* Columbia, S.C.: Gonzales and Bryan, State Printers, 1916–1926.

Journal of the Senate of the General Assembly of the State of South Carolina. Columbia, S.C.: Gonzales and Bryan, State Printers, 1916–26.

"Report of Pardons, Paroles and Commutations, 1916." *Reports and Resolutions
of the General Assembly of the State of South Carolina.* Columbia, S.C.: Gonzales and Bryan, 1917.

"Report of the Directors and Superintendent of the South Carolina State
Penitentiary, 1917." *Reports and Resolutions of the General Assembly of the State
of South Carolina.* Columbia, S.C.: Gonzales and Bryan, 1918.

*Report of the Joint Committee on Economy and Consolidation, Submitted to the
Regular Session 1921.* Columbia, S.C.: Gonzales and Bryan, 1922.

Report of the Joint Special Committee on Revenue and Taxation: Appointed by the General Assembly Session of 1920. Columbia, S.C.: Gonzales and Bryan, 1921.

Report of the Special Committee on Industrial Investigation, 1923. Columbia, S.C.: Gonzales and Bryan, 1924.

"Third Annual Report of the State Board of Charities and Corrections, 1917." *Reports and Resolutions of the General Assembly of the State of South Carolina.* Columbia, S.C.: Gonzales and Bryan, 1918.

U.S. Bureau of Education. *Negro Education: A Study of the Private and Higher Schools for Colored People in the United States.* Bulletins 38 and 39. Washington, D.C.: GPO, 1917.

U.S. Bureau of the Census. *Fourteenth Census of the United States Taken in the Year 1920.* Vol. 6, *Agriculture.* Washington, D.C.: GPO, 1922.

————. *Fourteenth Census of the United States Taken in the Year 1920.* Vols. 1 and 3, *Population.* Washington, D.C.: GPO, 1922.

————. *Fourteenth Census of the United States Taken in the Year 1920.* Vol. 4, *Occupations.* Washington, D.C.: GPO, 1922.

————. *Historical Statistics of the United States, Colonial Times to 1970.* 2 vols. Washington, D.C.: GPO, 1975.

————. *Report on Population of the United States in the Eleventh Census, 1890.* Washington, D.C.: GPO, 1897, pts. 1 and 2.

————. *Thirteenth Census of the United States Taken in the Year 1910.* Vol. 2, *Population.* Washington, D.C.: GPO, 1913.

————. *Wealth, Debt, and Taxation,* 1913. Washington, D.C.: GPO, 1914.

U.S. Congress. *Congressional Record,* 57th Cong., 2nd sess., 24 February 1903.

————. *Congressional Record,* 66th Cong., 1st sess., 25 August 1919.

U.S. Department of Labor. Division of Negro Economics. *The Negro at Work during the World War and Reconstruction.* Washington, D.C.: GPO, 1919.

————. Division of Negro Economics. *Negro Migration in 1916–17.* Washington, D.C.: GPO, 1919.

U.S. Senate. *Hearings before the Committee on Military Affairs.* 65th Cong., 2nd sess., 10–18 June 1918.

Published Pamphlets, Speeches, and Miscellaneous Documents

Bethea, Power W. *Suggested Plan for Financing the State School System.* Columbia, S.C.: State Department of Education, 1923.

Cooper, Roberts A. *Annual Address of Governor Robert A. Cooper, to the General Assembly of South Carolina 1919.* Columbia: Gonzales and Bryan, 1919.

————. *Annual Address of Governor Robert A. Cooper, to the General Assembly of South Carolina 1920.* Columbia, S.C.: Gonzales and Bryan, 1920.

————. *Annual Message of Governor Robert A. Cooper, to the General Assembly of South Carolina, 11 January 1921.* Columbia, S.C.: Gonzales and Bryan, 1921.

Farmer, Jim. "Eulalie Salley and the South Carolina Woman Suffrage Campaign." Photocopy, in author's possession.

Bibliography

Fort Jackson Museum. "1917." Chap. 1 in *History of Fort Jackson*. http://www
.jackson.army.mil/Museum/History/CHAPTER%20I.html.

Gibbs, J. Wilson. *Legislative Manual of the 75th General Assembly of South Carolina*. Columbia, S.C.: State Printers, 1924.

Hart, Hastings H. *The War Program of the State of South Carolina: A Report*. New York: Russell Sage Foundation, February 1918.

Manning, Richard I. *Annual Message of Governor Richard I. Manning to the General Assembly of South Carolina, 9 January 1917*. Columbia: Gonzales and Bryan, 1917.

McLeod, Thomas G. *Annual Message of Thomas G. McLeod to the General Assembly of South Carolina*. Columbia, S.C.: Gonzales and Bryan, 8 January 1924.

———. *Inaugural Address of Thomas G. McLeod to the General Assembly of South Carolina*. Columbia, S.C.: Gonzales and Bryan, 13 January 1925.

Meares, R. A. "An Analysis of '6-0-1' School Law and Its Effect in Fairfield County." Pamphlet. McLeod Papers, South Carolina Department of Archives and History. Columbia, S.C.

The 6-0-1 Law. Columbia, S.C.: State Department of Education, 1924.

Smith, Reed. *Tax Reform in South Carolina*. Bulletin of the University of South Carolina 101. Columbia: Gonzales and Bryan, 1921.

South Carolina Development Board. "Some Notes on the South Carolina Development Board." Ca. 1920.

South Carolina Federation of Colored Women's Clubs. *Fortieth Anniversary of the South Carolina Federation of Colored Women's Clubs, 1909–1949*.

Swearingen, J. E. "J. E. Swearingen Candidate for State Superintendent of Education." Columbia, S.C.: Sloane Printing, n.d.

———. "Progress without Extravagance." Columbia, S.C.: Allied Printing, n.d.

Books, Articles, Dissertations, and Theses

Alston, Lee J., and Robert Higgs. "Contractual Mix in Southern Agriculture since the Civil War." *Journal of Economic History* 42 (1982):327–53.

Anderson, James D. *The Education of Blacks in the South, 1860–1935*. Chapel Hill: University of North Carolina Press, 1988.

———. "Northern Foundations and the Shaping of Southern Black Rural Education, 1902–1935." *History of Education Quarterly* 19 (1978):371–96.

Arnesen, Eric. "Whiteness and the Historians' Imagination." *International Labor and Working Class History* 60 (Fall 2001): 3–32.

Ayers, Edward L. *Promise of the New South: Life after Reconstruction*. New York: Oxford University Press, 1992.

Ayres, Leonard P. *An Index Number for State School Systems*. New York: Russell Sage Foundation, 1920.

Bailey, N. Louise, Mary L. Morgan, and Carolyn R. Taylor, eds. *Biographical Directory of the South Carolina Senate 1776–1985*. Vol. 2. Columbia: University of South Carolina Press, 1986.

Ball, Edward. *The Sweet Hell Inside: The Rise of an Elite Black Family in the Segregated South.* New York: Perennial, 2001.

Barbeau, Arthur E., and Florette Henri. *The Unknown Soldiers: Black American Troops in World War I.* Philadelphia: Temple University Press, 1974.

Barnes, Oliver Lee. "The Economics of Tax Reform in South Carolina during the Decade 1920–1930." M.A. thesis, University of South Carolina, 1948.

Beardsley, Edward H. "Allied against Sin: American and British Responses to Venereal Disease In World War I." *Medical History* 1976 (20):189–202.

———. *A History of Neglect: Health Care for Blacks and Mill Workers in the Twentieth-Century South.* Knoxville: University of Tennessee Press, 1987.

Benson, Sumner. "A History of the General Property Tax." In *The American Property Tax: Its History, Administration, and Economic Impact.* Claremont, Calif.: Institute for Studies in Federalism and Lincoln School of Public Finance, 1965.

Biographical Dictionary of the South Carolina House of Representatives. Vol. 1, *Session List 1673–1973.* Columbia: University of South Carolina Press, 1974.

Bland, Sidney R. "Fighting the Odds: Militant Suffragists in South Carolina." *South Carolina Historical Magazine,* January 1981, 32–43.

Boggs, Doyle W. "John P. Grace and the Politics of Reform in South Carolina, 1900–1931." Ph.D. diss., University of South Carolina, 1977.

Boris, Joseph J., ed. *Who's Who in Colored America: A Biographical Dictionary of Notable Living Persons of African Descent in America.* New York: Who's Who in Colored America, 1927.

Brice, James Taylor. "The Use of Executive Clemency under Coleman Livingston Blease, Governor of South Carolina, 1911–1915." M.A. thesis, University of South Carolina, 1965.

Brundage, W. Fitzhugh. *Lynching in the New South: Georgia and Virginia, 1880–1930.* Urbana: University of Illinois Press, 1993.

Burke, W. Lewis, and William C. Hine. "The South Carolina State College Law School: Its Roots, Creation, and Legacy." In *Matthew J. Perry: The Man, His Times, and His Legacy,* edited by W. Lewis Burke and Belinda F. Gergel, 17–60. Columbia: University of South Carolina Press, 2004.

Burnside, Ronald D. "The Governorship of Coleman Livingston Blease of South Carolina, 1911–15." Ph.D. diss., Indiana University, 1963.

Burts, Robert Milton. *Richard Irvine Manning and the Progressive Movement in South Carolina.* Columbia: University of South Carolina Press, 1974.

Busbee, Cyril B. "Farm Tenancy in South Carolina." M.A. thesis, University of South Carolina, 1938.

Butts, R. Freeman, and Lawrence A. Cremin. *A History of Education in American Culture.* New York: Holt, Rinehart and Winston, 1953.

Caldwell, Arthur Bunyan. *The History of the Negro and His Institutions.* Vol. 3, *South Carolina.* Atlanta: Caldwell Publishing, 1919.

Caldwell, Joe Lewis. "Any Place But Here: Kansas Fever in Northeast Louisiana." *North Louisiana Historical Association Journal* 21 (1990):51–70.

Bibliography

"Calvin Coolidge." *South Carolina Education*, 15 October 1923, 12.

Campbell, Kenneth. "Starkly Different Views: A Historical Examination of Letters to the Editor Responding to the Lynching of Three Blacks in Aiken, S.C., 1926." Minorities and Communication Division, Association for Education in Journalism and Mass Communications Annual Convention, Miami Beach, Florida, August 2002. http://list.msu.edu/cgi-bin/wa?A2=in d0209c&L=aejmc&P=2693.

Cann, Mary Katherine Davis. "The Morning After: South Carolina in the Jazz Age." Ph.D. diss., University of South Carolina, 1984.

Carlton, David L. *Mill and Town in South Carolina, 1880–1920*. Baton Rouge, LA: Louisiana State University Press, 1982.

Carter, Wingard. "State Support for Public Schools in South Carolina Since 1895." M.A. thesis, University of South Carolina, 1936.

Catt, Carrie Chapman, and Nettie Rogers Shuler. *Woman Suffrage and Politics: The Inner Story of the Suffrage Movement*. New York: Charles Scribner's Sons, 1923.

Cell, John W. *The Highest Stage of White Supremacy: The Origins of Segregation in South Africa and the American South*. New York: Cambridge University Press, 1982.

Chambers, John Whiteclay, II. *To Raise an Army: The Draft Comes to Modern America*. New York: Free Press, 1987.

Coclanis, Peter A. "David R. Coker, Pedigreed Seeds, and the Limits of Agribusiness in Early Twentieth-Century South Carolina." *Business and Economic History* 28 (Fall 1999): 105–14.

Cohen, William. "The Great Migration as a Lever for Social Change." In *Black Exodus: The Great Migration from the American South*, edited by Alferdteen Harrison, 72–82. Jackson: University Press of Mississippi, 1991.

"Colored Teachers in Charleston Schools," *Crisis*, June 1921, 58–60.

Cooper, William J., Jr. *The Conservative Regime: South Carolina, 1877–1890*. Baltimore: Johns Hopkins University Press, 1968.

Cortner, Richard C. *A Mob Intent on Death: The NAACP and the Arkansas Riot Cases*. Middletown, Conn.: Wesleyan University Press, 1988.

Crawford, Vicki L., Jacqueline Anne Rouse, and Barbara Woods, eds. *Women in the Civil Rights Movement: Trailblazers and Torchbearers, 1941–1965*. Bloomington: Indiana University Press, 1993.

Cripps, Thomas R. "The Reaction of the Negro to the Motion Picture *Birth of a Nation*." *Historian* 25 (1963):344–62.

Dailey, Jane, Glenda Gilmore, and Bryant Simon, eds. *Jumpin' Jim Crow: Southern Politics from the Civil War to Civil Rights*. Princeton, N.J.: Princeton University Press, 2000.

Daniel, Pete. *Breaking the Land: The Transformation of Cotton, Tobacco, and Rice Cultures since 1880*. Urbana: University of Illinois Press, 1985.

DeSantis, Alan. "Selling the American Dream Myth to Black Southerners: The *Chicago Defender* and the Great Migration of 1915–1919." *Western Journal of Communication* 62 (Fall 1998): 474–511.

Devlin, George Alfred. "South Carolina and Black Migration 1865–1930: In Search of the Promised Land." Ph.D. diss., University of South Carolina, 1984.

Dittmer, John. *Black Georgia in the Progressive Era, 1900–1920.* Urbana: University of Illinois, 1977.

Drago, Edmund L. *Initiative, Paternalism, and Race Relations: Charleston's Avery Normal Institute.* Athens: University of Georgia Press, 1990.

DuBois, W. E. B. "Close Ranks." *Crisis*, July 1918, 111.

———. "Returning Soldiers." *Crisis*, May 1919, 13–14.

DuBow, Saul. *Racial Segregation and the Origins of Apartheid in South Africa, 1919–36.* London: Macmillan, 1989.

Duffy, John Joseph. "Charleston Politics in the Progressive Era." Ph.D. diss., University of South Carolina, 1963.

Edgar, Walter. *South Carolina: A History.* Columbia: University of South Carolina Press, 1998.

Egerton, John. *Speak Now against the Day: The Generation before the Civil Rights Movement in the South.* New York: Alfred A. Knopf, 1994.

Ellis, Mark. "'Closing Ranks' and 'Seeking Honors': W. E. B. DuBois in World War I." *Journal of American History* 79 (June 1992): 96–124.

———. *Race, War, and Surveillance: African Americans and the United States Government during World War I.* Bloomington: Indiana University Press, 2001.

Everett, Robert Burke. "Race Relations in South Carolina, 1900–1932." Ph.D. diss., University of Georgia, 1969.

Farewell, Robert H. *Woodrow Wilson and World War I, 1917–1921.* New York: Harper and Row, 1985.

Fields, Barbara. "Ideology and Race in American History." In *Region, Race and Reconstruction: Essays in Honor of C. Vann Woodward*, edited by J. Morgan Kousser and James M. McPherson, 143–77. New York: Oxford University Press, 1982.

Fields, Mamie Garvin, with Karen Fields. *Lemon Swamp and Other Places: A Carolina Memoir.* New York: Free Press, 1983.

Finnegan, Terence. "'At the hands of Parties Unknown': Lynching in Mississippi and South Carolina, 1881–1940." Ph.D. diss., University of Illinois, 1993.

———. "'The Equal of Some White Men and the Superior of Others': Racial Hegemony and the 1916 Lynching of Anthony Crawford in Abbeville County, South Carolina." *Proceedings of the South Carolina Historical Association 1994*, 54–60.

Fite, Gilbert. *Cotton Fields No More: Southern Agriculture, 1865–1980.* Lexington: University Press of Kentucky, 1984.

Fligstein, Neil. *Going North: Migration of Blacks and Whites from the South, 1900–1950.* New York: Academic Press, 1981.

Foner, Eric. *Free Soil, Free Labor, Free Men: The Ideology of the Republican Party before the Civil War.* New York: Oxford University Press, 1970.

———. *Reconstruction: America's Unfinished Revolution, 1863–1877*. New York: Harper and Row, 1988.

Ford, Lacy K., Jr. *Origins of Southern Radicalism: The South Carolina Upcountry, 1800–1860*. New York: Oxford University Press, 1988.

———. "Rednecks and Merchants: Economic Development and Social Tensions in the South Carolina Upcountry, 1865–1900." *Journal of American History* 71 (September 1984): 294–318.

Franklin, John Hope. *From Slavery to Freedom: A History of Negro Americans*. 3rd ed. New York: Alfred A. Knopf, 1967.

Fraser, Walter J., Jr. *Charleston! Charleston! The History of a South Carolina City*. Columbia: University of South Carolina Press, 1989.

Fredrickson, George M. *The Black Image in the White Mind: The Debate on Afro-American Character and Destiny, 1817–1914*. New York: Harper and Row, 1971.

———. *Racism: A Short History*. Princeton, N.J.: Princeton University Press, 2002.

———. "Social Origins of American Racism." In *The Arrogance of Race: Historical Perspectives on Slavery, Racism, and Social Inequality*, edited by George M. Fredrickson, 189–205. Middletown, Conn.: Wesleyan University Press, 1988.

———. *White Supremacy: A Comparative Study in American and South African History*. New York: Oxford University Press, 1981.

Fultz, Michael. "Charleston, 1919–1920: The Final Battle in the Emergence of the South's Urban African American Teaching Corps." *Journal of Urban History* 27 (July 2001): 604–32.

Gaines, Kevin K. *Uplifting the Race: Black Leadership, Politics, and Culture in the Twentieth Century*. Chapel Hill: University of North Carolina Press, 1996.

Galloway-Wright, Brenda. "Matilda Arabella Evans." In *Black Women in America: An Historical Encyclopedia*, edited by Darlene Clark Hine, Elsa Barkley Brown, and Rosalyn Terborg-Penn, 2:401–2. Bloomington: Indiana University Press, 1994.

Garris, Susan Page. "The Decline of Lynching in South Carolina, 1915–1947." M.A. thesis, University of South Carolina, 1973.

Geertz, Clifford. "Ideology as a Cultural System." In *Ideology and Discontent*, edited by David E. Apter, 47–76. London: Free Press of Glencoe, 1964.

Genovese, Eugene D. *Roll, Jordan, Roll: The World the Slaves Made*. New York: Vintage, 1974.

Gilmore, Glenda. *Gender and Jim Crow: Women and the Politics of White Supremacy in North Carolina, 1896–1920*. Chapel Hill: University of North Carolina Press, 1996.

Goldfield, David R. *Cottonfields and Skyscrapers: Southern City and Region, 1607–1980*. Baton Rouge: Louisiana State University, 1982.

———. "The Urban South: A Regional Framework." *American Historical Review* 86 (December 1981): 1009–34.

Goodwin, E. Marvin. *Black Migration in America from 1915 to 1960: An Uneasy Exodus*. Lewiston, N.Y.: E. Mellen Press, 1990.

Goodwyn, Lawrence. *Democratic Promise: The Populist Movement in America*. New York: Oxford University Press, 1976.

Gordon, Asa H. *Sketches of Negro Life and History in South Carolina*. 2nd ed. Columbia: University of South Carolina Press, 1971.

Grantham, Dewey. "Contours of Southern Progressives." *American Historical Review* 86 (December 1981): 1035–59.

———. *Southern Progressivism: The Reconciliation of Progress and Tradition*. Knoxville: University of Tennessee Press, 1983.

Green, Elna C. *Southern Strategies: Southern Women and the Woman Suffrage Question*. Chapel Hill: University of North Carolina Press, 1997.

Greenwood, Janette Thomas. *Bittersweet Legacy: The Black and White "Better Class" in Charlotte, 1850–1910*. Chapel Hill: University of North Carolina Press, 1994.

Grossman, James R. *Land of Hope: Chicago, Black Southerners, and the Great Migration*. Chicago: University of Chicago Press, 1989.

———. "The White Man's Union: The Great Migration and the Resonance of Race and Class in Chicago, 1916–1922." In *The Great Migration in Historical Perspective: New Dimensions of Race, Class, and Gender*, edited by Joe William Trotter Jr., 83–105. Bloomington: Indiana University Press, 1991.

Hahn, Steven. *A Nation under Our Feet: Black Political Struggles in the Rural South from Slavery to the Great Migration*. Cambridge, Mass.: Harvard University Press, 2003.

Hale, Grace Elizabeth. *Making Whiteness: The Culture of Segregation in the South, 1890–1940*. New York: Pantheon Books, 1998.

Hall, Jacquelyn Dowd. *Revolt against Chivalry: Jessie Daniel Ames and the Women's Campaign against Lynching*. New York: Columbia University Press, 1979.

Hall, Jacquelyn Dowd., et al. *Like a Family: The Making of a Southern Cotton Mill World*. Chapel Hill: University of North Carolina Press, 1987.

Harlan, Louis R. *Separate and Unequal: Public School Campaigns and Racism in the Southern Seaboard States, 1901–1915*. Chapel Hill: University of North Carolina Press, 1958.

Harris, J. William. *Deep Souths: Delta, Piedmont, and Sea Island Society in the Age of Segregation*. Baltimore: Johns Hopkins University Press, 2001.

Harris, Thomas E. *Analysis of the Clash over the Issues between Booker T. Washington and W. E. B. DuBois*. New York: Garland, 1993.

Harrison, Alferdteen, ed. *Black Exodus: The Great Migration from the American South*. Jackson: University Press of Mississippi, 1991.

Hawes, Robert, ed. *The Age of Segregation: Race Relations in the South, 1890–1945*. Jackson: University Press of Mississippi, 1978.

Haynes, George. "Negroes Move North: I. Their Departure from the South." *Survey*, 4 May 1918, 115–22.

Haynes, Robert V. *A Night of Violence: The Houston Riot of 1917*. Baton Rouge: Louisiana State University, 1976.

Bibliography

Hemmingway, Theodore. "Beneath the Yoke of Bondage: A History of Black Folks in South Carolina, 1900–1940." Ph.D. diss., University of South Carolina, 1976.

———. "Prelude to Change: Black Carolinians in the War Years, 1914–1920." *Journal of Negro History* 65 (Summer 1980): 212–27.

Henri, Florette. *Black Migration: Movement North 1900–1920.* Garden City, N.Y.: Anchor Press, 1975.

Herndon, Eliza. "Woman Suffrage in South Carolina, 1872–1920." M.A. thesis, University of South Carolina, 1953.

Hewitt, Nancy. *Southern Discomfort: Women's Activism in South Florida, 1880s–1920s.* Urbana: University of Illinois Press, 2001.

Heywood, Chester D. *Negro Combat Troops in the World War: The Story of the 371st Infantry.* Worcester, Mass.: Commonwealth Press, 1928.

Hickel, K. Walter. "War, Region, and Social Welfare: Federal Aid to Servicemen's Dependents in the South, 1917–1921." *Journal of American History* 87 (March 2001): 1362–91.

Hine, Darlene Clark. "The Corporeal and the Ocular Veil: Dr. Matilda A. Evans (1872–1935) and the Complexity of Southern History." *Journal of Southern History* 70 (February 2004): 3–35.

Hine, Darlene Clark, Elsa Barkley Brown, and Rosalyn Terborg-Penn, eds. *Black Women in America: An Historical Encyclopedia.* 2 vols. Bloomington: Indiana University Press, 1994.

History of the Bar of Richland County 1790–1948. Columbia, S.C.: Sloane Printing, 1948.

Holden, Charles J. *In the Great Maelstrom: Conservatives in Post–Civil War South Carolina.* Columbia: University of South Carolina Press, 2002.

Hollis, Daniel W. "Cole Blease: The Years Between the Governorship and the Senate, 1915–1924." *South Carolina Historical Magazine,* January 1979, 1–17.

———. "Cole L. Blease and the Senatorial Campaign of 1924." *Proceedings of the South Carolina Historical Association 1978,* 53–68.

Holt, Thomas. *Black over White: Negro Political Leadership in South Carolina during Reconstruction.* Urbana: University of Illinois, 1977.

Hope, James H. "To the People of South Carolina." *South Carolina Education,* 15 January 1923, 3–4, 9.

Houston, Charles H. "Need for Negro Lawyers." *Journal of Negro Education* 4 (January 1935): 49–52.

Hudson, Janet. "From Constitution to Constitution, 1868–1895: South Carolina's Unique Stance on Divorce." *South Carolina Historical Magazine,* January 1997, 75–96.

———. "Maintaining White Supremacy: Race, Class, and Reform in South Carolina, 1917–1924." Ph.D. diss., University of South Carolina, 1996.

———. "South Carolina's 6-0-1 Law of 1924: A Study of Educational Reform." M.A. thesis, University of South Carolina, 1992.

Hunter, Tera W. *To 'Joy My Freedom: Southern Black Women's Lives and Labors after the Civil War.* Cambridge, Mass.: Harvard University Press, 1998.

Ignatiev, Noel. *How the Irish Became White*. New York, Routledge, 1995.

Jaynes, Gerald David. *Branches without Roots: Genesis of the Black Working Class in the American South, 1862–1881*. New York: Oxford University Press, 1987.

Jenkins, Barbara Williams. "Marion Birnie Wilkinson." In *Notable Black American Women*, edited by Jessie Carney Smith, 2:710–12. New York: Gale Research, 1996.

Johns, Roe L., Edgar L. Morphet, and Kern Alexander. *The Economics and Financing of Education*. 4th ed. Englewood Cliffs, N.J.: Prentice-Hall, 1983.

Johnson, Charles S. "How Much Is the Migration a Flight from Persecution?" *Opportunity* 1 (1923):272–74.

———. "The Negro Migration: An Economic Interpretation." *Modern Quarterly* 2 (1925):314–26.

Johnson, Christopher Leevy. "Undertakings: The Politics of African-American Funeral Directing." Ph.D. diss., University of South Carolina, 2004.

Johnson, Guion Griffin. "Ideology of White Supremacy." In *Essays in Southern History Presented to Joseph Gregoire de Roulhac Hamilton*, edited by Fletcher Green, 194–256. Chapel Hill: University of North Carolina Press, 1949.

Johnson, Joan Marie. *Southern Ladies, New Women: Race, Region, and Clubwomen in South Carolina, 1890–1930*. Gainesville: University Press of Florida, 2004.

Jones, Lewis P. *South Carolina: A Synoptic History for Laymen*. Columbia, S.C.: Sandlapper Press, 1971.

Jordan, Frank E., Jr. *The Primary State: The Story of the Democratic Party in South Carolina 1876–1962*. N.p., n.d.

Kantrowitz, Stephen. *Ben Tillman and the Reconstruction of White Supremacy*. Chapel Hill: University of North Carolina Press, 2000.

Keith, Jeanette. *Rich Man's War, Poor Man's Fight: Race, Class, and Power in the Rural South during the First World War*. Chapel Hill: University of North Carolina Press, 2005.

Kellogg, Charles Flint. *NAACP: A History of the National Association for the Advancement of Colored People*. Baltimore: Johns Hopkins University Press, 1967.

Kennedy, David M. *Over Here: The First World War and American Society*. New York: Oxford University Press, 1980.

Key, V. O. *Southern Politics in State and Nation*. New York: Alfred A. Knopf, 1949.

Kirby, Jack Temple. *Darkness at the Dawning: Race and Reform in the Progressive South*. Philadelphia: J. B. Lippincott, 1972.

———. *Rural Worlds Lost: The American South, 1920–1960*. Baton Rouge: Louisiana State University Press, 1987.

Kohn, August. *The Cotton Mills of South Carolina*. 1907. Reprint, Spartanburg: Reprint Co., 1975.

Kohn, Erin Spence. "Dr. Wil Lou Gray." *South Carolina's Distinguished Women of Laurens County*. Columbia, S.C.: R. L. Bryan, 1972.

Bibliography

Kornweibel, Theodore, Jr. *"Investigate Everything": Federal Efforts to Compel Black Loyalty during World War I.* Bloomington: Indiana University Press, 2002.

Kousser, J. Morgan. "Progressivism—For Middle-Class Whites Only: North Carolina Education, 1880–1910." *Journal of Southern History* 46 (May 1980): 169–94.

———. *The Shaping of Southern Politics: Suffrage Restrictions and the Establishment of the One-Party South, 1880–1910.* New Haven, Conn.: Yale University Press, 1974.

Kraditor, Aileen S. *The Ideas of the Woman Suffrage Movement, 1890–1920.* Garden City, N.Y.: Doubleday, 1971.

Krawczynski, Keith. "World War I." In *A Historic Context for the African American Military Experience,* edited by Steven D. Smith and James A. Ziedler. Champaign, Ill.: U.S. Army Corps of Engineers, Construction Engineering Research Laboratories, 1998.

Lamon, Lester C. "(Document) W. T. Andrews Explains the Causes of Black Migration from the South." *Journal of Negro History,* 63 (October 1978): 365–72.

Lander, Ernest M., Jr. *The History of South Carolina 1865–1960.* Chapel Hill: University of North Carolina Press, 1960.

Lau, Peter F. *Democracy Rising: South Carolina and the Fight for Black Equality since 1865.* Lexington: University Press of Kentucky, 2006.

Lebsock, Suzanne. "Woman Suffrage and White Supremacy: A Virginia Case Study." In *Visible Women: New Essays on American Activism,* edited by Nancy A. Hewitt and Suzanne Lebsock, 62–100. Urbana: University of Illinois Press, 1993.

Leloudis, James L. "Schooling and the New South: Pedagogy, Self, and Society in North Carolina, 1880–1920." *Historical Studies in Education* (1993): 202–29.

Lemann, Nicholas. *The Promised Land: The Great Black Migration and How It Changed America.* New York: Alfred A. Knopf, 1991.

Lewis, D. L. "Division of Rural Schools." *South Carolina Education,* 7 March 1926, 232.

Lewis, David Levering. *W. E. B. DuBois: Biography of a Race 1868–1919.* New York: Henry Holt, 1993.

Link, Arthur S. "What Happened to the Progressive Movement in the 1920s?" *American Historical Review* 64 (July 1959): 833–51.

Link, William A. *A Hard Country and a Lonely Place: Schooling, Society, and Reform in Rural Virginia, 1870–1920.* Chapel Hill: University of North Carolina Press, 1986.

———. *Paradox of Southern Progressivism, 1880–1930.* Chapel Hill: University of North Carolina Press, 1992.

Litwack, Leon. *Trouble in Mind: Black Southerners in the Age of Jim Crow.* New York: Alfred A. Knopf, 1998.

Lupold, John Samuel. "The Nature of South Carolina Progressives 1914–1916." M.A. thesis, University of South Carolina, 1968.

Margo, Robert A. *Race and Schooling in the South, 1880–1950: An Economic History.* Chicago: University of Chicago Press, 1994.

Marks, Shula. "Natal, the Zulu Royal Family and the Ideology of Segregation." *Journal of Southern African Studies* (April 1978): 172–94.

McFadden, Grace Jordan. "Septima P. Clark and the Struggle for Human Rights." In *Women in the Civil Rights Movement: Trailblazers & Torchbearers 1941–1965,* edited by Vicki L. Crawford et al., 85–97. Bloomington: Indiana University Press, 1990, 85–97.

McLaurin, Melton A. *Paternalism and Protest: Southern Cotton Mill Workers and Organized Labor, 1875–1905.* Westport, Conn.: Greenwood, 1971.

McMath, Robert C. *American Populism: A Social History, 1877–1898.* New York: Hill and Wang, 1993.

McMillen, Neil R. *Dark Journey: Black Mississippians in the Age of Jim Crow.* Urbana: University of Illinois Press, 1989.

McNeely, Patricia G. *Fighting Words: The History of the Media in South Carolina.* Columbia: South Carolina Press Association, 1998.

Megginson, W. J. "Black South Carolinians in World War I: The Official Roster as a Resource for Local History, Mobility, and African-American History." *South Carolina Historical Magazine* 96 (1995): 153–73.

Meier, August. *Negro Thought in America, 1880–1915.* Ann Arbor: University of Michigan Press, 1963.

Michie, Allen A., and Frank Ryhlick. *Dixie Demagogues.* New York: Vanguard, 1939.

Miller, Anthony B. "Coleman Livingston Blease, South Carolina Politician." M.A. thesis, University of North Carolina, 1971.

"Minutes of the 38th Annual Meeting, South Carolina Teachers Association." *South Carolina Education,* 15 April 1924, 3–4.

Mitchell, Broadus. *The Rise of Cotton Mills in the South.* Baltimore: Johns Hopkins Press, 1921.

Mitchell, Sandra Corley. "Conservative Reform: South Carolina's Progressive Movement, 1915–1929." M.A. thesis, University of South Carolina, 1979.

Mixon, Kenneth W. "Senatorial Career of Coleman Livingston Blease, 1925–1931." M.A. thesis, University of South Carolina, 1970.

"Modern Exiles." *Crisis,* December 1919, 70–72.

Montgomery, Mabel. *South Carolina's Wil Lou Gray: Pioneer in Adult Education.* Columbia: Vogue Press, 1963.

Moore, John Hammond. *Columbia and Richland County: A South Carolina Community, 1740–1990.* Columbia: University of South Carolina Press, 1992.

———. *The South Carolina Highway Department, 1917–1987.* Columbia: University of South Carolina Press, 1987.

Moore, Winfred B., Jr., Joseph F. Tripp, and Lyon G. Tyler Jr., eds. *Developing Dixie: Modernization in a Traditional Society.* Westport, Conn.: Greenwood Press, 1988.

Morgan, David. *Suffragists and Democrats: The Politics of Woman Suffrage in America.* East Lansing: Michigan State University Press, 1972.

Bibliography

Morrison, Fred W. *Equalization of the Financial Burden of Education among Counties in North Carolina*. New York: Teacher's College, Columbia University, 1925.

Mort, Paul R. *State Support for Public Education*. Washington, D.C.: American Council on Education, 1933.

Mort, Paul R., and Walter C. Reusser. *Public School Finance: Its Background, Structure, and Operation*. New York: McGraw-Hill, 1941.

Mullins, Jack Simpson. "Lynching in South Carolina, 1900–1914." M.A. thesis, University of South Carolina, 1961.

Nash, Roy. "The Lynching of Anthony Crawford: South Carolina Declares an End to Mob Rule." *Independent*, 11 December 1916.

Newby, Idus A. *Black Carolinians: A History of Blacks in South Carolina from 1895 to 1968*. Columbia: University of South Carolina Press, 1973.

———. *Jim Crow's Defense: Anti-Negro Thought in America, 1900–1930*. Baton Rouge: Louisiana State University Press, 1965.

———. *Plain Folk in the New South: Social Change and Cultural Persistence, 1880–1955*. Baton Rouge: Louisiana State University Press, 1989.

Nolen, Claude H. *The Negro's Image in the South: Anatomy of White Supremacy*. Lexington: University Press of Kentucky, 1967.

Odem, Mary E. *Delinquent Daughters: Protecting and Policing Adolescent Female Sexuality in the United States, 1885–1920*. Chapel Hill: University of North Carolina Press, 1995.

Painter, Nell Irvin. *Exodusters: Black Migration to Kansas after Reconstruction*. New York: Alfred A. Knopf, 1976.

Parkinson, B. L. Editorial. *South Carolina Education*, 15 November 1923, 13.

———. "Why the SCTA Supports the New School Finance Law." *South Carolina Education*, 15 April 1924, 12–13.

Parsons, Sam. "Lever's Great Act." *Clemson World Online* 57, no. 2 (Spring 2004). http://www.clemson.edu/clemsonworld/archive/2004/spring04/cemetery.htm.

Payne, Charles. *I've Got the Light of Freedom: The Organizing Tradition and the Mississippi Freedom Struggle*. Berkeley and Los Angeles: University of California Press, 1995.

Pell, Robert P. "Citizens' Educational Association of South Carolina." *South Carolina Education*, 15 October 1921, 3–4.

Phillips, Ulrich B. "The Central Theme of Southern History." *American Historical Review* 34 (October 1928): 30–43.

Pickens, William. "The Woman Voter Hits the Color Line." *Nation*, 6 October 1920, 372–73.

Powell, Ruth Gilliam. "History of the Southern Commission on Interracial Cooperation." M.A. thesis, University of South Carolina, 1935.

"Public School Membership in SCTA." *South Carolina Education*, 15 April 1924, 29.

Quint, Howard H. *Profile in Black and White: A Frank Portrait of South Carolina*. Washington, D.C.: Public Affairs Press, 1958.

Rabinowitz, Harold. "From Exclusion to Segregation: Southern Race Relations, 1865–1890." *Journal of American History* 43 (1976):325–50.

———. *Race Relations in the Urban South, 1865–1890.* New York: Oxford University Press, 1978.

Ransom, Roger, and Richard Sutch. *One Kind of Freedom: The Economic Consequences of Emancipation.* Cambridge: Cambridge University Press, 1977.

Reynolds, Emily, and Joan Faust, eds. *Biographical Directory of the Senate of South Carolina 1776–1964.* Columbia: South Carolina Archives Division, 1964.

Robertson, David. *Sly and Able: A Political Biography of James F. Byrnes.* New York: W. W. Norton, 1994.

Rodgers, Daniel T. "In Search of Progressivism." *Reviews in American History* 10 (December 1982): 113–32.

Roediger, David R. *The Wages of Whiteness: Race and the Making of the American Working Class.* New York: Verso, 1991.

Roefs, Wim. "The Impact of 1940s Civil Rights Activism on the State's 1960s Civil Rights Scene: A Hypothesis and Historiographical Discussion." Paper presented at the Citadel Conference on the Civil Rights Movement in South Carolina. Charleston, S.C., March 5–8, 2003. http://www.citadel.edu/civilrights/papers/roefs.pdf.

Rogers, James A. *Mr. D. R.: A Biography of David R. Coker.* Hartsville, S.C.: Coker College Press, 1994.

Rubin, Hyman, III. *South Carolina Scalawags.* Columbia: University of South Carolina Press, 2006.

Saville, Julie. *The Work of Reconstruction: From Slave to Wage Laborer in South Carolina, 1860–1870.* New York: Cambridge University Press, 1994.

Schneider, Mark Robert. *"We Return Fighting:" The Civil Rights Movement in the Jazz Age.* Boston: Northeastern University Press, 2002.

Schultz, Mark. *The Rural Face of White Supremacy: Beyond Jim Crow.* Urbana: University of Illinois Press, 2005.

Scott, Anne Firor. *The Southern Lady: From Pedestal to Politics, 1830–1930.* Chicago: University of Chicago Press, 1970.

Scott, Anne Firor, and Andrew M. Scott. *One Half the People: The Fight for Woman Suffrage.* Philadelphia: J. B. Lippincott, 1975.

Scott, Emmett J., ed. "Letters of Negro Migrants of 1916–1918." *Journal of Negro History,* July and October 1919: 290–340; 412–65.

———. *Negro Migration during the War.* 1920. Reprint, New York: Arno Press, 1968.

———. *Official History of the American Negro in the World War.* 1919. Reprint, New York: Arno Press, 1969.

Seligman, Edwin R. A. *Essays in Taxation.* 10th ed., rev. New York: Macmillan, 1928.

———. *The Income Tax: A Study of the History, Theory, and Practice of Income Taxation at Home and Abroad.* New York: Macmillan, 1911.

Shaffer, E. T. H. "A New South: The Negro Migration." *Atlantic Monthly*, September 1923, 403–4.

Shealy, W. A. "Procedures in Financing the Schools under the 6-0-1 Law." *South Carolina Education*, 1 November 1924, 16–17.

Shenk, Gerald E. *"Work or Fight!" Race, Gender, and the Draft in World War One*. New York: Palgrave, 2005.

"Should SC Teachers Support an Official Organ." *South Carolina Education*, 15 February 1924, 12–13.

Simkins, Francis Butler. *Pitchfork Ben Tillman: South Carolinian*. Baton Rouge: Louisiana State University Press, 1944.

Simon, Bryant. "The Appeal of Cole Blease of South Carolina: Race, Class, and Sex in the New South." *Journal of Southern History* 62 (February 1996): 56–86.

———. *A Fabric of Defeat: The Politics of South Carolina Millhands, 1910–1948*. Chapel Hill: University of North Carolina, 1998.

Slaunwhite, Jerry. "The Public Career of Nathaniel Barksdale Dial." Ph.D. diss., University of South Carolina, 1978.

Sloan, James P. "The Blease Movement in South Carolina." M.A. thesis, Tulane University, 1938.

Smith, Alfred G., Jr. *Economic Readjustment of an Old Cotton State: South Carolina, 1820–1860*. Columbia: University of South Carolina Press, 1958.

Smith, C. Calvin. "The Houston Riot of 1917 Revisited." *Houston Review* 13 (1991): 85–102.

Smith, J. Douglas. *Managing White Supremacy: Race, Politics, and Citizenship in Jim Crow Virginia*. Chapel Hill: University of North Carolina Press, 2002.

Smith, Jessie Carney, ed. *Notable Black American Women*. Bk. 2. New York: Gale Research, 1996.

Smith, Seldon K. "Ellison Durant Smith: A Progressive, 1909–1929." Ph.D. dissertation, University of South Carolina, 1972.

South Carolina State Council of Defense. *The South Carolina Handbook for the War*. Columbia: The State Co., 1917.

Stark, John. *Damned Upcountryman: William Watts Ball; A Study in American Conservatism*. Durham, N.C.: Duke University Press, 1968.

Strayer, George D., and Robert M. Haig. *The Financing of Education in the State of New York*. Report of the Educational Finance Inquiry Commission, Vol. 1. New York: Macmillan, 1923.

Stockley, Grif. *Blood in Their Eyes: The Elaine Race Massacres of 1919*. Fayetteville: University of Arkansas, 2001.

Stoddard, J. A. "American Education Week." *South Carolina Education*, 15 November 1922, 5.

Stokes, Allen H. "Black and White Labor and the Development of the Southern Textile Industry, 1800–1920." Ph.D. diss., University of South Carolina, 1977.

Stroup, Rodger. "John L. McLaurin: A Political Biography." Ph.D. diss., University of South Carolina, 1980.

Suttles, William L. "The Struggle for State Control of Highways in South Carolina, 1908–1930." M.A. thesis, University of South Carolina, 1971.

Swearingen, Mary Hough. *A Gallant Journey: Mr. Swearingen and His Family.* Columbia: University of South Carolina Press, 1959.

Sweeney, W. Allison. *History of the American Negro in the Great World War.* New York: Negro Universities Press, 1919.

Synnott, Marcia G. "Replacing 'Sambo': Could White Immigrants Solve the Labor Problem in the Carolinas?" *Proceedings of the South Carolina Historical Association 1982:* 77–89.

Taylor, A. Elizabeth. "South Carolina and the Enfranchisement of Women: The Later Years." *South Carolina Historical Magazine,* October 1979, 298–310.

Tetzlaff, Monica Maria. *Cultivating a New South: Abbie Holmes Christensen and the Politics of Race and Gender, 1852–1938.* Columbia: University of South Carolina Press, 2002.

Tindall, George Brown. "The Campaign for the Disfranchisement of Negroes in South Carolina." *Journal of Southern History* 15 (May 1949): 212–34.

———. *The Emergence of the New South, 1913–1945.* Baton Rouge: Louisiana State University Press, 1967.

———. "The Question of Race in the South Carolina Constitutional Convention of 1895." *Journal of Negro History* 37 (July 1952): 277–303.

———. *South Carolina Negroes 1877–1900.* Columbia: University of South Carolina Press, 1952.

Tolnay, Stewart E., and E. M. Beck. "Rethinking the Role of Racial Violence." In *Black Exodus: the Great Migration from the American South,* edited by Alferdteen Harrison, 20–35. Jackson: University of Mississippi Press, 1991.

Trotter, Joe William, Jr. "Introduction: Black Migration in Historical Perspective; A Review of the Literature." In *Great Migration in Historical Perspective: New Dimensions of Race, Class, and Gender,* edited by Joe Trotter, 1–21. Bloomington: Indiana University Press, 1991.

Tullos, Allen. *Habits of Industry: White Culture and the Transformation of the Carolina Piedmont.* Chapel Hill: University of North Carolina Press, 1989.

Turner, James. "Understanding the Populists." *Journal of American History* 67 (September 1980): 354–73.

Tuttle, William, Jr. *Race Riot: Chicago and the Red Summer of 1919.* New York: Atheneum, 1970.

Tyson, Timothy B. "Robert F. Williams, 'Black Power,' and the Origins of the African American Freedom Struggle." *Journal of American History,* 85, no. 2 (September 1998): 540–70.

Underwood, James L. *The Constitution of South Carolina.* 4 vols. Columbia: University of South Carolina Press, 1986–1994.

Wallace, David Duncan. *The History of South Carolina.* 4 vols. New York: American Historical Society, 1934.

Wardlaw, Frank H., ed. *Men and Women of Carolina: Selected Addresses and Papers by J. Rion McKissick*. Columbia: University of South Carolina Press, 1948.

Wells, Alvin Leslie. "Wealth and Taxation in South Carolina." M.A. thesis, University of South Carolina, 1922.

Wells, B. J. "Mr. Swearingen's Administration." *South Carolina Education*, 15 December 1922, 3–4.

Whayne, Jeannie M. "Low Villains and Wickedness in High Places: Race and Class in the Elaine Riots." *Arkansas Historical Quarterly* 58 (1999): 285–313.

Wheeler, Marjorie Spruill. *New Women of the New South: The Leaders of the Woman Suffrage Movement in the Southern States*. New York: Oxford University Press, 1993.

Who's Who in South Carolina. Columbia, S.C.: McCaw of Columbia, 1921.

Wiebe, Robert H. *The Search for Order, 1877–1920*. New York: Hill and Wang, 1967.

Wiener, Jonathan M. "Class Structure and Economic Development in the American South, 1865–1955." *American Historical Review* 84 (October 1979): 970–93.

Williams, George Croft. *A Social Interpretation of South Carolina*. Columbia, S.C.: University of South Carolina Press, 1946.

———. *Social Problems of South Carolina*. Columbia, S.C.: The State Co., 1928.

Williamson, Gustavus, Jr. "Cotton Manufacturing in South Carolina, 1865–1892." Ph.D. diss., Johns Hopkins University, 1954.

Williamson, Joel. *After Slavery: The Negro in South Carolina during Reconstruction, 1861–1877*. Chapel Hill: University of North Carolina Press, 1965.

———. *The Crucible of Race: Black-White Relations in the American South since Emancipation*. New York: Oxford University Press, 1984.

Woodman, Harold D. "Sequel to Slavery: The New History Views the Postbellum South." *Journal of Southern History* 43 (November 1977): 523–54.

Woods, Barbara. "Modjeska Simkins and the South Carolina Conference of the NAACP, 1939–1957." In *Women in the Civil Rights Movement: Trailblazers and Torchbearers, 1941–1965*, edited by Vicki L. Crawford, Jacqueline Anne Rouse, and Barbara Woods, 99–120. Bloomington: Indiana University Press, 1993.

Woodson, Carter G. *A Century of Negro Migration*. Washington, D.C.: Association for the Study of Negro Life and History, 1918.

Woodward, C. Vann. *Origins of the New South, 1877–1913*. Baton Rouge: Louisiana State University Press, 1951.

———. *The Strange Career of Jim Crow*. New York: Oxford University Press, 1955.

Woofter, T. J., Jr. *Black Yeomanry: Life on St. Helena Island*. New York: Henry Holt, 1930.

Work, Monroe N. "The Negro Migration." *Southern Workman* 53 (May 1924): 202–12.

Wright, Gavin. *Old South, New South: Revolutions in the Southern Economy since the Civil War*. New York: Basic Books, 1986.

Index

The letter *t* following a page number denotes a table. The letter *m* following a page number denotes a map.

Index

Port Royal (S.C.), 57, 68
progressives. *See* black reformers;
    white reformers
property classification as tax reform
    opposed, 256, 258–60, 309
    recommended, 226, 229, 244, 246,
    251, 255
    See also tax reform; tax structure,
    South Carolina
property tax
    constitutionally mandated, 244–
    45, 259
    funds education, 267, 276
    heavy reliance on, 223, 226–29
    reductions recommended, 240–41,
    245–46, 251, 257, 263
    on types or classes of property,
    228–29, 233, 238, 259
    See also tax reform; three-mill
    property tax
public education. *See* education fund-
    ing, public; schools, public
public health
    disease prevention, 31–32
    poor quality of, 70
    STDs, 70, 107
    tuberculosis sanitarium, 105–6

racial violence
    anticipated (1919), 6, 132, 134–39
    armed preparation for, 134–38
    associated with migration, 158–59
    in Elaine, Arkansas, 137
    fear of, 146–47
    opposition to, 142
    race riots (1919), 132–34, 139–41
    See also Houston riot (1917);
    lynching
Ragsdale, Glenn, 256
Rainey, John, 248–49
Reconstruction, 27
    amendments, 17–18, 45–46, 213
    imagery of, 189, 213
    as "unfinished revolution," 40,
    121, 155

reformatory, juvenile, 22, 33, 37, 108
reform legislation
    localism v. state activism, 49, 62–
    63, 66, 70–71, 180, 239
    successes prior to 1917, 65–66
    See also education funding reform;
    localism; tax reform
Republican conventions, 159, 201
Republican Party, 191, 200–210
    black members of, 17, 25, 28–29,
    105, 122, 308
Republicans, 190–91, 194, 197–98
    Black and Tan, 200
    white Sumter, 202
Rhame, Charles L., 80
Rhett, R. Goodwin, 88
Rhodes, Lillian, 31–32, 124
Rice, James Henry, Jr., 98, 211
Richards, John G., 28
Richardson, Thomas E., 89
Richland County, 30, 57, 109, 112,
    121, 125
Robertson, Edwin W., 86
Rock Hill (S.C.), 81
Rodgers, Daniel T., 321n2
Rodgers, Robert S., 284, 289, 293–94

sales tax, 228
    considered, 278, 280–81, 283
    rejected, 244, 288–89
Salley, Eulalie Chafe, 211, 216
Samaritan Herald, 197
Sapp, Claud N., 57
    as education reformer, 276–77,
    280, 283, 292–93, 295
    on tax reform, 255
Saturday Service League, 97
Sawyer, Edward J. (E. J.), 26, 104,
    308, 320n37
Saxon, Celia D., 33
Schofield Normal and Industrial
    School (Aiken, S.C.), 30
schools, public
    improvements, 7, 267–69
    length of term, 62–63, 264, 286, 298